Macmillan Computer Science Series
Consulting Editor
Professor F. H. Sumner, University of Manchester

S. T. Allworth and R. N. Zobel, *Introduction to Real-second edition*
Ian O. Angell and Gareth Griffith, *High-resolution Computer Graphics Using FORTRAN 77*
Ian O. Angell and Gareth Griffith, *High-resolution Computer Graphics Using Pascal*
M. A. Azmoodeh, *Abstract Data Types and Algorithms*
C. Bamford and P. Curran, *Data Structures, Files and Databases*
Philip Barker, *Author Languages for CAL*
A. N. Barrett and A. L. Mackay, *Spatial Structure and the Microcomputer*
R. E. Berry and B. A. E. Meekings, *A Book on C*
G. M. Birtwistle, *Discrete Event Modelling on Simula*
T. B. Boffey, *Graph Theory in Operations Research*
Richard Bornat, *Understanding and Writing Compilers*
Linda E. M. Brackenbury, *Design of VLSI Systems – A Practical Introduction*
J. K. Buckle, *Software Configuration Management*
W. D. Burnham and A. R. Hall, *Prolog Programming and Applications*
J. C. Cluley, *Interfacing to Microprocessors*
Robert Cole, *Computer Communications, second edition*
Derek Coleman, *A Structured Programming Approach to Data*
Andrew J. T. Colin, *Fundamentals of Computer Science*
Andrew J. T. Colin, *Programming and Problem-solving in Algol 68*
S. M. Deen, *Fundamentals of Data Base Systems*
S. M. Deen, *Principles and Practice of Database Systems*
Tim Denvir, *Introduction to Discrete Mathematics for Software Engineering*
P. M. Dew and K. R. James, *Introduction to Numerical Computation in Pascal*
M. R. M. Dunsmuir and G. J. Davies, *Programming the UNIX System*
K. C. E. Gee, *Introduction to Local Area Computer Networks*
J. B. Gosling, *Design of Arithmetic Units for Digital Computers*
M. G. Hartley, M. Healey and P. G. Depledge, *Mini and Microcomputer Systems*
Roger Hutty, *Fortran for Students*
Roger Hutty, *Z80 Assembly Language Programming for Students*
Roland N. Ibbett, *The Architecture of High Performance Computers*
Patrick Jaulent, *The 68000 — Hardware and Software*
J. M. King and J. P. Pardoe, *Program Design Using JSP — A Practical Introduction*
H. Kopetz, *Software Reliability*
E. V. Krishnamurthy, *Introductory Theory of Computer Science*
V. P. Lane, *Security of Computer Based Information Systems*
Graham Lee, *From Hardware to Software — an introduction to computers*
A. M. Lister, *Fundamentals of Operating Systems, third edition*
G. P. McKeown and V. J. Rayward-Smith, *Mathematics for Computing*
Brian Meek, *Fortran, PL/1 and the Algols*
Barry Morrell and Peter Whittle, *CP/M 80 Programmer's Guide*
Derrick Morris, *System Programming Based on the PDP11*

(continued overleaf)

Pim Oets, *MS-DOS and PC-DOS — A Practical Guide*
Christian Queinnec, *LISP*
L. R. Redfern, *Introduction to Pascal for Computational Mathematics*
Gordon Reece, *Microcomputer Modelling by Finite Differences*
W. P. Salman, O. Tisserand and B. Toulout, *FORTH*
L. E. Scales, *Introduction to Non-linear Optimization*
Peter S. Sell, *Expert Systems — A Practical Introduction*
Colin J. Theaker and Graham R. Brookes, *A Practical Course on Operating Systems*
J-M. Trio, *8086–8088 Architecture and Programming*
M. J. Usher, *Information Theory for Information Technologists*
B. S. Walker, *Understanding Microprocessors*
Peter J. L. Wallis, *Portable Programming*
Colin Walls, *Programming Dedicated Microprocessors*
I. R. Wilson and A. M. Addyman, *A Practical Introduction to Pascal — with BS6192, second edition*

Non-series
Roy Anderson, *Management, Information Systems and Computers*
J. E. Bingham and G. W. P. Davies, *A Handbook of Systems Analysis, second edition*
J. E. Bingham and G. W. P. Davies, *Planning for Data Communications*

Mini and Microcomputer Systems

M. G. Hartley
Information Systems Engineering Group
Department of Electrical Engineering and Electronics
University of Manchester Institute of Science and Technology

M. Healey
Department of Electrical and Electronic Engineering
University College, Cardiff

P. G. Depledge
Application Engineering Organisation
Hewlett–Packard Ltd

MACMILLAN
EDUCATION

First published 1988

Published by
MACMILLAN EDUCATION LTD
Houndmills, Basingstoke, Hampshire RG21 2XS
and London
Companies and representatives
throughout the world

Printed in Hong Kong

British Library Cataloguing in Publication Data
Hartley, Michael G.
   Mini and microcomputer systems.—2nd ed.
   —(Macmillan computer science series).
   1. Microcomputers 2. Mini computers
   I. Title II. Healey, M. III. Depledge, P.
   IV. Hartley, Michael G. First course in
   computer technology
   004.16   QA76.5

ISBN 0–333–41758–5
ISBN 0–333–41759–3 Pbk

Contents

1 Introduction

1.1 The Background

The early history of digital computers (refs. 1.1, 1.2, 1.3, 1.4 and 1.5) is of considerable interest and serves to emphasise that many of the ideas fundamental to modern machines had been incorporated into computers as early as 1950 or thereabouts (ref. 1.6). Thereafter the progress with respect to the physical equipment, the *hardware*, though spectacular, has been confined largely to the use of enhanced technology. Progress on the programming side, the *software*, has been spectacular also, involving the provision of a *hierarchy of programming languages*, the development of software aids to programming, so-called *debug facilities* and finally *software-based operating systems* which permit the overall control of machines, large and small, and their associated peripheral equipment.

The earliest machines were built with relays and were electromechanical in operation (ref. 1.7) though thermionic valves and other discrete components such as resistors and capacitors were quickly incorporated. While a modular approach, coupled with miniature valves and components, was later adopted, machines were of large physical size and limited computing power (comparable to that of a modern programmable pocket calculator, for example). By about 1954–5 ferrite-core stores were beginning to be used for fast random-access stores. Such stores may still be found today though they are no longer incorporated in new equipment except in special circumstances.

A technological breakthrough came with the advent of quantity production of reliable discrete-circuit-element transistors by the late 1950s. Their use reduced voltage and power levels for computers and permitted further significant miniaturisation (ref. 1.8).

It was during the early 1960s that process-control computers of modest computing power and also reasonably small size began to be used to control continuous processes such as chemical plant. This use sprang out of military applications involving a similar philosophy. The period was the zenith of the analogue computer age and hybrid computation and analogue/

1

digital simulation relating to real-time became a possibility. Thus, for example, an analogue machine might be used to represent the behaviour of a plant while a small digital machine acted as the real-time controller (ref. 1.9). Indeed the first illustrative example of chapter 6, involving a 24-bit word computer, is modelled upon the architecture of a process-control computer of the period, the Argus 300 of Ferranti Ltd, UK.

1.2   The Advent of Integrated Circuits

The advent of the Integrated Circuit (IC) in the mid 1960s which used semiconductor technology to fabricate complete Small-Scale Integrated Circuits (SSI) on a single chip of semiconductor material provided further impetus to hardware technology. At first such circuits were expensive and each performed only one or two combinational or sequential functions, for example AND or OR (see chapter 4), but by the early 1970s unit prices had fallen dramatically and reliability was good.

For example, a pair of flip-flop circuits engineered using valves and mounted on a plug-in module might have cost £100 in 1956. Two decades later, the same circuits in integrated circuit form would cost less than 50p for quantity. This is a spectacular price reduction. By the mid 1970s an individual chip could comprise a complete shift register. This constitutes Medium-Scale Integration (MSI). A decade later a very wide range of complete circuits are accommodated on a single chip. Typical examples taken at random from a manufacturer's catalogue, include

> Precision timer/stop watch
> Voltage-to-frequency/frequency-to-voltage converter
> A wide range of operational amplifiers
> Video amplifiers
> Analogue-to-digital converters
> Single-chip microprocessors
> A wide variety of semiconductor memories including, for example,
> > 64K 1-bit dynamic volatile random access
> > 16K 4-bit dynamic volatile random access
> > 8-word 4-bit non-volatile random access
> > Various programmable read-only memories (ROM)

All these items are readily available at modest prices not greater than a few pounds. They constitute examples of Large-Scale Integration (LSI) or Very-Large-Scale Integration (VLSI).

The advent of significant price reduction, enhanced reliability and the possibility of substantial computing power achieved in small volume with low power consumption, has produced a situation in which computer hardware costs now represent only a fraction of the total *system cost*. The remainder relates to peripheral equipment and the cost of system software.

The second illustrative example of chapter 6 relating to a modern minicomputer is based on the PDP-11 range of computers manufactured by the Digital Electronics Corporation (DEC). Here fullest advantage is taken of the latest technology. The machines are small and fast and can support a wide variety of peripherals. They are capable of supporting several, or many, interactive users simultaneously.

1.3 The Present and the Future

Progress in computer technology, both hardware and software, is continuous and fast. The purpose of this section is to give a rapid sketch of the present position with some thoughts for the future.

It is important to stress that computing power represents a continuum ranging from hardwired logic through the smaller machines to the largest computing complex. Distinctions between levels of computing power are artificial and in any event become blurred as smaller computers, in a physical sense, rapidly achieve the computing power of larger machines.

The continuum begins with *hardwired logic*. This lies below the computer proper but finds its place in simple controllers and in the past as the heart of a microprogramming unit. Its modern analogue is the pre-programmed read-only memory (ROM), engineered typically using an LSI semiconductor chip where a set of micro-instructions perform the same microfunctions as the hardwired logic.

The microprocessor first appeared on the scene in the early 1970s. Initially it constituted a semiconductor chip with a 4-bit word-length capable of executing a limited set of arithmetic and logic instructions. It required a number of support chips to provide input/output and memory. Since those early days the microprocessor has evolved rapidly. Most microprocessors employ an 8-bit or 16-bit word-length. The *single-chip microcomputer* incorporates a basic microprocessor together with a limited amount of *random-access memory* (RAM), *read-only memory* (ROM) and *input/output ports*. In a very real sense the system comprises a complete computer on a single chip. With substantial production runs the unit cost is low.

The exploitation of the potential of the microprocessor has been facilitated greatly in recent years through the use of *development systems* of considerable power which permit rapid development and testing of programs intended for microprocessor use.

Both the above subjects are considered further in chapter 9.

The success of the microprocessor owes much to the rise of the semiconductor industry through the very rapid development of the pocket calculator. The mass market for the calculator created conditions favourable for the commercial development of the microprocessor. An excellent account of the 'microprocessor revolution' from a commercial viewpoint is to be found in ref. 1.8. Many books provide technical coverage of microprocessors. A selection is to be found at the end of chapters 9 and 11.

The *operating system* co-ordinates overall activity of a computer system and the peripheral equipment. With a minimal computing system such as a home computer the operating system is comparatively simple, but with larger installations the operating system assumes significant importance. An operating system such as UNIX (ref. 1.10), for example, is responsible for the co-ordination of all the activities of a *real-time interactive multi-user system*. It controls resource allocations relating to random-access store, store/disc transfers, peripheral devices such as printers, graph-plotters and the like as well as being responsible for editing, compilation and such house-keeping activities as the setting up of files, directories and the control of word processing. The development of an efficient and comprehensive operating system is a most labour-intensive activity and as such is expensive. The important subject of operating systems is discussed further in chapter 8.

The use of multiple microprocessors as an integral part of larger computers offers the promise of significant increase of speed. This arises through the development of *highly parallel processors* and also the use of microprocessors as *special-purpose* peripherals.

The transputer family, announced by INMOS in 1984, is an example of a set of devices which incorporated the then latest technology and offered flexibility of use for the future.

Thus the transputer comprises a VLSI single-chip microcomputer incorporating processor, memory and communication links. The use of concurrent elements provides a processing power of 10 million instructions per second (10 MIPS). For highest performance a network of transputers will operate in highly parallel fashion. Such processing power is required when dealing with real-time high data-stream applications. Typical requirements might include that of image processing with a requirement for processing power behind each individual element in the matrix constituting a picture (that is, each *pixel*). Alternatively a requirement might be for substantial computing power relating to speech synthesis and analysis or in the field of artificial intelligence. All such applications require large quantities of computing power and frequently relate to real-time applications. Computers to satisfy such needs are often called *fifth-generation* machines.

1.4 Summary

This chapter takes the reader from the earliest days towards a glimpse into computers of the future. In this context, re-reading of the chapter in the light of knowledge gained through the remainder of the book is strongly recommended. After such a revision, the reader should be able to proceed to more advanced works, such as ref. 1.11.

Above all, the hope is that this chapter serves to encourage the reader to share in the excitement which computer technology has always provided. The references associated with this chapter are directed to this end. Indications are that such excitement will be increased by future developments.

References

1.1   Bowden, B. V. (Ed.), *Faster than Thought*, Pitman, London, 1953.

1.2   Morrison, P. and Morrison, E., *Charles Babbage and his Calculating Engines*, Dover Publications, New York, 1961.

1.3   Hyman, A., *Charles Babbage — Pioneer of the Computer*, Oxford University Press, 1982.

1.4   Randell, B. (Ed.), *The Origins of Digital Computers*, Springer-Verlag, Berlin, 1975.

1.5   Atherton, W. A., *From Compass to Computer*, Macmillan, London, 1984, chapter 11.

1.6   'Joint IEE/IERE Coloquium on the "25th Anniversary of the Stored Program Computer" November 1974', published in the *Radio and Electronic Engineer*, July 1975.

1.7   Aiken, H. H. and Hopper, G. M., 'The Automatic Sequence Controlled Calculator', Electrical Engineering, **65** (1946) pp. 384–391, 449–454 and 522–528. (Reprinted in full in ref. 1.4, pp. 199–218.)

1.8   Braun, E. and Macdonald, S., *Revolution in Miniature*, Cambridge University Press, 1982.

1.9   Hartley, M. G., 'Versatile Analogue Computer for G. W. Studies', *Control* **4** (1961) pp. 98–101 and 103–104.

1.10   Brown, P., *Starting with UNIX*, Addison-Wesley, London, 1984.

1.11   Lewin, D., *Theory and Design of Digital Computer Systems*, Nelson, London, 1980.

2 General Concepts of Digital Computers

Objectives

This chapter is used to give a simplified overall view of a digital computer. A schematic viewpoint is used which can be related to more practical details in the following chapters. The potential of the digital computer is considered by indicating the diverse nature of common applications. The importance of human communication with the computer is explained with reference to a simple keyboard/display, such as the Visual Display Unit (VDU).

2.1 What is a Digital Computer

A digital computer is a calculating machine, but a calculating machine with a difference. It is capable of performing a number of simple operations, one at a time. Typical operations are *add two numbers together* and *store a piece of data*. An instruction of the form *test to see if one number is bigger than another*, is an example of a *conditional* instruction fundamental to computer operation. To perform more sophisticated tasks the machine must execute a number of these simple functions, one at a time, in a given sequence. Thus the task X = A + B + C + D is performed by adding A to B, then C to the previous result and finally D to that sum. One computer differs from another in the range of the simple *machine-level* operations available and in the speed and efficiency of execution.

To perform a given task the computer is made to execute a particular sequence of its own machine-level operations. The request for a specific operation is called an *instruction* and the list of instructions required for a given task is called a *program*. It is most important to realise that by giving the machine another program of instructions it can be made to perform a totally different and independent task from that of the previous program. It is also clear, since the computer follows the program explicitly, that any errors in the logic will be faithfully reproduced, giving wrong answers from the user's viewpoint.

The term *digital* stems from the use of binary representation of information in the computer. A two-state technique for the representation of information is much more easily achieved than say a ten-state, especially since with only a two-state arrangement a high degree of variation of the representative voltage levels can be tolerated without error. For example, if logical 0 is represented by 0 volts and logical 1 by +5 volts, then the range 0 volts to 1.5 volts is still clearly logical 0. Note however that since $99_{10} = 1100011_2$ then 7 binary digits are required to be equivalent to 2 decimal digits. This binary representation must also create some problems of human communication since we all tend to think in decimal terms. It will also be shown in the next two chapters that binary arithmetic is a relatively simple process, easily incorporated into the electronic circuits that go to make up a computer.

If a computer can perform only a limited repertoire of simple operations, so that even the most trivial problem must be presented as an accurately arranged sequence of these operations, what has it got to offer? The answer is high speed and accuracy. By way of comparison it is claimed that the human error rate is such that we cannot invert a 5×5 matrix without making a mistake. A computer can invert a 2000×2000 matrix with the upper limit set by accumulated *round-off* errors in the arithmetic, rather than random errors in calculation.

It is important that the student has some feel for the actual speed of a digital computer. Typically some 500 000 instructions can be executed each second. Thus with a typical typist capable of typing perhaps 10 characters per second, the computer has time to execute 50 000 instructions in between each character typed.

2.2   Classification of Digital Computers

Computers are classified very loosely as *microcomputers, minicomputers* and *mainframe computers*. Microcomputers are frequently specifically tailored to dedicated applications, such as home computers, small business machines, etc., based on an integrated circuit device called a *micropro-cessor*. Minicomputers are general-purpose machines. Sometimes they may be used as part of a larger piece of equipment — for example, as the switching controller in an automatic telephone exchange. Mainframe computers are the large machines used for commercial data processing and scientific calculations.

From a simplistic viewpoint, machines could be placed in one category or another on the basis of size, power and cost. This approach however is invalid in that a large minicomputer may be far more powerful and much cheaper than a small mainframe machine.

The situation is confused by the differing costs of marketing equipment in different applications areas. Thus for an accounting system, the user, who is not a computer specialist, needs support for systems analysis, programming, operator training, etc., so that the cost of the computer itself can be less than half the total system cost. A machine of similar power can be sold to a University Engineering Department for research work with little further support from the machine supplier at an appropriately lower cost. The example quoted in section 2.5 serves to emphasise the above case.

It is very important to realise that computers are an area of continuing development. In particular, the advances in the techniques of manufacturing electronic devices continue to result in cheaper, simpler and faster components. This enables the manufacturer to produce functionally more sophisticated machines which are more powerful and more reliable but nevertheless cheaper. However, never lose sight of the fact that a computer *system*, with all the associated services, is considerably more expensive than the computer itself.

2.3 The Need for Computing Power

One should not gloss too quickly over the question *is a computer needed?* Quite simply, a computer offers the ability to perform tedious and repetitious tasks quickly, accurately and relatively free from errors. It also has the ability to store large amounts of information which can be accessed very rapidly. There are many areas where a computer is essential — for example, in scientific calculations such as inversion of large matrices, accounting and transaction processing for a large bank, etc. The problem is one of scale as to when it becomes economical to use a computer. Thus it would be absurd to calculate the payroll for a company with 10 000 employees without a computer, while it would be equally unwise to consider a computer for a company with two employees. To decide whether the break-even point is 10 or 100 employees is not easy. It should be noted that the problem of scale means that in certain circumstances a computer is not only an economical but an essential solution since human errors in the early stages of processing build up and create further errors to a level where they are very difficult to trace and correct.

2.4 Schematic Organisation of a Computer

To help to understand the basic organisation of a computer consider the clerk shown in figure 2.1. He receives new data in readable form in his IN tray. His eyes convert the data from printed form to *memory images*. Output, in a *hard copy* form is produced by pen on paper. The role of the human brain in this context is rather complex but it can be simplified to three major roles:

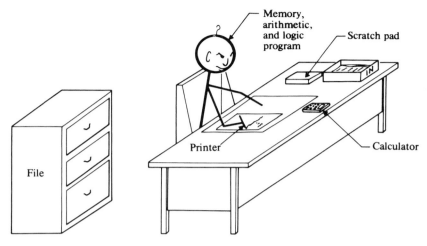

Figure 2.1 The human operator at work

(a) Processing, both arithmetic processing (for example, +, −, ×) and logical processing (for example, if A is bigger than B do one thing, otherwise do another). Note that processing efficiency can be improved with the aid of a scratch pad, used for saving intermediate values, and a calculator.
(b) The knowledge of what is to be done with the data. The clerk has been trained to study the input information, to manipulate it, to extract pertinent facts, to make amendments to ledgers and to write any desired output information.
(c) Memory, which gives rapid recall of the most salient facts. This serves two functions: (i) storage of the steps in the calculation, and (ii) storage of current input data and the regularly used common data.

While the human memory is extremely quick and versatile, it is not very good at storing large volumes of data. Nor is data stored in the brain accessible to others except by word of mouth. Thus a filing cabinet is used to save the bulk data. However, to process any of this data it must be temporarily transferred to the human memory.

Now consider the schematic diagram of a computer, shown in figure 2.2, and draw a comparison with the human system just described. The heart of the computer is called the *central processing unit* (CPU). This has two major components, the *arithmetic and logic unit* (ALU) and the *control unit*.

The ALU performs arithmetic and logical operations on any data presented to it. The control unit accepts an instruction, decodes it and as a

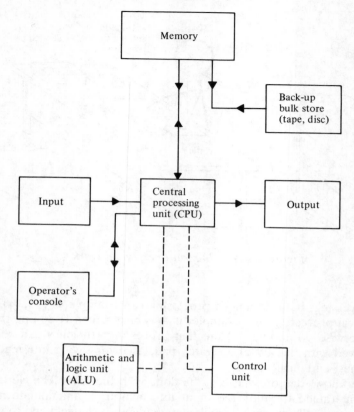

Figure 2.2 Block schematic of a digital computer

result organises the actions in and around the CPU. Chapters 5 and 6 discuss the operation of the CPU in considerable detail.

The computer memory is a store of information, both program instructions and data. All information is stored in binary form. This information must be identified so that it can be stored and recalled at will. The computer memory is *address organised*. It is arranged as a number of locations, each with a unique address. Information is located by the address at which it is stored rather than by its significance. Thus a program, being a sequential string of instructions, is stored in contiguous (consecutive addressed) locations. As will be seen in chapter 5 and again in chapter 6, a major requirement of computer memory is that information can be stored or extracted from any location just as quickly as any other — that is, to access locations 1, 20 562 and 2 takes the same time as access to locations 21, 22 and 23. This approach leads to the main store being termed *random-access memory* (RAM).

Ideally some instructions need more bits of information than others. The same is true of the number of significant digits required for data, such as 7 compared with 77. However, this situation could mean that some memory locations would store a different number of bits than others. To preserve generality, all instructions comprise the same number of bits. The same constraint is placed on data. Since information, instruction or data, is located solely by its address, then if both data and instructions use the same number of bits as a standard, they can use the same common memory. Accordingly a machine can run either a large program with only a low volume of data or a small program with masses of data. The whole machine is designed around a unit of information made up of a fixed number of bits, termed a *word*. Mini and microcomputers use 8, 16 or 32-bit words, and mainframes up to 64. Sometimes words are grouped together internally to provide in effect longer words — for example, a 16-bit instruction but stored in two consecutive 8-bit word memory locations. An 8-bit unit is termed a *byte* and is commonly used to store one *alphanumeric* character as will be explained later in chapter 3.

Words are also *concatenated* to give higher numeric precision; for example, one floating point number (see chapter 3) is stored in, say, two 16-bit memory locations. Thus while there is some variety in effective word-length, the length is always in multiples of the basic fixed word-length of the machine.

There are a number of computer input devices. The information must be presented in a machine-readable form, so that automatic equipment, controlled by the computer, can be used to convert this information into a binary form which can be stored in the memory. Typical input media are keyboards (usually associated with visual display units (VDUs)), punched paper tape, punched cards, magnetic-tape cassettes and analogue-to-digital converters (ADCs). Apart from the keyboard and ADC, the other devices require special equipment to prepare the data away from the machine (off-line).

Output is fundamentally displayed in a human-readable form (for example, as output to line printers, terminal printers or VDU displays), apart from on-line control applications, where output is provided via a digital-to-analogue converter (DAC), or binary data which is employed to open or close relays, etc. Variants do occur, however, when one computer is used to prepare data for another machine. In these cases, card and paper tape punches or magnetic-tape cassettes are employed. A further form of output is to a variety of graph-plotting devices.

The remaining item relating to the analogy between the computer and the clerk is the data storage system. The ideal solution for the computer is a bigger RAM. This approach, however, is impractical since it is too costly. In any case no matter how big, the random-access memory will eventually fill up. Thus in practice only active information will be kept in RAM, with other information filed away. Typically, *magnetic disc* and *tape* storage systems are used as back-up to the RAM. The processor does not use information direct from these *bulk* stores but will initiate a transfer to RAM from where the information will be used normally.

Thus the computer has a *storage hierarchy*, dictated by cost. The cost per unit becomes cheaper as the speed of access reduces. Further information on the subject of storage and input/output peripheral devices will be found in chapter 7.

2.5 Hardware and Software

A computer system comprises two major components: the computer itself with its storage devices and terminals, and the programs to make it perform a specified task. The physical devices are termed *hardware*, the programs *software*.

This book is largely devoted to an explanation of the computer itself. The other hardware, such as disc systems, printers, VDUs, etc., collectively referred to as *peripherals*, are only discussed as necessary in chapter 7 and as space allows. Software is discussed in broad terms in chapter 8. This approach is totally acceptable in an introductory text such as this present book but it must not be implied that topics other than the processor are of little importance. In a disc-based minicomputer business system, for instance, the total cost breakdown, which while not the only measure of importance is indicative, is typically:

processor	5 per cent
RAM memory	9 per cent
2 VDUs	12 per cent
disc system	20 per cent
printer	8 per cent
system software	3 per cent
application software	18 per cent
system analysis	10 per cent
services (documentation, training, etc.)	15 per cent

In addition, space must be provided for the system, and staff to run it, together with an annual maintenance charge of approximately 10 per cent of the above total.

The software is simply a suite of programs. The programs of the individual user are *applications orientated* and written by a *computer programmer* to a specification produced by a *systems analyst* in co-operation with the user. Dependent upon the solution, the user, programmer and analyst could be the same person. Now any program can be written as a list of binary instructions, but this is impossibly tedious. Thus the computer manufacturer provides a number of standard programs with the computer to help the programmers. These programs, which are general purpose and related to the specific computer, are collectively termed *system software*, as opposed to the user-specific programs, termed the *application software*.

System software, discussed in detail in chapter 8, falls into two broad categories:

(a) Aids to program development. These allow programmers to develop programs using English-like statements which a system program can convert into binary machine code, such as a Compiler, Assembler, Editor, etc.

(b) Aids to running the system. A number of operations are common to most application programs — for example, print a character, copy a block from disc to memory, etc. These routines can be held in a *library* and merged as necessary into the applications programs. Far more sophisticated programs, called *Operating Systems*, are used to make communication with the machine easy for the user — for example, typing RUN TESTPROG at the terminal causes a program with the identifier TESTPROG to be located on the disc, *loaded* (copied into memory), and executed. A sophisticated operating system will permit multiple use of the machine and takes care of resource scheduling and allocation.

System software is complex and expensive but its provision is the responsibility of the computer supplier so that since it is machine, rather than user orientated, the cost can be spread over many users. Hence the relatively low cost percentage in the system quoted above. Note, however, that this percentage would be increased significantly if a variety of Compilers and more complex Operating Systems were required.

A computer must be assessed not merely by the hardware price/performance but rather in terms of the hardware, system software and the support from the vendor.

2.6 Man–Machine Communication

Man–machine communication is achieved in various ways. The use of a Visual Display Unit (VDU) is a typical method. The VDU comprises two devices: a keyboard and a display. Information is transmitted to the computer from the keyboard (*input*) and from the computer to the display (*output*). Unlike a typewriter, the character struck on the keyboard will only be printed if the computer is programmed to accept the input and to *echo back* to the display. The character set is more extensive than a typewriter, including non-printing *control characters*, used to initiate actions in the computer. Again there is nothing special about these characters at the keyboard, the computer is programmed to look for them and to take special action when they are input.

Each character is represented by a unique binary code, the most common being the American Standard Code for Information Interchange (ASCII). This uses 8 bits (a byte), seven of which define $2^7 = 128$ characters and 1 bit provides a measure of error detection and is termed a *parity* bit. Further details are given in section 3.4.1. Thus one word of memory in a 16-bit computer can store 2 characters in ASCII code. When a key is depressed a total of 10 bits are transmitted serially to the computer — 1 start bit, 8 bits of the character and 1 stop bit. At the computer, the start and stop bits are used to synchronise an electronic circuit which places the 8 bits (byte) of code into a register from which the byte is then passed, in parallel fashion, to the computer. Alternatively the serial transmission mode may be used to economise on wires, since the terminal may be a long way from the computer and may even use telephone lines. Thus each terminal is linked to the computer proper by an interface. A system with multiple peripherals is shown in figure 2.3. Note that the computer is so fast that it uses the one Input/Output data *highway* or *bus*, interleaving programs and data transfers to support the multiple terminals.

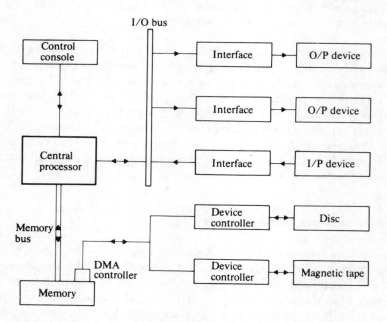

Figure 2.3 Connection of peripheral devices to a processor

Data transmitted direct to memory via the *direct memory access* (DMA) channel by-passes the processor and thus cannot be directly processed. An example of a simple computer based on a bus system is discussed in detail in section 6.4.

2.7 Applications of Digital Computers

The scope for applications of calculators and computers, considering that prices range from £5 to £5 million, is vast. Thus it is only intended here to quote the more typical applications and to arouse a general interest.

Applications can be categorised in many ways. It will suffice here to consider the following major groups:

1. Personal computing
2. Commercial data processing
3. Office automation
4. Scientific data processing
5. Instrumentation and control
6. Communications
7. Factory automation

The following subsections are intended to give a brief review of the applications of digital computers. Unavoidably, terminology and concepts will be mentioned which may be quite new to the reader. Indeed one of the objectives of this book is for the reader, after initially going through this section, to return to it when a broader grasp of the subject has been acquired from the following chapters.

2.7.1 *Personal Computing*

Computers for personal use have now become commonplace. They were created by the microprocessor, an electronic device which allowed a simple computer to be produced at prices low enough to encourage its use in homes and schools. Intended for playing games as well as carrying out simple calculations, domestic computers, despite their low cost, are designed with reasonable colour graphics capabilities, a feature which is relatively expensive in traditional computing. Leading examples have been the BBC micro, Sinclair Spectrum and Apple II. The Amstrad range of word processors and personal computers intended for the home user is a remarkable example of low cost and powerful equipment.

As microprocessors have improved, so new personal computers have evolved. Full 16-bit, high-speed computers are on the market with high resolution displays, disc storage and printers at domestic appliance prices. They are still, however, packaged with low cost a prime objective and with software and communications that are somewhat unsuited to professional applications. Examples are the Apple Macintosh and Atari ST 520.

The traditional computer manufacturers recognised the potential of microcomputers to provide personal computing for individuals in large organisations as alternatives to terminals attached to large computers. Prices were much higher than for the domestic market but greater attention was given to packaging and more suitable applications and communications peripherals were introduced. The leading example in this sector is the Personal Computer of International Business Machines, the IBM PC, an extremely low standard product, technically inferior to many cheaper products but, backed by the world's largest computer manufacturer, it has become a *de facto* standard and is copied by many other manufacturers.

There is a trend in many cases to replace the bigger shared computer by a multiplicity of single-user personal computers, joined together by a communications network called a Local Area Network (LAN). In this way a system can be created with all the advantages of the personal computer plus some of the advantages of shared resources offered by the bigger computer.

The personal computer development has also accelerated developments in associated areas. Specific examples are matrix printers and small (3 inch, $3\frac{1}{2}$ inch or $5\frac{1}{4}$ inch) disc drives, both floppy and Winchester, which have shown dramatic improvement in price/performance over a very short period. The reader will find further details in chapter 7.

2.7.2 Commercial Data Processing

Commercial data processing (DP) is the automation of accounting functions such as sales and purchase ledger keeping, payroll, invoice production, etc. It can also extend to stock control, recording stock quantities in hand, on order or to be ordered. There are also very sophisticated production scheduling applications where the work-load for a machine on the shop floor is computed from the current stock and order information.

Commercial DP dominates computer applications, accounting for about 75 per cent (by value) of all computer work.

This is the traditional market for mainframe computers, dominated by International Business Machines (IBM), with 50 per cent of the total computer industry output, followed by Unisys, Honeywell, NCR and International Computers Limited (ICL). Commercial DP programs are largely written in the high-level language called COBOL.

At the lower end of the scale simpler time-sharing computers are employed, called *Small Business Computers* (SBC). Sometimes there are specially designed machines, such as the IBM System/36, ICL 25, Nixdorf, Philips, etc. Others are based on general-purpose minicomputers, such as Digital Equipment Corporation (DEC) or Data General. There are a whole new generation of SBC manufacturers, such as Convergent Technology or Altos, that are designing machines around common microprocessors. Another natural trend is to introduce special software so that personal computers can be used as SBCs. The first generation based on the IBM PC architecture were not powerful enough, but the new generation (for example, the IBM PC/AT) are sufficiently powerful. Note that in many cases the same hardware can be used for a variety of applications. Thus DEC use the same CPU, etc. in process control applications as they use in SBCs. Different specialised software and peripherals tailor the computer to one application or another.

As a typical application of commercial data processing consider a weekly payroll system. The identification (ID) number, name, address, tax code, pension scheme and year-to-date data for each employee are all saved on a disc file. As will be explained later, bulk data is stored on a magnetic disc organised into files that can be identified easily by the computer. Thus the computer can readily access data from the disc as required. The hours worked by each employee are taken from the clock card. Normally these are gathered into batches and the total hours for the batch calculated. All the data is then entered into the computer either by punching on to cards to be read into the machine later, a *batch system*, or via a VDU, an *on-line system*. With an on-line system a high degree of data validation can be achieved. The ID number is typed in, which the computer then uses to search an appropriate disc file to extract the corresponding data, in this case the name, which is then displayed. The operator can then compare the name with the clock card so as to be certain that the data for the correct person is being updated. As the data is keyed in, it is checked for obvious *out-of-limit* errors and stored in a computer file. The computer carries out a running sum on the total hours entered which can be displayed when the batch is finished and compared with the previous hand-calculated value. If the totals disagree the data entered and the batch total must be checked. When they agree the computer is instructed to accept the batch of data. A program is then executed which looks up the employees' files for standard figures such as hourly rate, etc., multiplies the hours worked by the rate, calculates tax, bonuses, etc., and saves this data on a *print file*. The new data is then used to update the basic files for use in the following week. When all employees' data has been processed the print file data is output to a printer to produce pay slips for the current week. If a company has hourly, weekly and monthly paid staff, with varying bonus and pension schemes, the payroll program can become extremely complex.

The fact that a computer may have files of rapidly accessible data extends the commercial use to cover *information retrieval*. Important areas are banking and finance in general, library information, monthly breakdown of sales statistics, etc. A more complex problem is *transaction processing*, such as seat-reservation systems, where the information may be accessed from multiple terminals and possibly updated. The system must not allow the same seat to be sold simultaneously from two locations.

2.7.3   Office Automation

The catalyst for the use of computers as automation aids in offices came when microprocessor technology enabled manufacturers to produce Word Processing (WP) machines at prices low enough to become practical alternatives to typewriters. Word processors allow the typist to create a document using an image on a VDU screen. End-of-line and movement of the cursor to the beginning of the next line for a new word are automatic. Further, the typist can edit the text by inserting, deleting and moving blocks of words. Formatting for output printing can also be automated. More advanced systems include mechanisms for footnotes, indexing, automatic section numbering, page numbering and spelling checking.

The earlier word processors were specialised machines. However the current trend is to use a conventional personal computer with a word-processing software package. In this way the PC can be used for a variety of functions.

The second major office automation function introduced on PCs is the spreadsheet. A spreadsheet program such as *Lotus 1-2-3* or *SuperCalc* allows the screen to image a large sheet of paper, broken up into rows and columns. Data can be typed into certain *cells* in the matrix but the others can be filled in by calculations — for example, column 3 = column 1 + 0.5 × column 2. In this way complex models of financial data can be built. It is now relatively easy to study the effects of changes; for example, if the cost of a particular component increases, what effect does it have on overall profit?

By using a shared minicomputer or by networking PCs, users can share resources such as high-quality laser printers, mainframe communication links, databases, etc. Given a shareable system, new office automation functions become possible. Examples are *Electronic Mail* and *Messaging* (EMM) whereby a user can create a note or document using WP facilities and then either send it direct to another user (Messaging) or place it into an *electronic mail box*. Users are then responsible for checking their own mail box, a disc storage system in practice, to extract and delete their own mail. The system can be used for archiving and retrieving documents. Interfaces with the outside world, to send and receive Telex messages for example, are common extensions.

2.7.4 Scientific Data Processing

While commercial work currently dominates the use of computers, they were developed to solve complex mathematical problems.

It is correct to assert that engineering and science have progressed hand-in-hand with the computer. Thus as one problem became solvable, research workers looked deeper into their problems and demanded and achieved more and more processing power.

Frequently, a scientific problem is characterised by large complex programs which run for long periods but work on relatively little initial data, whereas commercial work involves relatively simple, repetitive programs with large amounts of data. This means that, ideally, a scientific machine must be most efficient at processing data while the commercial machine must be most efficient at data input, data output and data retrieval.

In general, despite the differing accent on requirements, the same mainframe machines are used for scientific problems as for commercial work. The same manufacturers in general are involved. In addition there are two further companies, Cray and Control Data Corporation (CDC), who make the biggest machines. Scientific or mathematical programs are mostly written in FORTRAN or Pascal. Unquestionably, the Space Age has greatly enhanced the potential of scientific computing. Extremely complex optimisation problems have been solved, computing trajectories, burn-times, etc. of space craft.

A big problem with the older mainframe systems, which work on a *batch* principle, is that the program, probably punched on cards, is submitted to the machine and queued with other jobs for processing. It may thus be hours and even days before printed results are available for error checking, etc. If processing requirements are high, this situation is virtually unavoidable. To overcome this problem in a teaching environment, however, a language called BASIC was developed in which a number of terminals are interactively connected to one machine. Statements are *executed* — that is, the computer performs the operations demanded by the statement, and results are immediately displayed at the terminal so that an *interactive* response is achieved. Remembering the comments made earlier about the speed of computers, each terminal is given total use of the machine for say 0.1 second when the machine is switched to the next terminal, etc., and then back to the first and so on. Bearing in mind the speed at which any user can type, the user appears to have the sole use of the whole computer. This technique is called *time-sharing*. Subsequently, BASIC has been commonly adopted to single-user personal computing.

Modern mainframe and super-minicomputers have extended this interactive technique to cover a wide variety of languages together with development tools such as Editors, Compilers, etc.

Mini and microcomputers are not used for large-scale scientific calculations, but are extensively used for small to medium-sized problems. Systems using FORTRAN, Pascal, C and BASIC are readily available. 16-bit microcomputers are being increasingly used in interactive scientific work where their superior graphic display capabilities can be utilised.

2.7.5 *Instrumentation and Control*

This is the application area for which the minicomputer was originally developed, predominantly by Digital Equipment Corporation (DEC), followed by Hewlett-Packard (HP), Data General and many others. These systems are characterised by the fact that the computer has a specific, dedicated task to perform. Indeed the computer becomes an integral part of a larger system.

The original example is that of process control. The computer is connected directly to the process, say a chemical reactor (for example, a petroleum plant), by sensors. The analogue voltages from these sensors are sampled and converted by *analogue-to-digital convertors* (ADC) to binary form and fed to the computer. The sampling is repeated at a sufficient rate whereby the signals do not change appreciably between samples. Too low a sample rate causes erroneous representation of the signal, too high a rate unnecessarily loads the computer. The data can be processed (for example, scaled, linearised, etc.), checked for alarm conditions, recorded and printed. Dependent variables, such as horse-power from speed and torque measurements, can also be produced at each sample.

Such a system can be extended to give *automatic* or *feedback control*. The sampled data from the transducers is processed to compute a value of an input to the process which will cause the state of the process to behave in some desired way. The computed binary variable is fed to a *digital-to-analogue-converter* (DAC) and thus as an equivalent analogue voltage to the process. This procedure is repeated at a fixed sampling rate, the analogue voltage from the DAC remaining constant during the sample interval until reset. In practice a computer is so fast that it can read one transducer signal, process the data and reset the DAC in a fraction of the sample period, so that multiple control loops can be *multiplexed* as shown in figure 2.4. It is the responsibility of the computer program to control which loop is being updated at any one instant.

This is a special form of an *on-line* system referred to as a *real-time system*. It is important to distinguish between a computer used, as here, as a component in the control system and a scientific machine used to solve the mathematical equations used in the design of such a system.

Other application areas lie in sophisticated instrumentation, such as spectrum analysers, factory data capture, etc.

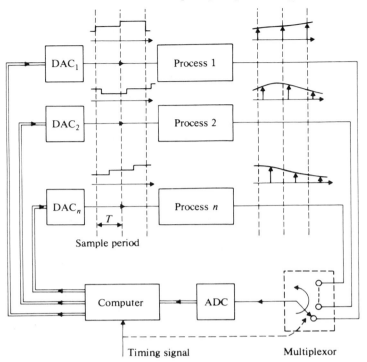

Figure 2.4 A closed-loop digital-computer control system

Some of the smaller computers are built to extremely high standards to withstand harsh environments, and are used in military systems, aircraft, spacecraft, and the like. Redundant techniques, such as those using two similar systems and comparing the results, have been developed to give a very high degree of reliability. These techniques are now used in more conventional computers for data processing in banks and other *high-availability* applications.

Microcomputers are now being used for a number of these applications, usually where less versatility is required. Thus consider the problem of control of traffic flow in a large city. The individual traffic light controller is an electro-mechanical switching unit. The unit could be improved by a specially programmed microcomputer which varies its timing sequences and priorities based on time of day or flow of traffic fed to the microcomputer from sensors set in the road. However, to give total integrated control of traffic flow, control of one set of lights will be influenced by traffic conditions at other localities.

Thus a large centralised mini is required to co-ordinate the control of all the lights. Perhaps the most interesting aspect of the falling cost of microcomputers is the distinct possibility of a smaller centralised minicomputer sending only supervisory control information to a number of local microcomputers which control the detailed timing, etc.

Simple microcomputers have become so cheap that they are now built into vehicles and washing machines. Indeed the pocket calculator, which is the original source of inspiration behind the microprocessor, has proved just how low the price of a device can be brought down if made in large enough quantities. In the motor car industry, control of fuel injection/ ignition systems for optimum efficiency and braking systems for anti-skid control are major examples, not to mention the use of microprocessors in instrument display.

Computers used in these dedicated tasks appear to violate the major concept of the general-purpose computer in which totally different work loads can be run simply by changing the program. If the program is fixed, why use a programmable device, as opposed to a specially designed electronic circuit? The answer lies in versatility. Any design errors can be corrected simply by modifying the program. Equally, design changes or enhancements can be introduced progressively. Further, in many applications the project may be completed in a few months so that the computer can be reprogrammed and used for another task. In laboratories, minicomputers are used for part of the day on dedicated instrumentation and control work, and at other times for developing and running mathematical calculations using, say, FORTRAN, BASIC or Pascal. Personal computers, with appropriate *real-world* I/O subsystems are now commonly employed as general-purpose laboratory computers. They can log data, control experiments and provide an element of local processing.

2.7.6 Communications

Communications systems carry mixtures of voice, data and image signals. Occasionally they are simple point-to-point systems, such as the cable joining a VDU to a computer port. More often, however, systems need a switching facility to make and break connections and to share a single physical system among a number of separate logical services (multiplexing). Thus computers can be used effectively as intelligent nodes in communications systems, acting as switches, multiplexors, demultiplexors and protocol convertors. In the latter case, messages can be received in one format and transmitted in another, thus acting as a bridge between different systems.

Consider two basic services: voice and data. The former is analogue, the latter digital. Voice services, such as the Public Switched Telephone Network (PSTN), dominate communications. Historically, Telex is the only true digital service. Thus to transmit data via the PSTN, it must first be modulated on to a carrier (digital-to-analogue conversion) and at the far end demodulated (analogue-to-digital conversion). Since both ends of the system usually send and receive, it is common to have both a modulator and a demodulator, called a *modem*, at each end. Nowadays, however, voice services are being digitised. The analogue signal is sampled at 8 kHz and each sample converted to an 8-bit binary *amplitude*, creating a 64 kbit per second data stream. This approach offers great potential for data communications services, eliminating the modem.

As an example of a computer-controlled communications switch, consider the Private Automatic Branch Exchange (PABX) which provides telephone services within a building and access to external public service lines. The earlier PABX used analogue circuits with relays to create connections. A computer sensed the dialling pulses or multi-tone frequency signals (touch tone), decoded this as address information and activated signals to close the required relays. Nowadays the PABX is totally digital. The voice signals as well as the dialling data are converted to digital form and the routeing is performed by addressing packets of data within the computer. The PABX hardware is of course highly specialised, but is nevertheless an example of a digital computer application.

Because of the computerised control of the circuits, many extended functions became available such as abbreviated dialling, conferencing, automatic redial, dial-back, etc.

Specialised data communications equipment for joining computers into networks, for connecting terminals to computers, for protocol conversion, multiplexing, etc., all use specialised digital computing techniques. Quite often a general-purpose mini or microcomputer is tailored to a communications application by using special interface hardware and appropriate real-time software.

2.7.7 *Factory Automation*

Factory production lines, particularly in the motor industry, have long been automated. Historically, production lines used simple sequential relay logic, but the scope can be greatly expanded by using computer-controlled logic. By applying the control techniques outlined in section 2.7.5, machines can be designed that can be programmed. Thus a numerically controlled (NC) machine tool can be programmed to machine a particular part by feeding the computer controlling the machine with basic geometrical data defining the paths, velocities, etc., of the cutters and tables.

The automatic control concept has been applied to materials handling, particularly to robotics. Here a machine can be programmed to manipulate and move material from one machine to another and into automatic warehouses.

Thus the whole concept of automating factories is beginning to come together. Some major areas are:

(a) Computer-aided draughting: the use of graphics displays to draw diagrams. The drawing can be created from basic shapes, stored in libraries on discs, and can be repeated and edited interactively.
(b) Computer-Aided Design (CAD). The draughting process can be extended so that instead of producing only a conventional drawing as the output, data sets can be produced in the format required to feed a machine tool. Extended design features such as stress calculations, automatic layout of printed circuit boards (PCBs), etc. can be incorporated.
(c) Computer-Aided Engineering (CAE). Computers can be used to schedule machine loading, stock control, etc. The approach is often called *Manufacturing Resource Planning* (MRP). This technique can be integrated with more conventional DP applications such as order processing, accounting, delivery scheduling, etc. The key to the success of any CAE system is adequate, accurate and timely data capture, particularly from the shop floor.
(d) Computer Integrated Manufacturing (CIM). If the machine tools are computer controlled, robots handle materials, designers use CAD to create direct control of the machines, etc., then a fully automated, unmanned factory becomes a possibility.

2.8 Summary and Conclusions

This chapter has given a broad introduction to digital computers, with a general view of where and how they are used. The concepts of hardware and software have been introduced, highlighting the fact that a computer system is much more than just an electronic box. The explanation of how a computer works has largely been from a schematic viewpoint. The chapters which follow pick up these concepts and consider in greater detail just how they are implemented.

Bibliography

Evans, C., *The Mightly Micro — The Impact of the Computer Revolution*, Gollancz, London, 1979.

Frates, J. and Moldrup, W., *Computers and Life, an Integrative Approach*, Prentice-Hall, Englewood Cliffs, New Jersey, 1983.

Stevens, R., *Understanding Computers — A User Friendly Guide*, Oxford University Press, 1986.

Walsh, V., *Computer Literacy*, Macmillan, London, 1985.

3 Data Representation, Number Systems and Arithmetic Processes

Objectives

The basic concepts of digital computers have been introduced in the first two chapters in a largely descriptive way. In this chapter and the next, the fundamental techniques necessary to construct a working computer to implement the concepts discussed are presented. The importance of the binary technique has been stressed as a practical method of achieving the inherent speed and accuracy by removing tight tolerances from the actual voltage levels used by the electronics. The representation of non-numeric data, such as alphabetic characters, is also important. This chapter reviews the commonly used techniques.

Having established the concept of binary representation of information, then the manipulation of binary data can be treated as a logical two-state process — for example, on or off, open or shut, true or false. For simplicity the two logical states are represented as 0 or 1, drawing an immediate parallel with binary numbers. Indeed it is shown in some detail in the next chapter how logic circuits are used to implement binary arithmetic units, such as an adder.

3.1 Data Types

In this chapter, attention is paid to the representation and manipulation of data. It should be remembered, however, that instructions are also coded into binary words. Both appear as patterns of binary digits. Inspection of the contents of a randomly selected memory location gives no indication as to its meaning. Data and instructions are differentiated only by the specific memory locations in which they are placed. If an incorrect program inadvertently jumps to a location containing data, rather than an instruction, then that data word will be assumed to be an instruction, which will be loaded and executed with very strange results.

In the present chapter, data is considered as two distinct types: numeric and non-numeric.

3.2   Representation of Numbers in Binary Systems

3.2.1   *Radix Number Systems*

A general form for an n digit number with *radix* or *base r* is

$$(a_{n-1}a_{n-2} \ldots a_1 a_0)_r$$

Each digit, a_i, can have a value between 0 and $r-1$. By convention, the most significant (MS) digit is to the left. The position of each digit in the number corresponds to the *weighting* factor so that the digit a_i indicates the corresponding value of r^i. Thus any quantity can be equated to a decimal number by the expression

$$a_{n-1}r^{n-1} + a_{n-2}r^{n-2} + \ldots + a_1 r + a_0 r^0 = N_{10}$$

where $r = 10$ and where a takes values between 0 and $r-1$ (that is, between 0 and 9). Remember that $r^0 = 1$ for all r.

Since they are so well known, decimal numbers will be assumed when no subscript is shown — that is, $372_{10} = 372$. In other words, if no radix subscript is appended to a number it is to be assumed decimal throughout this book. Thus a number in decimal notation is represented by a set of coefficients with the radix omitted in each case. The same approach is adopted for other common bases.

The common bases encountered in computer work are

binary	$r = 2$, $a = 0$ or 1
octal	$r = 8$, a between 0 and 7
decimal	$r = 10$, a between 0 and 9
hexadecimal	$r = 16$, a between 0 and 15

The representation of the larger values of a digit in the hexadecimal system creates a problem. This is overcome by using letters to extend the representation of numbers — that is, $A \equiv 10_{10}$, $B \equiv 11_{10}, \ldots, F \equiv 15_{10}$. A table of equivalent numbers in different base systems is shown in figure 3.1. The table shows that the binary system requires the maximum number of digits while hexadecimal is the most concise.

Some examples of conversion from other number systems to decimal are

$$101101_2 = 1 \times 2^5 + 0 \times 2^4 + 1 \times 2^3 + 1 \times 2^2 + 0 \times 2^1 + 1 \times 2^0$$
$$= 32 + 8 + 4 + 1 = 45$$
$$673_8 = 6 \times 8^2 + 7 \times 8 + 3 \times 8^0 = 443$$

and

$$B7D_{16} = 11 \times 16^2 + 7 \times 16 + 13 \times 16^0 = 2941$$

Decimal	Binary	Ternary	Octal	Hexadecimal
0	00000	0	0	0
1	00001	1	1	1
2	00010	2	2	2
3	00011	10	3	3
4	00100	11	4	4
5	00101	12	5	5
6	00110	20	6	6
7	00111	21	7	7
8	01000	22	10	8
9	01001	100	11	9
10	01010	101	12	A
11	01011	102	13	B
12	01100	110	14	C
13	01101	111	15	D
14	01110	112	16	E
15	01111	120	17	F
16	10000	121	20	10
17	10001	122	21	11

Figure 3.1 Equivalent numbers in different radix systems

Hexadecimal numbers are often identified by a subscript h rather than 16, for example, $B7D_{16} = B7D_h$.

In computer terminology, 1024 is referred to as 1K, rather than the traditional 1000. This is because 1024 is the nearest binary power (2^{10}) to 1000. Thus $2^{16} = 65\ 536$ is referred to as 64K.

Octal and hexadecimal numbers are of particular importance in computers since they can be used as convenient alternatives for binary numbers. This is because three binary digits representing the numbers 0 to 7 can be indicated by a single octal digit, while four binary digits representing the numbers 0 to 15 can be shown by a single hexadecimal digit. Thus a binary number can be converted to octal by grouping the bits in threes from the right and converting each individual group. Similarly the conversion to hexadecimal is achieved by splitting into 4 bit groups, that is

$$1\ 001\ 111\ 011\ 000\ 011_2 = 117\ 303_8$$

or

$$1001\ 1110\ 1100\ 0011_2 = 9EC3_{16}$$

Binary numbers are commonly organised as a fixed number of digits. This is the reason for adopting a fixed number of digits in each number represented in figure 3.1. Each binary digit is referred to as a *bit*, the right one being the least significant (LSB) and the left one the most significant (MSB). An n-bit word can have 2^n possible combinations which may represent positive numbers in the range 0 to $2^n - 1$ (that is, 2^n numbers including zero). Commonly an 8-bit combination is termed a *byte* and 4-bit a *nibble*. Note that a byte may be directly expressed as a 2-digit hexadecimal number — for example, $00111101 \equiv 3D_{16}$.

While the relationship between binary and decimal is not so simple as that between binary and octal or hexadecimal, it must be given special consideration because of its common everyday use. One system that is used is to code each decimal digit as an individual group of 4 bits, although only 10 of the 16 possible combinations will be used. This is referred to as *Binary-Coded Decimal (BCD)*. Thus

$$169 = 0001\ 0110\ 1001_{BCD}$$

Alternatively the decimal number 169 or any decimal number can be expressed as a pure binary number by repeated division by 2. For example

$$169 \div 2 = 84 \text{ remainder } 1 \text{ (LSB)}$$
$$84 \div 2 = 42 \text{ remainder } 0$$
$$42 \div 2 = 21 \text{ remainder } 0$$
$$21 \div 2 = 10 \text{ remainder } 1$$
$$10 \div 2 = 5 \text{ remainder } 0$$
$$5 \div 2 = 2 \text{ remainder } 1$$
$$2 \div 2 = 1 \text{ remainder } 0$$
$$1 \div 2 = 0 \text{ remainder } 1 \text{ (MSB)}$$

The binary number is formed from the values of the successive remainders, with the final remainder in the most significant bit, MSB, position:

$$169 = 10101001_2$$

Note that the pure binary number requires only 8 bits compared with 12 for the BCD number. With a 16-bit word, the maximum decimal number that may be represented using BCD is 9999 while that using binary is 65 535 (that is, $2^n - 1$) for $n = 16$.

Consider a normal 4-bit binary number. Since the left-hand bit determines whether (1) or not (0) an 8 is needed, the next bit a 4, the next a 2 and the right-hand bit a 1, this is often termed an 8421 code.

3.2.2 Signed Numbers

Signed numbers can be represented in binary notation by using the MSB to indicate the sign. While there are a number of codes encountered in specific applications in computers, it is sufficient here to consider only three possibilities. Five-bit numbers will be used in most examples, not because they are ever encountered in practice but because they are easiest for the reader to follow.

(i) Sign and Magnitude

The MSB is set to 0 to represent positive and 1 for negative. The remainder of the word is used to represent the magnitude of the number as a normal unsigned number — for example, $+5 = 00101$ and $-12 = 11100$. With a 5-bit number the range would be -15 to $+15$. Note that 00000 and 10000 both represent 0, which leads to arithmetic manipulation problems.

(ii) Complements of Numbers

(a) Two's Complement Method

The negative number is made up thus:

$$\tilde{N} = 2^{n+1} - N$$

where $\tilde{N}$ = negative number

$\quad n$ = number of digits representing the numbers (exclusive of the sign bit)

$\quad N$ = the number to be negated.

The complement of N is with respect to 2^{n+1}, that is, one order of magnitude higher than that of the sign bit.

Example. Evaluate -15 decimal. Take 4-digit representation, say, when $n = 4$. Hence $N = 15$ and $\tilde{N} = 2^{n+1} - N = 2^{4+1} - 15 = 32 - 15 = 17$.

Thus the two's complement of 15 with respect to 32 is 17_{10} (or 10001) and is written as

sign bit ┆ complement
_____
1 ┆ 0001

Retrieval of the original negative number is achieved thus:

$$N = 2^{n+1} - \tilde{N} = 32 - 17 = 15$$

Hence the negative number is -15.

Note that, when evaluating the negative number, the correct answer may be obtained merely by regarding the sign bit as the negative part of the number and the remainder of the expression as the positive part. Thus

$$-16 \nearrow \overset{1 \mid 0001}{\underset{\mid}{}} \searrow +1 \qquad \text{yielding } -16 + 1 = 15$$

However, this approach is dangerous. The use of 2^{n+1} rather than 2^n ensures that the negative quantities always have a sign bit of 1.

Consider the same example taken in the forward direction for $N = 15$ and taking $n = 4$ when $\tilde{N} = 2^n - N$ gives $2^4 - 15 = 16 - 15 = 1$ written as

$$
\begin{array}{c|c}
\text{sign bit} & \text{complement} \\
\hline
0 & 0001
\end{array}
$$

This is seen to be incorrect.

Summary. We must complement with respect to one order higher than that of the sign bit. In this example $n = 4$, so the sign bit is given by

$$2^n \text{ is sign bit} \nearrow \overset{2^4 \mid 2^3 2^2 2^1 2^0}{\underset{\mid}{}} \qquad \begin{array}{l} \text{Hence we take } 2^{n+1} \\ = 2^5 = 32 \end{array}$$

It is important to realise that our *range of numbers* depends on the value of n we choose. Here with $n = 4$, the range is $+15_{10} \rightarrow 16_{10}$.

Subtraction. Take the example of a larger positive number from which a smaller positive number is subtracted — for example, $9 - 5$. Then

$$
\begin{array}{r}
9 \\
-5 \\
\hline
4
\end{array}
\qquad
\begin{array}{r}
0 \mid 1001 \\
\text{SUBTRACT } 0 \mid 0101 \\
\hline
0 \mid 0100
\end{array}
\qquad \text{thus result of } 9 - 5 = +4
$$

sign $\nearrow$

Alternatively, complement the smaller number and ADD. Thus $\tilde{N} = 2^{4+1} - 5 = 32 - 5 = 27$ written as $1 \mid 1011$ in complement form. Hence

$$
\begin{array}{r}
0 \mid 1001 \\
\text{ADD } 1 \mid 1011 \\
\hline
(1) \quad 0 \mid 0100
\end{array}
\qquad
\begin{array}{r}
9 \\
(-5) \\
\hline
4
\end{array}
\qquad \text{result } 9 + (-5) = 4
$$

$\nearrow$
carry out

Note that with two's complement, the *carry-out* is neglected. The exercise of subtracting a larger positive number from a smaller positive number, for example, 7 − 13, is left to the reader.

Useful Rules. When negating a number, either positive or negative, in two's complement notation, start from the least significant (LS) end; leave the bits unchanged up to and including the first 1. Thereafter invert all bits — that is, 1 to 0 and 0 to 1 (including the sign bit). For example

0 0101 =   5
1 1011 = −5

Figure 3.2 provides a representation of the number range −16 to +15 in binary two's-complement form.

Decimal	Sign and magnitude	One's complement	Two's complement
15	01111	01111	01111
:	:	:	:
2	00010	00010	00010
1	00001	00001	00001
0	00000⎫ 10000⎭	00000⎫ 11111⎭	00000
−1	10001	11110	11111
−2	10010	11101	11110
:	:	:	:
−15	11111	10000	10001
−16	—	—	10000

Figure 3.2 Representations of signed binary numbers

(b) One's Complement Method
Here negative numbers are obtained using the relation

$$\bar{N} = 2^{n+1} - N - 1$$

The same notation is employed as previously except that $\bar{N}$ is one's complement. Hence the extra item in the equation.

Note that with subtraction, any *overflow* from the most significant bit must be added in at the least significant end. This is the *end-around carry*.

Useful Rules. When inverting numbers in one's complement, invert *all* the individual bits; for example

since   5 is ¦ 0 0101
then −5 is ¦ 1 1010

This property is extremely useful on occasions since the one's complement is always immediately available on the reset side of a set of flip-flops constituting a register.

+5	0	0	1	0	1	SET
−5	1	1	0	1	0	RESET

Notes
(a)   For two's complement, zero has unique representation 0 ¦ 0000 with no equivalent to +0, −0
    For one's complement, zero may be

    0 ¦ 0000   or   1 ¦ 1111

    positive zero   negative zero

    In both cases:
(b)   A negative number of small absolute magnitude commences with a string of 1's
(c)   A negative number of large absolute magnitude has 1 for sign bit but followed mostly by 0's.

3.2.3 Binary Fractions

With the number systems so far described, the smallest increment is 1. These are termed *integer* numbers. The general number representation can be extended to include fractions by introducing a *radix point* — that is, decimal or binary point. (Strictly speaking, the fraction is that part of the number to the right of the radix point, the part to the left being the integer.) Thus:

$$(a_2a_1a_0 \cdot f_1f_2f_3)_r = a_2r^2 + a_1r + a_0r + f_1r^{-1} + f_2r^{-2} + f_3r^{-3}$$

The radix point is not physically represented in the binary word but is implied by the programmer as being in a fixed position, hence the term *fixed-point* arithmetic.

3.2.4 Floating-point Representation

Using integer and fixed-point notations, the range of numbers which can be represented is limited by the word-length. An alternative method is to represent the magnitude of the number by a fraction with a separate counter to locate the radix point. The following number equalities illustrate this point:

$$106.372_{10} = 0.106372 \times 10^3$$
$$-0.00032_{10} = -0.32 \times 10^{-3}$$
$$110.1010_2 = 0.110101 \times 2^3$$

In general, the number is represented by

$$\pm m \times r^e$$

where m is called the *mantissa* and e the *exponent*, r being the radix. If the mantissa is adjusted so that the digit immediately following the radix point is the most significant non-zero digit, as in the above examples, the number is said to be *normalised*.

Floating-point numbers can be stored inside a computer by saving m and e only, r being implied. A typical representation is shown in figure 3.3. Since special software or hardware is required to manipulate floating-point numbers, there is no special advantage to be gained in two's complement representation of the mantissa which is stored as sign and magnitude. Two's complement can be used for the exponent.

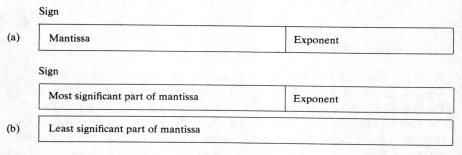

Figure 3.3 Representation of numbers in floating-point format: (a) single precision; (b) double precision

The number of bits in the mantissa determines the number of significant figures, the exponent determines the range of numbers. With a double precision word, the whole of the second word is used to extend the mantissa, thus more than doubling the number of significant figures without increasing the range of numbers.

Single precision in a high-level language, such as FORTRAN, is typically 32 bits — 1 bit for the sign, 23 for the normalised mantissa and 8 for the exponent. Since $2^{23} = 8\ 388\ 608$, approximately 7 decimal places of accuracy are represented. The range of exponent is -128 to 127 so that the largest (normalised) number is

$$0.11 \ldots 1 \times 2^{127} \approx 0.17 \times 10^{38}$$

and the smallest is

$$0.10 \ldots 0 \times 2^{-128} \approx 1.47 \times 10^{-38}$$

With double precision the mantissa is increased to 55 bits, giving approximately 17 decimal places of accuracy.

3.3 Binary Arithmetic

3.3.1 *Unsigned Numbers*

Addition

The normal rules of addition apply, except that a carry is generated when the result exceeds 1. The table shows the possible combinations of adding two 1-bit numbers A and B.

A	B	$A + B$	Carry
0	0	0	0
1	0	1	0
0	1	1	0
1	1	0	1

Subtraction

When subtracting binary numbers the rules of the following table can be applied, borrowing when necessary from the next more significant bit.

A	B	$A - B$	Borrow
0	0	0	0
1	0	1	0
0	1	1	1
1	1	0	0

Multiplication

The rules for multiplication are given in the table below.

A	B	$A \times B$
0	0	0
1	0	0
0	1	0
1	1	1

Example

Multiplicand	101010	42
Multiplier	× 11011	27

```
        101010
        101010
        000000
        101010
        101010
```

Product	10001101110	1134

The 5 intermediate numbers in the above example are termed *partial products*. Note that the product is longer than the multiplicand and multiplier A full 32-bit product must be allowed for when multiplying two 16-bit numbers. The 32-bit product must thus be allocated two 16-bit words. Further details of the technique are given in section 4.9. With binary numbers, since each digit is either 1 or 0, each partial product is either the multiplicand or zero.

The individual partial products need not be saved. The first is calculated by copying the multiplicand or zero, dependent upon whether the LSB of the multiplier is 1 or 0 respectively. The second partial product is similarly obtained and added to the first, but displaced one place to the left. This is repeated *n* times. This technique of adding a number to the previous result (shifting in this special case) is called *accumulation*. In practice if the multiplier bit is zero, the addition can simply be skipped, but not the shift of course. This method of binary multiplication is referred to as *shift-and-add*. A hardware implementation of the multiplier is shown in section 4.9.

Division

Division can be performed by the conventional *long division* techniques as shown in the following example. 42 is the dividend, 27 the divisor and the answer the quotient.

Example

```
            1.10001            Result      = 1.10001
    11011  ⌐101010       that is, 1 + 1/2 + 1/32 = 1.531
            11011
          ─────────
           0011110
           11011
          ─────────
            0110000
            11011
           ─────────
            101010
```

Note that the error introduced in the truncated answer given above is quite large (42 ÷ 27 = 1.5556). This example serves to show that appreciably more binary places must be retained to give the equivalent decimal accuracy.

3.3.2 Signed Numbers

Since the MSB is used to represent the sign of the number, it is most important to treat all numbers as a fixed number of bits with leading zeros as necessary. In the following examples, 5-bit numbers will be used — that is, four significant bits together with a sign bit.

Sign and Magnitude

The actual operation must be determined by a logical test of the sign bits involved and the operation demanded: for example, $A - B$ can involve the following, where $| \cdot |$ means the magnitude or *modulus*:

  (i) A and B positive $|A| > |B|$ *subtract* $|B|$ from $|A|$
  (ii) A and B positive $|A| < |B|$ *subtract* $|A|$ from $|B|$
        and set sign bit of answer to negative
 (iii) A positive, B negative, *add* $|A|$ and $|B|$
  (iv) A negative, B negative, *subtract* $|A|$ from $|B|$
   (v) A negative, B positive, *add* $|A|$ and $|B|$ and
        set sign bit of answer to negative

For multiplication (or division) the moduli can be multiplied (divided) and the sign bit set to positive if the signs of A and B are the same, negative otherwise.

3.3.3   Floating-point

Addition and Subtraction

The smaller number is adjusted by shifting the mantissa right, filling in with leading zeros and incrementing the exponent by one for each shift. This proceeds until the exponents are equal, when the mantissas can be directly added (subtracted) as sign and magnitude numbers. The resultant mantissa may exceed 1, in which case it must be shifted right one place and the exponent incremented.

$$0.11011 \mid 001 = + 0.843375 \times 2^1 = 1.6875$$
$$+ \ 0.10001 \mid 110 = + 0.53125 \times 2^{-2} = 0.1328$$

becomes

$$0.11011 \mid 001$$
$$+ \ 0.00010 \mid 001$$
$$\overline{0.11101 \mid 001} = + 0.90625 \times 2^1 \ \ = 1.8125$$

Note that in shifting the smaller number, significant bits are lost, resulting in a loss of precision.

Multiplication and Division

If

$$A = m_1 r^{e_1} \text{ and } B = m_2 r^{e_2}$$

then

$$A \times B = (m_1 \times m_2)\, r^{(e_1 + e_2)}$$

and

$$\frac{A}{B} = \frac{m_1}{m_2}\, r^{(e_1 - e_2)}$$

Thus to multiply two floating-point numbers, the mantissas must be multiplied as sign and magnitude numbers and the exponents added. The mantissa may result in a 0 in the left-hand bit in which case it must be shifted left and the exponent decremented.

3.4 Non-numeric Data

3.4.1 Alphanumeric Characters

A number is stored and manipulated inside the computer as a binary number but must be printed for external display as an equivalent decimal number. This in turn means that the number must be represented as a string of characters and fed to the printer one at a time in sequence. Thus in order to drive the printer the computer must have a standard internal representation for each possible character. In addition to the numeric characters 0, 1, . . . , 9 the character set must include 26 upper and 26 lower case alphabetic characters, the usual symbols, $+ - \times \div$, full stop, comma, etc., and a number of special *non-printing* characters to issue control commands mixed in with alphanumeric messages. The most common set is called the ASCII code (American Standard Code for Information Interchange) which uses 7 bits since $2^7 = 128$. A set of 128 characters is thus defined. An eighth bit, termed a parity bit, is appended to give the standard 8-bit byte per character. The parity bit is appended as a 1 or 0 such that the total number of 1's in the eight bits is an even (or odd) number for every character. By checking the number of 1's at any time, a single bit error can be detected. Some typical ASCII characters are:

Alphanumeric	ASCII Code	Value of p to achieve even parity
Space	$p0100000$	$p = 1$ for even parity
0	$p0110000$	$p = 0$
1	$p0110001$	$p = 1$
⋮		
9	$p0111001$	$p = 0$
A	$p1000001$	$p = 0$
B	$p1000010$	$p = 0$
⋮		
Z	$p1011010$	$p = 0$
etc.		

Thus the decimal number 5741 may be stored inside the computer as a 16-bit binary number

0001011001101101

For transmission to a printer a special program is run which reconverts this number to the equivalent decimal number 5741, and then codes each decimal digit as individual ASCII characters, which are stored in memory; for example

00110101 = ASCII (5)
00110111 = ASCII (7)
10110100 = ASCII (4)
10110001 = ASCII (1)

The print routine is finally completed by transmitting the string of characters, one at a time, to the printer. Note that while the 10 numeric characters can be coded using only 4 bits, as in BCD, for input and output purposes the numeric characters are 10 of the 128 alphanumeric characters defined for ASCII and thus require the full 8-bit code.

3.4.2 Logical Variables

When a computer is used in a control system the external data variables may be numeric (for example, output from an analogue-to-digital converter), but more often they are simple two-state signals. Typically these signals are related to opening or closing of switches, such as limit switches, overload indicators, turn on or off, etc. In computer terms these can all be interpreted as being in a 0 or 1 state. For output from the computer the voltage levels can be used to open (0) or close (1) a relay, the contacts of which can switch power as required. For input to the computer an external switch contact can be connected in series with a 5 volt battery, the computer receiving 0 or 5 volts when the switch is open or closed respectively.

Now any logical variable can be represented by the state of a single bit. However, computers are orientated fundamentally towards binary words and not single bits. Two techniques are used to handle logical variables:

(a) Allocate a full word, set to the numbers 0 or 1. Alternatively the MSB can carry the 0 to 1 so that the logical state can be interpreted as a positive or negative number.
(b) Allocate specific bits of a word to a variable so that, for example, 16 logical variables are represented in one 16-bit word.

The first method is wasteful of internal storage space, the second method is economic. For the first method, however, no special instructions are required; for example, a normal output instruction transmits the full word from the computer, the appropriate relay being connected to the one specific wire, all the others being ignored. With the second method, special instructions are required to manipulate particular bits inside the word; for example, instructions to set or clear the mth bit in a word without affecting the other bits, and similar instructions to test the state of a bit. With the second method, 16 output lines can be controlled by one output *port*, while the first method requires 16 separate ports. Both techniques are commonly encountered, the first method being more suitable for low numbers of variables, the second for high numbers.

Coding

In the above examples it has been assumed that each logical variable is independent of every other, so that m wires are required to control m outputs. The number of wires required to transmit information can be reduced by coding data. Consider the switching for a traffic signal, which has three logical variables, red, amber and green (logical variables since they are either lit or not). The standard sequence is red, red/amber, green, amber, red, etc. With 3 output wires (r, a and g), this sequence can be controlled by the logical conditions:

red	amber	green
1	0	0
1	1	0
0	0	1
0	1	0
1	0	0	repeating

etc.

While there are eight possible combinations of the three variables only four are used, which can therefore be coded into a 2-digit variable thus:

    00 = red only
    01 = red and amber
    10 = amber only
    11 = green only

With the first method, three wires are required but the lamp relays can be directly switched. With the second scheme, only two wires are needed but the traffic-signal controller must decode the data to determine which lights to switch. The technique is explained in section 4.6.2.

Coding of data requires fewer digits to store and transmit information, but requires equipment to code the data initially and to decode it before use.

3.5 Summary and Conclusions

This chapter has presented a review of the differing techniques used to represent information in a binary form suitable for internal storage and manipulation in a digital computer.

It has been stressed that there is more than one method of representing the same information, different methods having advantages in specific cases. For example, 16-bit integer numbers are much easier to manipulate than floating-point numbers, but if the range of numbers is wide, then the penalty for using floating-point cannot be avoided as the integer number is inadequate.

It has also been stressed that provision must be made for other than numeric data.

The problems of storage and manipulation of binary data necessary to implement the techniques just introduced are considered in the next chapter.

Bibliography

Richard, R. K., *Arithmetic Operations in Digital Computers*, Van Nostrand, New York, 1955.

Problems

3.1 Convert the following unsigned binary numbers into decimal numbers:
(a) 11011101110 (b) 100100111 (c) 0110110001
(b) 0011011 (e) 1010·1010 (f) 0110111·1001111

3.2 Convert the binary numbers of problem **3.1** into octal numbers.

3.3 Convert the binary numbers of problem **3.1** into hexadecimal numbers.

3.4 Convert the following decimal numbers into binary numbers:
(a) 376 (b) 221 (c) 999 (d) 2376 (e) 167.32 (f) 0.01135

3.5 Convert the decimal numbers of problem **3.4** into octal numbers.

3.6 Convert the decimal numbers of problem **3.4** into hexadecimal numbers.

3.7 Convert the following octal numbers into hexadecimal numbers
(a) 63 (b) 216 (c) 3472 (d) 2376
(*Hint*: convert to binary first.)

3.8 Convert the following hexadecimal numbers into octal numbers:
(a) AB (b) 3AA (c) 79FF (d) A111E

3.9 Convert the following hexadecimal numbers to eight-bit two's complement binary numbers:
(a) 6 (b) −6 (c) 100 (d) −100
(e) 64 (f) −32 (g) 150

3.10 Using eight-bit two's complement numbers and two's complement arithmetic, calculate $A + B$ and $A - B$ for:
(a) $A = 6, B = -6$ (b) $A = 120, B = 4$
(c) $A = -32, B = 64$ (d) $A = -16, B = -32$
(e) $A = 100, B = 64$ (f) $A = 64, B = -80$
Note: Check for overflow.

3.11 By using the examples of problem **3.10**, show that the MIC *algorithm* for subtraction, for example, $A - B = (\overline{A} + B)$, is valid for all two's complement numbers.

3.12 Calculate by using binary numbers and the shift-and-add technique the following products:
(a) 2×2 (b) 8×3 (c) 15×15 (d) 12×7
Use four-bit numbers and an eight-bit product, unsigned.

3.13 Assuming the same floating-point number format as in section 3.2.4., express as unsigned, normalised mantissa and an eight-bit two's complement exponent, the following numbers:

(a) 872   (b) 0.103   (c) 3727.62

(d) 1.2×10^{-3} (e) 0.67×10^4

3.14 Assuming the same floating-point number format as in problem **3.13**, express the following as decimal numbers:

(a) 011100000000000000001100

(b) 111100000000000000001100

(c) 010110100000000010010000

3.15 From the information given in Section 3.4.1 complete the table for the eight-bit-with-odd-parity ASCII representation of the letters of the alphabet and the numbers 0 to 9.

4 The Building Blocks

Objectives

A digital computer is an interconnected network of logic circuit elements. Different features of the machine are created by specific combinations of the basic elements. These elements, the building blocks, are discussed in this chapter. Some specific examples of building blocks such as a binary adder and a counter are provided. A complete computer is left to chapters 5 and 6.

It is most important for the reader to understand the concepts introduced here since they will be used freely in constructing more complete computer systems in later chapters.

The fundamental elements of *combinational logic*, AND, OR, NOT, NAND and NOR gates, are described from a *black-box* viewpoint, rather than an electronic one, in keeping with the current trend towards widespread use of *integrated circuits*. *Sequential logic* elements with memory capability which comprise the various forms of flip-flop, are developed from *combinational* logic gates.

The algebra of logic, *Boolean algebra*, is introduced together with *truth tables*. Only sufficient depth to help promote basic understanding is provided.

The concept of *data flow* is stressed, an idea which is fundamental to the understanding of computer operation.

4.1 Logic Systems

As previously explained, information in a digital computer is represented by two-state devices. The basic binary digit *(bit)* can take one of two states, 0 or 1. Inside the computer these two states are represented by different voltage levels. If logic 1 is represented by a more positive voltage than logic 0, *positive logic* is employed; for example, $1 \equiv +5$ volts, $0 \equiv 0$ volts. Conversely if logic 1 is represented by a more negative voltage than logic 0, *negative logic* is involved; for example, $1 \equiv 0$ volts, $0 \equiv 5$ volts.

In practice, the power supply voltage to the component will determine the voltage levels employed for logic signals. The supply voltage specifications are relatively high and can only be allowed to vary from the specification by 2 to 5 per cent. The signal levels on the other hand can vary considerably before causing errors. As an example, the common standard is that 0 is represented by 0.7 volts and 1 by 2.5 volts with a 5 volt power supply. The 5 volt power supply must not vary by more than 250 mV while 0 can be any voltage below 0.7 volt and 1 any voltage above 2.5 volts. As a result, a designer will aim at *nominal* values of, say, 0.5 volt for logic 0 and 3.5 volt for logic 1. This is important since outputs may be required to feed one or many inputs (the number of connected inputs an output can accommodate is called *fan-out*) along various lengths of wiring circuits and therefore will not be totally consistent. It is most important in practice that the power supplies are heavily decoupled to avoid transient switching signals getting into the chip. There is a standard nominal load that an input places on an output device. Actual chips will vary in the actual load they present which is specified in an equivalent number of nominal loads, the *fan-in*. The total number of unit loads connected to an output must not exceed the specified maximum *fan-out*.

Each logic element, and there are thousands in each computer, is made from a circuit of transistors, diodes, resistors, etc. However each element, say one of the gates described in this chapter, is usually available as a single *integrated-circuit* (IC) entity compared with the discrete circuit components used in earlier computers. In fact not only single gates but specific combinations of a number of gates can be manufactured on one IC, referred to as a *chip*, since they are constructed on a small chip of silicon, encapsulated in plastic or ceramic. Thus a chip with, say, four AND gates is termed *small-scale integration* (SSI) while a memory chip with 4000 storage elements is referred to as *large-scale integration* (LSI).

Each element, such as a gate, a memory cell, etc., comprises a number of transistors, so that there can be many thousands in practice on one LSI chip. There are two basic types of transistor, the *bipolar* and the *field effect* (FET), which lead to whole families of MSI and LSI systems. The most dominant are the bipolar-based *transistor–transistor logic* (TTL) circuits and the FET based *metal–oxide–silicon* (MOS) units. The former are used mostly for fast MSI and the latter for slower LSI. Typically the *central processor* of a computer will be made from TTL elements while the computer *memory* will comprise MOS elements, although the simpler processors, such as calculators and microprocessors, are MOS LSI chips.

Details of integrated circuit electronics are not required in this book and the reader should turn to other books (for example ref. 4.1) which include a more detailed treatment. The following table is included to give some feeling for the effects which the different technologies will have on speed, power consumption and size. *Emitter-coupled logic* (ECL) is included as typical of one of a number of lesser-used technologies which have special attributes, in this case high speed.

Type	Switching speed (nanosecond)	Power consumption (mW/gate)	Density (gate/mm²)	Typical voltages logic 0	logic 1	Power supply
TTL	2–25	1–20	15	0	3.5	5
MOS	10–300	0.05–1	150	0	4.0	5
ECL	0.3–1	30–250	10	−1.58	−0.75	

To improve interconnection of various chips, small MOS components today are made with TTL-compatible signal levels at their pins.

Having noted that LSI technology reduces cost, size and power consumption and improves reliability, little further mention will be made in this book of the details of the physical implementation of integrated circuits.

Logic circuits, systems constructed from logic components, can be broken into two classes: *combinational* and *sequential*. The output from a combinational circuit is a function of the present inputs. On the other hand a sequential circuit relies on the present inputs *and* previous states (outputs, inputs or intermediate signals). In practice this means that combinational circuits consist of gates only whereas a sequential circuit contains both combinational and memory elements. These memory elements are termed *flip-flops*. A typical example of a *combinational* circuit is an adder, while a counter is a *sequential* circuit. These circuits are explained more fully later.

4.2 AND, OR and NOT Gates

A logic gate is a basic element with an output which takes on the value 1 or 0 dependent upon the combination of the logic levels of the inputs to the gate. There may be any number of inputs, although there is a practical limit, and 2, 3 or 4 are common per element.

A simple method of specifying the characteristics of a gate is the truth table in which there is one entry for each possible combination of the inputs together with the corresponding output state. Thus there are $2^2 = 4$ entries for two inputs, $2^3 = 8$ entries for three etc. Typical examples are shown in figures 4.1, 4.3, 4.4, etc.

The two basic elements are the AND and the OR gates. The AND function is the same as the *intersect* ($\land$) of set theory and the OR function is the *union* ($\cup$). In the computer field a dot (multiplication symbol) is used to mean AND while a plus sign is used for OR. Thus if an output variable,

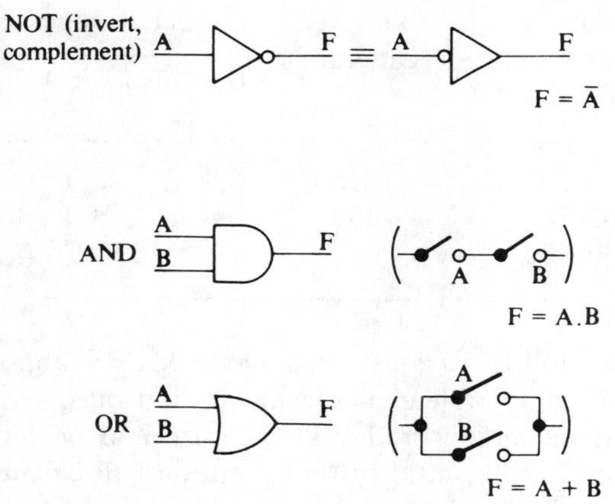

A	F
0	1
1	0

NOT (invert, complement)

$F = \bar{A}$

A	B	F
0	0	0
1	0	0
0	1	0
1	1	1

AND

$F = A.B$

A	B	F
0	0	0
1	0	1
0	1	1
1	1	1

OR

$F = A + B$

Figure 4.1 NOT, AND and OR logic elements

F, is defined as the logical AND of three inputs A, B and C, then this is written

$$F = A \cdot B \cdot C \ (\equiv A \wedge B \wedge C)$$

Effectively the AND function means that the output will be 0 unless *all* the inputs are 1 when the output will be 1. Similarly the OR function is defined such that

$$F = A + B + C \ (\equiv A \cup B \cup C)$$

This means that the output will be 1 as long as any of the inputs are 1 and will be 0 only if all inputs are 0. To express this more clearly refer to figure 4.1 where the AND and OR functions for two-input gates are shown in terms of their truth tables. Note the logic symbols introduced in this figure and the equivalent switch circuits.

Also shown in figure 4.1 is a NOT gate. This has one output and one input and is said to *invert* or *complement* the input as shown in the truth table. Note that diagrammatically the small circle on an input or output line is used to indicate when a signal is complemented.

Unfortunately there is a variety of sets of symbols in use. Figure 4.30 at the end of the chapter provides common alternatives to the set used in this book. Consistency as to the set of symbols used should be regarded as important.

4.3 Boolean Algebra

Just as there is a well defined algebra for numbers, there is an appropriate algebra for logical variables, called Boolean algebra after its originator, George Boole.

Each variable of Boolean algebra can take one of two states, on or off, open or closed, true or false, or in the simplest notation 0 or 1. A complement is represented by a bar over the variable; for example $\bar{A}$ is the complement of A. 0 is the complement of 1. Hence $\bar{0} = 1$. The table overleaf defines the fundamental Boolean relationships and should be studied carefully. The laws may be verified by substitution of combinations of 0's and 1's for the variables A and B.

If table 4.1 is studied, it can be seen that the AND of two logical variables produces the same results as multiplication applied to the binary numbers 0 and 1. Similarly, with one exception, the OR function is similar to binary addition. The exception is the OR of 1 and 1, which is 1, while 1 plus 1 is 0 (carry 1). Thus the standard OR function is more specifically called the *Inclusive-OR* while an alternative *Exclusive-OR* function is defined and denoted by the symbol $\oplus$ such that $1 \oplus 1 = 0$. This concept is expanded at the end of this section.

The laws included in the table are obviously devised to help simplify complex Boolean equations. Some examples of simplification will be included in this book, but at a very simple level. Further design simplification is important as it can result in a reduction in the number of gates required to implement a complex logic circuit. It becomes less important however as the cost of logic components falls. Details as to traditional approaches to logic design may be found in many books (for example refs 4.2 and 4.3), while more modern approaches are discussed in ref. 4.4.

An example of the simplification of a Boolean expression is shown in figure 4.2 and relates to the function

$$X = A \cdot B + \bar{A} \cdot B + \bar{A} \cdot \bar{B}$$

This is implemented in figure 4.2 (a) using six gates. Simplification of the Boolean expression gives

$$X = A \cdot B + \bar{A}(B + \bar{B}) \text{ since } (B + \bar{B}) = 1$$
$$X = A \cdot B + \bar{A}$$

which is implemented in figure 4.2(b) using three gates. If now the third of the three absorption laws is utilised we have

$$X = \bar{A} + B$$

Table 4.1 The fundamental relations of Boolean algebra

AND		OR		
$1 \cdot 1 = 1$		$1 + 1 = 1$		
$1 \cdot 0 = 0$		$1 + 0 = 1$		
$0 \cdot 0 = 0$		$0 + 0 = 0$		
$A \cdot 1 = A$		$A + 0 = A$		
$A \cdot 0 = 0$		$A + 1 = 1$		
$A \cdot A = A$		$A + A = A$	Indempotence	
$A \cdot \bar{A} = 0$		$A + \bar{A} = 1$	Complementarity	
$A \cdot B = B \cdot A$		$A + B = B + A$	Commutativity	
$A \cdot (B \cdot C) = (A \cdot B) \cdot C$		$(A + B) + C = A + (B + C)$	Associativity	

$\bar{\bar{A}} = A$ Involution

$$A + AB = A$$
$$A(A + B) = A$$
$$A + \bar{A}B = A + B$$
   Absorption Laws

$$\overline{A + B} = \bar{A} \cdot \bar{B}$$
$$\overline{A \cdot B} = \bar{A} + \bar{B}$$
   De Morgan's Theorem

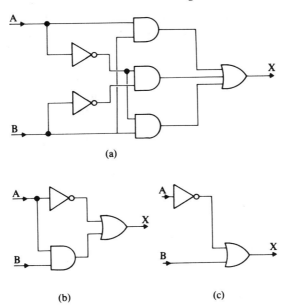

(a)

(b)   (c)

Figure 4.2 Different implementations of the function
$$X = A \cdot B + \bar{A} \cdot B + \bar{A} \cdot \bar{B}$$

which requires only two gates as shown in figure 4.2(c). Note that one of the gates in figure 4.2(a), the OR gate, has three inputs.

The truth tables shown for the various gates on figure 4.1 define all possible states of the input variables. Truth tables can also be constructed for more complex Boolean expressions. Thus for the example used above, which simplified to

$$X = \bar{A} + B$$

the truth table is

A	B	$X = \bar{A} + B$
0	0	1
1	0	0
0	1	1
1	1	1

This truth table is constructed by substituting the appropriate values of the variables in any row into the defining equation. In practice the inverse situation is more common whereby the truth table is constructed from the physical requirements of the system so that the problem is then to find the equivalent Boolean expression. This is simply done by writing down the combinations of each row of the truth table which gives a logical 1 as the result. Thus from the above truth table $X = 1$ when $A = 0$ and $B = 0$ (1st row) — that is, $X = \bar{A} \cdot \bar{B}$. Also $X = 1$ when $A = 0$ and $B = 1$ (3rd row) — that is, $X = \bar{A} \cdot B$. Finally, from the 4th row $X = A \cdot B$. Thus $X = 1$ for any of these combinations of A and B, the first row, or the third row, or the fourth row, so that

$$X = \bar{A} \cdot \bar{B} + \bar{A} \cdot B + A \cdot B$$

Note that the expression derived direct from the truth table is the unsimplified form. Each term in the expression is a combination of *all* variables. No term has A or B only before simplification. This form of expression is called the *sum of products* and each term is called a *minterm*.

An immediately simpler expression can often be obtained by considering the combinations for which the result is 0. For the above example there is only one row, so that combinations do not need to be OR-ed together. Thus, for the second row $X = 0$ when $A = 1$ and $B = 0$, that is

$$\bar{X} = A \cdot \bar{B}$$
$$X = \overline{A \cdot \bar{B}}$$
$$= \bar{A} + \bar{\bar{B}} = \bar{A} + B \text{ (De Morgan's Theorem)}$$

Thus we have seen that a truth table gives an exact defining Boolean expression directly. This Boolean expression is not necessarily the simplest one.

Figure 4.3 shows the details of the Exclusive-OR function, differing from the normal OR function in the fourth row. The defining Boolean equations can be derived from the truth table.

Some examples of the use of Boolean algebra appear in chapter 5 where the logic of the arithmetic and control unit of a minimal computer is

$$F = A \oplus B$$
$$= A.\bar{B} + B.\bar{A}$$
$$= \overline{\bar{A}.\bar{B} + A.B}$$

A	B	F
0	0	0
1	0	1
0	1	1
1	1	0

Figure 4.3 The exclusive-OR logic element

considered. The reader is invited to work that material in the light of the treatment of Boolean algebra given here.

4.4 NAND and NOR Gates

A NAND (NOT-AND) gate is a combination of a conventional AND gate (two or more inputs) and a NOT gate. Thus the output is the complement of the AND gate.

A NOR (NOT–OR) gate is similarly an OR gate cascaded with a NOT gate.

Both the NAND and NOR gates are summarised with their symbols and truth tables in figure 4.4. Note the use of De Morgan's theorem to give the alternate forms in which the input signals are complemented.

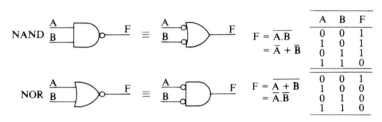

A	B	F
0	0	1
1	0	1
0	1	1
1	1	0
0	0	1
1	0	0
0	1	0
1	1	0

NAND $F = \overline{A.B}$
       $= \bar{A} + \bar{B}$

NOR $F = \overline{A + B}$
       $= \bar{A}.\bar{B}$

Figure 4.4 The NAND and NOR logic elements

The importance of the NAND gate is that it can be used to synthesise all other gates as shown in figure 4.5. Thus *any* combinational logic circuit can be implemented exclusively with NAND gates. This would appear at first sight to be clumsy since, for example, the one OR gate requires three

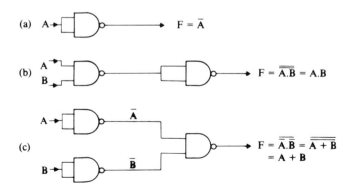

(a) $F = \bar{A}$

(b) $F = \overline{\overline{A.B}} = A.B$

(c) $F = \overline{\bar{A}.\bar{B}} = \overline{\bar{A}} + \overline{\bar{B}}$
     $= A + B$

Figure 4.5 Use of NAND gates to synthesise other functions

NAND gates. In practice, more complex circuits can often be more simply implemented in NAND logic. An example is the half-adder described in the next section. This approach is accentuated further by the fact that certain logic elements, particularly registers, give both the output and its complement so that if both A and $\bar{A}$ and B and $\bar{B}$ are available, the one OR gate requires only the one NAND gate, see figure 4.5(c). The whole concept of NAND gate implementation is based on manipulation of complements using De Morgan's theorem. The position is indicated on figure 4.5.

It is left as an exercise to show that all functions can similarly be synthesised exclusively with NOR gates.

NAND gate logic dominated in the early days of integrated circuits, since they were the easiest to fabricate and avoided a proliferation of elements. The single chip with four independent two-input NAND gates was the most common component. Nowadays all types of gate are equally available and circuits are implemented in the most convenient combination. The standard MSI chip is packaged typically as a 14-pin entity approximately $\frac{3}{4}$ inch $\times$ $\frac{3}{8}$ inch; two pins are required for power supplies, the other twelve being used for data pins. Examples of commercial components utilising the 12 data pins are

> Quad 2-input AND, OR, NAND, etc., gates
> Hex (6) inverter (NOT) gates
> Triple 3-input AND, OR, etc., gates

4.5 The Two-input AND Gate, Bus-bars and Data Flow

The basis of the operation of a digital computer is the control of transfer of data from one point in the system to another. It is most convenient descriptively to think of data *flowing* from a source to a destination. Data of course does not flow, the voltage levels available at the data source are simple *switched* to a connecting wire so that they are applied as inputs to the destination, but the idea is very simple to understand. The switch must be a high-speed electronic device which can be opened or closed by application of an appropriate control voltage so that specific flow paths can be connected selectively when an instruction is decoded. The two-input AND gate provides the ideal switch.

The two-input AND gate is redrawn in figure 4.6. This is the same gate as shown in figure 4.1 but the inputs are now termed X_i and C while the output is labelled X_0. By inspection of the truth table it can be noted that $X_0 = 0$ when $C = 0$ but $X_0 = X_i$ when $C = 1$. Thus C acts as a *control signal*. A lot of confusion can occur with the most obvious terms, *open* and *closed*, so that a gate is said to be *inhibited* with $C = 0$ and *enabled*

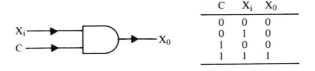

C	X_i	X_0
0	0	0
0	1	0
1	0	0
1	1	1

Figure 4.6 Use of two-input AND gate to control data flow

with $C = 1$. Examples of this use of AND gates are given in chapter 5 (section 5.7).

Now consider figure 4.7 where there are two possible data sources, A and B, one of which is to flow to X. With $C_1 = 1$ and $C_2 = 0$, $X = A$ while with $C_1 = 0$ and $C_2 = 1$, $X = B$. If $C_1 = C_2 = 0$, then $X = 0$ independently of $A + B$. If $C_1 = C_2 = 1$, then $X = A + B$, which is allowable but achieves nothing in terms of control of data flow and is simply avoided by the control unit of a computer. In practice, there may be more than two data sources in contention and there may be more than one destination device. The actual physical source output and destination input wires may be some distance away, in computer terms, so that the concept of a *data bus* or *bus-bar*, is commonly used. Data is asserted on the bus and all receiving devices copy that data. One and only one source device can be connected at any one time or else one source might try to establish logical 1 while another source wants to establish logical 0. Such a system is shown in figure 4.8. The first thing to note is that the OR gate used in figure 4.7 has been dispensed with, the outputs from the AND gates being wired in parallel by the bus. This is simply not allowable with standard gates since if one asserts logical 1 while another demands logical 0 then circulating currents flow which burn out the device. Special gates, termed *open-collector* (OC) gates, are available for which the outputs can be wired together to perform a NOR function, figure 4.9(a). This is referred to variously as *Dot-OR* or *Wired-OR* and gives similar results to figure 4.7, apart from the data inversion.

The simpler alternative to the open-collector gate is a *tri-state* gate as shown in figure 4.9(b). The tri-state gate is similar to a two-input AND gate, enabled when $C = 1$ but when $C = 0$ the output is not clamped to

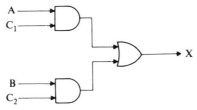

Figure 4.7 Use of gates to route data flow

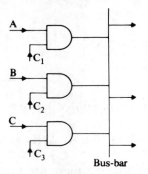

Figure 4.8 A bus-bar system

logical 0 but is disconnected — that is, it floats. Thus the outputs of tri-state gates can be freely wired together as in the bus-bar system. However if more than one control signal is set to 1 then damage can occur when the two enabled data sources differ in logic levels. Thus with the tri-state gates used in figure 4.8, care must be taken to ensure that only one control (or enable) signal is set to 1 at any instant.

The bus-bar concept is common in practical computers. Examples of the use of bus-bars are given in chapter 6.

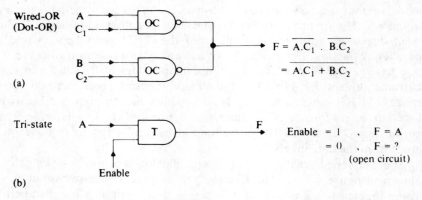

Figure 4.9 (a) Open-collector and (b) tri-state gates

4.6 Combinational Logic Systems

4.6.1 Binary Adders

The basic element of a binary adder is a logic unit which generates two outputs, one the sum and the other carry, of three input binary digits.

Three inputs are required, the two units of data being added plus a possible carry from a lower significant addition. Such a device is called a *full-adder*, figure 4.10(b). The simpler device with just two bits of input is called a *half-adder*, figure 4.10(a).

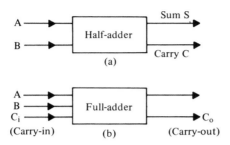

Figure 4.10 Schematic diagram of (a) half-adder and (b) full-adder

Since data is word orientated, it is frequently necessary to add two n-bit words together. This addition can be achieved either by a *serial* or a *parallel* technique. To demonstrate these techniques, consider the addition of two n-bit binary numbers A and B, such that $A = A_{n-1}A_{n-2} \cdots A_1A_0$ where A_0, A_1, etc. are the binary digits with A_{n-1} the most significant bit (MSB) and A_0 the least significant (LSB). Similarly for B.

Serial Adder

The full addition takes n time intervals. In the first interval the LSBs A_0 and B_0 are presented to the full-adder input with $C_i = 0$. The output S is now the LSB of the sum, S_0, and is saved. The carry bit, C_0, is also saved. In the next time interval A_1, B_1 and the value of C_0 saved from the previous addition are presented to the full-adder, generating S_1 and any carry for the next more significant addition. This continues until after the nth time interval the full n-bit sum $S = S_{n-1} S_{n-2} \cdots S_1S_0$ has been produced. Any carry out remaining from the nth addition is the carry due to the full n-bit addition. All n S-bits generated must be saved while only the one C-bit needs saving, being over-written at each interval. Since the C-bit must be saved at each interval for use in the next interval, the n-bit serial adder is a sequential logical circuit, although the full-adder itself is combinational. The need for storing bits of data is thus demonstrated. The use of such an adder is described in detail in chapter 5.

Parallel Adder

A parallel adder uses one time interval and n full-adders as shown in figure 4.11. Consider the rth adder along the chain. The inputs A and B are

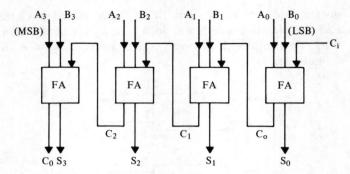

Figure 4.11 A four-bit parallel adder

immediately available but the value of C will be affected by the result of the $(r-1)^{th}$ sum, which in turn depends on the $(r-2)^{th}$ sum, etc. Thus the carry bits propagate from the LSB upwards and the more significant sum bits change transiently until all the less significant full-adders have completed. This is termed *ripple-through* and the n-bit sum is not complete until n times the time taken for the individual carry bits to set. This time is significantly shorter, however, than the n time intervals required for the serial addition. In practice, more complex circuits are used, called *carry-look-ahead* logic, to speed up the operation.

Implementation of the Half-adder

The truth table for the half-adder of figure 4.10(a) is

A	B	S	C
0	0	0	0
1	0	1	0
0	1	1	0
1	1	0	1

By using the rules previously described in section 4.3:

$$S = A \cdot \bar{B} + \bar{A} \cdot B = A \oplus B$$

and

$$C = A \cdot B$$

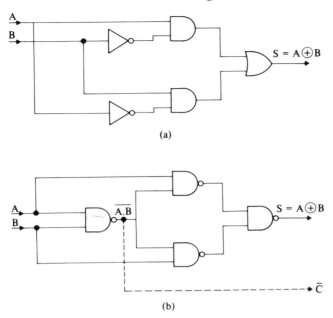

(a)

(b)

Figure 4.12 Implementations of the half-adder

The direct implementation of S is shown in figure 4.12(a). However, by using De Morgan's theorem and involution:

$$S = A \cdot \bar{B} + \bar{A} \cdot B = \overline{(\overline{A \cdot \bar{B}}) \cdot (\overline{\bar{A} \cdot B})}$$

Now

$$\overline{A \cdot \bar{B}} = \overline{A \cdot \bar{A} + A \cdot \bar{B}} = \overline{A \cdot (\bar{A} + \bar{B})}$$
$$= \overline{A \cdot \overline{A \cdot B}}$$

Similarly

$$\overline{\bar{A} \cdot B} = \overline{B \cdot \overline{A \cdot B}}$$

Thus, as shown in figure 4.12(b), the exclusive-OR function can be implemented entirely with NAND gates. Note that this is an example where the NAND gate implementation requires fewer gates than the direct method. Further the complement of C is directly available.

Implementation of the Full-adder

The truth table for the full-adder of figure 4.10(b) is

A	B	Carry-in C_i	Sum S	Carry-out C_0
0	0	0	0	0
1	0	0	1	0
0	1	0	1	0
1	1	0	0	1
0	0	1	1	0
1	0	1	0	1
0	1	1	0	1
1	1	1	1	1

Hence

$$S = A\bar{B}\bar{C_i} + \bar{A}B\bar{C_i} + \bar{A}\bar{B}C_i + ABC_i$$

and

$$C_0 = AB\bar{C_i} + A\bar{B}C_i + \bar{A}BC_i + ABC_i$$

It can be shown by more advanced techniques than those introduced here that S is the minimal realisation. C_0 can be minimised by OR-ing the term ABC_i twice more and grouping, thus

$$C_0 = AB\bar{C_i} + ABC_i + A\bar{B}C_i + ABC_i + \bar{A}BC_i + ABC_i$$
$$= AB(\bar{C_i} + C_i) + AC_i(\bar{B} + B) + BC_i(\bar{A} + A)$$
$$= AB + AC_i + BC_i$$
$$= \overline{\bar{AB} \cdot \bar{AC_i} \cdot \bar{BC_i}}$$

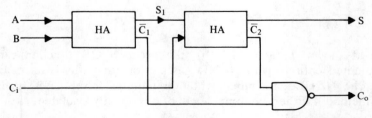

Figure 4.13 Construction of half-adder using two half-adders

Rather than implement the above Boolean functions directly, the full-adder can be constructed from two half-adders and a NAND gate as shown in figure 4.13.

4.6.2 Decoders

One-out-of-n Decoder

A decoder is a device which activates one specific output line, selected by a binary number on the input lines. Since there are 2^n ways of arranging n bits, a decoder with 3 input lines can select one-out-of-8 output lines, with 4 inputs one-out-of-16 outputs, with five inputs one-out-of-32 (see the example of chapter 5, section 5.7.3).

The truth table for a one-out-of-8 decoder is

Input			Output							
A_2	A_1	A_0	F_0	F_1	F_2	F_3	F_4	F_5	F_6	F_7
0	0	0	1	0	0	0	0	0	0	0
0	0	1	0	1	0	0	0	0	0	0
0	1	0	0	0	1	0	0	0	0	0
0	1	1	0	0	0	1	0	0	0	0
1	0	0	0	0	0	0	1	0	0	0
1	0	1	0	0	0	0	0	1	0	0
1	1	0	0	0	0	0	0	0	1	0
1	1	1	0	0	0	0	0	0	0	1

Thus 8 defining Boolean expressions can be written, one for each output, for example

$$F_2 = \bar{A}_0 \cdot A_1 \cdot \bar{A}_2$$

and

$$F_7 = A_0 \cdot A_1 \cdot A_2$$

This can be directly implemented with three inverters and eight 3-input AND gates as shown in figure 4.14. Practical examples of the use of one-out-of-n decoding are given in chapter 6 and in chapter 7, sections 7.5.2 and 7.5.3 relating to the addressing of random-access memories.

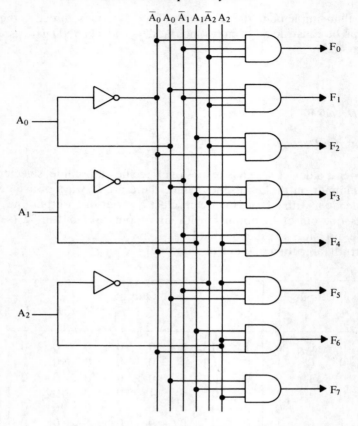

Figure 4.14 A one-of-8 decoder

Traffic-light Decoder

From the example discussed in chapter 3, section 3.4.2, a two-bit coded variable is used to select the state of the three traffic lights red, R, amber, A, and green, G. The truth table was defined as

X	Y	R	A	G
0	0	1	0	0
0	1	1	1	0
1	0	0	1	0
1	1	0	0	1

$$R = \bar{X} \cdot \bar{Y} + \bar{X} \cdot Y = \bar{X}$$
$$A = \bar{X} \cdot Y + X \cdot \bar{Y} = X \oplus Y$$
and $G = X \cdot Y$

The decoder defined here is more general than the one-of-n decoder, in that specific input combinations can activate combinations of outputs. Also note from the example that in general there may be fewer than the maximum 2^n outputs for n inputs.

4.7 Sequential Logic Systems

Sequential logic systems must contain memory elements to save the logic level of a present state, which may be used to effect some future state. The analysis of sequential circuits is beyond the scope of this book, but some knowledge of the basic memory elements is required. Such devices are collectively called *bistables*, *latches* or *flip-flops*. As with gates, they can be constructed in positive or negative logic and in a variety of technologies, such as bipolar or MOS technology, so that they can be made compatible with each range of gates. There is a number of variants on the basic flip-flop, largely determined by specialised input gating. The variants are outlined below.

4.7.1 Flip-flops

The R–S Flip-flop

The term R–S stands for reset–set where *reset* means to establish the logical output variable at level 0 and *set* at level 1. Alternatively the term 'clear' is used rather than reset, but here clear–preset will be used as a rather special R–S function, as will be explained later. The basic R–S flip-flop is the basis of all other flip-flops.

Two implementations of the R–S flip-flop are shown in figure 4.15, one using NOR gates and the other NAND gates. They are similar except for the case of $R = S = 1$, a state which is to be avoided, since the outputs are not then a complementary pair.

Consider the NOR gate system. Then the Boolean equations defining each output are

$$Q = \overline{R + P} \text{ and } P = \overline{S + Q}$$

Thus for $R = 1, S = 0$:

$$Q = \overline{1 + P} = 0 \text{ and } P = \overline{0 + Q} = \bar{Q} = 1$$

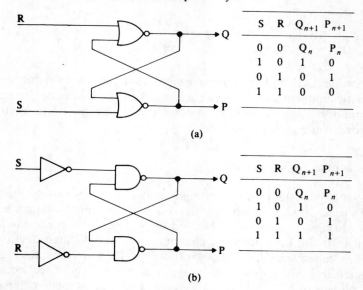

Figure 4.15 Basic R–S flip-flops

For $R = 0$, $S = 1$:

$$Q = \overline{0 + P} \text{ and } P = \overline{1 + Q} = 0$$

Therefore

$$Q = 1$$

For $R = 0$, $S = 0$:

$$Q = \bar{P} \text{ and } P = \bar{Q}$$

Thus for $S = R = 0$, the flip-flop is in a *do-nothing* state which maintains the logical levels of P and Q which have been determined by some previous value — for example, at power-on either state may occur at random. Note however that, except for $R = S = 1$, $P = \bar{Q}$. Thus the two outputs from a flip-flop are the true output, Q, and its complement, $\bar{Q}$, as shown diagrammatically in figure 4.16.

Refer to the truth table of figure 4.15 and consider the quiescent state of the inputs R and S to be 0. Q can then be set to 1 (and $\bar{Q}$ to 0) by raising S to 1. Once Q has reached its stable state, S can be returned to 0 and that state will be retained. Similarly, raising R to 1 will make $Q = 0$, a state which will again be retained when R returns to 0. Thus the flip-flop is a

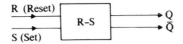

Figure 4.16 Schematic diagram of R–S flip-flop

memory device, its output retaining the last information that was on the input lines, assuming that both were not simultaneously 1, even though that input information may be transient.

Clocked R–S Flip-flops

The basic R–S flip-flop is an asynchronous device in the sense that the outputs will respond to the inputs as soon as they are applied. A synchronous version can be derived by additional input gating, as shown in figure 4.17. In this case either R and the *clock pulse* (CP) or S and the clock-pulse must both be 1 to reset or set Q. Thus information contained on either R or S is only memorised by the flip-flop when the clock pulse occurs. The clock pulse must stay at 1 long enough for any transitions to take place, but preferably no longer. S and R must not change while the pulse is high and $S = R = 1$ must be avoided. The initial state of the flip-flop can be pre-established by retaining asynchronous entry points after the input gating, labelled PS and C, (preset and clear) for example. Normally, RS and C will stay at logical 0.

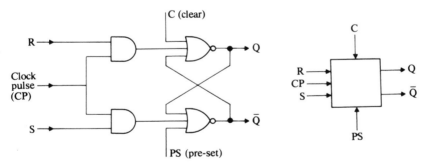

Figure 4.17 Clocked R–S flip-flop

D-Type Flip-flops

It has been stressed previously that the $R = S = 1$ state must be avoided. With a clocked input, however, the quiescent state $R = S = 0$ need not be maintained (CP = 0 has the same effect) so that an unambiguous input system can be used, as shown in figure 4.18. This is termed D-type input.

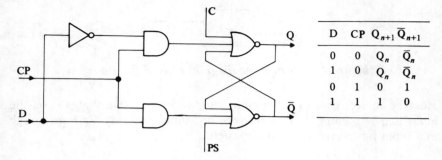

D	CP	Q_{n+1}	$\overline{Q}_{n+1}$
0	0	Q_n	$\overline{Q}_n$
1	0	Q_n	$\overline{Q}_n$
0	1	0	1
1	1	1	0

Figure 4.18 D-type flip-flop

The CP will set Q to 1 if $D = 1$ and reset Q to 0 for $D = 0$ — that is, Q copies and saves D. This type of flip-flop is used to store data, hence the term D-type.

Edge-triggering

In a number of cases, to be introduced later, it is important that the transfer of data from D to Q is timed so that once the CP initiates any change in Q, D can immediately begin to accept a new value while Q completes the copy of the original D. Nevertheless, a new value of D must await a new CP before Q will respond again. This can be achieved by making the CP duration just long enough to initiate the response of Q to D, falling back to zero while Q completes any possible change and effectively blocking any effect of new changes in D. Too short a clock pulse will not supply enough energy to initiate the response in Q, while too long a pulse could see Q responding to a new D. In practice, detailed electronic circuitry is provided inside the gate to modify the CP to avoid dependence upon external accurate timing.

The CP is differentiated, generating a positive pulse as the CP rises and a negative pulse as it falls back to zero. The output of the differentiater is then rectified, resulting in a controlled-width pulse being fed to the flip-flop, synchronised to the leading-edge of the CP, independent of its duration. If an inverter is included before the rectifier, then the positive pulse fed to the flip-flop is generated by the trailing-edge of the CP, independent of the rising edge. This is shown in figure 4.19. Trailing-edge switching is usually indicated on block diagrams by an inverter *dot* on the CP input. An example is shown in figure 4.21.

J–K Flip-flops

Figure 4.20 shows a modification to the clocked R–S flip-flop of figure 4.17 in that feedback is now employed from the output to the input.

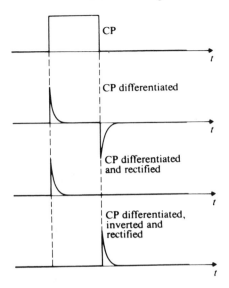

Figure 4.19 Clock-pulse modification for trailing and leading-edge triggering

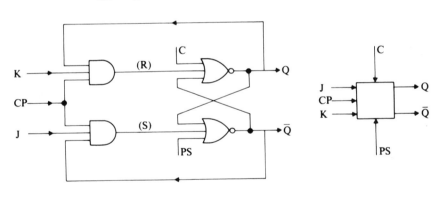

J	K	Q_{n+1}	$\bar{Q}_{n+1}$
0	0	Q_n	$\bar{Q}_n$
1	0	1	0
0	1	0	1
1	1	$\bar{Q}_n$	Q_n

CP = 1

Figure 4.20 Logic diagram, block diagram and truth table for J–K flip-flop

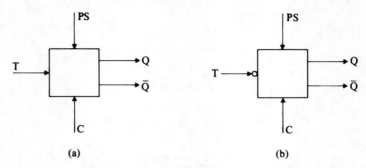

Figure 4.21 (a) Leading-edge-triggered and (b) trailing-edge-triggered toggling flip-flop

It can easily be verified that for the input conditions $J = K = 0$; $J = 0$, $K = 1$ and $J = 1$, $K = 0$, the feedback has no effect and $J = S$ and $K = R$ of a normal R–S type.

The difference occurs when $J = K = 1$. Assume for the moment that CP is also held at 1. Then while this condition exists, Q is directly connected to R and $\bar{Q}$ to S. Thus if $Q = 1$ and $\bar{Q} = 0$, the flip-flop will be reset, changing Q to 0 and $\bar{Q}$ to 1. Now however the input to S is 1 so that Q changes back to 1 and $\bar{Q}$ to 0. In fact an unstable state has been reached and Q and $\bar{Q}$ will continue to oscillate. If now, however, the clock pulse is timed so that it stays at logic 1 long enough to initiate the transition in output state, but then falls to 0 before the transition is complete, the input gates will be inhibited and the second and subsequent transitions will not be allowed. Thus the net effect of $J = K = 1$, combined with an accurately timed pulse or edge-triggering circuitry, results in the flip-flop simply changing state — that is, the output is complemented.

Toggling or T-type Flip-flops

If a flip-flop is to be used exclusively for complementing, individual J, K and CP inputs are not required; effectively they can be paralleled into one input. This type of flip-flop is known as a *toggle*, the output of which is complemented by the application of a pulse at the input, T. Either leading or trailing-edge triggering can be incorporated as indicated in figure 4.21.

Master–slave Flip-flops

Master–slave flip-flops employ two cascaded clocked flip-flop elements. The outputs of the first (master) flip-flop are coupled into the inputs of the second (slave) flip-flop. A common CP is used, except that it is inverted before being fed to the slave as shown in figure 4.22(a). The master in

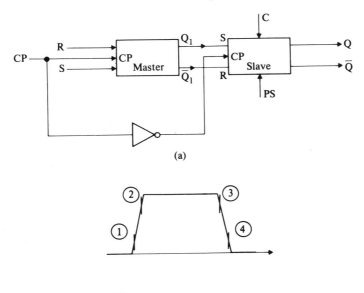

(a)

① Isolate slave from master

② Enter signal into master

③ Inhibit inputs to master

④ Transfer data from master to slave

(b)

Figure 4.22 (a) Logic diagram and (b) timing diagram for master–slave flip-flop

figure 4.22 is shown with R–S inputs; they could equally well be J–K or D-type.

While the CP is at zero, the slave is enabled, as a result of the CP inversion, and the output from the master is copied into the slave; for example, if $Q_1 = 1$, Q is set to 1.

When the CP is raised to 1, input information is transmitted to the master flip-flop, setting or resetting Q_1 and $\bar{Q}_1$ as required. However, the slave is now inhibited so that Q and $\bar{Q}$ do not yet change. Thus while the clock pulse is high the master–slave flip-flop stores both the new and the old information, in the master and slave respectively. When the CP falls back to zero the new data is copied to the slave and the old data lost. A typical timing diagram is shown in figure 4.22(b).

The use of this type of flip-flop in a shift register and an accumulator will be shown later. One immediate use, however, is that the output Q can be fed back to the input R and $\bar{Q}$ to the input S to create a toggling flip-flop, the buffer created by the master stopping the oscillation possible with a normal clocked J–K flip-flop as mentioned above. Thus a flip-flop as shown in figure 4.22 could be used as a trailing-edge toggle simply by external wiring connecting Q to R and $\bar{Q}$ to S and using CP as T.

Master–slave flip-flops can be used as alternatives to edge-triggered flip-flops. They are free from pulse timing problems and can be used over a wide range of speeds.

Applications of Flip-flops

Having now reviewed the range of flip-flops available as the basic building blocks for sequential logic systems, the following two sections outline some typical applications.

4.7.2 Binary Counters

Figure 4.23 shows a 4-bit binary up-counter. Trailing-edge triggered toggles are employed in this case, although it is possible to use other types. A pulse is applied initially to the clear line to clear each flip-flop to 0. The train of pulses to be counted is applied to the first flip-flop. Q_0 switches from 0 to 1 when the first input pulse falls back to 0. The input T_1 is now

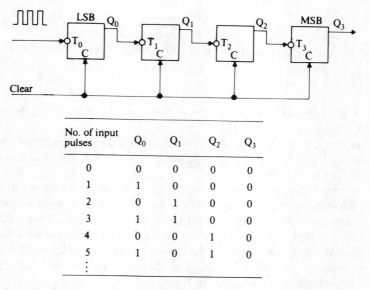

No. of input pulses	Q_0	Q_1	Q_2	Q_3
0	0	0	0	0
1	1	0	0	0
2	0	1	0	0
3	1	1	0	0
4	0	0	1	0
5	1	0	1	0
⋮				

Figure 4.23 Binary up-counter with state diagram

high, but does not trigger Q_1. The second pulse rising to 1 does nothing but when it falls back to 0, T_0 is again triggered, changing Q_0 from 1 to 0. This in turn causes T_1 to fall to 0 and complements Q_1 from 0 to 1, etc.

The above circuit may be modified to provide a BCD counter by noting that $10_{10} = 1010_2$. Thus when Q_1 and Q_3 are both 1, a carry should be generated to the next 4-bit counter representing the next most significant decimal digit and the first 4 bits must be cleared. This is shown in principle in figure 4.24. It is left to the reader to verify that this is correct by construction of a table similar to that in figure 4.23.

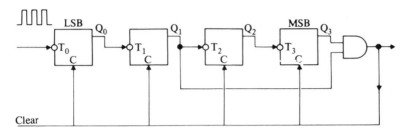

Figure 4.24 A decade counter

4.7.3 Shift Registers

A shift register is used to store a serial string of binary digits, synchronously — that is, timed by a separate clock. Referring to figure 4.25, each bit of input data is applied sequentially to the D line and is transferred into the shift register by a synchronous clock pulse. Thus the rate at which the input data is presented must be related to the clock pulse rate. The shift register must have as many *cells* as there are bits to be stored. The MSB is shown at the left-hand end of the register in conventional fashion.

Master–slave or edge-triggered flip-flops must be used since any one cell will be receiving new input data and yet using its existing output as input to the next stage. In the case of the master–slave flip-flop shown in figure 4.25, the contents of one cell are shifted into the master of the next while the slave of that cell provides the correct data to the next master. When the clock pulse falls back to 0, the masters copy to the slaves but communication between the cells is inhibited. The system shown will only shift-right. By appropriate reconnections of the outputs to inputs, a shift-left can be achieved. In practice, appropriate gating can be incorporated to shift either right or left, determined by whether a control signal, SC, is 1 or 0; for example

$$S_n = Q_{n+1} \cdot \overline{SC} + Q_{n-1} \cdot SC$$

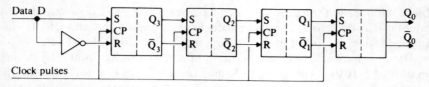

Data	Q_3	Q_2	Q_1	Q_0
0	0	0	0	0
1	1	0	0	0
0	0	1	0	0
1	1	0	1	0
1	1	1	0	1
0	0	1	1	0
⋮				

Figure 4.25 Shift register

where S_n is the input to the nth flip-flop, Q_{n-1} is the output from the left-adjacent flip-flop and Q_{n+1} the output from the right-adjacent flip-flop. Such an approach is necessary for the single register at the CPU of the teaching computer MIC. Shift-right and shift-left instructions relating to the contents of this register require the interconnections above (see chapter 5, section 5.6.2).

4.8 Word-orientated Registers

4.8.1 Registers

An n-bit word of data can be stored in a register comprising n flip-flops. For serial mode a shift register is used. Data is shifted in at the MSB and out at the LSB by the application of n shift pulses. The original contents are normally lost so that arrangements must be made for recycling if this is to be avoided. For the circuit of figure 4.26, new data can be loaded into the A register by enabling gate *a* only for 4 shift pulses. By enabling gate *b* only, 4 shift pulses will copy the data from A to B and clear A at the same time. Enabling *b* and *c* allows the contents of A to be copied to B, but also recycles the data in A leaving A unaltered.

By including connections to the outputs of all the flip-flops, data could be read as a parallel word. Figure 4.27 shows an arrangement of a parallel in-parallel out, word-length register connected to a bus-bar. Note that

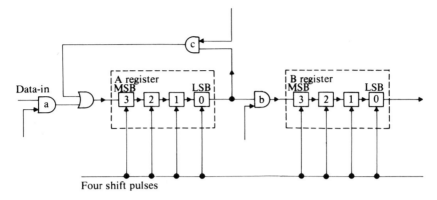

Figure 4.26 Data transfer (serial) using shift registers

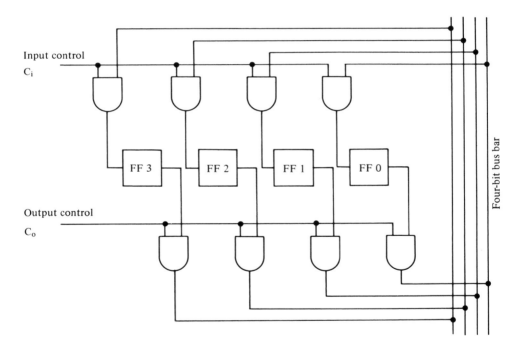

Figure 4.27 Parallel-in/parallel-out register using a bus-bar

while each bit requires independent data lines, the input gating control, C_i, is common to each bit of the word. The same applies to the output control, C_0. With such a system, the common one in practice, individual bits of the word cannot be manipulated separately.

4.8.2 *Accumulators*

An accumulator is a register used in conjunction with an adder. One input number to the adder is supplied from the accumulator and the other from another independent source. The resulting sum is then returned to the register, over-writing the original contents, hence the term 'accumulator'.

Note that the adder used with such an accumulator has no storage capacity itself, so that at one instant the register must be providing the original number as input to the adder and storing the sum. Again, master–slave flip-flops are commonly employed to achieve this and to stop the new sum being cycled back to the adder. Figure 4.28 shows a simple schematic diagram for a parallel accumulator/adder. An example of a serial accumulator/adder system is shown in detail in chapter 5, section 5.6.2.

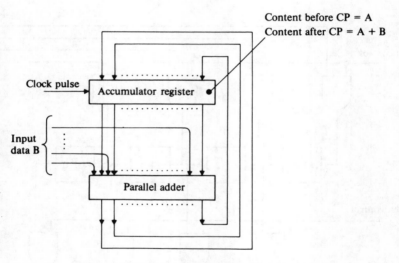

Figure 4.28 A parallel accumulator/adder

4.9 A Binary Multiplier

The shift-and-add technique for multiplying two n-bit numbers together was explained in chapter 3, section 3.3.1. Since the resulting product can be up to $2n$ bits long, 2 n-bit registers will be needed to save the answer. In practice, the first partial product is formed and then shifted *right* one place. The second partial product is then added to the most significant n bits and the result shifted-right one place, this result now being $(n + 2)$ bits long. This is repeated until all n partial products have been added and shifted.

With binary numbers, the ith partial product is simply the multiplicand when bit $(i - 1)$ of the multiplier (remember, bit 0 is defined as the LSB) is 1 and zero when it is 0.

Referring to figure 4.29, the multiplicand is stored in a register, B, and the multiplier in a register, MQ (this stands for multiplier/quotient, as it is also used in division). The result must be stored in two registers, the most significant half in register A and the least significant half in an extra register (A0).

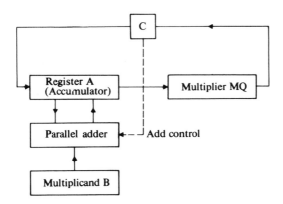

Figure 4.29 Shift-and-add register

The basic algorithm for multiplication is thus:

   (i)   clear A

  (ii)   if bit $(i - 1)$ of MQ is 1, add B to A

 (iii)   shift contents of the A and AO linked together one place right, moving any carry from (ii) into the MSB of A

 (iv)   repeat (ii) and (iii) n times, $i = 1, 2 \ldots n$.

In practice, the convenient way to test the bit of the multiplier is to shift MQ right in such a way that the LSB, bit 0, is in a separate one-bit carry register. A second shift puts bit 1 into the carry, etc. Accepting that this destroys the original contents of MQ, the multiplier register MQ can thus serve as A0, since the accumulated sum of the partial products *grows* into A0 at the same rate as the multiplier is shifted into the carry. An initial shift on MQ is required to load carry with bit 0. The algorithm, related to figure 4.29, then becomes:

   (i)   clear A

  (ii)   shift MQ right; bit 0 to carry

(iii)   if carry is 1, add B to A, re-establishing carry
(iv)   shift (rotate) right A and MQ through C — for example, LSB
        of A to MSB of MQ, LSB of MQ to C and original C to MSB
        of A
(v)   repeat (iii) and (iv) *n* times.

The double precision product is left in A and MQ. The multiplier is destroyed, but the multiplicand is left unaffected.

4.10   Summary

The standard logical components have now been described with a relatively simple introduction to the methods of analysing and designing circuits. There are a number of ways in which these gates can be constructed electronically from transistors, etc. which are not even considered here.

The primary objective of this chapter has been to develop a set of standard, simple elements which can be used in the following chapters to show how computers work and to give an idea as to how they can be constructed. Binary logic has been used throughout and indications have

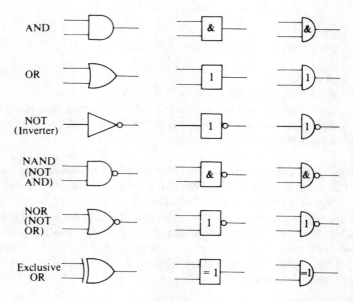

Figure 4.30 Alternative symbols for logic elements

been given as to how pure logical functions, such as a decoder, and binary arithmetic functions, such as an adder, use the same basic elements.

Figure 4.30 is included to show that other sets of symbols are employed beside the set used in this text.

References

4.1 Bannister, B. R. and Whitehead, D. G., *Fundamentals of Modern Digital Systems*, 2nd edn, Macmillan, London, 1987.

4.2 Lewin, D., *Logical Design of Switching Circuits*, Van Nostrand Reinhold, Wokingham, 1974.

4.3 Lewin, D., *Computer-Aided Design of Digital Systems*, Arnold, London, 1977.

4.4 Green, D., *Modern Logic Design*, Addison-Wesley, Wokingham, 1986.

Problems

4.1 Prove the following Boolean identities by constructing the truth tables:

(a) $A + AB = A$

(b) $A + \bar{A}B = A + B$

(c) $(A + B)(A + C) = A + BC$

(d) $(A + B + C)(\bar{A} + B + C)(\bar{A} + B + \bar{C}) = B + \bar{A}C$

4.2 A *majority* gate is a circuit the output of which is logic 1 if more of its inputs are logic 1 than are logic 0; the output is logic 0 otherwise. Construct a truth table and hence write down the minterm expression for a three and a five-input majority gate.

Solution. The truth table is as shown in the table below. Therefore $F_3 = \bar{A}BC + A\bar{B}C + AB\bar{C} + ABC = A \cdot B + A \cdot C + B \cdot C$.

A	B	C	F_3
0	0	0	0
0	0	1	0
0	1	0	0
0	1	1	1
1	0	0	0
1	0	1	1
1	1	0	1
1	1	1	1

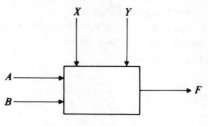

Figure 4.31

4.3 BCD subtraction can be achieved by taking the nine's complement of each digit and then adding 1. Construct a truth table to convert the four-bit BCD number $A_3A_2A_1A_0$ to its nine's complement number $C_3C_2C_1C_0$ and hence construct a circuit of AND and OR gates to implement the code conversion.

4.4 The system shown in figure 4.31 has an output F which is a function of the two inputs A and B. The Boolean relation between F, A and B changes as a function of the control inputs X and Y such that:
  (a) $X=1$ and $Y = 1$: AND gate
  (b) $X = 0$ and $Y = 1$: exclusive-OR gate
  (c) $X = 1$ and $Y = 0$ or if $X = 0$ and $Y = 0$: OR gate.
      Write down the Boolean expression defining F as a function of A, B, X and Y.

4.5 A *comparator* is required, the output of which, F, is 1 if, and only if, two n-bit binary input numbers are equal. Derive a logic system for this function for three-bit input numbers.

4.6 Design the logic circuit to convert the three-bit binary code to the three-bit Gray code defined by the truth table shown in the following table:

	Binary			Gray		
	a_2	a_1	a_0	g_2	g_1	g_0
0	0	0	0	0	0	0
1	0	0	1	0	0	1
2	0	1	0	0	1	1
3	0	1	1	0	1	0
4	1	0	0	1	1	0
5	1	0	1	1	1	1
6	1	1	0	1	0	1
7	1	1	1	1	0	0

4.7 Write down the truth table for the system shown in figure 4.32.

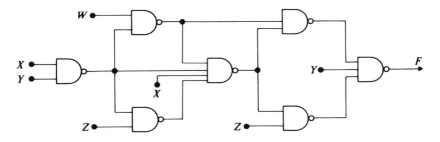

Figure 4.32

5 A Simple Teaching Computer

Objectives

This chapter introduces for the first time a simple computer and in so doing draws together material from earlier chapters. The relevance of binary representation of data and instructions is explained as is the importance of the three basic computer elements: the control unit, the arithmetic unit and the store. The concept is introduced of a binary word of standard length — an instruction word — which may be used to represent both orders and the locations, the addresses, at which data is stored. In this simple machine which has an eight-bit word-length, eight simple orders are possible and only thirty-two locations containing data may be addressed. Nevertheless, in spite of the limited instruction set and the small number of address locations, the chapter and its various figures illustrate in detail how data is routed within the machine, how orders are executed and how store locations are addressed. For simplicity, the machine operates in serial fashion in contrast to most modern machines which operate in parallel mode.

The chapter concludes with consideration of the serious limitations of the simple machine which has just been discussed. The Problems at the end of the chapter encourage students to consolidate their knowledge by drawing out a complete diagram of the machine using the detailed information contained in this chapter supplemented by limited design work.

5.1 Introduction

In chapter 2 it was seen that a computer comprises three essential parts — a control unit, an arithmetic unit and a store — together with input and output devices which permit communication between the machine and the outside world. Chapter 3 dealt with binary representation of data and with number systems. Practical details of combinational and sequential logic were discussed in chapter 4. The present chapter builds upon earlier chapters to provide the first detailed explanation of computer operation. Since real computers are very complex, the discussion is with reference to a small teaching computer operating in serial fashion. In spite of its limited performance however, the machine incorporates many of the features to be found in a practical computer. Its limitations, and these are considerable, are discussed towards the end of the chapter. In the section devoted to problems, students are invited to carry out simple design work with a view to enhancing machine performance. More ambitious ways of improving the scope of the teaching aid are also mentioned.

5.2 Preliminary Ideas

In this chapter the emphasis is on simplicity. Accordingly, in the machine to be described, *MIC (Minimal Instruction Computer)*, only essential features are included. Perhaps the most basic of all the design parameters of a digital computer is the decision as to the number of binary bits used to form the standard word-length for the machine. With the simple machines to be described here and in the first part of chapter 6, instructions are stored in the computer as binary words of standard length. It will be seen in the sections below that for such machines the decision as to word-length determines the total storage capacity possible for a particular computer and, equally important, restricts the range of orders which the machine can execute. Since data is also stored as binary words of standard length, the decision as to word-length places a restriction on the precision to which numbers, either in fixed or floating-point notation, may be represented.

For MIC the word-length is fixed at *eight bits*. The machine operates in serial rather than parallel fashion. This reduces the total number of circuit elements required and simplifies construction. As a result a single full-adder is required rather than the complete set of adders necessary with parallel operation.

Arithmetic operations are limited to addition and subtraction together with multiplication and division by powers of two achieved by shift-left and shift-right respectively of binary words. In order to avoid the need for a specific subtractor at the arithmetic unit, subtraction is achieved via complementing and addition. In common with practical computers, two's complement arithmetic is used, employing the subtraction algorithm described in chapter 3. The eight-bit word-length of MIC limits signed numbers to be within the range.

to $\begin{cases} \text{decimal } -128 \text{ represented by } 10000000 \text{ binary} \\ \text{decimal } + 127 \text{ represented by } 01111111 \text{ binary} \end{cases}$

with the most significant bit acting as the sign bit (see chapter 3). Unsigned numbers lie in the range 0 to 255 represented by

to $\begin{cases} 0 \text{ or } 00000000 \text{ binary or } \quad 0 \text{ decimal} \\ 2^8 - 1 \text{ or } 11111111 \text{ binary or } 255 \text{ decimal} \end{cases}$

Note that the limitations apply to both data and the results of arithmetic operations or logic shift. The programmer must decide which arithmetic mode to employ. Signed and unsigned data cannot be freely mixed. Signed numbers, in two's complement form, will be employed hereafter unless an alternative designation is mentioned explicitly.

In this simple machine a pair of specific instructions is devoted to input and output respectively. Input, both of data and instructions, is achieved via binary numbers set up on hand-switches or at a keypad. Thus the correct setting of hand-switches or keypad constitutes the input device. Output is observed as the condition of a set of small lamps equal in number to the length of the standard word of eight bits. An illuminated lamp corresponds to 1, and an extinguished lamp represents a 0. Thus the condition of the set of lamps constitutes the output device. The lamps are connected to consecutive stages of an *output register* comprising eight flip-flops arranged in series.

Program is inserted via the hand-switches on an instruction-by-instruction basis, and each instruction is stored immediately upon insertion via a store-transfer instruction. In this, MIC is similar to real machines in that in the majority of the latter, a complete program is entered into store and then executed at a later time.

After this preliminary consideration of the machine, a more detailed treatment of the subject now follows.

5.3   The Idea of an Instruction

Instructions are stored as binary words of the standard length. Eight bits is the word-length for MIC. Under normal circumstances instructions must contain at least two element or *fields*. The first is an *order* which specifies an operation to be carried out on an *operand*. Typically the order will be represented by a unique binary code, called the *operation code* or *op-code*, specifying an arithmetic operation performed on a piece of data. The second element to be found in a simple instruction word is an *address* which specifies the location of the operand under consideration. The address comprises a unique binary code which designates the location in store of the piece of data involved in the arithmetic operation.

Thus, for example, an elementary instruction may relate to addition. The instruction commands: *add the contents of a specified address location to the current contents of the register situated at and forming part of the arithmetic unit*. This particular register is frequently called the *accumulator*. In simple cases such as this one, in which only a single location is specified explicitly, it may be assumed that the second of the two locations involved in the arithmetic operation is the accumulator. The question of multiple accumulator working is discussed in chapter 6.

In the case of instructions, three of the bits designate *orders* (*operation codes* or *op-codes*) while the remaining five are allocated as *address labels* (*operand pointers*). Thus, instruction words have the format shown in figure 5.1, where XYZ respectively may take independently the value 0 or 1. The letters XYZ are chosen in arbitrary fashion to represent each of the three bits of the order. The choice of XYZ is merely for convenience. With larger machines having, say, a word-length of 16 bits, the individual bits of the instruction words may be identified conveniently by the decimal numbers 0 to 15. In this latter case, letters may be used to designate groups of bits having specific functions within the instruction word. Examples of this convention will be seen in chapter 6.

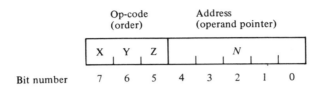

Figure 5.1 Instruction format for MIC

Since with MIC three bits are used to designate orders, there is a total of eight possible op-codes in the *instruction set* (*order code*). For any computer the complete set of orders forming the instruction set is at the discretion of the computer designer. MIC is no exception. The instruction set is unique to a particular model of computer. It is because of their unique instruction sets that computers with the same word-length begin to exhibit their different characteristics and performance.

In a similar fashion the five binary bits allocated as an address label, N, yield a total of $2^5 = 32$ unique binary patterns each of which represents a specific address location. Address locations will contain individual items of both data and stored program placed in storage locations identified by specific address labels.

The binary codes which identify eight op-codes and 32 addresses are shown in figure 5.2.

5.4 The Orders of the Instruction Set

As already pointed out, the computer designer chooses orders in the instruction set depending on the applications required of the computer under consideration. In this simple case, eight representative orders have been chosen. These are listed in figure 5.3.

The first pair of instructions are *transfer instructions*. In the first of the pair the contents of the accumulator at the arithmetic unit are transferred to a specified location (address) in the store. The accumulator contents are

Bit no.	7	6	5	
	X	Y	Z	
	0	0	0	
	0	0	1	
	0	1	0	
	0	1	1	8 op-codes
	1	0	0	
	1	0	1	
	1	1	0	
	1	1	1	

Address N					
Bit 4	3	2	1	0	
0	0	0	0	0	
0	0	0	0	1	
0	0	0	1	0	
0	0	0	1	1	32 address labels
1	1	1	1	0	
1	1	1	1	1	

Figure 5.2 Op-codes and address labels for MIC

regenerated in case they are required again later. With the second order, data is transferred to the accumulator. The contents of the store location are regenerated in case data at that location is required on a subsequent occasion. Note the shorthand notation used to describe these two orders:

$$(Acc) \rightarrow Address$$
$$(Address) \rightarrow Acc$$

which associates very closely the contents of a location with the location itself. This notation is very widespread and frequently becomes a source of confusion for the student. Contents of a register or accumulator are

Op-codes		Orders
	X Y Z	
Transfer	0 0 0	Transfer contents of accumulator to address location Regenerate accumulator contents (Accumulator) → Address
	0 0 1	Transfer contents of address location to accumulator Regenerate address contents (Address) → Accumulator
Arithmetic	0 1 0	Add contents of address location to accumulator contents Place result in accumulator. Address contents regenerated (Address) + (Accumulator) → Accumulator
	0 1 1	Subtract contents of address location from contents of accumulator. Address contents regenerated (Accumulator) − (Address) → Accumulator
Logic shift	1 0 0	Shift accumulator contents left N places where N is the binary number in address field
	1 0 1	Shift accumulator contents right N places where N is the binary number in address field
Input/Output	1 1 0	Transfer contents of input register to accumulator (Input) → Accumulator
	1 1 1	Transfer contents of accumulator to output register (Accumulator) → Output

Figure 5.3 The eight orders of the instruction set of MIC with the equivalent op-codes

designated by the enclosure of the designated register or accumulator by brackets. The arrow implies transfer to the designated location which is quoted without brackets. With serial electronic registers, explicit regeneration is essential if contents are to be preserved, since the reading technique destroys or alters the original content. This problem is avoided in parallel electronic (semiconductor) memories as shown in chapter 7.

The second pair of orders relate to *arithmetic operations*. With the first of the pair, the contents of an addressed location are added to the present contents of the accumulator and the contents of the addressed location are regenerated. In the second of the pair, the final instruction of the arithmetic set, subtraction, takes place with the result placed in the accumulator. Notice that the accumulator is involved in all four instructions so far but need not be mentioned explicitly since in this simple machine there is no alternative accumulator. Instructions of the present type, in which only one address is specified explicitly, are sometimes called *single-operand* (*single-address*) instructions even though in reality two data locations are involved, the store and the accumulator. The concept of *double-operand* (*double-address*) instructions is introduced in chapter 6.

The third pair of orders provide left and right *cyclic shift* respectively of the contents of the accumulator. Such shift is useful in various ways. One obvious application is to permit multiplication of the contents of the accumulator by powers of 2 (left-shift) and division by powers of 2 (right-shift). Such manipulation is an essential feature of software routines for multiplication and division.

With logic shift the *address field*, N, of the instruction word is used in a new way. Rather than designate the address of an operand, the five bits 0 to 4 denote the number of places through which the accumulator contents must be shifted.

To retain simplicity, logic shift is confined to unsigned positive numbers. When the objective of the logic shift is as part of a multiplication or division routine, it is essential to ensure that problems due to rotation of bits back into the accumulator are avoided. An example of potential hazards is given later in section 5.7.1 which deals with data flow.

The final pair of orders relates to the input and output of information to and from the computer. Input is in respect of both data and program while output is restricted to results. For both input and output, information appears as patterns of ones and zeros in binary fashion. Since the machine is an eight-bit computer, input and output occur in blocks comprising eight-bit words. Since the machine is serial in operation, input/output is also serial.

The eight orders available with MIC are representative in that similar orders are available with real machines. In the latter case, however, the total number of orders is usually considerable. In the first machine to be described in chapter 6, for example, about thirty orders are' employed. Some of these might be regarded as essential, while others are included to facilitate programming.

It will be seen shortly (section 5.7) that with MIC, orders are executed via logic which identifies the three-bit op-code specifying an order; as a result, gates are activated to provide a data path between the appropriate parts of the machine — for example, between the store and the accumulator. Since both the accumulator and the store locations comprise shift registers, data flows between them in serial fashion at a rate controlled by *clock pulses* generated within the machine. Overall synchronisation is achieved since the same clock pulses also control the operation of the serial adder of the arithmetic unit. Real computers usually operate in parallel fashion and at high speed. As a result the data flows in parallel fashion along a *parallel data highway* (*bus*) which is as wide as the number of bits constituting the word-length used in the machine. However, MIC illustrates in a simple way the basic principles by which orders are executed in real machines, although far more extensive logic will be required to implement the wide range of orders of such machines than the eight orders of MIC.

5.5   Specification of Addresses

So far the eight instructions of the instruction set have been specified. It is also necessary to designate the address locations. With five address bits, $2^5 = 32$ address locations may be specified. While this number must be regarded as trivial it is sufficient to illustrate principles. A small semiconductor memory comprising 32 eight-bit registers, each of which may be accessed equally readily, rather than in sequence, would constitute a simple implementation in this case. More realistic implementations of semiconductor memory are discussed in chapter 7.

As with real machines, it is necessary to achieve access to one or other of the 32 stores at will. Since this access is not necessarily sequential, it is usually described as *random access*. In the case of MIC, random access is achieved by logic which recognises the specific five-bit address code associated with each of the store locations. Upon recognition a data path is provided to the appropriate store. In a practical computer the number of store locations which may be accessed in random fashion is considerable. For example, a random-access store with

$$2^{16} = 65\ 536\ (64\text{K})$$

eight-bit (that is, one-byte) locations is commonplace. Nevertheless, the approach to random access used with MIC serves to illustrate the technique.

Methods of storage of digital information are so important that a complete chapter of this book (chapter 7) is allocated to this subject.

5.6   Hardware of the Minimal Instruction Computer (MIC)

The three principal elements of MIC have been discussed in earlier sections. The way in which program steps are executed through the implementation of orders from the instruction set has been considered briefly. At this point it is necessary to discuss further how orders are executed and access to specified store locations achieved.

Figure 5.4 shows an overall schematic diagram of the machine. The four principal elements, the *control unit*, the *arithmetic unit*, the *store* and *input/output* (I/O), appear as separate items. At this stage, attention is drawn to general features with emphasis on data flow and overall control. A detailed treatment of specific points follows later.

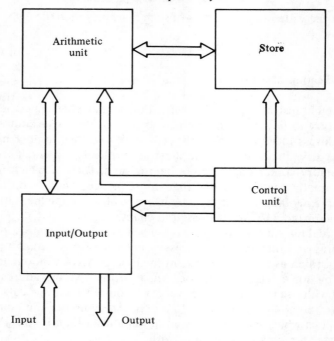

Figure 5.4 Schematic diagram of MIC

5.6.1 Overall Control and Synchronisation

Serial data paths are employed. Flow of data along the various paths is achieved by virtue of control signals generated in the control unit and applied selectively to one or more of the 2-entry AND gates, A to V, as a result of which the appropriate path is held open for sufficient time for the data to be transmitted. Store selection too is attained as a result of control signals generated in the control unit. Overall synchronisation occurs as a result of clock pulses also generated in the control unit. Since the word-length is eight bits and operation is serial, eight clock pulses are required to execute the majority of orders.

Since the store is restricted to 32 locations, only very small programs operating on most limited amounts of data may be implemented. Nevertheless MIC follows the common practice of working upon a complete program of instructions which have been placed in sequential locations before program execution commences.

5.6.2 The Arithmetic Unit

Since MIC is a serial machine, the arithmetic unit which constitutes a simple Central Processing Unit (CPU) (figure 5.5(a)) incorporates a single full adder just as that already described in chapter 4. Numbers are represented in two's complement form for which the most significant bit is the sign bit. As a result of the use of the two's complement technique, it is not necessary to provide a separate binary subtractor. This feature of the machine will be discussed in greater detail later. The full adder may be engineered either in discrete element circuitry to illustrate principles or alternatively, for convenience, a single integrated-circuit chip (IC) may be used.

The arithmetic unit also includes a special working register called the *accumulator*. One important function of the accumulator is to hold the result of addition (see chapter 4, section 4.8.2). In the present case, the working register is merely an eight-stage shift register. However, for this register it is necessary to have available both the output Q (the set output) and its complement $\bar{Q}$ (the reset output); figure 5.5(a) also shows two further registers.

The first is the *control register* which provides temporary storage for instruction words in transit from the store to the control unit. The contents of the instruction words are used in two ways at the control unit. Bits XYZ (alternative designation, bits 5, 6, 7) are decoded to determine which of the eight orders is to be implemented by the control unit. Bits 0 to 4 constitute a five-bit designation for the N address of the operand involved in execution of the order. Thus an instruction word

ORDER	ADDRESS
XYZ	43210
000	10000

requests the control unit to transfer the contents of the accumulator at the arithmetic unit (CPU) via order

000: (Acc) → Address

to the address specified by the address label 10000.

The second register is only five bits long and is called the *program counter* (PC). Initially its contents are set to a starting valve (typically by hand in a simple machine such as MIC). The initial contents correspond to the five-bit address of the first program instruction. After the execution of the first order the contents of the program counter are incremented

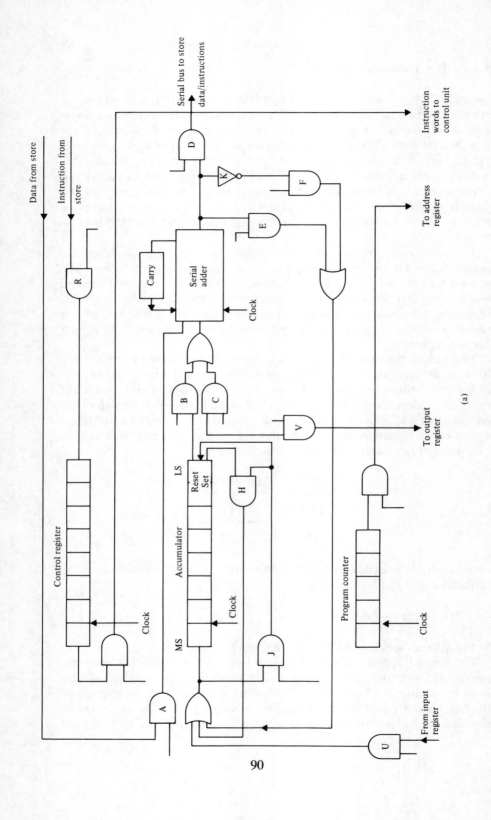

(a)

90

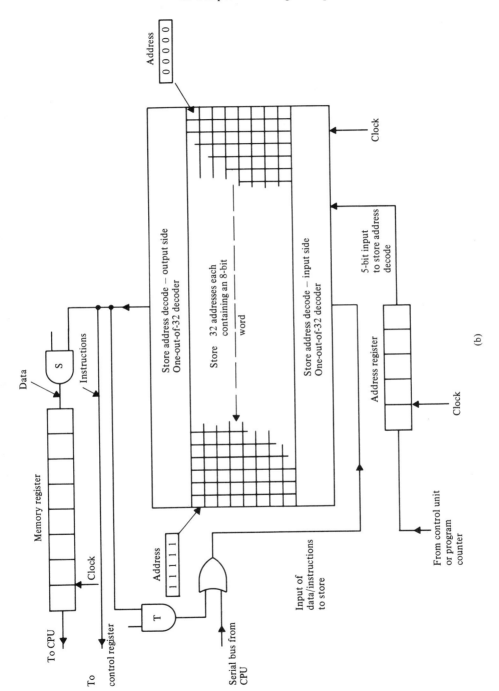

(b)

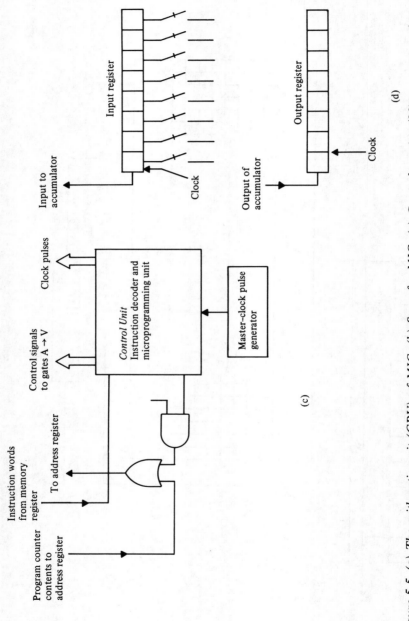

Figure 5.5 (a) The arithmetic unit (CPU) of MIC. (b) Store for MIC. (c) Control unit (Microprogramming Unit) for MIC. (d) Input/Output registers for MIC

automatically to provide the address of the next program instruction. This process is repeated with the execution of each instruction until the program is concluded. As will be seen later (in chapter 6) sequential execution of program is disrupted with implementation of *conditional instructions* as a result of which a new sequence is entered. The lack of a conditional instruction with MIC is a serious limitation to performance and will be mentioned again later in this chapter.

5.6.3   The Store

This consists of 32 eight-stage shift registers (figure 5.5(b)). Each of these is used to store an eight-bit piece of data. In practice, a single IC chip may well be used for each register. Five address bits, 0 to 4, of every instruction designate one or other of the storage locations. The five bits are applied to the *address register* (five bits long) associated with the store and thereafter to the one-out-of-32 decode which permits data flow to or from one or other of the 32 storage locations (see section 5.7.3). The *memory register* may be used for the temporary storage of an operand before presentation to the arithmetic unit.

5.6.4   The Control Unit

The *control unit* (figure 5.5(c)) accepts the three most significant bits of instruction words — that is, bits XYZ (bits 5, 6, 7) — and after decoding the specified op-code enables the appropriate gates to permit execution of the instruction involved. Section 5.7.2 provides details of the specific gating arrangements at the control unit.

Since operation of the machine is serial and eight-bit operands are involved, then the relevant gates normally will be held open for the duration of the eight clock pulses generated by the control unit to permit sequential operation of the eight-bit registers involved in transfer arithmetic, and input/output operations. However in the case of the shift instructions the number of clock pulses will correspond to the contents of the address field, N, in the instruction word. Thus if the contents of the address field are 00011 then three clock pulses will be generated to permit shift through three places.

5.6.5 Input/Output (I/O)

Input and Output (figure 5.5(d)) in the case of MIC are restricted, as might be expected, to the serial mode. Input is from the *input register*, each stage of which must be set up with hand-switches before the input of the corresponding eight-bit word of program or data. However, simple hardware, not discussed in detail, must be employed to act as a primitive *loader* permitting input of program and data to the store before the machine becomes operative. In addition, input and output under program control is possible as a program is executed.

	Op-code			Order	Gates											
	X	Y	Z		A	B	C	D	E	F	H	J	S	T	U	V
Transfer	0	0	0	Transfer to store			X	X			X					
	0	0	1	Load accumulator	X				X				X	X		
Arithmetic	0	1	0	Add	X		X		X				X	X		
	0	1	1	Subtract	X	X				X			X	X		
Logic shift	1	0	0	Left-shift by N								X				
	1	0	1	Right-shift by N							X					
Input/Output	1	1	0	Input											X	
	1	1	1	Output							X					X

Figure 5.6 Gating arrangements for MIC

5.7 Implementation of Orders

With MIC, orders such as addition are executed and results placed in specific locations as specified by the eight-bit instruction code. Figure 5.3 gave details of the instructions while figure 5.5 provides an overall view of the machine, together with its gating arrangements. It is important to determine which particular gates must be enabled to permit execution of the eight orders. Accordingly the eight orders are considered in turn. It must be remembered that all gates normally will be inhibited until enabled by application of logic 1 to their *control input*. The appropriate control signals will be generated by the control unit when decoding the op-code, bits X, Y and Z, of the instruction. See figure 5.7(a) by way of illustration.

5.7.1   Data Flow

(a)   Transfer Instructions

(i)   XYZ = 000 : Transfer (Acc) → Address;
            Accumulator contents regenerated

Reference to figure 5.5(a) and (b) indicates a data path from the output of the accumulator via gate C and through the network of the serial adder, and thence via gate D and the appropriate selection network into the store location designated by the address register. Note this common technique of using an active component of the processor as a passive data path. Thus with gate A inhibited and gate C enabled, the adder output is equal to C + 0 and simply transfers the data. A path is established back to the accumulator via gate H, enabled for this instruction, and thus the previous contents are regenerated. At the end of eight clock pulses, eight bits of data — that is, a complete byte of information — have been transferred to the store and the contents of the accumulator have been regenerated. In summary, to achieve data transfer from the accumulator to a specific address, gates C, D and H must be enabled for the duration of eight clock pulses.

(ii)   XYZ = 001 : Transfer (Address) → Acc;
             address contents regenerated

The second transfer order is achieved in a similar manner. Again reference to figure 5.5(a) and (b) indicates a suitable data path from a specific store location through the output selection network, gate S, the memory register, gate A and the adder, and hence via gate E to the accumulator. The contents of the address location are regenerated since data is also circulated to the appropriate address location via gate T and the input selection network of the store. Accordingly, gates S, A, E and T must be enabled for eight clock pulses to permit data transfer from the addressed location to the accumulator. Note that gate H is inhibited to prevent any original contents of the accumulator from recirculating during the transfer process and corrupting the new contents of the accumulator.

(b)   Arithmetic Instructions

Addition

XYZ=010 : Addition; (Address) + (Acc) → Acc;
             Sum placed in accumulator. Address contents
             regenerated. Previous contents of accumulator cleared

In this case, gates A, C and E together with gates S and T are enabled to permit the addition of two items of data, one from a store location, the other from the accumulator. Data is presented at the serial adder starting with the least significant pair of bits at the first clock pulse. With the second clock pulse the second pair of bits in the next least significant bit position is added, together with the carry bit from the previous addition. The process continues for a total of eight clock pulses as the corresponding pairs of bits of the words in the accumulator and the address location are shifted towards the least significant bit position. The results of the successive additions are stored sequentially at the most significant end of the accumulator as successive stages become vacant and are shifted down towards the least significant end with each clock pulse. Thus after eight clock pulses the final result of the addition is stored in the accumulator and its original contents are lost. Gate H is inhibited to prevent corruption of the results of the addition by the original contents of the accumulator. However, the contents of the store location are regenerated via gate T and the store selection network.

Subtraction

> XYZ = 011 : Subtraction; (Acc) − (Address) → Acc;
> Difference placed in accumulator. Address contents regenerated. Previous contents of accumulator cleared

Subtraction is achieved by a two's complement technique, adding the complement of the contents of the designated store location to the accumulator contents and inverting the result. Recall that the two's complement of a number, −(Qty), is related to the one's complement of that number, $\overline{\text{Qty}}$, by the relation

$$-(\text{Qty}) = \overline{\text{Qty}} + 1 \qquad\qquad (5.1)$$

(see chapter 3, section 3.3.2)
Hence

$$
\begin{aligned}
(\text{Acc}) - (\text{Address}) &= -\{-(\text{Acc}) + (\text{Address})\} \\
&= -\{\ (\overline{\text{Acc}}) + 1 + (\text{Address})\} \\
&\qquad\qquad\qquad\qquad\qquad \text{(equation 5.1)} \\
&= -\{\ (\overline{\text{Acc}}) + (\text{Address})\} - 1 \\
&= \{\ \overline{(\overline{\text{Acc}}) + (\text{Address})}\} + 1 - 1 \\
&\qquad\qquad\qquad\qquad\qquad \text{(equation 5.1)} \\
&= \overline{(\overline{\text{Acc}}) + (\text{Address})}
\end{aligned}
$$

where $(\overline{Acc})$ is the one's complement of the contents of the accumulator. Any carry is ignored since the algorithm employs the two's complement technique.

As was demonstrated in chapter 3, the one's complement of a binary number is obtained very readily by inversion of all the bits of the word. This is achieved here by taking the $\overline{Q}$ output (reset output) from the accumulator. Thereafter the process of subtraction follows closely that of addition. Data is presented sequentially, starting with the least significant pair, to the serial adder. The result of the addition is inverted, through the use of gate K, and then circulated to the most significant end of the accumulator. The process is complete at the end of eight clock pulses. Gates A, B and F together with gates S and T must be enabled during the process. Gate T permits the regeneration of address contents at the store. Gate H is inhibited to prevent the regeneration of the original contents of the accumulator. Such regeneration would corrupt the result of the subtraction which is placed in the accumulator.

(c)   Logic Shift

XYZ = 100 : left shift. Multiplication by 2^N
            Accumulator contents shifted left N places

In this case only the contents of the accumulator are involved when the order is executed. Gate J is enabled while the number of clock pulses corresponding to the contents of the address field, N, of the instruction word are applied to the accumulator. As a result the contents of the accumulator are shifted left by N places. As has been mentioned already the shift is cyclic. Thus it is important that when shift is applied to achieve multiplication by powers of 2, overflow is avoided. Thus consider the unsigned number 00000111

for $N = 3$ shift left yields   00111000
but for $N = 6$ the result is in error   11000001

XYZ = 101 : right shift. Division by 2^N
            Accumulator contents shifted right N places

Here the contents of the accumulator are shifted right by the number of places specified by the contents of the address field, N, of the instruction word. Gate H is enabled for the appropriate number of clock pulses. Again since the shift is cyclic, care must be exercised as to the range of numbers employed if errors in division are to be avoided.

Note that gating is required between the stages of the accumulator in order to permit data transfer in one direction or the other direction depending on whether left-shift or right-shift is required. In the interest of simplicity, the interstage gating is omitted from figure 5.5(a). The reader is referred to chapter 4, section 4.8.1, for further details relating to shift registers.

(d)   Input/Output

XYZ = 110 : transfer the contents of the input register
to accumulator
(input) → Accumulator

The individual stages of the input register are set up, typically with the aid of hand-switches to contain an appropriate piece of eight-bit data. On receipt at the control register of an instruction with XYZ = 110, the eight-bit data word is transferred to the accumulator. Note that to achieve this, transfer gate U must be enabled for eight clock pulses. With this order, no address in store is involved. Hence the *N* part of the order contains no information. With a rearrangement of circuits it would be possible to carry out a *direct memory-access* for which the *N* address specified the address in store to which the data would be directed from the input register. Figure 5.5(a) and (d) illustrates the position.

XYZ = 111 : transfer of the contents of the accumulator to the
output register
(Accumulator) → Output
Accumulator contents regenerated

In this case the contents of the accumulator are transmitted serially via gate V to the output register. After eight clock pulses the new contents of the output register are the previous contents of the accumulator. Note that the previous contents of the accumulator are regenerated via the use of gate H. The position is shown in figure 5.5(a) and (d).

5.7.2   Gating Arrangements for Implementing Orders

Figure 5.6 gives a table showing in summary form the gating requirements for the execution of the eight orders of the instruction set for MIC. The table is derived from the material of the subsequent sections. As orders are executed, instruction words from the control register are supplied to the control or microprogramming unit, figure 5.5(c), where the control logic decodes the op-code and enables specific gates as a result. How this is achieved is best considered by taking the gates in turn.

It will be recalled that values for XYZ, the op-code, are provided each time an instruction is read from a store location.

Gate A. Reference to the table of figure 5.6 indicates that gate A must be enabled when XYZ has one or other of the following values:

001, 010, 011

Thus gate A is enabled for

$$\bar{X}\bar{Y}Z + \bar{X}Y\bar{Z} + \bar{X}YZ$$

Implementation of this Boolean logic expression is simply achieved and the result is shown in figure 5.7(a). Thus for any one of the three possibilities XYZ = 001, 010 or 011, data present at the input of gate A is transferred to the output of the gate. The control logic ensures that the data path established via gate A is held open for the duration of the eight clock pulses necessary to transfer eight-bit data through the gate.

In the interest of simplicity, no attempt at minimisation of the logic has been made either here or in respect of the other logic gates. This is left as a simple exercise for the reader (see the Problems at the end of the chapter).

Gate B. From the table of figure 5.6 it is clear that gate B is enabled only for XYZ =011 — that is, in the presence of $\bar{X}YZ$. The logic circuit is shown in figure 5.7(b).

The logic arrangements for the remaining gates are given in figure 5.7(c), (d), (e), (f), (h), (j), (s), (u) and (v). They may be deduced very readily from figure 5.6.

It must be stressed that in executing an instruction, control waveforms generated from a clock-pulse generator at the control unit, figure 5.5(c), ensure that signals corresponding to the op-code XYZ are presented to the logic of figure 5.7 for the duration of eight clock pulses. This permits the successive departure of the eight bits of 8-bit words from accumulator, store location, input register or output register as appropriate. The only departure from this procedure occurs for the cases of figure 5.7(j) and (h) which relate to cyclic shift through *N* places.

5.7.3 *Store Selection*

The methods of achieving store selection discussed here for MIC employ the same principles as are used in real machines especially when a random-access store is used. In the present case the arrangements are very simple since only 32 locations and hence a 5-bit code are involved. The five-bit code is taken from the address register whose contents are derived

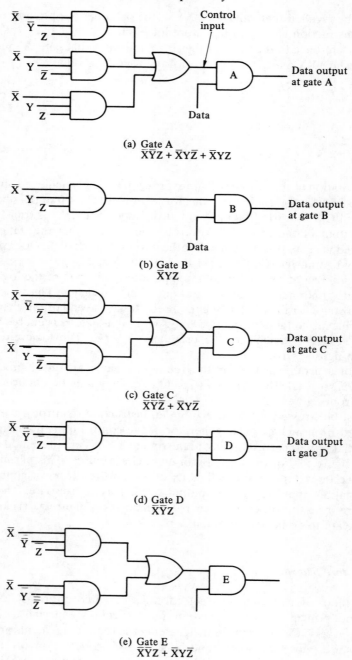

(a) Gate A
$\overline{X}\overline{Y}Z + \overline{X}Y\overline{Z} + \overline{X}YZ$

(b) Gate B
$\overline{X}YZ$

(c) Gate C
$\overline{X}\overline{Y}\overline{Z} + \overline{X}Y\overline{Z}$

(d) Gate D
$\overline{X}\overline{Y}Z$

(e) Gate E
$\overline{X}\overline{Y}Z + \overline{X}Y\overline{Z}$

Figure 5.7 Logic implementation for MIC

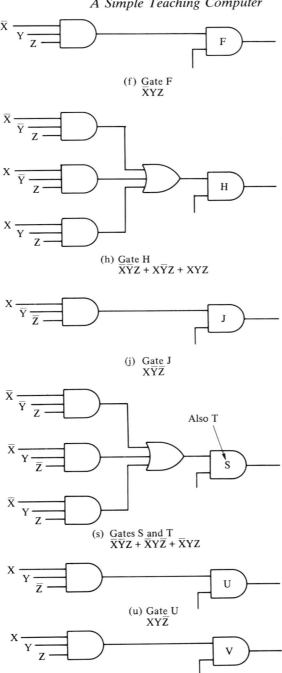

(f) Gate F
$\overline{X}YZ$

(h) Gate H
$\overline{X}\overline{Y}Z + X\overline{Y}Z + XYZ$

(j) Gate J
$X\overline{Y}\overline{Z}$

(s) Gates S and T
$\overline{X}\overline{Y}Z + \overline{X}Y\overline{Z} + \overline{X}YZ$

Also T

(u) Gate U
$XY\overline{Z}$

(v) Gate V
XYZ

either from the program counter or from the N address of instruction words obtained via the control unit. In either case the bits are designated N_4 to N_0 (see figure 5.5(b)). The five-bit code provides the basis for a one-out-of-32 decode at store input and output as illustrated by figures 5.8 and 5.9 (see also chapter 4, section 4.6.2), on decoders).

Control of input to one or other of the 32 store locations S_0 to S_{31} from the data input line is achieved via 5-entry AND gates connected to the appropriate N_0–N_4 and $\bar{N}_0$–$\bar{N}_4$ lines determined by the table of figure 5.8 and shown in figure 5.9. Data from the serial data bus forms one input to a second AND gate while the other input is the control signal. Only when an appropriate all-ones pattern is set at a control gate is data flow permitted. Thus, for example, store location S_0 is selected when N_4–N_0 corresponds to 00000. This is achieved by applying the corresponding pattern $\bar{N}_4$–$\bar{N}_0$ — that is, 11111 to the appropriate control gate S_0 for the duration of eight clock pulses corresponding to the passage of an eight-bit word. The clock pulses are directed to the correct store location by a one-out-of-32 decoder similar to that employed for store selection itself. For clarity, the decoder is omitted from figure 5.5(b).

Input					Output							
Address bits					Corresponding store location							
N_4	N_3	N_2	N_1	N_0	S_0	S_1	S_2	S_3	S_4	S_{29}	S_{30}	S_{31}
0	0	0	0	0	x							
0	0	0	0	1		x						
0	0	0	1	0			x					
0	0	0	1	1				x				
1	1	1	1	0							x	
1	1	1	1	1								x

Figure 5.8 N addresses designating the 32 store locations

Similarly, store location S_1 is selected by pattern N_4–N_0 set as 00001. This is achieved by applying $\bar{N}_4\,\bar{N}_3\,\bar{N}_2\,\bar{N}_1\,N_0$ — that is, 11111, to control gate S_1. To provide a path to store S_{31}, pattern N_4–N_0 is set to 11111. The application of $N_4\,N_3\,N_2\,N_1\,N_0$ to control gate S_{31} achieves the required objective.

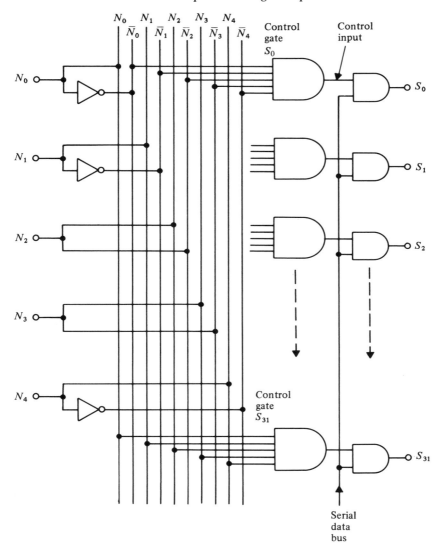

Figure 5.9 Store selection for MIC, one-out-of-32

Control of output from the store is achieved in similar fashion. The design of detailed circuit arrangements is left as a student exercise — see the Problems at the end of the chapter.

Note that the data-input and data-output line to or from the store act as rudimentary *data buses* in that data from the lines is available to or from any or all store locations subject to the presence of the correct 5-bit control codes. With real computers the selection code would involve significantly more bits but the principle would be the same. Certain codes would be allocated to permit access of data to peripheral equipment rather than to the store. Thus, for example, one code would permit data access to a printer, another to a visual display unit (VDU), and so on.

Note that the serial read-out of data removes the contents of a store location as successive clock pulses are applied (see chapter 4, section 4.7.1). Hence with MIC, store contents must be regenerated at read-out. An appropriate path is achieved via gate T (see figure 5.5(b)).

Note also that the successive clock pulses must be applied only to the specific eight-bit shift register constituting the store location. To achieve this end a further one-out-of-32 decoder is used to direct the clock pulses to the selected store location. In the interests of clarity this decoder is not shown on the figure.

5.7.4 Physical Realisation and Mode of Operation of MIC

It is useful to conclude this section with some practical details as to the circuits and operation of MIC when engineered as a teaching aid. For example, the accumulator and the 32 store locations might each comprise master–slave flip-flops connected as eight-stage shift registers and operating in serial fashion on receipt of clock pulses. Typically each shift register would constitute a single integrated circuit chip. For high-speed operation, clock pulses would be provided from a multivibrator on receipt of a start pulse from the control unit with operation of the multivibrator inhibited after eight successive outputs. Alternatively, low-speed clock pulses might be provided singly to illustrate detailed operation.

Program and data would be set into the computer manually via hand-switches and the input register before program execution. The provision of two rates for the master clock ensures that, when the program runs, execution of each order takes place automatically either at high speed or alternatively at low speed. In the former case, final results may be inspected as the contents of the output register. With low-speed operation, intermediate results can be displayed at the output register. In the present case, a lamp indicates the contents of each stage of the output register but more satisfactory arrangements can be made.

In both cases, execution of each instruction of the program involves two steps. In the first, the instruction stored in the location specified in the program counter is retrieved from store and is decoded. The decode indicates the order to be executed and the location in store of the operand involved. The second step relates to the execution of the order and frequently involves a second store access. During this *two-beat* cycle, the program counter is incremented to permit retrieval of a further instruction from store and continuance of the program. The process is repeated until the program is complete. A two-beat cycle is typical of much computer operation. The subject will be considered in greater detail in chapter 6.

5.8 Limitations of the Minimal Computer

Earlier sections of this chapter have discussed the features of a simple teaching computer intended to illustrate fundamental ideas. This present section points out the limitations of such a machine. These limitations are both numerous and substantial.

5.8.1 Limitations due to Word-length

Perhaps the most serious limitation of MIC arises from the short word-length. It is from this deficiency that most of the other shortcomings arise. For a real computer, a word-length of eight bits is a most serious limitation. With care, eight bits can be used to good advantage in a small computer by using double-length working but sixteen or even thirty-two bits are both more common and permit versatility.

5.8.2 Stored Programs

With a real machine, both program and data are stored typically in a semiconductor memory prior to program execution. This has been mentioned already in chapter 2 and the subject will receive further attention in chapters 6 and 7. With MIC, storage space is so limited that space can be found only for the storage of very short programs with most limited data.

5.8.3 Increase in the Total Number of Orders

With an increase in word-length, more bits can be allocated to the op-code and an increase in the total number of orders of the instruction set is possible. This means that essential instructions such as conditional orders may be accommodated. Without conditional instructions, an aid to calculation cannot be classed as a computer. Such instructions are related to similar instructions in high-level language. Examples are the GO TO in BASIC and the IF...THEN in Pascal. The notion of the importance of the conditional order was appreciated during the earliest days of computers as is evident from the work of Babbage and his colleague Lady Lovelace (ref. 5.1). Thus, in all but the simplest calculations, one or more conditional instructions which break the sequential order of instruction execution are essential and inevitable.

Thus, for example, the solution of a problem using an iterative procedure must be terminated after a finite number of steps, typically when two successive solutions differ by no more than a pre-determined amount. Otherwise the iterative procedure will continue indefinitely. The machine does not share the intuitive feel of the human operator who usually appreciates when the iterative procedure has reached a satisfactory conclusion. Accordingly, conditional instructions of the form

$$
\begin{array}{ll}
\text{Jump} & \text{unconditional} \\
\left.\begin{array}{l}
\text{Jump if } X > 0 \\
\text{Jump if } X = 0 \\
\text{Jump if } X < 0
\end{array}\right\} & \text{conditional}
\end{array}
$$

must be provided.

Other instructions permit transfer of data to and from peripheral equipment such as keyboards, visual display units and the like, while further orders allow communication with paper tape and card punches and readers, line printers, graph-plotters and other items. Special facilities are required to support bulk storage devices such as magnetic tape and disc.

The instructions discussed above may be regarded as essential to computer operation. In addition, it may be thought desirable to include additional instructions which make for efficiency and speed in programming at low level and by implication at higher level also. Obvious examples are multiply and divide achieved with the aid of a hardware multiplier and divider. Another help is an interchange instruction which *swaps* two items of data between an accumulator and a store location. Such an instruction is not essential but will reduce a swap procedure to a single instruction. Other examples of useful but non-essential instructions spring readily to mind. Thus, while multiple conditional instructions may be reduced to the single instruction, such as

$$
\left.\begin{array}{l}
\text{Jump if } X < 0 \\
\text{Jump if } X = 0
\end{array}\right\} \equiv \text{Jump if } X \leqslant 0
$$

the more versatile set earlier in this section is to be preferred.

Some illustrations of typical instructions are given in chapter 6 which discusses a simple but practical computer and goes on to consider briefly features of a more modern and versatile machine.

5.8.4   Additional Elements in the Instruction Words

So far, instruction words comprising op-codes and addresses only have been considered. With increased word-length, further possibilities are available. For example, a real computer incorporates several working registers which can be used as accumulators. Such provision makes for flexibility in programming and speed in operation. If several registers are used then it becomes necessary to specify which register is to be used in the execution of a particular instruction. Accordingly, bits must be allowed to designate individual registers. In practice two bits, permitting four registers, or three bits, allowing eight registers are typical.

For ease in programming on machines with multiple registers it may be useful to include one or more *mode* or *modifier* bits in instruction words. Typically, such a bit (or bits) designates modifier (index) register(s), the contents of which are added to the address forming part of the instruction to provide an effective address from which an operand may be retrieved and upon which arithmetic or logical operations may be performed. This technique is termed *relative addressing*. The registers used are called *modifier registers* or *index registers* (see chapter 6, section 6.3.4). Other similar techniques are considered later in chapter 6 in the context of a 16-bit machine.

5.8.5   Increase in Store Locations

The further and immediate advantage of an increase in word-length relates to the increase in the number of store locations which may be addressed. As seen already, a word-length of n bits permits the *direct addressing* of 2^n locations. Thus, if 12 bits are allocated as address bits

$$2^{12} = 4096$$

locations may be addressed. A block of store with 4096 locations is normally described as a 4K word store ($1K = 1024$ or 2^{10} locations). With modern technology, a random-access store of 64K locations is commonplace even for the home computer based on a microprocessor implementation.

With a word-length of eight bits or more, *indirect addressing* systems become a possibility. A special *flag bit* forming part of the instruction word is set at 1 to indicate that indirect addressing is being used (see chapter 6). Indirect addressing enhances total store size and provides increased programming flexibility. Typically, too, storage such as disc storage involving floppy discs or cartridge discs, magnetic tape storage and the like are involved in addition to the random access storage already considered. The subject is beyond the scope of the present chapter but will receive further consideration later (chapter 7).

5.8.6   *Variety of Instruction Formats*

In many cases, increased versatility is achieved through the use of alternative *instruction formats*. In such cases, restrictions imposed by the rigid structure of a single format are avoided. With one or more alternative formats, emphasis can be devoted to particular aspects of operation depending on circumstances. Thus one instruction format can be particularly relevant to store access while another can provide a wide variety of op-codes to permit flexibility in programming.

In order to distinguish between the various formats which are in use in a particular case, one or more specific bits in every instruction must be designated as a *flag bit* indicating which format is in use. With two formats a single flag may be set to indicate the alternative format. With four formats, the four conditions of a pair of flag bits must be examined. This important subject is carried further in chapter 6.

5.8.7   *Enhanced Precision of Data*

With short word-length, data cannot be specified with precision. With increased word-length, a sign bit may be provided and a choice of fixed or floating point arithmetic is possible. In either case, data may be specified with substantial precision. This is important to ensure accurate answers after lengthy arithmetic manipulation. Double and higher precision is achieved by employing a pair of words or multiple words to represent a number.

5.8.8   *Input and Output of Instructions and Data*

MIC provides data and instruction input via hand keys and output of results through visual inspection of a set of illuminated bulbs. In practice, such input and output arrangements are inadequate. Man–machine communication involves a variety of input and output peripherals. At this point it is sufficient to reiterate that they include input via punched cards or paper tape or input directly from the keyboard of a Teletype or Visual Display Unit (VDU). Output of data may be on punched cards, paper tape, printer or on the screen of a VDU. Alternatively, a permanent record may be necessary. In this case the display would be complemented by a *hard copy* using some form of printer. Often in engineering applications a graphical record using a *graph-plotter* is convenient. Frequently, output of data takes place at high speed through transference of information to disc or magnetic tape. In this case, data is output later in more convenient form as a visual record via a printer or as a graph. This *off-line* method of data handling is useful since the high-speed operation of the computer cannot be matched by the comparatively low speed of electro-mechanical devices.

5.9 Summary

This chapter has discussed a simple eight-bit serial computer, MIC, in some detail. As a result, the student can appreciate its features in full. The importance of word-length as the ultimate design criterion has been stressed. The Problems which follow encourage students to consolidate the knowledge gained in this chapter by preparing as a single diagram the constituent parts of the teaching-aid MIC, adding as much of the detail as possible down to the level of individual gates.

The importance of word-length was emphasised when the limitations of MIC were considered. Later chapters of this book will draw upon the present chapter and will explain how the limitations of the teaching-aid are overcome in real computers.

Reference

5.1 Bowden, B. V., *Faster than Thought*, Pitman, London, 1953.

Problems

This section of the chapter is of particular importance since it permits a check by the student on how well the material has been understood. The Problems draw the attention of the student to the considerable limitations of the machine described in the chapter. The chapter serves as a bridge, linking the fundamental ideas discussed in the preliminary chapters with the description of real computers contained in the remaining chapters. The problems and exercises described here are relevant to this link.

5.1 Figure 5.7 shows gating arrangements to permit implementation of orders within the machine. As mentioned in the text, no attempt has been made to minimise the logic used. It is evident from the Boolean expression for the logic at gate A that minimisation is possible. How may this be achieved?

Solution. Gate A is enabled for $W\overline{X} + WX + \overline{W}\overline{X}$. This expression may be simplified thus:

$$
\begin{aligned}
W\overline{X} + WX + \overline{W}\overline{X} &= W(\overline{X} + X) + \overline{W}\overline{X} \\
&= W + \overline{W}\overline{X} \\
&= W + \overline{X} \text{ (absorption law)}
\end{aligned}
$$

Similarly minimisation is possible at gate E where

$$
W\overline{X} + WX = W(\overline{X} + X) = W
$$

Is is possible to carry out minimisation for any other gate?

5.2 Figure 5.9 provided a detailed circuit for store selection using a one-out-of-32 decoder. The diagram related to selection of a store location at the *input* side of the store. A detailed circuit to choose one-out-of-32 store locations for the *return* of data to the CPU via the serial data bus was not given.

Draw up a modified version of figure 5.9 which will achieve the desired objective. As with the case of the text supporting figure 5.9, make specific provision for the fact that for successful operation of store selection eight clock pulses must be applied to the eight-state shift register constituting the required store location. The clock pulses must not be applied to the other 31 eight-stage shift registers. Add the appropriate decode circuit to your diagram.

5.3 Draw up a detailed circuit diagram for the accumulator at the CPU. Assume initially that individual flip-flop stages will be provided which must be equipped with gating between the stages to allow data transfer in both directions to permit left-shift and right-shift as necessary to accommodate multiplication and division by powers of 2. See section 5.7.1(c).

5.4 Chapter 5 gives the outline of a simple computer with an eight-bit word-length. In order to consolidate the material of chapter 5 it is useful to prepare a complete diagram of the computer including sufficient detail to permit construction.

The task is quite substantial and might be attempted in stages using a very large sheet of drawing paper. The following steps indicate a logical progression.

(a) Draw out the four diagrams comprising figure 5.5(a), (b), (c) and (d) to a substantial size with control lines between the parts sketched out.

(b) Complete the logic minimisation begun in problem **5.1** and insert the gating for the execution of the eight orders into the control (microprogramming) unit.

(c) Include the detailed one-out-of-32 decode logic at the input and output of the store together with similar logic for the selection of the clock pulses necessary to clock out the operands from selected locations.

(d) Add the interstage gating at the accumulator to permit left and right shift. See problem **5.3** above.

(e) Draw out the circuit for the single full-adder at the CPU.

(f) It is now appropriate to add the detailed control and clock-pulse lines from the microprogramming (control) unit to individual elements within the complete computer.

(g) Prepare a circuit for a basic two-speed clock.

Note that the detailed circuit for the machine is now almost complete. Note, however, that certain important items are still lacking. Missing elements include provision for the following features:

(i) Explicit circuit arrangements to permit left and right shift.

(ii) Provision for initial setting of the Program Counter (PC) and subsequent increments as orders are executed.

(iii) Detailed arrangements relating to machine start and the initial loading of program. These features might well be provided by a set of read-only instructions stored in a small read-only memory (ROM). Greater appreciation of the need for primitive *bootstrap* and *loader* programs will be apparent after studying chapter 8 which deals with software utilities.

The reader is invited to reconsider items (i) and (ii) above after further study. The inclusion of the features discussed under items (i) and (ii) completes the overall design of the simple eight-bit machine.

5.5 On the basis of your understanding of chapter 5, devise a set of simple laboratory experiments which might be carried out by a student using MIC. Pay particular attention to the balance between experiments which serve to illustrate overall machine operation and experiments which provide practice with simple programs.

5.6 Consider a redesign of the minimal teaching aid MIC in which word-length is extended to twelve bits. Allocate

4 bits to orders (instructions)
8 bits to store addresses

Choose appropriate orders additional to those for the minimal computer MIC.

How many store locations may now be addressed? What will be the effect on machine performance?

Outline Solution. With the 12-bit machine the instruction format will be as below:

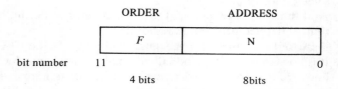

ORDER   ADDRESS

bit number   11   0

4 bits   8bits

Orders. 4 bits are allocated, so $2^4 = 16$ orders are possible. Now with the machine already discussed, 3 bits were allocated permitting $2^3 = 8$ instructions as follows:

Transfer   (Accumulator) → Address
          (Address)   → Accumulator

Arithmetic
   Addition
     (Address) + (Accumulator) → Accumulator

   Subtraction
     (Accumulator) − (Address) → Accumulator

Logic Shift   left by N places
          right by N places

Input/Output   (Input)   → Accumulator
          (Accumulator) → Output

The present problem requests 8 additional orders. There are various possibilities. A set of 8 orders is suggested below. These may be regarded as rather important.

Additional Orders

Addition   with the result placed in *store*, that is
          (Address) + (Accumulator) → Address

Subtraction with the result placed in *store*, that is
          (Accumulator) − (Address) → Address

Multiplication

Division

Subroutine   jump to subroutine
          return from subroutine

Conditional jump to N if x > 0
          jump to N if x ⩽ 0

Total Store Locations. A total of $2^8 = 256$ locations may be addressed.

Changes to machine. Necessary changes to machine to permit implementation of the above orders are:

1. Provision of auxiliary register Q associated with multiplication and division.
    Hardware multiplier and divider.
2. Extra control gating in respect of all orders.
3. Increase in the length of the program counter (PC) register to 8 stages from 5 stages.

Note. This final problem provides a bridge to the material which will be covered in chapter 6. This chapter begins with consideration of a machine with a word-length of twenty-four bits permitting a reasonable range of orders, access to a substantially larger store and, through two additional fields in instruction words, substantial versatility in programming.

6 Principal Features of Small Digital Computers

Objectives

By this point in the text, readers should appreciate how small computers, minicomputers, operate upon data in response to orders presented sequentially by the instructions of the instruction set according to the Von Neumann concept of a computer. The importance of word-length in determining the range of possible orders and the maximum size of store which may be addressed directly has been stressed in the light of the teaching-aid MIC. However, many important features of real minicomputers remain to be considered. This chapter discusses particularly relevant aspects of computer architecture. Initially a simple 24-bit machine is taken as the example though later the machine is contrasted against a more sophisticated 16-bit minicomputer representative of current computer practice. Detailed gating arrangements necessary to achieve machine operation are not emphasised since they detract from the attempt to provide an overview of computer architecture. Instead, throughout the chapter, the emphasis is on the effect of word-length on instruction set and store capacity. The role of the computer designer as to the choice of the orders of the instruction set is considered.

6.1 Introduction

It is useful to point out that real-world computers at the present time employ word-lengths which for the most part are multiples of eight. Thus eight-bit microcomputer systems represent the lower end of computing power. These microcomputers frequently employ a simple 8-bit microprocessor as their central processor and arithmetic unit. Other semiconductor chips provide essential features such as clocks, input/output ports, semiconductor memory and the like. As a result the complete machine is accommodated on a single printed circuit board (PCB) of moderate physical size. In other cases, a single chip provides all the essential features of the central processor unit together with input/output and some limited memory capability. The present performance of such machines is of necessity rather limited with programming typically restricted to low-level languages. Inevitably, instructions involve more than a single 8-bit word.

Sixteen-bit machines are frequently represented by the 16-bit minicomputer. Here the architecture tends to reflect an evolution from the mainstream of computer development. Often a complete range of 16-bit machines employing the same overall architecture will be provided by each manufacturer. Substantial compatability in respect of the running of software on each machine in the range is likely. The distinguishing features between machines within the range will relate to total memory size, variety of peripherals which may be attached, speed and cost. At the same time, however, there is an increasing trend towards 16-bit implementations of microprocessor-based systems including single-chip microcomputers.

Larger, faster and more powerful minicomputers employ a 32-bit architecture. A 32-bit word-length permits very powerful instruction sets, high precision arithmetic and the possibility of ready access to large main memory. Such machines will employ powerful operating systems such as UNIX (ref. 6.1) which permit multi-user, multi-task work and the flexible deployment of a wide variety of peripherals. Again, however, microprocessor-based 32-bit microcomputer systems including single-chip versions are becoming available. However, unless sufficient memory can be provided on the single-chip minicomputers to accommodate enough space for a powerful operating system, then neither the 16-bit nor 32-bit single-chip microcomputer system is able to compete with the well established 16 or 32-bit minicomputer systems for general-purpose applications.

While it is very difficult to generalise with respect to a rapidly evolving field, it is probably correct to state that the single-chip microcomputer system is particularly appropriate for dedicated specific applications in industry. Outside the specialist area of single-chip systems, it is also probably correct to assert that it is increasingly difficult to distinguish between mini and micro systems and their architectures. This statement will become increasingly apparent when specific features of microprocessor-based systems are considered in chapter 9.

Large *mainframe* machines often employ a 64-bit word-length. They may be used in large industrial organisations, government departments or to provide a central service in colleges and universities. Such machines will be very powerful and will be provided with most extensive storage facilities both in terms of main store and backing store. Their architecture will incorporate both the latest designs and the most recent technologies. The unit cost of the machine and supporting software may well exceed £1 million. Such machines are beyond the scope of this introductory volume and will not be discussed further.

In this chapter, important features of real minicomputers are introduced though with the space available only an outline treatment is practicable. An approach via the hardware of specific computers has been avoided since inevitably considerable detail will be introduced and too much stress may be placed on a particular machine. Instead, an alternative and more general treatment is employed in which the emphasis is on the effect of adopting a particular word-length and instruction format. Initially a simple minicomputer with 24-bit word-length is considered in some detail and later this is contrasted with a more sophisticated machine in which a 16-bit word-length is used.

The illustrations relating to the implementation of orders in the earlier part of the chapter refer to machine language coded in binary and octal while the examples of the latter part of the chapter refer to assembly language involving mnemonic codes in which the mnemonic is substituted for a binary or octal code usually on a direct one-for-one basis. In either event, the discussion of the codes should not be regarded as an attempt to teach low-level programming but rather as providing illustrative examples to emphasise machine architecture and general features.

6.2 A Simple 24-bit Machine

In this section a simple 24-bit machine is discussed. The computer considered is typical of an early minicomputer. Modern mini and micro-computers are invariably more complex in their architecture than the machine under consideration. Nevertheless the discussion is valuable since it brings out essential features of all small computers and introduces the relevant technical terms. The machine is sufficiently simple for its overall architecture to be discussed in considerable detail though not to the level of the individual gating arrangements as was the case for the teaching-aid of chapter 5. The material serves as a bridge to the 16-bit machine discussed briefly later in the chapter and the more sophisticated computers consi-dered elsewhere in advanced texts (ref. 6.2.).

Figure 6.1 shows the instruction format adopted for the machine. The letters X, F, M, N designate the four sections or *fields* of the instruction

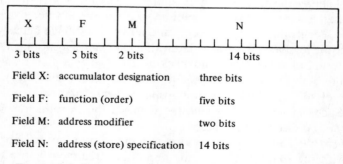

Figure 6.1 Instruction format for simple 24-bit machine

format. While the letters used for the designation of the particular fields have no special connotation, they are widely used in the literature to denote the fields specified.

The first part (or field) of the instruction format is the three-bit code, X, designated to distinguish between one or other of the eight working registers at the Central Processor Unit (CPU). Recall that there are 2^3 ways of arranging the three binary bits of the 3-bit field X. Hence 8 registers can be labelled each with a unique 3-bit code. In accordance with common usage, such working registers are frequently designated the title *accumulator* though it will be seen that such designation is restrictive and in reality their applications are wider. This usage is an example of computer jargon which may confuse students. Unfortunately the use of such jargon is widespread in computer technology.

The five-bit field F permits a maximum of 32 orders in the instruction set. While 32 orders are far fewer than is currently the practice, they are sufficient to be representative and to illustrate the features of a typical simple instruction set.

A two-bit code M is used to permit reference to those four of the registers also used as *index* or *modifier registers*.

The address selection field N is 14-bits long and permits direct access of up to $2^{14} = 16\,384$ (16K) locations. 16K locations represent only a small memory by current standards but the memory size is sufficient to illustrate important features of current practice. Note the convention by which 1024 locations are referred to as 1K locations.

In this machine, arithmetic and other logical operations are performed at the CPU which is more sophisticated than the simple arithmetic unit of the teaching-aid MIC of the previous chapter. The accumulator and index (modifier) registers are situated at the CPU. The system is basically single-address in that most orders relate to an arithmetic or logical operation carried out on the contents of a single memory location. Although the contents of one or more of the registers at the CPU are likely to be involved also, only one location external to the CPU is specified in the address field N, hence the designation *single-address* or *single-operand*. Later in the chapter the concept of *two-address* or *double-operand* working will be introduced in connection with a 16-bit machine.

In writing programs at low level — that is, at machine-code level — instructions are often designated in octal rather than binary since this makes for programming convenience. Conversion to binary might be via a very simple assembler program. An example of a format written in octal is given in figure 6.2. which indicates how the 14 bits of an N address appear. The representation might be either

*12 000 or 12 000$_8$

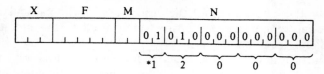

Figure 6.2 An address in store designated in octal as *12 000 or 12 000$_8$ and in binary as 01 010 000 000 000

The machines discussed in this chapter, like almost all modern machines, are *parallel in operation* in contrast to the teaching-aid MIC considered in chapter 5. The implications of parallel operation are discussed later in the chapter. Initially, however, the features of the instruction format of the 24-bit minicomputer are considered in more detail.

6.2.1   The Role of the X Accumulators (Field X)

These registers (accumulators), each 24-bits long, are situated at the CPU. Each is analogous to the single eight-bit accumulator of MIC. Since X is specified by 3 bits, there are eight such accumulators ($2^3 = 8$). In executing program, intermediate results may be held in one or more of the accumulators. Since the operation of store access is time consuming, reduction of the number of times access is required improves overall machine speed. Accordingly, multi-accumulator working enhances overall efficiency and speed (see chapter 7, section 7.4). The question of store access will be considered again when a 16-bit machine is discussed later in the chapter (section 6.6). The use of multiple register working also facilitates arithmetic operations carried out repetitively on the contents of contiguous store locations. In this case they are used in association with the index (modifier) registers. An example of such use is to be found in section 6.3.6.

In this text the registers are designated X0 to X7. Typically, the eight registers each comprise bi-polar integrated circuit elements and form part of the CPU. As a result, they are capable of access at very high speed compared with main memory. Such registers represent the highest level of the storage hierarchy. A set of bi-polar registers, situated at and forming part of the CPU, and ranging in number from, say, 4 to 32 is typical of current practice with mini and microcomputers. The registers may also be regarded in certain circumstances as a small slave or cache store. The detailed treatment of slave or cache stores is outside the scope of the present book but ref. 6.3, for example, may be consulted.

The important topic of storage hierarchy will be considered at length in chapter 7.

6.2.2 The Instruction Set (Field F)

Since five bits are designated to represent orders or functions, F, a maximum of 32 orders is possible from the 5-bit op-code. The orders chosen are at the discretion of the computer designer, not the user. The choice depends upon the range of work which it is expected the machine will encounter and also reflects, as does the complete instruction format, the evolution of the machine. A detailed consideration of the orders chosen for the present machine appears in the sections which follow. It must be recalled that the execution of orders takes place in the same way as occurred with MIC. As an order is decoded the appropriate gates are enabled to permit, under controlled conditions, the circulation of data between accumulators and memory locations and also the execution of arithmetic and logical operations. The implications of parallel rather than serial operation will become apparent later in the chapter (see section 6.4).

In the second part of the chapter the orders of this simple machine will be contrasted with the more versatile arrangements to be found in a more modern machine. As usual, however, the price of enhanced flexibility is increased complexity.

6.2.3 The Modifier (Field M)

Frequently it is necessary to carry out the same sequence of operations on data held in a set of store, often contiguous, locations. One method is to write out the set of program instructions the requisite number of times, merely changing the relevant store address labels on each occasion. This leads to a very lengthy program and is inelegant. It is convenient both in program writing and in the storage of a program if a single cycle of instructions can be used. This requires some means whereby the address specified in the program can be changed in a controlled manner each time the contents of a new store location are to be accessed. The index (modifier) registers permit such *modification* of a set of store location addresses.

The M part of an order is used to designate one or other of the registers X1, X2 or X3, specified by M = 01, 10 or 11 whose contents, (M), are added to the address part of an order before the order is obeyed. By convention, modification is avoided when M = 00. Thus an *effective address*, E, is achieved where

$$\text{effective address} = E = (M) + N$$

Note the use of (M) to indicate the contents of a location, here an index register M. It must be appreciated that the addition (M) + N will add to the execution time for the order (see chapter 7, section 7.4).

When the modifier technique is used to perform the same set of operations a number of times, the contents of the relevant register X1, X2, X3 must be incremented or decremented as appropriate each time a subsequent cycle of operations is entered. For example, with operations involving data in contiguous locations, increment or decrement must be by unity. The example of section 6.3.6 makes the position clear and illustrates the power of the technique. The registers used for address modification are often called *index registers*.

The use of the modifier in the case of the simple 24-bit machine is contrasted against the *index mode* used with the 16-bit machine later in the chapter (section 6.6.5).

6.2.4   The N Address (Field N)

In this case the N address comprises 14 bits. This allows the direct addressing of

$$2^{14} = 16\ 384\ (16K)$$

decimal locations. In some cases a store of maximum size is not employed either because of financial constraints or because the particular application required of the machine does not justify a store of this size. Recall the analogy of the home computer with a basic memory capable of later extension. In the case of the 24-bit minicomputer the total store capacity has been partitioned into four sections or blocks each of 4K locations to illustrate the position. Note that a total store of only 16K words would be regarded as small by current practice. Figure 6.3 shows a typical arrangement. Note that within the store the instruction words and data are indistinguishable. They appear as patterns of zeros and ones expressed in terms of the storage medium employed. The context in which the binary words, *operands*, appear reveals whether they are instructions or data. In all cases the operands are of the standard word-length for the machine — that is, 24-bits long.

Block number	Address locations (decimal)	Address locations (octal)
0	0 to 4095	0 to 7777_8
1	4096 to 8191	10000_8 to 17777_8
2	8192 to 12287	20000_8 to 27777_8
3	12288 to 16383	30000_8 to 37777_8
	Last eight addresses reserved for registers X0 to X7	

Figure 6.3   Organisation of a 16K store for a small computer

For convenience, the contents of block 0 might comprise simple conversion programs from octal to binary, together with a variety of simple *assemblers* or *compilers* which might be retained in store on a semi-permanent basis. In some cases it would be convenient to restrict the *compiled program* currently under execution to block 1, with data held in block 2 say. Much depends on the type of program encountered: the compiler, the need to use available store to best advantage and, especially when working with low-level languages, the inclination of the programmer. The significance of the above terms will become more apparent when chapter 8 has been studied.

Semiconductor store is used almost universally as the main storage medium for micro and minicomputer systems. However, such store usually forms only a part of a complete storage hierarchy. Since there is a trend towards data processing on an ever-increasing scale, even with the home computer, the problems associated with storage become increasingly important. Accordingly the subject of storage is accorded a complete chapter (chapter 7) in this book.

6.3 Implementation of the Instruction Set of the 24-bit Machine

Some instructions of the set may be regarded as essential, while others are included at the discretion of the designer to improve speed and efficiency and to facilitate programming. This section discusses a complete set of instructions, stressing important features as they arise. The orders should be regarded as a simplified sub-set of orders used in current micro and minicomputer systems. The addressing techniques and instructions discussed in connection with the 16-bit computer later in the chapter extend the subject further. It must be stressed that throughout the chapter the intention is to highlight features of machine architecture and operation and that the material is not intended as an introduction to programming at machine-code level.

The various orders of the 24-bit machine fall into groups. For convenience they have been allocated octal designations. The octal numbers do not constitute a consecutive set.

6.3.1 Elementary Functions

The first pair are *transfer instructions* moving data between a working accumulator and a store location. In this they are similar to the pair of transfer instructions in MIC. Hardware execution of the orders occurs in analogous fashion though a parallel data bus is employed in the present case. This pair of orders permitting exchange of data between CPU and store must be regarded as essential.

Function 00_8 Transfer Function: (Address) $\rightarrow$ Accumulator

This function causes an operand in an address location designated by an N address (possibly modified) to be transferred into the accumulator specified by X. The previous contents of accumulator X are naturally lost in the process. Notice that in the above notation the contents of a location are identified very closely with the location itself. This approach was first observed with the MIC computer. The brief specification for this instruction is written as

> *Function* 00_8 : $x' = n$; $n' = n$

The concise notation adopted here is widely used. Capital letters are used to denote locations themselves and either parentheses or small letters to denote the contents. Hence

> $n = (N)$, that is, quantity n is the contents of address N
> $x = (X)$, that is, quantity x is the contents of accumulator X

The contents of a location before an instruction is obeyed are denoted by unprimed symbols while primed symbols are used after an instruction is obeyed. An arrow symbol or equals sign is used to indicate transfer of data from one location to another.

Typically an order is written in the following format:

> X F   M   N

So by way of example in this particular case we might have

> X F   M   N
> 1 00   0   *20 000

This instruction transfers the operand in location *20 000, typically a piece of data, into accumulator X1. No address modification takes place since M = 0.

The order is written more concisely as

> | 1   00   0   *20 000|

Recall that the 5-bit code, F, enables the gates which permit transfer from the store to the accumulator X1 while the 14-bit code, N, defines the relevant location N within the store. The activities involved are similar to those described in chapter 5 in relation to the teaching-computer MIC. Now, however, the gating and decode arrangements are more complex since code F is 5 bits while N is 14 bits. (For MIC, F was 3 bits, N was 5 bits.)

Since any accumulator may be used with any store location, we might write three consecutive steps of program as:

$$\begin{vmatrix} 5 & 00 & 0 & *20\ 000 \\ 6 & 00 & 0 & *20\ 001 \\ 7 & 00 & 0 & *20\ 001 \end{vmatrix}$$

which transfers the contents of location *20 000 into accumulator 5 and the contents of location *20 001 into both accumulators 6 and 7. Implicit in this procedure is the retention of the contents of address locations unless the locations are cleared explicitly of current contents as fresh operands (data or instructions) are written into the locations specified.

In listings such as the above, the convention is to write the address of the program steps (instructions) to the left of the program listing and program notes to the right. An example will appear in figure 6.6. Note that in many cases the addresses of the instructions of the program will be allocated automatically by the assembler program when the program is assembled prior to running (see section 6.3.2 and chapter 8).

Function 10_8 Transfer Function: (Accumulator) $\rightarrow$ Address

This function transfers the contents of a specified accumulator to a designated address (possibly modified). The accumulator contents are unchanged. This specification is written:

$$10_8 : n' = x; x' = x$$

Thus

$$\begin{vmatrix} 6 & 10 & 0 & *12\ 000 \\ 6 & 10 & 0 & X7 \end{vmatrix} \quad \begin{array}{l} (X6) \rightarrow *12\ 000 \text{ with X6 unchanged} \\ (X6) \rightarrow \quad X7 \quad \text{with X6 unchanged} \end{array}$$

Notice that by a slight extension we are permitting *transfer of data to accumulators* as well as to store locations. This may prove a useful programming aid and obviates the need for the allocation of a separate instruction for the purpose.

Within the context of the present instruction set, this desirable feature could be achieved by allocating the last eight addresses specified by N as alternate designations for the accumulators X0 to X7, that is

$X0 = 37770_8$ to $X7 = 37777_8$

(compare figure 6.3). Note now that the normal memory address space has been reduced from 16K by eight locations. Adopting this approach the symbol X7 used in the instruction above would be replaced by the assembler with the binary equivalent of 37777_8. When the program ran, a data path would be established to accumulator X7 rather than to a store location.

Function 02_8 Addition : (Accumulator) + (Address) → Accumulator

With this function, *addition* of the contents x of accumulator X and the contents n of store location N takes place. The result is place in accumulator X. Hence we may write

$02_8 : x' = x + n; n' = n$

As before, the contents of N remain unchanged.

Function 12_8 Addition : (Address) + (Accumulator) → Address

This function is *complementary* to function 02_8. The result is placed in store location N and the original contents of accumulator X remain. Hence we may write

$12_8 : n' = x + n; x' = x$

Function 03_8 subtraction : (Accumulator) − (Address) → Accumulator

$03_8 : x' = x - n; n' = n$

Function 13_8 Subtraction : (Accumulator) − (Address) → Address

$13_8 : n' = x - n; x' = x$

This pair of functions performs *subtraction* with reference to the contents of an accumulator and the contents of a specific store location. Typically, subtraction is achieved by taking the two's complement of the data to be subtracted and performing addition. Thus a separate subtractor is not required at the arithmetic unit of the CPU. All that is necessary is logic to obtain the two's complement of the relevant quantity. Note that this is the same process as was the case with MIC.

A further pair of useful functions is included among the elementary functions as follows.

Function 01_8 : $x' = -n$; $n' = n$
Function 11_8 : $n' = -x$; $x' = x$

These orders are like 00_8 and 10_8 in that they *transfer* data but the data is *negated* in the process. It is left for the reader to decide if they are essential.

Function 14_8 : $x' = n$; $n' = x$

This *interchange* function is the final one in the set of elementary functions which involve the exchange and manipulation of data between CPU and store. As with functions 01_8 and 11_8, function 14_8 is not essential, but it is a useful aid to concise programming.

6.3.2 Execution of Simple Instructions

In a simple computer of the type under discussion, each instruction comprises a single word of standard length and each piece of data is also a single word. The program is stored sequentially starting at some convenient address in store — for example, at location *10 000. The computer has at the CPU a special unit called the *program counter* (PC), *main counter*, *sequence register* or *order-number register* which contains the address at which the *next* instruction is to be found. In very simple machines there may be provision for setting the program counter by hand to the address of the first order in a program. The setting may be achieved by employing a set of switches with which the appropriate binary address is set up or alternatively by using thumb wheels coded in octal. In larger machines this is done without reference to the user through the executive program of the operating system (see chapter 8).

While the first instruction is being obeyed, the counter is advanced by 1 to provide the address where the next instruction is to be found. Normally, orders are obeyed in sequence with the computer in a *two-beat cycle*, fetching and executing orders alternatively. Such a two-beat cycle involves for the most part two store accesses for each order carried out. The first access is to fetch the instruction, the second to execute the order. It will be seen later that this approach is a fundamental limitation to the speed and flexibility with which program may be executed. Ways in which the problem may be overcome in part will be considered later in this chapter.

Figure 6.4 shows a schematic diagram which illustrates the above situation. In the figure, program instructions are shown in sequential locations starting at *10 000 and data in sequential locations starting at

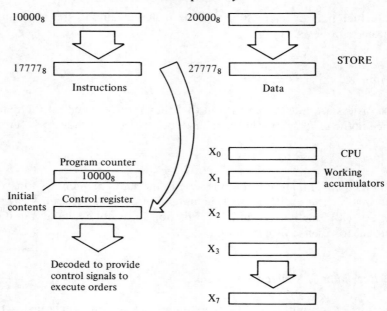

10000_8

20000_8

17777_8

27777_8

STORE

Instructions

Data

Program counter
10000_8

X_0 CPU

X_1 Working accumulators

Initial contents   Control register

X_2

X_3

Decoded to provide control signals to execute orders

X_7

Figure 6.4 Illustration of execution of simple order

*20 000. The program counter is shown at its initial setting of *10 000. As an instruction is read down from the store, it is placed in the *control register* (*instruction register*) and then decoded to permit execution of the order through the action of the microprogramming unit (see chapter 7, section 7.4).

The regular execution of orders obeyed sequentially is lost when *jump* or *conditional* orders are involved, in which case the N part of the order is used to specify an address at which the order to be obeyed next may be found. This address replaces the next address in the ordered sequence in the program counter. The sequential execution is interrupted temporarily. Such a scheme is typical of the execution of all conditional (jump) instructions. Jumps may be forward in the program or they may be backwards. In the latter case they permit loops or cycles in a program. Such an approach makes for a more concise approach to programming.

It is the conditional instruction which distinguishes the computer from other forms of aid to calculation. This important point has been understood from the earliest days of digital computers and indeed was fully appreciated by Babbage and Lady Lovelace in the 1830s. The lack of the conditional instruction was one of the fundamental limitations of the teaching-aid MIC considered in chapter 5.

6.3.3 Conditional Instructions

One of the important features of the accumulators is that operands held in them may be tested with certain conditional instructions. The X part of the order specifies which accumulator is used. The N part of the conditional instruction specifies where the next instruction is to be found should the test prove successful. Note that this is an entirely new use for the N part of an instruction. At this point it is convenient to consider some typical conditional instructions. A set of typical conditional instructions is discussed below. It will be appreciated that this set could be reduced in extent if so desired. The result would be a reduction in flexibility in the use of the computer.

Function 20_8 : If $x = 0$, jump to N, where N is the address of the next instruction

This causes a jump only if the contents x, of accumulator X, are zero. Otherwise the next instruction in sequence will be obeyed. Hence there are two possibilities:

(i) Test fails: advance the program counter by 1,

or (ii) Test successful: replace the contents of the program counter by N. Should $M \neq 0$ (that is, if the modifier is involved), then the contents of the program counter become the effective address

$$E = N + (M)$$

Figure 6.5 illustrates the position. It also indicates the unconditional jump required in the main program at the point at which control is restored to the main program. This will be necessary to ensure that in the event of the condition not being satisfied, the course of the main body of the program is not corrupted by the program step or steps resulting from the jump. With this computer an unconditional jump would be achieved by testing for zero a location which had been cleared explicitly. If further orders had been available an order

Jump to N unconditionally

could have been included in the instruction set.

The provision of additional jump instructions makes for programming flexibility, so further jump instructions are included in the instructions set of the 24-bit machine as follows:

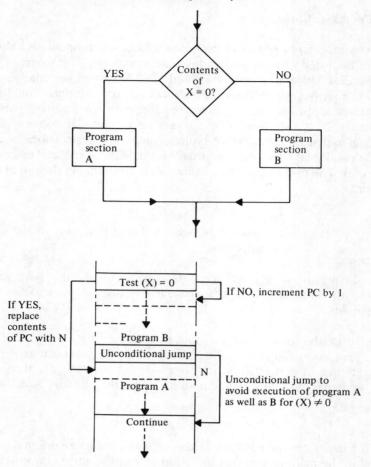

Figure 6.5 Execution of a jump instruction

Function 21_8 : Jump to N if $x \neq 0$ (that is, inverse of 20_8)
Function 22_8 : Jump to N if $x \geqslant 0$
Function 23_8 : Jump to N if $x < 0$

It should be noted that the provision of additional jump instructions makes for programming convenience. Thus, for example, functions 22_8 and 23_8 allow a number to be tested to determine the appropriate sign bit. An example of a piece of program including a simple jump instruction is shown in figure 6.6. Note the provision of the second and unconditional jump instruction, since the contents of X0 have been set to zero, in order to overcome the hazard mentioned in connection with figure 6.5.

Steps	Address	Program				Notes
Test	*14023	7	20	0	*14047	Jump to *14047 if (X7)=0
	*14024	2	10	0	*12000	(X2) → *12000, thus continuing main
				etc.		program if test fails
Program B			•			
			•			
			•			
Unconditional Jump to *14060	*14046	0	20	0	*14060	Jump to *14060 if (X0)=0, that is, an unconditional jump, since X(0) has been cleared in advance to ensure that the contents of X0=0
	*14047	2	10	0	*12001	(X2) → *12001
				etc.		
Program B			•			
			•			
			•			
			•			
Main program continues	*14060					

Figure 6.6 An example of a simple jump instruction

6.3.4 Relative Address Notation

In writing program at low level, the programmer is conscious of the locations into which the instructions will be placed. So far we have been concerned with *absolute address* notation. This is not always convenient especially in cases where programs are built up by a team of writers or where library routines are involved (see chapter 8). In particular, it is important to be able to write addresses *relative* to the address of a particular instruction rather than necessarily quote an absolute address.

Consider the case of a jump instruction

7 22 0 v0 + 3	Jump forward 3 locations if $(X7) \geqslant 0$
next instruction next instruction next instruction	

In the convention adopted here, v0 is decoded by the assembler as the address at which the instruction is stored, to which 3 is added to give N in the instruction proper. Should v0 turn out to be *15 676 for example, then the jump instruction is

7   22   0   *15 701

With the technique described above, the mapping relative to an absolute address is performed by the assembler *before* the program is run. Note that v0 is merely a code to denote that relative addressing is invoked. There is no special reason why this code is used. Any other code could be substituted provided the assembler is constructed in such a way as to respond correctly.

6.3.5   *Provision for Insertion of Constants into Programs*

When programming at low level it may be convenient to be able to manipulate constants directly within a program itself. Functions 04_8, 05_8, 06_8 and 07_8 make this provision. Here the N part of the order is used as the data, rather than as an *operand pointer*. The 14 binary bits constituting the N part of the order are placed in a specified accumulator either directly or after addition to or subtraction from the existing contents of the specified accumulator. The position is made clear by reference to each of the instructions in turn.

Function 04_8 : x' = C where C is the quantity specified in the N part of the order

For example:

| 4   04   0   ⨀*27* | places *27 in accumulator X4

The constant *27 is encircled merely in order to draw attention to the fact that it is a constant. It is often referred to as the *literal mode* of addressing.
   Similarly:

Function 05_8 : x' = −C, that is, placing of constant C in accumulator X after negation

Increment of the existing contents of an accumulator by constant C is possible using the instruction:

Function 06_8 : x' = x + C, that is, *increment* x by C

Similarly decrement of the existing contents of an accumulator is achieved by:

Function 07_8 : x' = x − C, that is, *decrement* x by C

A simple example of the value of such provision will be seen in the next section, which relates to the modification of orders.

6.3.6 Modification of Orders

This topic has been discussed briefly in section 6.2.3. The subject is taken further at this point through consideration of an example. As already explained, the M part of an order is used to specify a register whose contents are added to the N part of an order immediately before execution, for example

effective address $E = N + (M)$

For this particular computer, M has been allocated two bits and relates to registers X0, X1, X2 and X3 though no modification takes place when M=0 is specified. For example

$$\begin{vmatrix} 7 & 00 & 1 & *12\ 000 \end{vmatrix}$$

produces a copy of data to X7 from a location specified by *12 000 plus the contents of register X1 rather than from address *12 000 alone — that is, an effective address

$E = *12\ 000 + X1$

Modifiers find considerable use in cycles (loops) in that they permit operation on operands held in a batch of addresses, frequently sequential addressed (that is, an *array*). This may be illustrated with a simple example. The example is also useful since it shows the value of functions 06_8 and 07_8 — that is, increment and decrement by constants, the use of a jump instruction, function 21_8, and the convenience of relative addressing.

Suppose we wish to clear the contents of a block of sixteen sequential locations *15 000 to *15 017 — that is, 20_8 locations in all. This may be achieved with a program loop involving multi-accumulator working. Suppose we use, say, accumulator X1 as the modifier (index) register and X4 as a counter. Then the program may be specified as in figure 6.7.

The stages in the program execution are as follows. A constant of zero value is set into accumulator X0 to set up a null register. The counter X4 is set to 20_8 and the index register X1 is cleared. The loop of four orders then follows. The first time round the loop (X1) = 0 and 15 000_8 itself is cleared. The contents of the index register X1 are incremented by unity and the counter X4 is decremented by unity. Thus the second time round the loop we have

$(X1) = 1$ while $(X4) = 17_8$

This arrangement permits the clearing of location (15 000 + 1_8) during the cycle. The process continues until on the sixteenth time round we enter the

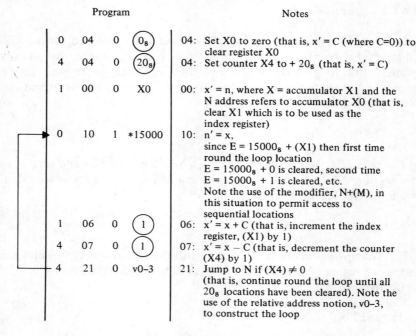

	Program				Notes
0	04	0	(0_8)	04:	Set X0 to zero (that is, x' = C (where C=0)) to clear register X0
4	04	0	(20_8)	04:	Set counter X4 to + 20_8 (that is, x' = C)
1	00	0	X0	00:	x' = n, where X = accumulator X1 and the N address refers to accumulator X0 (that is, clear X1 which is to be used as the index register)
0	10	1	*15000	10:	n' = x, since E = 15000_8 + (X1) then first time round the loop location E = 15000_8 + 0 is cleared, second time E = 15000_8 + 1 is cleared, etc. Note the use of the modifier, N+(M), in this situation to permit access to sequential locations
1	06	0	(1)	06:	x' = x + C (that is, increment the index register, (X1) by 1)
4	07	0	(1)	07:	x' = x – C (that is, decrement the counter (X4) by 1)
4	21	0	v0–3	21:	Jump to N if (X4) $\neq$ 0 (that is, continue round the loop until all 20_8 locations have been cleared). Note the use of the relative address notion, v0–3, to construct the loop

Figure 6.7 An example of the use of the modifier

loop with (X1) = 17_8 and thus 15 017_8 is cleared. At the end of the loop, register X4 is decremented to yield (X4) = 0. The test shown in the last line of the program fails with the result that exit from the routine occurs.

The routine corresponds to the DO instruction in FORTRAN or **repeat...until** in Pascal. It is important to note particularly the use of the modifier and to appreciate the convenience of multiple accumulator working in this case. Note, however, that the program loop could be simplifed by combining the roles of counter and index register. The example is carried a little further in the Problems at the end of this chapter (see problem **6.2**).

It is important to note that provision must be made in the hardware of the computer for the rapid addition of the contents of the index register M to the N part of the contents of the control register before addressing the memory — that is, the operation

$$E = N + (M)$$

The arithmetic unit of the CPU is used for this purpose in the same way as for normal addition which occurs on the decode of such orders as 02_8 and 12_8, and the same hardware is utilised. Naturally a time penalty is incurred.

With a high-speed parallel adder, employing parallel carry, the time penalty is small. For example, parallel addition with parallel carry might be achieved within 100 ns for both the 24-bit additions of such orders as

$$02_8 : \text{(accumulator)} + \text{(address)} \rightarrow \text{accumulator}$$

and the 14-bit addition required for

$$\text{effective address } E = N + (M)$$

With parallel carry, true parallel addition takes place typically only across blocks of 4 bits. *Block carry* which is sequential then follows. Accordingly a time penalty is exacted for the addition. Further details of this fascinating topic will be found in more advanced texts. See, for example, ref. 6.3.

6.3.7 *Multiplication and Division*

Multiplication and division are more complicated processes than addition and subtraction. In addition, the result of multiplication of two words of standard length (that is, the product) appears as a double-length word, while for division, divisor and quotient of standard length implies a dividend of double length. Such double-length working requires the provision of an additional register or registers. For example, a special register may be used to accommodate the least significant half of double-length operands with the more significant half held in one or other of the regular working accumulators. The double-length word in this case would be a sign bit followed by 47 digits. This is illustrated in figure 6.8. In order to facilitate subsequent working, the double-length operand would be truncated later to single length. In the 24-bit machine under consideration, the lower half of the double-length operand is held in an auxiliary register, sometimes known as the *Q register*, as contents q. (The term Q register may arise from its possible use in division to hold a quotient. See order 37_8 relating to division.)

Various possibilities and requirements occur for multiplication and division. For example, a hardware multiplier and divider may be provided. This is typically the case with the minicomputer where speed is important

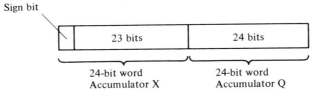

Figure 6.8 Arrangements for double-length working with 24-bit machine

and the cost of the integrated-circuit multiplier and divider chips may be justified. Alternatively in minimal microprocessor-based microcomputer systems, cost considerations may be predominant. Here multiplication and division may be achieved via special software routines. Sometimes the basic minicomputer of a range of machines uses software multiplier and divider routines in the interest of cost considerations while a more expensive machine in the range employs hardware and operates at faster speed.

For both hardware and software multipliers, the algorithms employed mirror the basic processes of long multiplication and long division as carried out by hand. Thus multiplication becomes a shift and add process. With two n-bit numbers the final result may be two n-bits wide. However, multiplication in particular differs in one important respect from the hand calculation in that the computer algorithm adds successive partial products sequentially rather than provides the addition of all the products at the end of the calculation.

On reflection it will be seen that the addition of just two numbers across the maximum width of $2n$ bits is a standard computer procedure involving parallel addition with parallel carry. On the other hand, to emulate the hand calculation of long multiplication with its simultaneous addition of n numbers to yield a $2n$-bit wide result would require formidable hardware. Accordingly, in the computer case, pairs of numbers are added as partial products increment the running total in an accumulator at the CPU. As a result of the successive additions, multiplication of two n-bit numbers is a relatively slow process though there are variations of the basic multiplication algorithm to reduce the number of successive additions. Unfortunately, discussion of these ingenious methods lies outside the scope of this book (see ref. 6.3, however).

Each element in the basic software routines for multiplication and division is the left or right shift of bits of an operand corresponding to multiplication and division respectively by powers of 2 followed by addition or subtraction. (Naturally though, the position is more complicated in the case of signed operands and when floating-point arithmetic is employed.)

Thus orders to achieve left and right shift must be provided. These are similar to other orders which rotate bits of a word left-hand or right-hand in closed-loop fashion. Such orders find application in various logical operations such as the assembly of sub-words into complete data words, the disassembly from complete data words and in process-control situations in addition to their role in multiplication and division. The versatile orders included in this final group and discussed below reflect the above needs. Provision is also made for orders to implement multiplication and division achieved directly through hardware.

Function 30_8 : $(XQ)' = 2^{-N} \cdot (XQ)$ $0 \leqslant N \leqslant 24$

With this function, the digits held in the double register XQ are shifted right by N places where the N part of the order quotes the number of places involved. Accordingly this is arithmetic division by an integral power of 2. Provision is made to retain the sign bit. Round-off takes place automatically to retain only the 23 most significant bits.

Function 31_8 $x' = 2^N \cdot x$ $0 \leqslant N \leqslant 24$

Here the contents of a register X are shifted left by up to 24 places. The least significant bits are filled with zeros. Clearly this function may be used as part of a software multiplication routine.

Function 32_8 : logic shift right of (XQ) by N places

Here the whole array of bits in the double register XQ is moved right N places. The most significant end of the double register is filled with zeros. Since no account is taken of a sign bit and no round-off occurs, the operation should be regarded as a logical shift only.

Function 33_8 : cyclic shift x left N places

In this case the bits in a single-length register X are rotated N places to the left with the bits at the most significant end of the word reappearing at the least significant end. This function finds use in logical operations such as occur when unpacking shorter words. A typical application might be in a process control situation where a 24-bit word might comprise three 8-bit sub-words or bytes.

Function 34_8 : cyclic shift (XQ) left N places

This function is similar to 33_8 but now the contents of the double-length register XQ are involved. Again, logic shift alone is involved.

Function 36_8 multiplication $(XQ)' = x \cdot n$

The function forms the product of a pair of 24-bit words held in locations X and N as a double-length word held in XQ. (XQ) comprises a sign bit plus 47 significant digits.

Division 37_8 division : $q' = \dfrac{xq}{n}$; $x' =$ remainder

Here a dividend xq of double length held in XQ is divided by divisor n held in address location N to yield a quotient q' held in register Q. The remainder appears in register X.

6.3.8   Subroutines

It will have become apparent already that program writing at machine-code level is a time-consuming task. Even at the rather higher level of assembly language, coding remains a time-consuming task. It was appreciated from the earliest days of computers that program sequences which were likely to be used frequently should be regarded as part of the permanent *program library* associated with a complete system. Such sequences became known as *routines* or more commonly as *subroutines*. Other routines might well be written by a programmer who would use them frequently in later work. Often such routines are known by other names. Thus, for example, Pascal uses the term *function* for shorter routines and *procedure* for longer and more complex routines.

Subroutines are entered by an unconditional jump and are terminated by an unconditional jump back to the relevant location in the main program. However, such unconditional jumps differ from those considered so far in that provision must be made to save the appropriate main-program return address — that is, the contents of the program counter, (PC), in a specified location in order to restore control to the main program at the end of the subroutine. When higher-level languages employing mnemonic code are used, then a subroutine is entered by specifying JSR (*Jump to Subroutine*) followed by the name of the subroutine. Thus JSR (SINX) would permit the calculation of sine X using an appropriate subroutine.

In the present case, octal instruction 40_8 is allocated to specify JSR with the N part of the order indicating the start address for the subroutine. Before executing the jump the current contents of the PC are saved so that, at the end of the subroutine, control is restored to the next instruction of the main program via an unconditional jump. The contents of the PC must be stored in a location previously defined otherwise a special order will be required for the unconditional jump back.

A typical arrangement might be as follows. The first address of the subroutine is location N as specified in the instruction JSR. Before the subroutine begins the current contents of the program counter (PC) are written into location N. (Recall that PC contains the *next* address to be accessed by the main program.) The subroutine proper starts at location N + 1.

At the conclusion of the subroutine, instruction RET N (41_8) ensures a return to location N whose contents are the next address in the main program. In this way control is restored to the main program. Figure 6.9 illustrates the position.

An alternative approach, very popular with microprocessor-based systems, is to store return addresses in a set of special registers known as a *stack*. This technique is discussed further in chapter 9.

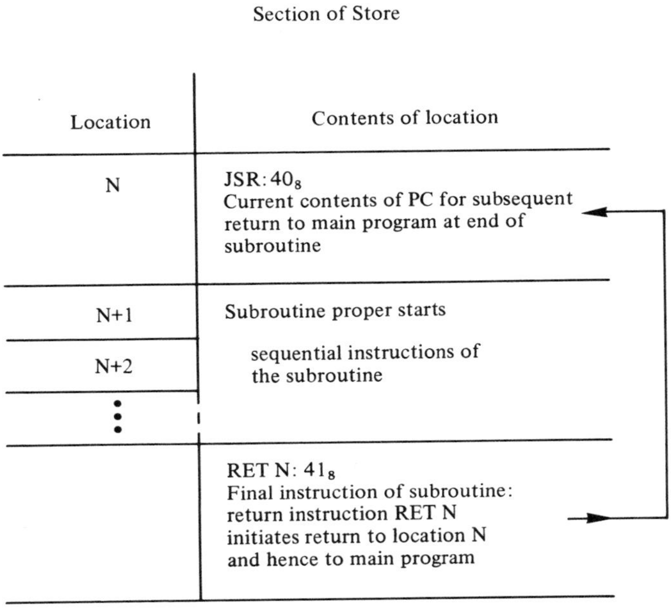

Section of Store

Location	Contents of location
N	JSR: 40_8 Current contents of PC for subsequent return to main program at end of subroutine
N+1	Subroutine proper starts
N+2	sequential instructions of the subroutine
$\vdots$	
	RET N: 41_8 Final instruction of subroutine: return instruction RET N initiates return to location N and hence to main program

Figure 6.9 Execution of instructions: JSR and RET N to carry out a subroutine

6.3.9 Input/Output (I/O)

Here one or more of the remaining orders of the instruction set may be allocated to operations involving peripherals. For example, one order might permit output of data to one or other of several output peripheral devices. Another order would relate to input of data from one or other peripheral device.

Typical orders relating to peripherals include an order, say 50_8, to permit output of data to a device, for example, a tape punch and an order, say 51_8, which permits input of data from a device, for example, a tape reader. Note that in a computer installation with multiple peripherals, the N part of the order specifies which particular device is involved. Accordingly no less than $2^{14} = 16$K peripherals may be accessed. The X part of the order specifies the processor register to which or from which the data is transferred.

Function	Result	Comments
Elementary functions		
00_8	$x' = n$ with $n' = n$	⎫ Transfer orders.
10_8	$n' = x$ with $x' = x$	⎭
02_8	$x' = x + n$ with $n' = n$	⎫ Addition orders.
12_8	$n' = x + n$ with $x' = x$	⎭
03_8	$x' = x - n$ with $n' = n$	⎫ Subtraction.
13_8	$n' = x - n$ with $x' = x$	⎭
01_8	$x' = -n$ with $n' = n$	⎫ Transfer with negation.
11_8	$n' = -x$ with $x' = x$	⎭
14_8	$x' = n;\qquad n' = x$	Interchange function.
Conditional instructions		
20_8	Jump to N if $x = 0$	Conditional instructions 'Jump to N' where N is address of next order to be obeyed.
21_8	Jump to N if $x \neq 0$	
22_8	Jump to N if $x > 0$	
23_8	Jump to N if $x < 0$	
Manipulation of constants		
04_8	$x' = C$	Storage of constant C at accumulator X.
05_8	$x' = -C$	Storage of inverse of constant C.
06_8	$x' = x + C$	Addition of a constant C to existing contents of accumulator X.
07_8	$x' = x - C$	Subtraction of a constant C from existing contents of accumulator X.
Logical functions		
30_8	$(XQ)' = 2^{-N}(XQ)$	Shift right of contents of XQ by N places.
31_8	$x' = 2^N x$	Shift left of contents of X by up to 24 places.

Figure 6.10 Summary of the instruction set of a simple 24-bit computer

32_8	Logic shift right of (XQ) by N places	The vacant places at the left-hand end of the register are filled with zeros.
33_8	Cyclic shift left of (X) by N places	Bits overflowing at the left-hand end of the register reappear at the right-hand end.
34_8	Cyclic shift left of (XQ) by N places	Similar comments to 33_8 but double-length register involved.

Multiplication		
36_8	$(XQ)' = x.n$	$(XQ)'$ is the product of a pair of operands x and n held in X and N, respectively.

Division		
37_8	$q' = (XQ) \div n$	Dividend xq held in XQ divided by divisor n in location N to yield quotient q' in register Q.

Jump to subroutine 40_8 JSR	$(PC) \longrightarrow N$ $(N + 1) \longrightarrow PC$	Contents of PC saved to permit control to be restored to main program at the end of the subroutine.
RETN Return 41_8	$(N) \longrightarrow PC$	

Output to peripheral 50_8	Output of data to a buffer register of peripheral device	Instructions to transfer information between a CPU register and a peripheral device with a specified address P.
Input from peripheral 51_8	Input of data from a buffer register of a peripheral device	

Figure 6.10—continued

6.3.10 Further Instructions

A summary of the instructions included in the instruction set is provided in figure 6.10. It will be noted that they fall into the following categories:

Elementary functions: transfer, addition, subtraction and interchange

Conditional: four jump instructions

Manipulation of constants: associated with such activity as the use of the modifier

Logical functions; various types of shift
Multiplication
Division
Jump to Subroutine
Input/Output (I/O)

A total of 28 orders is involved in all, whereas a maximum of 32 orders may be accommodated in the instruction set. Notice that, as already mentioned, the octal numbers associated with the various instructions of the instruction set are regarded as labels or identifiers and are arranged as groups. They do not form a consecutive set of octal numbers.

It is left to the reader to choose four final orders to complete the maximum of 32 orders possible for this machine with its 5-bit op-code.

6.4   Outline Architecture of the 24-bit Parallel Computer

The preceding sections have explained the operation of a simple 24-bit computer in terms of the instruction format and the orders of the instruction set. Notice that of the 32 orders possible via the 5-bit op-code, only 28 have been taken up. *Direct addressing* alone has been employed in contrast to the more elaborate methods to be discussed in sections 6.5 and 6.6. Since 14 bits are allocated to address store locations, the store is restricted to 16K words with no provision for necessary access to back-up store such as disc or magnetic-tape storage. Emphasis has been on programming at low level which requires substantial skill. Assembly of program has been restricted more or less to octal–binary conversion with some provision for such items as relative addressing. No mnemonic code has been involved.

In the light of the logic elements discussed in earlier chapters and the detailed design criteria of chapter 5, which related to the simple teaching-aid, MIC, it is now possible to consider briefly the outline hardware design of this present machine.

While MIC was a serial machine, parallel operation is used on almost all modern machines. Operands are routed between the store locations, working registers and the arithmetic unit along a *parallel bus* sufficiently wide to accommodate simultaneously all the bits of the instruction and data words.

Such a bus is bi-directional. Since the machine has a word-length of 24 bits, the common highway comprises 24 lines. Access to the bus from the various registers is by *tri-state gating* (see chapter 4, section 4.5). In addition to the 24-bit wide bus, the machine has two further principal buses. The first is the 14-bit wide *address-bus* linking the central processing unit, CPU, with the store. The second is the 10-bit wide *instruction-bus* linking the CPU to the control unit (the microprogramming unit).

At this point it is convenient to sketch an outline of the machine in the light of the requirements presented by the instruction format. A simplified block diagram is shown in figure 6.11. Most of the features have been discussed already but certain additional items must be stressed.

The diagram shows how parallel highways are used for data and instruction transfer with access controlled by appropriate gating provided by the *control unit*. Figure 6.11 indicates the several highways. For example, the 24-bit wide common data-bus links all the accumulators, miscellaneous registers and the arithmetic unit of the CPU with the memory register of the store.

Operation of the computer is best understood in terms of a two-beat cycle which starts with the beginning of the execution of an order.

In normal operation the address of the next order to be executed constitutes the current contents of the program counter (PC). The cycle of operations begins with the transfer of the N address from the program counter to the *store address unit* (via the *address register*) at the store. On receipt of the N address at the address register of the store address unit, one-out-of-*n* decodes take place (see chapter 4, section 4.6.2) to select the appropriate block of store and the correct location within the store. The process may be summarised as follows.

The first two bits of the 14-bit N address are used for block selection. The two bits provide inputs to a one-out-of-four decoder ($2^2 = 4$), according to the principles outlined in chapter 4, section 4.6.2. Thus the four lines leaving the store address unit constitute the block-selection bus. Whenever a store address request is made, only one of the four lines carries a 1 and thus enables gating to allow the selection of the appropriate block of store. With semiconductor random-access memory the 'chip-select' pin facilitates block selection (see chapter 7, section 7.5.3).

Within the 4K block of store, each of the 4096 24-bit words is identified by means of its *x* and *y* co-ordinates. Accordingly, the remaining 12 bits of the N address are split into two groups of six bits. Each group of six bits acts as input to a one-out-of-64 decoder ($2^6 = 64$). Accordingly, the location selection-bus leaving the store address units is 128 bits wide (64 lines for *x* plus 64 lines for *y*). Whenever a store-address request is made only one *x* co-ordinate line and one *y* co-ordinate line are held at 1. As a result, only a single 24-bit word is located. The detailed mechanism of reading and writing to and from semiconductor store is discussed in chapter 7 (see section 7.5.3).

Once located, information passes to the *memory register* located at the store and thence onto the *24-bit data-bus* to the CPU. At the same time the contents of the memory register are retained in the relevant store location to ensure that they will be present when accessed on a subsequent occasion. Since the operation corresponds to the *first beat* of a two-beat cycle, then the operand read from store will be an instruction, and accordingly, will be passed to the *control register* (sometimes known as the *instruction register*). From the control register the first 10 bits, corresponding to an instruction, will be passed to the *instruction decoder* of the control unit where control waveforms are generated by the microprogramming unit to permit the execution of the relevant order.

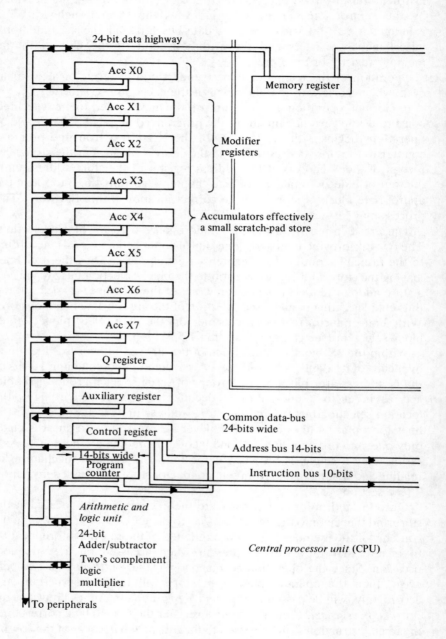

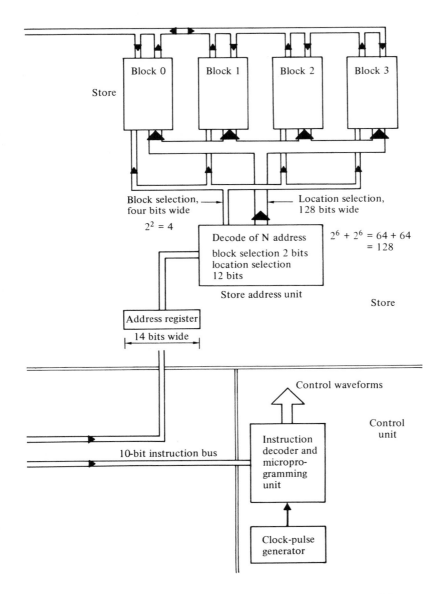

Figure 6.11 Overall block schematic of a simple 24-bit parallel computer

During the second beat of the cycle, the remaining 14 bits of the instruction (that is, address N) are presented to the store address unit and are decoded to permit transfer of data to or from the correct store location. The transfer takes place under the control of the waveforms generated by the microprogramming unit during the first of the two beats. The data is also manipulated as appropriate. Thus, for example, the data may be transferred from the store location to an accumulator (function 00_8) or taken from the store location and added at the *arithmetic unit* to the contents of an accumulator (function 02_8). In the case of a logical function such as cyclic rotation (function 32_8 or function 33_8, say), the contents of an *accumulator* may be cycled through a requisite number of places. In this latter case the alternative address designation for accumulators mentioned in section 6.3.1 is employed. Accordingly, in the second beat the 14-bit N address in the range 37770_8 to 37777_8 is decoded as a request for accumulator rather than store access. Thus the operand is taken from the appropriate accumulator, shifted through the appropriate number of places and placed in the *auxiliary register* before being restored to its original accumulator location. This auxiliary register is useful because of practical considerations relating to high-speed transfer to and from shift registers.

When operation is sequential, the contents of the program counter are incremented to permit the access of the next instruction in sequence. However, this orderly progression is interrupted on receipt of a jump instruction. In this case, the N part of the order specifies the next address should the condition be satisfied. It is for this reason that the 14-bit address-bus links the control register as well as the program counter to the store address unit.

When an instruction involves modification, the contents of the accumulator used as a *modifier register* are added to the N part of the control register contents before the second store access. This involves addition at the *arithmetic unit* and a path back to the address bus. Chapter 7, section 7.4, provides a useful illustrative example in this subject through consideration of an addition order involving modification. The important topics of synchronous and asynchronous operation are also discussed at this point.

The arithmetic unit provides the logic involved in the process of taking the 2's complement of numbers and thus provides subtraction as well as addition. If a hardware multiplier and divider are provided, they are located at the arithmetic unit. As already indicated, detailed consideration of high-speed addition and fast multiplication and division techniques are beyond the scope of this book. Further information should be sought elsewhere. See, for example, ref. 6.3.

It will be noticed that the common 24-bit data-bus in figure 6.11 is extended to permit access to peripheral devices through the use of I/O instructions.

6.5   Expansion of Store Capacity

As a bridge to a consideration of more elaborate instruction formats than the one discussed to date, it is useful to concentrate on methods of expanding store capacity when the word-length used in a machine is restricted. Thoughtful use of the modifer facility provides one possibility while the provision of an *indirect-address flag bit* yields a second approach. Both techniques may be used in conjunction. Accordingly, reconsider the case of the small computer with a 24-bit word-length but now change the instruction format slightly as shown in figure 6.12 to incorporate a single indirect-address flag bit I through the sacrifice of one of the bits of the N address. The indirect-address bit 1 is the first example in this book of the use of a *flag bit*. When a 1 is placed in the flag-bit position, the *flag* is set.

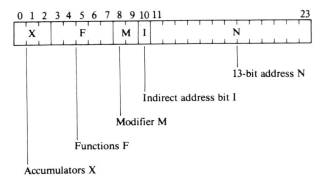

Figure 6.12 Instruction format to permit extension of store capacity for 24-bit word-length computer

6.5.1   Consideration of the Modifier Bits M

A non-zero bit pattern set into the modifer bit positions indicates that the contents of the modifier register must be added to the address specified in the N part of the instruction word before the instruction is obeyed. As a result, an *effective address* N + (M) is achieved. In that this modification permits loops and jumps and makes for economy in program writing, since it facilitates the provision of loops, it is in effect an extension of store capacity through more efficient usage. However, since the modifier register can hold addresses up to a length equal to total word-length, in this case 24 bits, it becomes possible to access a much wider range of addresses than that so far considered. In this case, $2^{24} = 16M$ addresses may be accessed, provided of course that the program counter and the address register are the full 24-bits wide. In these circumstances, it is important to make the necessary changes to figure 6.11 where both the program writer and address register are shown as only 14-bits wide. Note also that the maximum value of the effective address cannot exceed 2^{24}. Accordingly, $(N + (M))_{max} = 2^{24}$. Note that, by convention, $1M = 1024 \times 1024$ locations.

6.5.2　Use of the Indirect-address Bit I

The use of this bit goes beyond the idea of the modifier bit. If a 1 is set into the indirect address bit (that is, the flag is set), then the N address part of the instruction specifies the address of a further location where the actual operand is to be found. This *indirect-address technique* is complementary to the use of the modifer register in that with the technique one avoids the need for addition of the contents of the modifier register to the N address in order to achieve the new address location. However, the price that is paid is the need for an additional store access. In the present case, the emphasis is on increasing the effective store capacity. Indirect addressing is valuable here since the address referenced indirectly may exceed in length the normal address part N of the instruction. Since the location addressed indirectly contains no instruction part, the address bits may total the complete word-length. For example, in the present case 2^{24} (that is, 16M locations) are indirectly addressable. Naturally the program counter and the address register must be the full 24-bits wide.

6.5.3　An Apparent Paradox

It might appear that the above techniques would permit the addressing of only the same total number of addresses, though more widely distributed, as are available in the directly addressable store since it would seem that an address there is required in each case as a starting point for each indirectly addressed location. However, this is not the case. For example, a main program may be held in the directly addressable store. When it becomes necessary to call a routine, then a location indirectly addressed may be used to contain the first operand of the routine. It is this address which is loaded into the program counter. Thereafter, for the remainder of the routine, the program counter is incremented from this first address. Only at the end of the routine is there a jump back to the program in the directly addressed part of the store (see section 6.3.8). The only proviso is that the register used as the program counter and address register is sufficiently wide to accommodate the full word-length of the machine. It is not necessary therefore to refer to the directly accessed store for each of the sequential instructions of the routine which may be of considerable length. Figure 6.13 illustrates the situation.

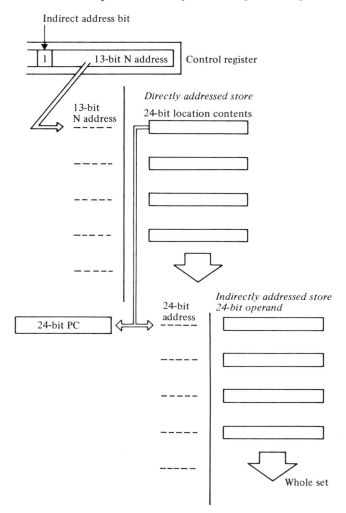

Figure 6.13 Illustration of indirect-addressing technique for 24-bit machine

6.5.4 Paging

One convenient way of designating a large store is to adopt the convention of paging. With this technique the store is considered descriptively as a number of *pages* each comprising a fixed number of lines. The technique is useful, for example, when a team effort is devoted to a substantial suite of programs since each programmer in the team, responsible for programs within the suite, can have an allocation of pages.

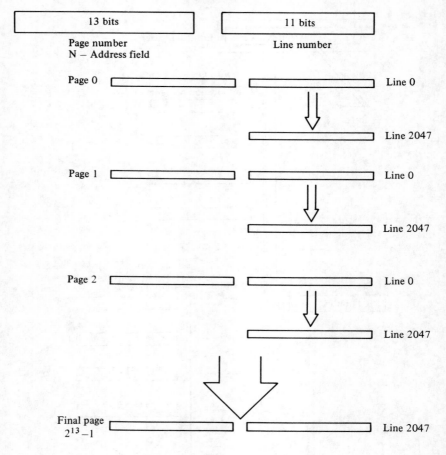

Figure 6.14 Illustration of paging

Figure 6.14 shows a schematic diagram of an arrangement which relates to the 24-bit machine in question. When the flag bit I is set to 1, indirect addressing is invoked and indirect access is available to 2^{13} (8K) locations since the address field N comprises 13 bits. Each of the 8K locations is regarded as the start address for a separate page of store. It has been seen already that the total store available for a 24-bit machine is 2^{24} locations. Accordingly each page of store contains

$$2^{24} - 2^{13} = 2^{11} = 2048$$

lines as shown in the figure. Page 0 starts with address

0000000000000   00000000000

and concludes with address

0000000000000   11111111111

The final page, $2^{13} - 1$, starts with address

1111111111111   00000000000

and concludes with address

1111111111111   11111111111

In order to implement the paging technique, provision must be made for the value in the N address field to be placed in the 13 most significant digit positions in the 24-bit program counter whenever store access takes place via indirect addressing. Zeros must be placed in the remaining 11 digit positions of the program counter to constitute the start address for the page in question. Thereafter, program is executed by PC increment within the page. Conditional instructions will result in non-sequential execution of program steps within the page but the process of indirect addressing will not be invoked again until access to a further page is required.

6.6   Modern Minicomputers

6.6.1   Introduction

At this point it is useful to consider briefly more advanced types of minicomputers. Such minicomputers typically employ a 16-bit word length with an appropriate architecture. In order to achieve high performance with restricted overall word-length, a variety of instruction formats is employed. These instruction formats permit a wide choice of addressing modes to allow flexibility in programming and a substantial number of instructions in the instruction set. Each manufacturer employs a different architecture corresponding to differing design philosophies and traditions. The position is made more complicated in that there is an increasing trend towards 16-bit microprocessors. These provide the central processing units for microcomputer systems. Indeed at the level of the 16-bit machine, the distinction between minicomputers and microcomputers begins to break down.

The choice as to which architecture to use to illustrate typical 16-bit mini and microcomputers is difficult. In the present case the discussion is based broadly on features of the DEC (Digital Equipment Corporation) family of 16-bit machines. Certainly the student will perceive differences, sometimes substantial differences, when comparing the present material with that relating to other 16-bit machines. Such comparisons serve to highlight specific design features of various families of 16-bit machines.

Inevitably coverage is restricted. Emphasis will be placed on comparison between the simpler 24-bit machine and 16-bit machines. Attention will be concentrated on the variety of instruction formats and on addressing techniques. Full details of current 16-bit machines must be sought elsewhere. In this context it must be recalled that the literature of the manufacturers is often the only route to up-to-date detailed information. In the present case, consult ref. 6.4 for example.

6.6.2 *Preliminary Ideas*

A typical modern minicomputer is a 16-bit machine in contrast to the simple 24-bit machine previously considered. The PDP-11 family manufactured by Digital Equipment Co. Ltd. (DEC) is typical of modern practice. The PDP-11 family ranges from the single-board Large-Scale Integrated Circuit LSI-11 through to powerful time-sharing multi-user machines. All the members of the family share a similar architecture which incorporates a UNIBUS and they have a common software.

With the PDP-11 family, the CPU contains eight working registers or accumulators. These are allocated as follows:

    Registers 0 → 5   General-Purpose Registers
    Register   6   Hardware Stackpointer (SP)
    Register   7   Program Counter (PC)

To illustrate the use of the registers and the various addressing modes, the instructions in figure 6.15 are used as examples. Notice that, in contrast to the octal or binary codes used to illustrate the performance of the 24-bit machine, *mnemonic code* at *assembler level* is employed by way of contrast. The use of such mnemonic code is a first introduction to assembler-level coding, very widely used with mini and microcomputers.

With the PDP-11 family of machines, the 16-bit instructions fall into seven categories as listed in figure 6.16. Thus there are seven instruction formats in contrast to the single instruction format discussed earlier in connection with the 24-bit machine. Specific bits in an instruction are used as flag bits to denote which of the instruction formats is currently in use.

Although not necessarily obvious to the user, three bits in any of the 16-bit instructions formats will constitute flag bits since the $2^3 = 8$ identifying codes thus made available will categorise one or other of the seven

Mnemonic	Description	Octal code
CLR	Clear (zero the specified destination word)	0050DD
CLRB	Clear byte (zero the specified destination byte)	1050DD
INC	Increment (add 1 to contents of destination word)	0052DD
INCB	Increment byte (add 1 to the contents of the destination byte)	1052DD
COM	Complement (replace the contents of the destination by its logical one's complement. Each 0 bit is set and each 1 bit is cleared)	0051DD
COMB	Complement byte (replace the contents of the destination byte by its logical one's complement. Each 0 bit is set and each 1 bit is cleared)	1051DD
ADD	Add (add the source operand to the destination operand and store the result at the destination address)	06SSDD

DD = destination field (6 bits)
SS = source field (6 bits)
( ) = contents of

Figure 6.15 Instructions used to illustrate operation of a 16-bit machine

1. Single operand
2. Double operand
3. Branch
4. Jump to subroutine
5. Trap
6. Miscellaneous
7. Condition code

Figure 6.16 Seven instruction formats

instruction formats. One code will not be required in this particular application but could serve to specify an eighth and final instruction-format if necessary.

Emphasis will be placed on a *single-operand* (*single-address*) and *double-operand* (*two-address*) instruction formats and their associated addressing modes. It will become apparent that the distinction between direct and indirect address observed in the case of the 24-bit machine becomes less clear in the case of the 16-bit machine with its various addressing modes.

6.6.3 Single-operand Instruction Format

The single-operand instruction format is as shown in figure 6.17. The figure shows that three bits, bits 0, 1 and 2, are used to designate one or other of

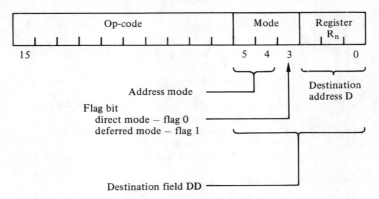

Figure 6.17 Single-operand instruction format, 16-bit machine

the eight working registers of the CPU. The working register is shown on the diagram as R_n and is also referred to as the *destination address D*. The designation destination address should be regarded as implying that the register is the destination to which the op-code is directed. It does not imply that the results of all arithmetic and logic operations are stored at that particular location. A single flag bit, bit 3, specifies direct or indirect addressing (that is, distinguishes between *direct mode* or *deferred mode*) and two further bits, bits 4 and 5, specify the specific addressing mode to be employed. Overall, bits 0 to 5 specify the *destination field DD*. Ten bits, bits 6 to 15, remain to specify the instructions of the op-code. The use of ten bits permits a very wide choice of instructions.

It must be recalled, however, that for this instruction format and for the other instruction formats, three bits are employed, at least implicitly, to designate which of the seven instruction formats is being used.

6.6.4   Double-operand Instruction Format

The double-operand instruction format is indicated in figure 6.18. It will be appreciated immediately that provision is now made for two operands rather than a single operand. Two working registers designated the *source* and *destination registers* S and D which are associated with *source* and *destination addresses* respectively. The overall *source field* is designated SS while the *destination field* is designated DD. Note that the titles source and destination are used very loosely. Since six bits are devoted to each of the two operands, only four bits remain to provide a much restricted set of op-codes and to designate which instruction format is being used.

Notice that for both single and double operand instruction formats, no bits designate store addresses explicitly. Their omission releases bits for

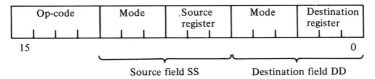

Figure 6.18 Double-operand instruction format, 16-bit machine

other purposes. The illustrative examples which follow indicate how operands are accessed either directly or indirectly through the thoughtful use of the eight working registers at the CPU.

6.6.5 Basic Addressing Modes

With the simple 24-bit machine, direct addressing was made more flexible through the use of the modifier M and Modifier Registers (Index Registers) and via indirect addressing. With the present family of machines there are *four* basic addressing modes to permit greater flexibility than was the case with the earlier machine. These are:

1. Register
2. Autoincrement
3. Autodecrement
4. Index (modifier)

Four modes are possible since two bits are allocated to select the *mode*. In addition, the use of a flag bit permits direct or deferred addressing with each of the four modes. Thus, for example, with single-operand format, bits 5 and 4 specify the mode while bit 3 specifies direct or deferred addressing.

With the simple 24-bit machine used with direct addressing, 14-bits of an instruction specified the address of an operand in store. However, the diagrams for single and double operand instruction formats indicate that a new technique has been adopted with the 16-bit machine. No bits in an instruction word denote an address in store explicitly. Instead emphasis is placed on the *contents* of the register(s) specified in the instruction. In some cases arithmetic and logic operations are carried out directly on the contents of the register(s) without reference to store. In other cases the contents of the register(s) provide the address(es) of operands in store.

In effect, the approach separates arithmetic and logic operations from memory access operations. It permits a wide range of op-codes since there is no longer any need to retain a substantial part of an instruction word to specify a store address explicitly. The memory size may be $2^{16} = 64K$

without difficulty. Various techniques, not described in this book, may be used to ensure an effective memory larger than the 64K *virtual* memory. This is particularly important when several users in a multi-user situation require a full-memory of 64K. Note that because the memory system is byte orientated, the 64K store means a 64K byte store.

6.6.6   The Basic Addressing Modes Explained

With each of the four addressing modes, either direct or indirect addressing (direct or deferred mode) is possible as indicated by the condition of the flag bit(s).

(i)   Register Direct Mode (Mode 0)

This mode provides the possibility of the fastest instruction execution, since with appropriate instructions there will be no need to reference memory to retrieve an operand. Any of the general registers can be used to contain the operand. The address is provided by the final three bits in the single-operand instruction format. With double-operand instruction format, bits 8 to 6 and 2 to 0 are used. The appropriate flag bit(s) set at 0 indicate that direct addressing is used. An example of a single-operand instruction involving the increment of the contents of register R3 is given in figure 6.19. Reference to figure 6.15 gives the op-code for increment as

$$00 \ 52 \ DD_8$$

where DD represent the mode and register respectively. Since register direct mode, with direct addressing, is employed and register R3 is used, the full op-code becomes

$$00 \ 52 \ 03_8$$

as shown in figure 6.19

In contrast, figure 6.20 illustrates a double-operand instruction relating to the addition of the contents of R2 and R4 with the result of the addition placed in register R4.

$$(R_2) + (R_4) \rightarrow R_4$$

that is

$$000003_8 + 000005_8 \rightarrow 000010_8$$

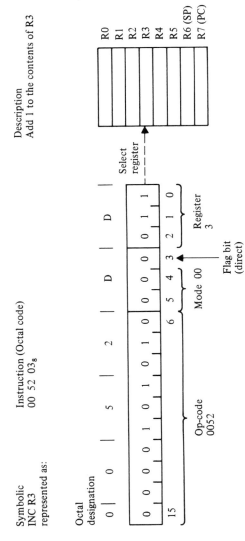

Register-mode Example
General form of increment order 00 52 DD₈

Symbolic   Instruction (Octal code)   Description
INC R3   00 52 03₈   Add 1 to the contents of R3
represented as:

Octal
designation

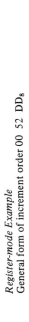

R0
R1
R2
R3
R4
R5
R6 (SP)
R7 (PC)

Figure 6.19 An example of the execution of a single-operand instruction

Register-mode Example
General form of add order 06 SS DD$_8$

Symbolic	Instruction (Octal code)	Description
ADD R2, R4	06 02 04$_8$	Add the contents of R2 to the contents of R4, replacing the original contents of R4 with the sum

Represented as:

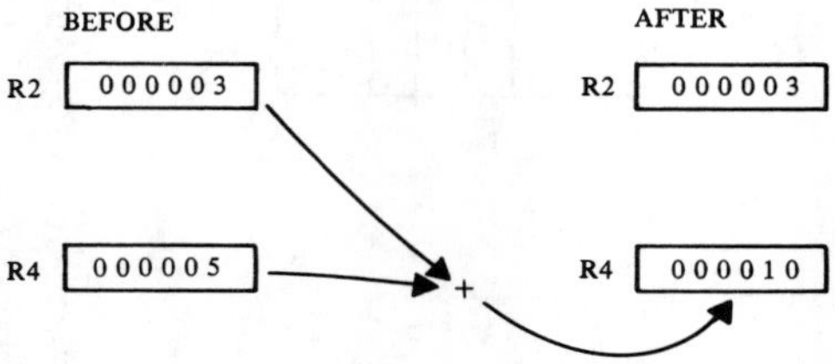

BEFORE

R2 [000003]

R4 [000005] ——→ +

AFTER

R2 [000003]

R4 [000010]

Figure 6.20 An example of the execution of a double-operand instruction (by courtesy of Digital Equipment Corporation)

The general form of the op-code for this add operation is

06 SS DD$_8$

where SS represent the mode and register relating to the source address and DD represent the mode and register relating to the destination address. The full op-code thus becomes

06 02 04$_8$

since, for both the source and destination addresses, register direct mode with direct addressing is employed.

In both the above examples, instruction execution is very fast since no time is expended in the transfer of operands between store and CPU. Memory reference, with consequent reduction of speed, is naturally required should transfer operations be necessary.

(ii)   Register Deferred Mode (Mode 1)

With the flag bit(s) set at 1, indirect addressing (deferred mode) is employed. Here the address of the operand, rather than the operand itself, is stored in the general-purpose register. Thus the address contained in the general-purpose register *directs* the CPU to the operand. The situation is similar to that of the case of indirect addressing for the 24-bit machine except that the address of the operand is to be found in a general-purpose register at the CPU rather than at a particular location in store. An example is given in figure 6.21 for which the contents of the location, 1700_8, specified by the contents of register R5 are cleared using the op-code

00 50 DD_8 that is, 00 50 15_8

Note that the figure shows location 1700_8 as following location 1676_8, recalling that the store is byte orientated with two bytes to each 16-bit location.

(iii)   Autoincrement Direct Mode (Mode 2)

In autoincrement direct mode, the register *contains the address of the operand*. The address is *automatically incremented* after the operand is retrieved from the address location. The address then references the next sequential operand. This mode allows automatic stepping through a list of operands stored in sequential locations in order to perform the same operation on the contents of each location. Accordingly, each single-operand instruction format is similar to the previous one while the access to the sequential locations continues. Clearly this is a useful and concise mode of operation which may be compared with the use of the modifier with the

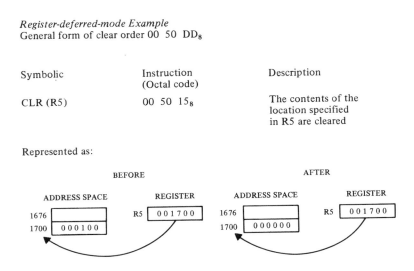

Register-deferred-mode Example
General form of clear order 00 50 DD_8

Symbolic	Instruction (Octal code)	Description
CLR (R5)	00 50 15_8	The contents of the location specified in R5 are cleared

Represented as:

Figure 6.21 *Clearing a store location using register-deferred-mode addressing (by courtesy of Digital Equipment Corporation)*

24 bit machine. Note that when byte instructions — that is, instructions relating to operands comprising only a single eight-bit byte — are employed, then the increment is by *one*. When instructions relate to operands of full word-length, the increment is by *two*. This approach is used because the store is addressed byte-by-byte rather than word-by-word.

Note that in the autoincrement direct mode the register contains the address of an operand rather than the operand itself. No longer is there close comparison with the direct addressing mode of the 24-bit machine. Figure 6.22 illustrated the mechanism of access to a sequential table of operands using autoincrement direct.

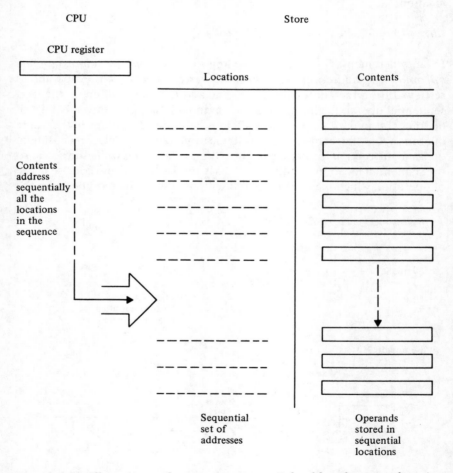

Figure 6.22 Illustration of access to sequential table of operands using autoincrement

A specific example of the use of autoincrement direct mode is shown in figure 6.23.

Autoincrement-mode Example
General form of the clear order 00 50 DD$_8$

Symbolic	Instruction (Octal code)	Description
CLR (R5)	00 50 25$_8$	Contents of R5 are used as the address of the operand. Clear selected operand and then increment the contents of R5 by 2

Represented as:

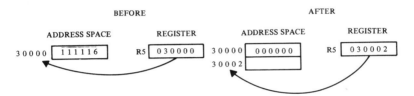

Figure 6.23 An example of the use of autoincrement direct mode to clear one of a set of consecutive locations. Note that the increment of the contents of R5 is by 2 to yield the next location (by courtesy of Digital Equipment Corporation)

(iv) Autoincrement Deferred Mode (Mode 3)

With autoincrement deferred (indirect addressing), the register *contains a pointer* to the address of the operand. The *pointer* is incremented by 2 (both word and byte operations) after the address is located. Autoincrement deferred is used to access operands which are not necessarily stored in consecutive locations. They may be anywhere in the store. Mode 3 (autoincrement deferred) is used to step though a *consecutive table of addresses*. The contents of these addresses are a further set of addresses — not necessarily in consecutive order. It is these addresses which contain the operands. Here the analogy with the indirect addressing of the 24-bit machine is close. Figure 6.24 illustrates the mechanism of access to a set of non-consecutive operands.

Thus, to summarise, autoincrement *direct* mode (that is, mode 2) is used to *access* operands in *consecutive locations*. On the other hand, autoincrement *deferred* mode (that is, mode 3) is used to *access* operands *anywhere* in the store.

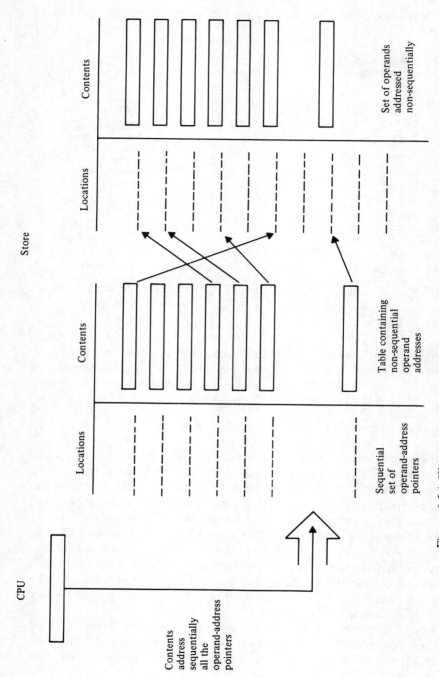

Figure 6.24 Illustration of access to a non-sequential table of operands using autoincrement deferred

A specific example of the use of autoincrement deferred is shown in figure 6.25. Here increment of an operand at location 001010 is involved. After execution of this order the contents of the register R2 are incremented by 2. Since autoincrement *deferred* is involved, the execution of the next order takes place on the contents of 175623 rather than 001012 as would have been the case with autoincrement direct which related to consecutive locations. Note the the symbol @ is introduced to indicate increment *deferred*.

Autoincrement-deferred Example

Symbolic	Instruction (Octal code)	Description
INC @ (R2)	005232	Contents of R2 are used as the address of the address of the operand. The operand is increased by 1, contents of R2 are incremented by 2

Represented as:

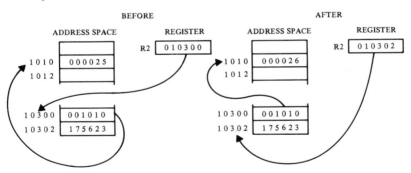

Figure 6.25 Illustration of the use of autoincrement deferred (by courtesy of Digital Equipment Corporation)

(v)   Autodecrement Direct Mode (Mode 4)

Here the register contains an address that is automatically decremented *before* the decremented address is used to locate an operand. This mode is similar to autoincrement but permits stepping through a list of words or bytes in reverse order. The address is decremented by 1 for bytes and by 2 for words.

(vi) Autodecrement Deferred Mode (Mode 5)

In this mode the register contains a *pointer* to the address of the operand. The pointer is decremented by 2, then the new pointer is used to retrieve an address. The mode is similar to autoincrement deferred but permits stepping through the *table of addresses in reverse order*.

(vii)   Index Mode (Mode 6)

In index mode a *base address*, stored in a register, here R4 by way of example, is added to an *index word*, which follows the current instruction, to produce the *effective address* of an operand. The base address specifies the starting location of a table or list. The index word then represents the address of an entry in the table or list relative to the starting (base) address. The resemblance to relative addressing employed with the 24-bit machine should be noted.

Figure 6.26 illustrates how the effective address of an operand is determined by adding the contents of register R4, address 001000_8, to an

Index-mode Example

Symbolic	Instruction (Octal code)	Description
CLR 200 (R4)	005064 000200	The address of the operand is determined by adding 200 to the contents of R4. The resulting location is then cleared

Represented as:

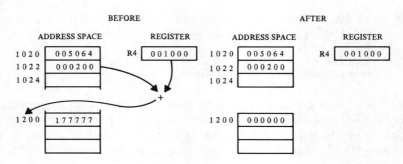

Figure 6.26 The use of the index mode to clear an address location (by courtesy of Digital Equipment Corporation)

index word, 000200_8, which follows the current instruction, 005064_8, to yield an effective address 001200_8; that is

$$001000_8 + 000200_8 = 001200_8$$

The address 001200_8 is then cleared since the mnemonic code indicates CLR 200 (R4) — that is, clear the location which is 200_8 places beyond the start address of 001000_8.

(viii) Index Deferred Mode (Mode 7)

Here a base address, stored in a register, here R4 by way of example, is added to an index word, which follows the current instruction, to produce an effective address. This *effective address* is used as a *pointer* to an address rather than as the address at which the operand is located. Thus mode 7 provides for the random access of operands using a table of operand addresses. Figure 6.27 illustrates the use of index deferred mode with the double-operand instruction format to permit the addition of the contents of register R1 (that is, 001234) to the contents, 2, of the location 1050, achieved via the index deferred mode. The result of the addition, 001236, is stored in register R1.

The eight modes given above permit flexibility in programming at assembler level. Note that they represent the maximum number of options available since 3 bits are allocated in the instruction format to selection of the relevant mode ($2^3 = 8$ modes).

6.6.7 Overall Performance of the 16-bit Machine

The case of this 16-bit machine with its various instruction formats, several addressing techniques and comprehensive instruction set is interesting especially when contrasted against the simpler 24-bit machine. It illustrates how limited word-length may be used to good effect though the price paid is substantial complexity. This in turn means that the logic circuitry of the instruction decoder and the microprogramming unit will also be more complex.

The machine may be used with various peripheral devices including magnetic-tape decks, cassette-tape decks, disc stores (including floppy disc), teletypes and a variety of visual display units. These items are dealt with briefly in chapter 7.

The machine requires a group of programs relating to overall control both of the machine itself and also its peripheral devices. Automatic shut-down on power failure, interrupt facilities to permit the efficient use of more than one peripheral and an operating system for disc store — that

Index-deferred-mode Example

Symbolic	Instruction (Octal code)	Description
ADD @ 1000 (R2), R1	067201 001000	1000 and the contents of R2 are summed to produce the address of the address of the source operand, the contents of which are added to the contents of R1. The result is stored in R1

Represented as:

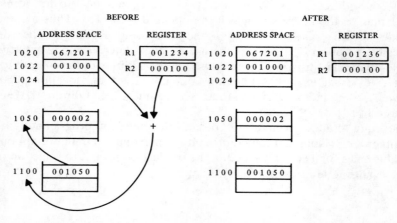

Figure 6.27 Addition using index-deferred mode and the double-operand instruction format (by courtesy of Digital Equipment Corporation)

is, a *Disc Operating System* (DOS) — must be provided. In addition, various Assemblers in the case of low-level programming and Compilers for high-level languages are also necessary. The cost of this software will amount to an appreciable fraction of the overall cost of the system. Such matters were introduced in chapter 2 and are considered in more detail in chapter 8.

6.7 Summary

This chapter has considered the overall operation of small but real computers. The approach has been via word-length as the ultimate design criterion. Two machines, one with a simple 24-bit instruction format, the other having a 16-bit word-length and a variety of instruction formats, have been contrasted. Emphasis has been placed on the broad outline of machine operation through implementation of orders decoded at the CPU on data read down from store locations. In the first case, such implementation involved for the most part two store accesses for the execution of each order. In the second case, with the 16-bit machine the functions of fetching data from store and executing orders on data were separated to some considerable extent. This procedure permits a variety of instruction formats and an enhanced instruction repertoire to compensate for the limitation of the shorter word-length.

Detailed hardware design was considered for neither case, though for the first machine a block diagram approach to overall architecture was discussed.

The material from the first part of the chapter dealing with the 24-bit machine is a natural link into storage and timing considerations discussed in chapter 7. The treatment of the 16-bit machine is a link to microprocessor architectures considered in chapters 9 and 11.

References

6.1 Brown, P., *Starting with UNIX* Addison-Wesley, London, 1984.
6.2 Garside, R. G., *The Architecture of Digital Computers*, Clarendon Press, Oxford, 1980.
6.3 Lewin, D., *Theory and Design of Digital Computer Systems*, Nelson, London, 1980.
6.4 Digital Equipment Corporation, *PDP-11 Architecture Handbook*, December 1983.

Problems

The exercises suggested in this section are intended to reinforce the ideas presented in chapter 6. Initial problems reinforce the value of multi-accumulator working and emphasise the versatility of the instruction set of the simple 24-bit machine. They point the way to the enhanced flexibility of the illustrative 16-bit machine with its variety of addressing modes and instruction formats.

Other problems provide practice in coming to terms with the hardware necessary for hardware multiplication and division. In this area the problems extend somewhat the material covered in the main body of the chapter. It is hoped that the experience gained by the student will prove an encouragement to consult more advanced texts.

6.1 This first problem serves merely to reiterate the basic ideas mentioned in the early part of the chapter.

A 24-bit machine has the instruction format shown below:

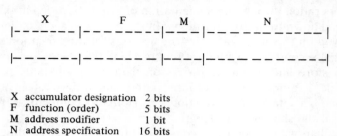

X	accumulator designation	2 bits
F	function (order)	5 bits
M	address modifier	1 bit
N	address specification	16 bits

What size of store may be accessed through the sole use of the N address? How may the instruction format above be used to advantage to permit access to a larger store? What penalties in time and equipment must be paid? What is the total size of store which may be accessed in this way?

Explain how similar results may be achieved through the use of the technique known as 'indirect addressing'. Again, explain the penalties incurred.

6.2 This problem serves to illustrate the advantages of multi-accumulator working and instructions devoted to increment and decrement. It reinforces the coverage relating to address modification and conditional instructions.

Draw up a flow diagram to illustrate the use of the modifier to clear the batch of 20_8 locations using the method discussed in section 6.3.6 and illustrated by the program shown in figure 6.7. How may the program be simplified?

Outline Solution. Reference to figure 6.7 indicates that a flow diagram as shown in figure 6.28 illustrates the clearing of 20_8 locations. The program may be simplifed very readily. Notice that there are effectively two counters in use, one counting down (Acc X4) and one counting up (Acc X1). These may be combined. Since the Jump instruction refers to 0, the simplest way is to clear the locations starting at 15017_8 and working backwards to location 15000_8. It is left to the reader to draw up a modified flow diagram and amend the program.

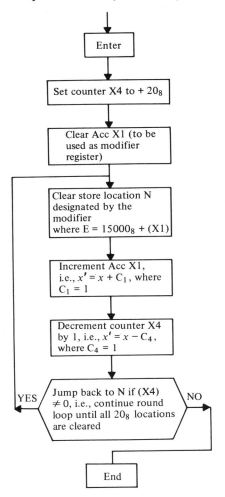

Figure 6.28 Flow diagram to illustrate use of the modifier

6.3 Multiplication and division may be achieved either through software routines or via special-purpose hardware, possibly regarded as peripherals. Based on your existing knowledge of conventional multiplication of decimal numbers by the method of partial products, multiply 1101 by 1001 and then sketch out a flow diagram relating to a software program to achieve binary multiplication. Using the instruction set of the 24-bit directly addressed machine of the earlier part of the chapter, attempt a suitable software routine. Thereafter refer to the outline design of the hardware multiplier given in chapter 4.

Part Outline Solution. The multiplication of 1101 by 1001 is readily achieved as follows:

```
    1101
    1001
```

1101	1st partial product
0000	2nd partial product
0000	3rd partial product
1101	4th partial product

1110101	sum of products

Notice the need for a double-length register for the product. In considering the software routine and later the hardware multiplier, it is useful to recall that provision for the *running total* of the partial products is more readily achieved than a final simultaneous addition of all products.

One convenient way of implementing the appropriate software routine is to store the complete routine in a dedicated read-only memory (ROM, see chapter 7), which is activated on receipt of the relevant instruction of the instruction set. This approach introduces the notion of *microprogramming*, a detailed discussion of which lies outside the scope of this book, but see chapter 7 for a preliminary consideration.

7 Storage of Digital Information

Objectives

The previous chapter looked at the overall architecture of a range of small computers. In the discussion it became apparent that storage played a very important role in machine design and performance. Because storage is so important the present chapter is devoted to the subject. Since new physical principles are being adopted continuously to provide storage media, the first part of the chapter discusses the various types of storage as categorised by their general properties. This systematic approach leads into a first consideration of storage hierarchy.

Thereafter a number of specific items are considered in detail. The important subject of overall computer speed as a function of speed of memory access is introduced through practical examples associated with synchronous and asynchronous operation.

Semiconductor store is considered in detail. Both RAM and ROM are discussed. Disc stores as illustrations of cyclic-access store are considered briefly both as examples of bulk stores and as one of a wide range of peripheral devices available with computers.

The chapter closes with consideration of a number of problems designed to reinforce the material covered.

7.1 Introduction

Chapter 6 introduced the basic ideas of machine architecture, stressing the notion that in computers both program and data are stored as binary words, usually of standard length, though double-length working was mentioned. It became clear during the chapter that the provision of an adequate amount of storage is essential for effective working. Indeed methods of addressing large stores, via indexing or indirect-addressing techniques, while retaining comparatively short instruction formats, received some prominence.

A wide variety of storage media is used with digital computers and new techniques are under development constantly. Accordingly, the chapter begins with a consideration of the various criteria used to categorise

169

storage together with brief reference to specific and typical examples within the different classes. This approach facilitates appreciation of the role of new storage media as they become available. The discussion leads naturally into consideration of storage hierarchy and the trade-off between speed and cost as the cost of storage continues to fall.

Semiconductor stores employ either 2-D or 3-D access techniques. Such stores are used either as *random-access memory* (RAM), or as *read-only memory* (ROM). Often they employ *Metal–Oxide–Silicon* (MOS) technology. Hence the term MOS RAM, for example. The importance of semiconductor memory is reflected by its role as the main storage medium in microcomputers, minicomputers and indeed in large mainframe machines.

Synchronous and *asynchronous* computer *operation* is considered principally through discussion of timing diagrams associated with memory access. As far as possible the treatment has been integrated with that of chapter 6.

A principal objective of chapter 7 is to emphasise that the speed of a computer system is substantially limited by the time required to store and retrieve information while the hardware cost of such a system is to a large extent determined by the overall store capacity. The types of store actually employed must of necessity represent a compromise between speed, capacity, reliability, convenience of use and the particular type of installation and its function. Inevitably, total budget will be of overriding importance in most cases. However, it must be appreciated that hardware costs constitute a decreasing fraction of the total cost of the system. Software costs escalate as increasingly elaborate operating systems and other software utilities are provided.

7.2 Basic Characteristics of Storage Devices

Each memory element must constitute a discrete storage location capable of being set into one or other of two distinct states corresponding to 1 or 0. In most cases an assembly of 1's and 0's constituting a word of standard length is regarded as the basic unit of storage. Sometimes a byte is taken as the basic storage unit. This is particularly the case in mini and microcomputer applications.

It is essential that operands are stored in pre-determined locations and retrieved under program control from these locations in a systematic manner. No distinction is made within the storage medium between operands comprising the instructions of the program, data or possibly addresses should indirect or deferred addressing be involved in program execution. Memory elements must remain in the set state either indefinitely or until placed into another state by an external signal. This attribute forms the basis of a pair of important and fundamentally opposite storage characterisations now to be discussed briefly.

7.2.1 Volatile and Non-volatile Storage

In the category of non-volatile storage fall those storage techniques in which no external energy is required either periodically or continuously to maintain the stable state representing the 1's or 0's of the stored word. An obvious example is that of punched-card storage where holes punched into a card constitute meaningful binary information. Short of destruction of the deck of cards, by fire for example, the program stored on the deck is retained indefinitely. The same is true of program stored on paper tape as rows of holes coded to represent program content. Certain types of semiconductor ROM fall into the same non-volatile category. More of this later however.

With volatile storage external energy is required to maintain the appropriate stable states. An obvious example concerns storage using a set of bistable electronic circuits, possible as a register at CPU. Here external power must be provided continuously, otherwise the stored contents will be lost. With certain types of semiconductor memory the same is true. With other types, however, periodic refresh of contents suffices (section 7.5). The two types are known respectively as *static* and *dynamic semiconductor stores*.

7.2.2 Categorisation by Access Time

This is a particularly significant parameter and relates to the speed with which a word may be written into or retrieved from store. Three elements are involved: the time taken for addressing or locating the word (this is typically a *decode* time), the *switching* or operation time for the storage elements and finally the *transmission times* between store and CPU. In many cases the final item may be disregarded, but this is not always the case. See, for example, section 7.4. Accordingly the true access time for data retrieval is the interval between generation of a store address at the CPU, typically at the Program Counter, and the receipt at a register of the CPU, say a working accumulator, of the information contained in the location so addressed.

Access of operands from a bi-polar semiconductor store adjacent to the CPU is rapid since retrieval time and transmission time are short. A retrieval time of substantially less than 100 ns is typical. Transmission time at 6 ns/m may well be sufficiently short to be disregarded. In the case of MOS RAM and ROM, access time is rather longer and may well be of the order of several hundred nanoseconds. With magnetic-tape storage on the other hand where serial access is involved retrieval times can extend to minutes. Disc systems with cyclic access have intermediate retrieval times of the order of 100 milliseconds.

7.2.3   Categorisation by Mode of Access

Three modes are considered. The first relates to retrieval of individual words while the other two are more suited to retrieval of blocks of information.

(i)   Random-access Store

This is the type of store which was highlighted in chapter 6 where an address in the Program Counter permitted access to the relevant location in the main store to retrieve an individual operand. Since any location may be addressed and there is no implication of retrieval of operands from contiguous locations, the process is called *random-access*. This is an unfortunate designation since there is no suggestion of access in a haphazard manner. Typical examples of random-access stores are given later in the chapter (section 7.5.1). The retrieval time for every operand is constant in the case of such a random-access store and typically is of the order of a few hundred nanoseconds. However, retrieval times continue to fall.

(ii)   Cyclic-access Store

With a *cyclic-access* store, large amounts of storage are involved and in most cases data is retrieved in blocks containing many words. Such transfers occur under the control of the operating system (see section 7.3, and also chapter 8). Indeed, since the bulk storage medium may well be used with a variety of types of machine each having a different word-length, it is common to quote such storage capacity in bytes, typically in megabytes. The disc store with data stored on one or more discs in a manner analogous to that of musical information on a record is a typical example of cyclic-access store (section 7.6).

   With such a store, access time is no longer constant but on average is half the time taken for a complete circulation of the whole body of information on an individual disc of the cyclic store. This occurs at high speed. However, in practice, further time may be required to move the reading head to the appropriate position on the disc as a result of which the overall retrieval time will be an appreciable fraction of a second. Further details of disc stores will be found in section 7.6.

(iii) Serial-access Store

Here *bulk storage* is involved as with the previous case. The total body of information passes a reading device in *serial fashion* and again the average retrieval time is half the total time necessary for a complete pass of the information. Typical serial-access devices include cassette and open-reel magnetic tapes and also paper tapes. It will be apparent that a complete pass of the information will take a considerable time — typically a substantial number of seconds or indeed minutes — and so average retrieval times are lengthy.

7.2.4 Other Categorisations of Storage Devices

Further categorisation of storage is possible. Thus we must distinguish between *destructive* and *non-destructive* read-out. Note that in the case of destructive read-out the need for rewrite effectively doubles access time. The classic case of destructive read-out concerns *ferrite-core* store which until comparatively recently was the principal type of main store. While ferrite-core store is no longer employed in new computers except in very special circumstances, it is still to be found in many well established installations. Good accounts of the physical principles and mode of operation of such stores are to be found in many texts (see, for example, ref. 7.1).

With non-volatile stores, *switching transients* may corrupt data unless care is taken. This is not the case with paper-tape storage and card storage, nor is it likely except under extreme conditions for such media as magnetic-tape storage. Accordingly such storage media may be regarded as *permanent*.

In many cases, storage media must possess the property of *erasability* but in some cases it is necessary to have *read-only memory*, (ROM). This is the case, for example, when a *programmable read-only memory*, a PROM, is used as the basis of a microprogramming unit at the CPU. As will be seen later in section 7.5.2, PROMS are widely used for many applications. Should a PROM require reprogramming from time to time, then a need arises for a reprogrammable read-only memory. This implies that the read-only memory is erasable. Hence the category of *erasable programmable read-only memory* (EPROM).

One important characteristic of the various types of semiconductor ROM is that they are non-volatile. The various types of RAM and ROM may be regarded as static memories whereas *dynamic memories* refer to those operating in the space domain such as disc stores and paper-tape storage. Note, however, that RAM semiconductor memories requiring periodic refresh are called *dynamic RAM* in contrast to those requiring continuous external energy which are classed as *static RAM*. This terminology may give rise to confusion as is the case with much computer jargon.

A further and most important categorisation is that relating to speed of access *versus* cost. As a general guide, *bulk storage* is *low cost* and *slow-speed access* while *high-speed access* is achieved only at *higher cost* and as a result is more limited in size. However, even high-speed storage is becoming cheaper in a manner which would have been unthinkable in even the recent past. The breakthrough came with the substitution of semiconductor memory for ferrite-core store. The latter with substantial assembly costs was intrinsically expensive.

It is important to realise that the above categorisations are far from exhaustive and merely outline the main types of store currently available. No account has been taken of size, convenience or running costs, factors which are of considerable practical importance. Thus, for example, some types of bulk store, especially those used in large installations, demand air-conditioned rooms which involve substantial capital expenditure and high running costs thereafter. These considerations must not be underestimated when planning an overall computer system.

7.3   Storage Hierarchy

In an ideal situation it would be convenient to have all operands available through random-access with fast retrieval time. However, this is not practical from various viewpoints. For example, while indirect addressing allows access to large areas of store, word-length sets a final limit to total store access unless more sophisticated techniques involving access to peripheral storage devices are employed. But the most significant limitation is that provided by cost considerations. Random-access high-speed storage with its associated electronics is more expensive than conventional bulk storage methods, and is likely to remain so for a considerable time in spite of recent spectacular advances in the field of semiconductor electronics.

Accordingly a hierarchy of storage is employed. Figure 7.1 illustrates the situation for a medium-size computer installation. Here the main store is semiconductor RAM and the bulk memory typically comprises disc store. Magnetic tape, paper tape or cards may be used as a further level of storage. Disc stores using floppy disc, cartridge or Winchester drive are popular. In the really small systems, cassette tapes find a place as miniature backing stores. With the bulk store, only cyclic or serial access is possible and to save time overall, data transfers to the main store take place in blocks. Thus, for example, a particular assembler required for assembly of a specific low-level user program will be transferred to the main store on a temporary basis and replaced by an alternative assembler when a new

Computer

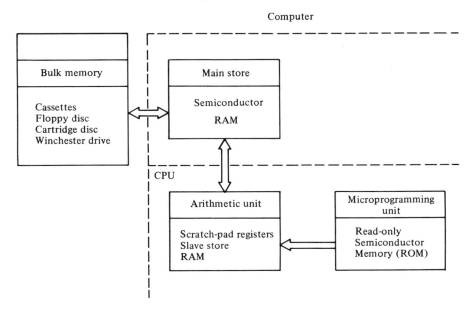

Figure 7.1 Storage hierarchy for a minicomputer

program written in a different low-level language is to be translated into machine code. With modern machines, facilities are available for *direct memory access* (DMA) from bulk store without involving the central processor to any considerable extent.

The main store, typically MOS RAM, contains the current program and data and also the programs comprising the *computer operating system* (OS). The operating system controls peripheral devices such as printers and of particular relevance in the present context the bulk-store device, say a disc store. Thus we refer to the *disc operating system* (DOS). In many cases the relevant compiler/assembler together with program-editing facilities is considered to form part of the operating system which then occupies on a more or less permanent basis a significant fraction of the total random-access store. Indeed with a small installation in which the main store comprises fewer than the maximum number of permitted blocks, it is possible to have a situation where an over-elaborate operating system occupies almost the whole of the store. As a consequence, only the shortest programs may be executed. Clearly this is a most unsatisfactory state of affairs.

At the arithmetic unit are to be found working registers (accumulators), a variety of auxiliary registers and possibly additional *scratch-pad* registers typically all comprising bistable stages involving bi-polar semiconductor technology in the interests of speed. In addition a *slave store* or *cache* may be provided. A detailed consideration of the role of master–slave stores lies outside the scope of this book (see ref. 7.1 for example). It is sufficient to point out that there is a variety of strategies by which instructions likely to require frequent program access are held in a slave store at the CPU where they may be accessed substantially more rapidly than from the main store. If small, such a slave store would be engineered in bi-polar technology to take advantage of the highest access speed. If rather larger, then very fast MOS RAM would represent a compromise between speed of access and cost.

Also at the CPU is the *microprogramming unit* (to be discussed further in section 7.4 below) associated with the instruction decoder. The unit comprises one or more high-speed ROM, again typically involving MOS technology.

Table 7.1 gives an indication of the principal types of storage together with the approximate cost/bit. In appropriate cases, the cost of the electronics immediately associated with the storage medium is included.

7.4 Store Access — Synchronous and Asynchronous Computer Operation

At this point it is instructive to consider the operation of a semiconductor store in the *time domain* in order to illustrate relevant *timing considerations*. The execution of a simple addition order serves as a useful example. The exercise serves to highlight the importance of fast switching in the search for high-speed operation. This section also serves to illustrate the difference between *synchronous* and *asynchronous* computer operation. Initially synchronous operation will be considered.

Consider the case of the simple 24-bit computer of chapter 6. For this simple machine, orders fall into two classes; *memory reference* and *non-memory reference*. As has been seen already, most of the orders are memory reference orders involving two store accesses, one to *fetch* an instruction, the other to *execute* such an instruction. Thus a typical memory reference instruction might be

Order 12_8 : n$'$ = x + n with x$'$ = x

while a non-memory reference instruction might relate to the addition of the contents of two of the accumulators at the CPU.

Consider the execution of the above memory-reference instruction and assume that operation is synchronous with a *memory cycle* of 1 μs. This implies that the operation of the computer is linked to a basic clock operating at interals of 1 μs and in particular that access to memory,

EXPENSIVE

CHEAP

Table 7.1 *Storage media and characteristics*

Type and characteristic	Approximate speed of access	Function	Approx. cost/bit
ECL and TTL bi-polar; volatile, non-dstructive read-out	tens of ns	CPU registers, scratch-pad, microprogramming unit, small slave store	c. 20p
Bipolar ROM; non-volatile, non-destructive read-out	50–200 ns	CPU microprogramming unit	< 0.1p
MOS RAM; volatile, static or dynamic refresh, non-destructive read-out	50–500 ns	CPU micrprogramming unit, general-purpose store	c. 0.1p
MOS ROM; non-volatile, includes PROM, fusible-link EPROM, UV erasable, non-destructive read-out	50–500 ns	Fixed-content store for assemblers, sub-routines, frequently accessed programs for small minicomputers and microprocessors	< 0.1p
Disc storage, cartridge, floppy disc; cyclic access, non-volatile	c. 100 ms / c. 300 ms	Backing store for programs, assemblers, compilers, routines and data	<< 1p (include cost of system and cartridge or floppy disc)
Magnetic tape, open-reel, cassette; serial access, non-volatile	seconds	Permanent record and backing store for programs, assemblers, routines, operating systems and bulk data	<< 1p
Paper tape and cards; serial access, non-volatile, permanent	seconds–minutes		

FAST

SLOW

typically involving say a read/write operation, cannot be initiated more frequently than once per μs.

The following principal steps are involved in the addition order above:

1. Fetch the instruction from the location specified by PC.
2. Increment the program counter (PC).
3. Identify as an add order.
4. Modify the address specified in the instruction using modifier M to determine the effective address E = N + (M).
5. Fetch contents n of modified address N + (M).
6. Execute addition order n′= n + x.
7. Place result n′ in the location N + (M).

In order to make the example specific, the following data is assumed:

1. *Medium-speed store*
   Address decode, gating and read-time   400 ns
   Address decode, gating and write-time   400 ns
2. *Cable Time*
   Length from CPU to store, 8 m say
   Transmission rate 6 ns/m approximately, so cable time
   approximately   50 ns
3. *Instruction*
   Decode time   30 ns
4. *Modification*
   Time for addition N + (M)
   24-bit parallel addition with fast parallel carry   80 ns
5. *Addition time*
   Time for fast addition n′ = x + n
   24-bit parallel addition with fast parallel carry   80 ns

Figure 7.2, which should be studied in association with figure 6.11, illustrates the procedure. The *fetch cycle* starts by transferring the initial contents of the program counter, PC, a 14-bit address, to the address register situated at the store. If a machine of some size is assumed, then 50 ns represents the transmission time. In most cases the time will be substantially less, particularly for microcomputers. The PC can be incremented to point to the next instruction in sequence as soon as the address register has been loaded. 30 ns has been allocated for this purpose. Note, however, that the increment may take place coincidently with activity at the store. This will not be the case when the first instruction of a subroutine is executed. With such an instruction the contents of the program counter are replaced by the start-address of the subroutine (see chapter 6, section

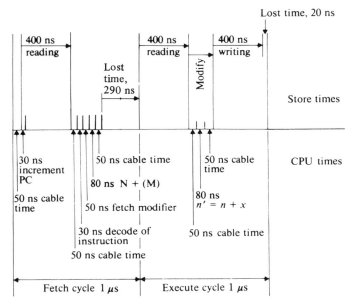

Figure 7.2 Execution of simple add order with synchronous operation and 1 μs memory cycle

6.3.8). Thereafter the PC is incremented with successive steps of the subroutine.

Decode of the 14-bit address as a 2-bit store-block identifier together with two 6-bit (x, y) co-ordinates then takes place to permit the reading of the contents of the relevant address (see section 7.5.3). This total process is assumed to take 400 ns and corresponds to operation of a medium-speed store.

The contents of the address comprise a 24-bit operand, consisting of an instruction word, which is placed in the memory register and at the same time is transmitted, with a cable time of 50 ns to the control register at the CPU. At the control register of the CPU the first ten bits of the operand corresponding to the instruction itself are decoded within 30 ns. On receipt of an appropriate bit pattern, the output of the instruction decoder initiates at the control unit one or other set of sequential control waveforms necessary to execute the relevant order — in this case the addition order. This is achieved in the *microprogramming unit*. The decoding logic is implemented as a very fast dedicated program, termed a *microprogram*.

In effect, the microprogramming unit is a computer in itself with its own micro-instruction register and microprogram counter. Each machine-level order, such as add, etc., selects a specific subroutine. The microroutines are very simple, merely enabling and inhibiting sets of gates in the desired sequence. They are stored in very fast ROM since several micro-instructions must be executed for one machine instruction. One special advantage of microprogramming over the hardwired logic frequently employed in the past is that the machine-level instruction set can be extended merely by defining more orders and storing the appropriate microprograms in the micro ROM.

The order decode also identifies the need for modification of the address N referred to in the instruction. This arises out of a non-zero value of the M bits. Accordingly, the orders of the microprogram fetch the contents of the relevant modifier register, taking 50 ns, and the addition

$$E = N + (M)$$

takes place to yield the address required in the next store access. 80 ns are allowed for this fast addition. Note that addition takes place over the full 24-bits since the contents of location M may be 24-bits in length (see chapter 6, section 6.5.1). It is now possible to access the modified address N + (M). After a cable delay of 50 ns the second access of store is possible, but with synchronous operation such access must wait until the expiry of the first 1 μs memory cycle. Thus there is a delay of 290 ns.

The *execute cycle* begins with the reading of data from store location N + (M). Again 400 ns is involved. After a further cable delay of 50 ns the addition order

$$n' = x + n$$

is executed. The order involves the writing of fresh data into location N + (M). The time allocated, 80 ns, implies the use of a fast parallel adder. Addition takes place across the full 24 bits of each of the two operands. While addition is parallel, carry must be propagated across the 24 bits. Sophisticated techniques are used to speed up the processes of the propagation of the carry (ref. 7.1). Nevertheless the total addition time still reflects the fact that addition is across the full 24 bits. The same situation of addition across the full 24 bits arose for the addition N + (M) involved in address modification. Since the full width of 24 bits was used and the same adder employed, a similar addition time of 80 ns was required.

The result of the addition is placed in the location immediately it is available at the memory register. This is the *read/modify/write* operation with the original contents of the store location over-written. The timing diagram shows that a lost time of only 20 ns is involved and this is due to synchronous operation.

Note that for orders such as

$$02_8 : x' = x + n \text{ with } n' = n$$

the result of addition is placed in an accumulator. In this case the execute cycle involves only read. The lost time is approximately 470 ns since the result of addition no longer needs to be written to store.

In either case, at the end of the second memory cycle the add instruction is complete and the machine can proceed to the execution of further orders, again typically in a two-beat cycle (see chapter 6, section 6.3.2).

The choice of cycle time is important. It must be sufficiently long to accommodate the execution of all the more elementary instructions but not so long as to contribute significant lost time in the majority of cases. Instructions such as multiply and divide clearly take considerably longer than transfer and addition/subtraction orders. Accordingly, multiplication and division are each allocated several complete cycles rather than the two cycles for the more elementary orders.

If asynchronous operation is adopted, then the position is rather different than with synchronous operation. In the example of figure 7.2 the fetch cycle would be followed immediately by the execute cycle. Accordingly 290 ns would be saved. The execute cycle would conclude with the end of the writing into store of the result of addition and a further 20 ns would be saved. In the case of the 02_8 order however, a saving of 470 ns would result. The price paid for asynchronous operation, however, is the increased complexity in timing arrangements.

Notice too that as switching speeds increase, cable-times become an increasingly important fraction of the unproductive time expended. Cable-times may be reduced only by a reduction in the physical proximity of CPU and store. The increase in the computing power of minicomputers and microprocessor-based systems with their small physical size is making cable-time less important as a design consideration.

7.5 Semiconductor Memory

Semiconductor memory of various types has been mentioned throughout this chapter. Accordingly, this section is devoted to a brief survey of the various types and a consideration of the external circuitry required for such semiconductor memory. Since the technology and applications of semiconductor memory are advancing very rapidly, the reader must look elsewhere for fuller information (refs. 7.1 and 7.2). Literature provided by manufacturers is a further important source of useful and up-to-date information.

The two principal technologies employed in semiconductor memory are the bi-polar based on the *bipolar transistor* and the MOS based on the *field effect transistor*. This latter comprises the *metal–oxide–silicon* technology (MOS) which divides into three sub-groups: p-channel (P-MOS), n-channel (N-MOS) and complementary MOS (C-MOS) which incorporates both P-MOS and N-MOS. A further variation is silicon-on-sapphire (SOS MOS).

7.5.1 Random-Access Memory (RAM)

For random-access memory, RAM, the storage medium is *volatile* with data disappearing on removal of the power supply. In the *static* case where the storage elements are effectively flip-flops irrespective of whether bi-polar or MOS technology is used, power must be provided continuously. A typical NMOS RAM storage element might constitute a 16-pin dual-in-line integrated circuit of size 1024 bits organised as 256 words each of 4 bits. Such a device might have an access time of 450 ns and a supply current of 50 mA maximum. The cost of approximately £1 (at 1987 prices) represents a price per bit of approximately 0.1 p/bit. An alternative N-MOS RAM chip might store 4096 bits, organised as 4096 words × 1 bit, and have an access time of only 55 ns together with a power requirement of 170 mA. The price of approximately £4 again represents a cost of about 0.1 p/bit.

In the *dynamic* case, sometimes referred as DRAM and restricted to MOS technology, storage takes place as charge on capacitors, one capacitor per element. In this case it suffices to refresh the capacitors periodically in order to preserve the data. Typically, refresh is required once every few milliseconds. Such a system requires an *operating power* comparable with the static type, but the *stand-by power* dissipation is significantly less, possibly only a fraction of 1 per cent of the operating power. This is a particularly attractive feature.

A typical example might be C-MOS low power dynamic RAM with a capacity of 4096 bits organised as 1024 words of 4 bits each. Access time might be about 300 ns, supply current 5 mA with a standby current of 2 μA. The standby current is seen to be only 0.04 per cent of the supply current. The cost per bit stored for such a device is significantly less than 0.1 p/bit, again at 1987 prices. By way of contrast, an alternative type of C-MOS RAM packaged in a 28-pin dual-in-line (d.i.l.) configuration has a size of 65 536 bits (that is, 64K bits) and is organised as 8K words of 8 bits. Access time is 150 ns. Supply current is 110 mA maximum with a standby current of 20 μA (approximately 0.02 per cent of the supply current). The price per bit is about 0.05 pence. A variation on the conventional random-access memory, RAM, permits retention of data during power loss. The resulting device is described as *non-volatile RAM* though this designation is not strictly accurate. The device consists of a RAM in parallel with a non-volatile N-MOS store which is used to save the contents of the RAM in the absence of power for substantial periods.

Random-access memory, RAM, finds particular application for the main memory of computers in view of its relative cheapness, speed of random access and the ease with which it is interfaced to the computer. The principal drawback is that such storage is volatile, contents disappearing on the removal of the power supply.

7.5.2   *Read-Only Memory (ROM)*

In contrast, in the case of read-only memory, ROM, storage is essentially non-volatile. ROMs are usually engineered in MOS technology which typically requires less operating power than the bi-polar types though they have longer access times. Several forms of ROM are available. The choice depends on the application required.

(i)   Mask-programmable PROM

This type is pre-programmed during the fabrication of the integrated circuit chip. Hence the term *mask-programmable* PROM. Both bi-polar and MOS FET transistors may be used as the basic storage element. The presence of a transistor at a location in the matrix corresponds to the presence of a 1, the absence of a transistor to a 0. In many cases the manufacturer specifies ROM content. This might be the case with code conversion, for example from ASCII code to a 7 × 5 dot matrix for a VDU. Here a single mask-programmed ROM permits keyboard–VDU conversion for a complete character set for one or other of a variety of languages including Japanese and Greek. A second example might be a speech synthesis system. Part of the system would be a set of specially prepared ROMs, each of which would respond to eight-bit control words to yield specific words from a specialist vocabulary. A typical supply current might be 130 mA maximum. A vocabulary of, say, 60 or 70 words would be achieved for a chip cost of, say, £10. In other cases a customer requiring special ROM contents, for a non-standard code conversion or for a microprogramming unit for example, will provide details in sufficient time for the necessary art-work to be incorporated at the fabrication stage of IC manufacture. Such a procedure is only economically viable for quantity production. The cost for each semiconductor is a function of the length of the production run and would range from tens of pence to many pounds.

(ii)   Fusible-link PROM

In this type of PROM the contents are set, once-for-all, by the customer. Hence the term programmable read-only memory or PROM. A typical configuration is a matrix of cells comprising a bi-polar transistor array. Initially all the transistors which comprise the cells in the matrix are operative with read-out yielding words comprising all 1's. In order to achieve an alternative bit pattern for a specific word, the individual cells comprising the word are selected, typically using a one-out-of-n technique (see chapter 4, section 4.6.2). A current of carefully controlled magnitude and duration is then passed through those cells for which an output 0 is required, causing fusible links at the output of the relevant transistors to melt. As a result the transistors are rendered inoperative, yielding 0's rather than 1's when read-out occurs. Naturally, the process is irreversible. Whenever the word in question is selected thereafter, the bit pattern achieved by virtue of the fusible-link technique is provided.

(iii)   UV Erasable PROM (EPROM)

The third case is particularly interesting. The memory cells comprise MOS FET transistors. Here certain of the FETs constituting the memory matrix are rendered conducting as the initial program is inserted through the provision of programming currents applied to specific cells of the matrix which produce a negative charge at the appropriate FET gates. The electrical insulation is sufficient to keep this charge more or less indefinitely and thus render the PROM non-volatile. Erasure of the data is achieved when the memory matrix is illuminated by intense ultra-violet light for a total period of a few minutes through a quartz window on top of the IC. As a result of this illumination, photocurrents discharge the gates leaving all the memory cells in the zero state. Since the ROM is both *erasable* and *programmable*, it is designated an *EPROM*.

(iv)   Electrically Erasable and Programmable PROM (E^2PROM or EEPROM)

Electrically erasable and programmable read-only memories (EEPROMs) are useful where permanent storage is normally required but where it may be necessary to change storage contents occasionally. In these circumstances fresh data can be written into read-only memory in a manner analogous to writing to static RAM. By way of illustration, an EEPROM with 256-bit storage organised as 16 registers of length 16 bits is available as an 8-pin dual-in-line package. Maximum supply current for read/write operation is 10 mA. The price reflects a cost of about 2 p/bit.

(v)   Electrically Alterable Read-Only Memory (EAROM)

Here the semiconductor memory is used as a read-only memory. A single word or block of words can be altered readily as required. A typical configuration is 4096 bits arranged as 1024 words of 4 bits each at about 0.2 p/bit.

   The five types of read-only memory contrasted above illustrate the current possibilities in this area of semiconductor electronics. Larger ROMS at lower cost together with further types of semiconductor read-only memory can be predicted for the future with some confidence.

7.5.3 Organisation of RAM and ROM Stores

In the case of the semiconductor store, both RAM and ROM, all the necessary ancillary circuits are incorporated on the IC chip itself. The external connections are TTL compatible for the most part while connections to data buses are tri-state (see chapter 4, section 4.5). Frequently, only a single +5 V supply is necessary.

Most straightforward memory systems use *position addressing* in which data occupies a specific location (that is, address) in store. Access to a location is achieved by recourse to its address. Two principal types of addressing system are employed: *word-organised* or *2-D addressing*, and *bit-organised* or *3-D addressing*. The two types will be considered in turn.

(i) Word-organised or 2-D Addressing

In this case, emphasis is on the reading to store (RAM only) or retrieval from store of complete words of standard length (both ROM and RAM). Typically these may be 8 bits long for simple microprocessor systems or 16 bits long for mini and microcomputer applications.

The address of the operand is achieved through the selection of the unique *word-line* which relates to the operand in question. The word-line is identified through a one-out-of-n decode of the address associated with the operand. Consider a simple case in which a teaching computer such as MIC, discussed in chapter 5, employs a standard word-length of eight bits. Within instruction words, five bits would be used as the N address permitting a 32-word store. A one-out-of-n decode for the N address yields $2^5 = 32$ unique word-lines (see chapter 4, section 4.6.2, and chapter 5, section 5.7.3).

Figure 7.3 shows a schematic diagram of the resulting 2-D memory with 32 word lines (N_0 to N_{31}) each encompassing the eight memory elements constituting individual 8-bit words. Each memory element or bit position, D_1 to D_8, of the 32 words is connected also to a corresponding digit-line. Since there are eight bit positions within the words there are eight digit-lines. The storage elements or cells are thus situated at the intersections of word-lines and digit-lines.

Reading and writing, the latter to RAM only, from and to store involves word selection as indicated above. When reading occurs, with either RAM or ROM, a word-line is selected and the logic levels at the output of the individual cells constituting the selected word are monitored. As a result, 1's and 0's appear in parallel on the digit lines D_1 to D_8 and are impressed on the 8-bit parallel bus system. When writing to store, which is possible only with RAM, appropriate signals from the CPU energise the digit lines, D_1 to D_8, and as a result 1's and 0's are set into the individual cells which constitute the word in question. The detailed circuit configuration of the

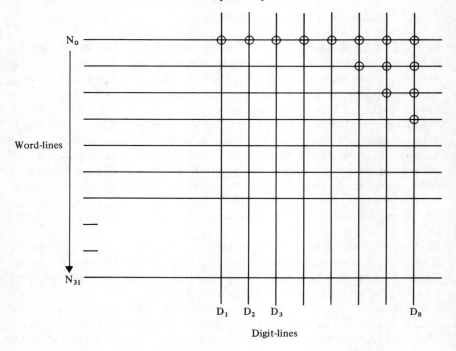

Figure 7.3 Word-organised or 2-D addressing schematic

individual cells depends on whether bi-polar or MOS transistor flip-flop technology comprises the cells, the case with static RAMs, or whether the cells are formed from single FET transistors in series with elemental capacitors, the case with dynamic RAMs. Readers should consult more specialist texts for specific details — see refs 7.1, 7.2 and 7.3.

A schematic diagram of a typical idealised random-access memory employing a 2-D word-organised store arrangement is shown in figure 7.4(a). The RAM provides 1024 words each of 8 bits. Accordingly a 10 bit N address is necessary. The resulting one-out-of-1024 decode selects one or other of the 1024 word-lines. Tri-state gating permits access to the 8-stage buffer register and the bi-directional data bus. Choice of writing (input of data) or reading (output of data) is achieved by providing a 1 or 0 at the read/write R/W pin. A *chip-select* line permits multiple-chip operation. Only when a logical 1 is applied to the chip-select line is the chip addressed. When not selected, the tri-state gates go into their high-impedance state which disconnects the RAM from the data bus. The memory-map of figure 7.4(b) shows how three additional higher address bits beyond the ten already provided permit activation of one or other of eight RAM chips via the chip-select line, thus increasing store size from 1K words to 8K words.

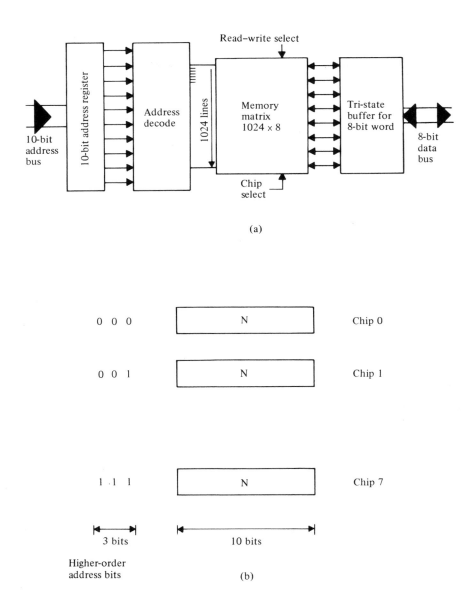

(a)

(b)

Figure 7.4 (a) Block diagram of 1024 eight-bit word 2-D static RAM.
(b) Memory map for extension to 8K

The provision of appropriate gating to achieve this end is left as a simple student exercise.

A consideration of the *pin-count* for the RAM shown in figure 7.4(a) is instructive. A list of the requirements shows:

memory address lines	10
input/output data bus lines	8
read/write select line	1
chip-select line	1
supply voltage	1
ground	1
Total lines	22

Hence the pin requirement is 22. This is a convenient number for the popular dual-in-line (d.i.l.) configuration.

It will be appreciated that the total number of pins on an IC memory package is a possible limitation to the size of memory which may be accommodated. When larger memories are required than the pin count indicates, then the problem is overcome by the judicious use of *multiplexing techniques*.

2-D memories are available for various word-lengths. Four-bit word-length memories and eight-bit word-length memories are popular. Also popular are one-bit word-length memories. In this latter case a set of chips is necessary, one chip for each significant bit position, when multi-bit words are to be stored. The technique employed shares some common features with the 3-D stores to be considered next.

(ii)   Bit-organised or 3-D Addressing

An alternative to the 2-D addressing method is the 3-D technique. With this technique an individual bit (cell) within a chip is identified rather than a complete word. With static RAM a flip-flop constitutes the cell, either using bi-polar or MOS technology. With dynamic RAM the cell comprises a single FET transistor in series with a capacitor which stores a 1 or 0 as necessary. Cell selection is achieved through application of a logic 1 to the appropriate (x, y) co-ordinates. Detailed circuitry considerations may be disregarded at this stage. It suffices to state that a logic 1 on both x and y co-ordinate lines simultaneously is necessary to select an individual cell permitting reading or writing thereafter via the sense lines. Lewin (ref. 7.1) provides useful technical detail.

Figure 7.5(a) shows a simplified block diagram of a 1024-bit static random-access MOS memory. The memory matrix comprises 32×32 elements with X (row select) and Y (column select) decodes each

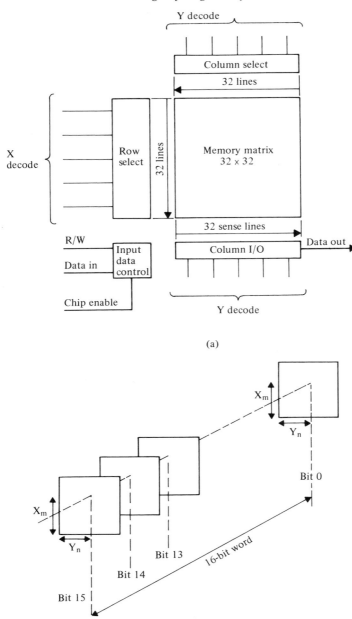

(a)

(b)

*Figure 7.5 (a) 3-D 1024-bit static random-access MOS memory.
(b) Schematic showing storage of 16-bit word using 16 bit-
organised static RAM chips*

constituting one-out-of-32 decodes. Reading and writing is to a single bit position via a sense line which links the 32 cells of an individual column of the matrix but receives an output from or activates only the cell in the selected row (that is, the cell selected by the X decode). Selection of the correct sense line requires a one-out-of-32 decode in order to address the appropriate column. In accord with the single-bit operation, only a single data-in and and a single data-out pin are necessary. Choice of read/write is provided by the R/W pin. A chip-enable pin is provided which can be used to inhibit operation if necessary. A list of the requirements is given below:

X decode lines	5
Y decode lines	5
read/write select line	1
chip-enable line	1
data-in line	1
data-out line	1
supply voltage	1
ground	1
Total lines	16

Since the bit-organised memory provides input/output only in respect of a single memory element at any one time, a set of chips is necessary to achieve storage of complete words. The number of chips equals the number of bits in the word. Accordingly, provision may be made for words of any length. This may be a useful design feature.

In a practical case the address lines are common to each chip in the set used to store a block of words. Thus an individual word is stored, one bit per chip, with co-ordinates $X_m Y_n$ for each chip. Data is written to or retrieved from the buffer register connected to the parallel data bus system on the basis of one bit per chip. Thus for a 16-bit word-length a set of 16 1024-bit RAM chips would provide a 1024 word store — that is, a 1K store corresponding to a 10-bit N address divided into X and Y decodes each of 5 bits. Figure 7.5(b) provides a schematic showing storage of a 16-bit word using 16-bit-organised (3-D) static RAM chips.

The chip-enable pin provides an easy way to extend store capacity through what is in effect higher-order address bits. Consider, for example, extension of the above store to 4K words. Access to one or other of four blocks of store each of 1K capacity can be achieved by an extension of the N address to 12 bits. X and Y decodes, each of 5 bits, select a word position common to all four blocks of store while a one-out-of-four decode applied to the chip-enable pin of each of the chips comprising one or other of the four blocks of store permits selection of the correct block of store. The technique is very similar to that discussed in respect of store extension in the case of the 2-D store.

Note that the number of address lines to achieve access to a store of given word size is the same for both the 2-D arrangement and the 3-D arrangement. In the example of figure 7.4, with the 2-D single-chip store a 10-bit address yields 1024 words. In this particular case the words are 8 bits long. In the 3-D case the 10-bit address also yields 1024 words. Since 16 chips are used, the word-length is 16 bits. The choice of 2-D or 3-D storage depends on practical considerations associated with chip-count, pin-count, chip availability, multiplexing problems and the inclination of the computer designer.

7.5.4 *Emerging Semiconductory Technology as New Storage Media*

Over the years since the earliest development of the digital computer in the 1950s, it has been appreciated that access to high-speed stores (preferably random access) of large capacity and low cost is the key to successful computer operation. Many types of store have been devised. Some had only a short life while others were popular for many years. The history of computer storage techniques forms a subject in its own right and mirrors the development of computers themselves.

Two newer types of semiconductor memory offer possibilities at the present time though it must be admitted that they have not yet achieved widespread popularity as evidenced by the anticipated easy availability and low cost forecast by their originators and developers. The substantial development of semiconductor RAM with rapid random access coupled with the huge storage capability of disc store, albeit achieved via cyclic access, has overshadowed the CCD and magnetic bubble memories discussed below. However, the situation may be reversed at any time. The two types are now discussed briefly. For further details of these and other types the specialist literature should be consulted.

(i) *Charge-Coupled Device (CCD) Memories* (refs 7.2 and 7.4)

The charge-coupled device (CCD) is a serial shift register which stores digital data through its circulation of a pattern of 1's and 0's along a CCD shift register providing amplification and regeneration as each digit reaches the end of the register. In this the charge-coupled device resembles the mercury delay-line of the earliest years of computers but avoids the very serious practical limitations of the former equipment. Commercial devices with capacities in excess of 64K bits are currently available.

(ii)   Magnetic-Bubble Device (MBD) Memories (refs 7.2 and 7.4)

The magnetic-bubble device memory is a storage device intermediate between semiconductor devices and electromechanical magnetic tape and disc units. Such MBD memories can be considered as integrated-circuit equivalents of the electromechanical magnetic memories. Information is stored in both cases in the form of magnetised regions. With the MBD memory the minute magnetised region is known as a magnetic bubble and is sufficiently small for a 16K-bit bubble memory to be mounted on a chip area as small as 25 mm^2. The memory is organised for serial access as a set of shift registers typically permitting cyclic access to a section of the memory containing 512 bubbles (that is, 512 bits of data in 5 ms). Thus access to an individual bit would be achieved on average in 2.5 ms.

Bubble memories are slower of access than semiconductor memories but are non-volatile with lower power consumption on read/write. The small size and lack of mechanical parts make bubble memories an attractive potential rival to electromechanical cyclic memories such as disc stores. As with CCD stores, bubble memories are not yet employed on a large scale. Their future application should be watched with interest. However, both CCD stores and bubble memory systems are rivalled by the ever-increasing capacity of disc stores. Recent developments in the area of optical-disc storage makes the adoption of CCD or bubble memory less likely than was anticipated at an earlier date.

7.6   The Disc Store — an Example of Cyclic Access

7.6.1   General Criteria

This section deals briefly with disc stores (for further details see refs 7.2 or 7.4). The disc store is widely used and serves as a typical example of a *cyclic-access non-volatile* bulk store of comparatively short access-time. The disc store rotates at high uniform speed so that the store may also be regarded as *dynamic* in contrast to, say, a ferrite-core store which was a static non-volatile bulk store. The disc store has come to be the principal non-volatile bulk store, taking over the role from the rotating magnetic-drum store so popular at an earlier time. The transition may be seen as analogous to that which occurred during the early part of the twentieth century in the field of sound recording and storage when cylindrical records were replaced by the more convenient discs currently employed.

With all disc systems, a coating of magnetic material (ferrite) is applied to the surface of the disc platter. Writing and reading of data are performed by a recording/playback head positioned above the disc. The head is moved radially to select one of a number of concentric tracks. Each head comprises a high-permeability split-ring core wound with a coil of fine wire.

In the write phase when a current pulse of short duration is passed through the coil, a magnetic field is generated across the core gap in the elemental area adjacent to the disc surface. As a result a minute magnetic dipole appears in the ferrite coating of the disc at that point. It will be recalled that the disc is rotating at high speed. Accordingly, the direction of successive current pulses determines the sense of the magnetic dipoles induced in contiguous elemental areas along tracks tangential to the axis of rotation of the disc. A dipole in one sense comprises a 1, a dipole in the other a 0. In the reading phase the passage of each of the sequential magnetic dipoles past the head induces a flux in the core and as a result small e.m.f.s are induced in the head coil. The direction of the e.m.f.s corresponds to the sense of the dipoles. Accordingly, 1's or 0's are retrieved as appropriate.

Earlier disc systems involved multiple fixed-position discs of substantial size, typically with moving heads which could be aligned to the required track with high-speed servo systems. An alternative modern arrangement often comprises a removable single or multiple *hard disc system*. A variant is a fixed disc with multiple heads, one per track. Since the time to position the head is eliminated, such drives are faster but more expensive. Low-capacity, low-cost drives use *floppy discs*.

With multiple platter disc systems, storage capacity is high with up to perhaps 100 megabytes per spindle. 2.5, 10 and 40 megabyte capacities are common. Data is recorded serially on concentric tracks divided into sections each containing a block of, say, 512 bytes. There may be as many as 250 tracks per inch. The serial bit stream comprising a block is read from a track and is collated into 16-bit words in buffer registers. Thereafter buffer contents are transferred to main store in blocks.

A disc system will transfer data at high speed once the relevant block of data has been located. The disc rotates at high speed, usually 3600 r.p.m. and, since the block of data required may be at any point with respect to the reading head, a time equal on average to that required for half a revolution of the disc is involved before transfer can begin. This location time is the *latency* and is a fundamental limitation of cyclic-access storage. With a 3600 r.p.m. disc, for example, the average latency is about 8 ms. In the case of systems with movable read/write heads, there is a further delay while the servo moves the appropriate head to the correct track. This may involve a delay of up to 100 ms. As a result, a total delay of 100 ms or thereabouts may be encountered with a disc system. This is a further reason why disc-to-memory transfers take place via blocks of data rather than as individual words.

7.6.2   The Winchester Disc System

The Winchester disc system is a typical example of a modern system. The set of discs, typically 133 mm ($5\frac{1}{4}$ inches) in diameter, stores up to 80 megabytes. The capacity of the larger 200.3 mm (8 inch) disc is substantially greater. Data transfer rates may be 5 megabytes/s with average access time of less than 100 ms. The disc drive is totally sealed and requires neither maintenance nor a controlled environment. Physical size is little more than that required to accommodate the discs themselves. The price of a typical Winchester system of about £500 for a 20 megabyte store reflects a cost/bit of the order of 2.5×10^{-3} pence/byte.

7.6.3   The Floppy Disc System

Floppy disc (discette) systems are cheaper disc systems. The discs themselves are smaller, substantially cheaper, more easily portable and have a more limited store capacity than the cartridge discs. A capacity of perhaps 500 kilobytes is typical. Speed is lower than with the more robust hard-disc drives, typically about 300 r.p.m. This gives an average rotational latency of 100 ms. Data transfer between disc and memory might be 250 kilobytes/s. A typical specification provides for 96 tracks per inch with each track of 10 sectors comprising 512 bytes and either a single or dual-disc arrangement. A moving head system is used with a seek time of about 10 ms to step in or out of a single track with the result that the total average latency, including head settle time, is of the order of, say, 300 ms. With the floppy disc the head is brought into direct contact with the disc, in contrast to the larger systems in which the head is positioned at a small distance from the rotating disc using an 'air-bearing' formed as a result of the aerodynamic design of the head.

7.6.4   The Optical Disc System

With the *optical disc system*, writing to individual magnetic storage locations and reading from such locations are achieved via optical means. The technique is in its early development but already storage of hundreds of Gigabytes on a single platter is possible. Further developments are to be expected. As a result of the huge capacity of such a system, provision for data erasure prior to rewrite is not made. In the unlikely event of filling the disc, a fresh disc must be provided.

Comparatively low-cost storage of this type which provides relatively fast access to an extremely large number of blocks of data offers completely new possibilities in such areas as artificial intelligence and image analysis. In both cases, huge amounts of storage are required. For example, in image analysis the storage of even a single image derived from a 100×100 matrix of picture elements (pixels) with 256 gray levels involves 10 kilobytes of information. With a data stream of, say, 200 images/s, 2 megabytes/s must be stored. Even a substantial Winchester disc store of 100 megabytes total capacity could provide storage for only 50 s of record.

7.7 Serial Bulk Stores

The previous section considered disc stores as examples of cyclic-access bulk storage systems. The present section moves on to a brief considera-tion of serial-access stores. These are characterised by low-cost/bit-stored achieved at the expense of long access times. It was pointed out that with cyclic access stores, data transfer is in blocks in order to minimise the effect of slow retrieval time. The need for transfer in blocks is even more relevant in the case of serial stores. Typically, the media used are *non-volatile* and may also be *permanent*. Media used include the following types.

(i) Magnetic-tape Systems

Here data is stored on magnetic tape as elemental magnetic dipoles using reading/writing techniques similar to those described already for the case of disc storage systems. Thus in the present case the magnetic-tape stores individual alphanumeric characters across the tape in binary code using, say, 8 tracks plus a parity track. In this way the standard ASCII character set can be accommodated directly.

Data is recorded in blocks known as *records* separated by *record gaps*. Records are grouped together into *files* also separated, this time by *file gaps*. Special codes on the tape identify records and files. Since individual files may be located at any point on the tape, average retrieval time is half the time taken for a complete pass of information. This may extend to minutes unless particular care is taken to group files in a special order on the tape. Such a procedure is restrictive on a programmer but may reduce retrieval time significantly for certain types of work.

Magnetic tape systems were once the principal bulk storage devices. However, they involve a considerable amount of electromechanical engi-neering, are somewhat inflexible and are generally regarded as less attractive than disc systems with their enhanced flexibility and significantly faster retrieval times.

(ii)   Cassette Storage

Here the storage medium is a miniature version of that described above. Small cassette tapes running at 47.4 mm/s ($1\frac{7}{8}$ inches/s) are employed. While speeds are slow and store capacity limited, cost is low both as to the medium itself and the record/playback equipment. Frequently, cheap commercial cassette recorders suffice. Cassette-based bulk storage finds a place with small minicomputers, microprocessor based systems and at 'intelligent' VDU terminals linked to large on-line computer systems.

(iii)   Paper-tape Systems

Paper tape is also used as a storage medium. Multi-track tapes are used, typically 5, 7 or 8 hole with sometimes one hole reserved for a parity bit. Each item of alphanumeric information is stored in binary fashion across the tape with the pattern of holes and absence of holes corresponding to the appropriate pattern of 1's and 0's. This approach is very popular with systems in which a keyboard machine such as a Teletype is used in tape preparation. A Teletype and paper-tape record is useful in small-scale off-line program and data preparation.

   If tape is punched directly from a Teletype, then the punching rate is determined by the skill of the operator and is slow of necessity. Fast paper tape punches and readers are used as computer peripherals to provide data for off-line analysis on the one hand and the input of program and data to a computer on the other.

   The serial nature of a paper tape system coupled with the comparatively low speed of even the fastest punches and readers makes paper-tape storage unattractive save for small-scale or special activities. The cost of such storage is low while its field of application is virtually unlimited.

   It must be pointed out, however, that direct input via VDU, both for scientific and business applications, has gained enormously in popularity for larger-scale program preparation. For the ever increasingly important area of home computing, input at keyboard and output at VDU are universal.

(iv)   Punched Cards

The use of punched cards for data storage extends even beyond the earliest days of computers and has been popular throughout computer history. The medium has much in common with paper-tape storage in that data is stored as alphanumeric characters coded in binary fashion as holes or absences of holes in the 12-position rows of 80-column rectangular cards. Both program and data take the form of a pack of cards. Program modification is easily achieved as an individual card or group of cards can be replaced in the pack as required. Usually a pack of punched cards relates to a single file so that delay relating to a search for a particular file is avoided. Nevertheless the fastest punched-card reader is comparatively slow. As with paper-tape systems, punched-card systems lack the flexibility of disc-based systems. While a disc system may be used directly in a real-time or multi-programming computer installation, paper-tape and punched-card systems are more appropriate to batch-orientated computer installations. Nevertheless, punched-card storage may be used as a back-up permanent record of the software of a complete computer system.

7.8 Summary

This chapter has considered storage of data for computer systems. The basic characteristics of storage media have been contrasted and the trade-off between cost/bit, speed of access, convenience of use, volatility and other features examined. The importance of hierarchy of storage types emerged. Particular attention was devoted to semiconductor storage of various types including the newer varieties. The chapter closed with consideration of bulk storage, both cyclic and serial of access.

References

7.1   Lewin, D., *Theory and Design of Digital Computer Systems*, Nelson, London, 1980.

7.2   Bannister, B. R. and Whitehead, D. G., *Fundamentals of Modern Digital Systems*, 2nd edn, Macmillan, London, 1987.

7.3   Simpson, R. J. and Terrell, T., *Introduction to 6800/6802 Microprocessor Systems Hardware, Software and Experimentation*, Newnes Butterworth, Sevenoaks, 1982.

7.4   Wilkinson, B. and Horrocks, D., *Computer Peripherals*, Hodder and Stoughton, London, 1980.

Problems

The problems in this chapter fall into two classes. General problems with non-specific answers (**7.1** to **7.3**) are followed by a more detailed problem (**7.4**) with specific answers.

7.1   A new computer is at the design stage. The word-length is fixed at 16 bits and since indirect addressing is provided, 16-bit address labels are possible. The intention is to organise the store into a number of

distinct blocks of convenient size. Discuss the criteria which determine an appropriate size for the blocks. Make provision for semiconductor store. Give preliminary consideration to the electronics
involved for address decode.

Comment. This problem may be taken at a superficial level
involving little more than a modification of the information given in
figures 7.4 and 7.5.

7.2 A ground station is to be set up in connection with a space
exploration programme. It is anticipated that the following items will
be included among its equipment.

(a) A steerable radio-telescope which will be used to track space
vehicles, transmit control signals to space vehicles, and collect data
from such vehicles.

(b) A process-control digital computer for continuous assessment of
the signals received at the telescope and the calculation of command
information for transmission to space vehicles.

(c) A general-purpose digital computer for long-term analysis of
results obtained from the programme of space exploration. It is also
intended that this computer will be used for the routine payroll
calculations for the staff of the ground station who will be about 1000
in number.

In the light of financial stringency, discuss the most appropriate
computer types storage hierarchy for efficient operation of the
station.

Comment. As in the case of problem **7.1**, an answer can be
provided readily in the light of knowledge gained from studying this
chapter. At a deeper level, brief reference may be made to books on
radio astronomy and accounting, to provide a more informed
background to the topic. Since storage methods are subject to
continuous revision in the light of developing technology, up-to-date
specialist texts and manufacturers' guides, including price lists,
should be consulted.

7.3 The reader will be well aware of the difficulty of providing detailed
guidance as to speed and cost of storage of various types in a book
such as the present one. Performance and cost reflect advances in
technology, especially semiconductor technology, and also the
marketing policies of the various companies. A useful exercise is
to revise table 7.1, using the latest performance characteristics
and price lists of the catalogues of the various manufacturers of
semiconductors.

7.4 Figure 7.2 showed the timing diagram for the synchronous operation
of an add order

$$n' = n + x$$

for a small minicomputer employing direct addressing with a semi-conductor, non-destructive read-out store. With this order, the contents, n, of store location N are added to the contents, x, of accumulator X, at the central processor unit (CPU) of the machine. The result of the addition becomes the new contents, n', of the store location N.

Timing arrangements are as follows:

1. Medium-speed store:
   400 ns address decode, gating and read-time.
   400 ns address decode, gating and rewrite-time.
2. Cable length from CUP to store, 8 m:
   transmission rate, 6 ns m^{-1}; therefore
   cable time, approximately 50 ns.
3. Order decode time, 30 ns.
4. Modification: time for addition N + (M), 80 ns.
5. Time for fast addition n' = x + n, 80 ns.

The fetch and execute cycles are 1 μs in duration.

Now consider alternative situations as indicated below. When drawing diagrams, use squared paper to ensure that the figures are to scale.

(a) With the retention of synchronous operation which of the following alternatives will result in a significant increase of speed?
  (i) Improvement in addition time from 80 ns to 40 ns.
  (ii) Improvement in store speed from 400 ns to 250 ns with no improvement in addition time.
  Draw out timing diagrams and suggest possible cycle times for synchronous operation.

(b) What would be the duration of the fetch cycle and the execute cycle for the addition order n + x if asynchronous operation was adopted in conjunction with the preferred option from section (a) above?

(c) Draw out a diagram to illustrate the effect of the introduction of indirect addressing on the overall cycle of operations. Assume that operation is synchronous, that the add order n + x is involved and that the preferred option from (a) above is employed.

Outline Solution

(a) Figure 7.2 shows the initial arrangement with the semiconductor store having non-destructive read-out and fetch and execute cycles each of 1 μs (that is, synchronous operation). Now consider alternatives.

(i) *Reduction of addition time to 40 ns*
Retention of synchronous operation but improvement in addition time from 80 ns to 40 ns. Figure 7.6(i) shows that no real change in overall speed can be expected with the retention of synchronous operation. All that occurs is a small increase in 'lost time' for the execute cycle.

(ii) *Reduction of store speed to 250 ns*
When the store speed is improved from 400 ns to 250 ns, overall speed is increased sufficiently to permit cycle time to be reduced to 700 ns though the addition time remains at 80 ns. Figure 7.6(ii) illustrates the position. Clearly this is the better option.

(b) *Asynchronous operation*
Asynchronous operation with option a(ii). Here the fetch and execute cycles are of different length and no 'lost time' is involved. Figure 7.6(ii) illustrates the position and indicates that the

$$\text{fetch cycle} = (700 \text{ ns} - 140 \text{ ns}) = 560 \text{ ns}$$
$$\text{execute cycle} = (700 \text{ ns} - 20 \text{ ns}) = 680 \text{ ns}$$

No separate diagram is required.

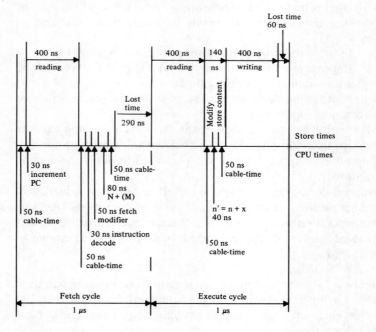

(i)

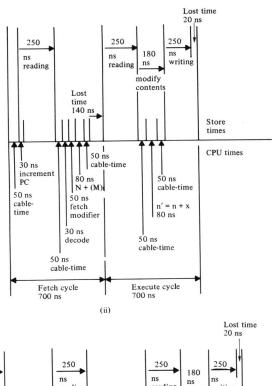

(ii)

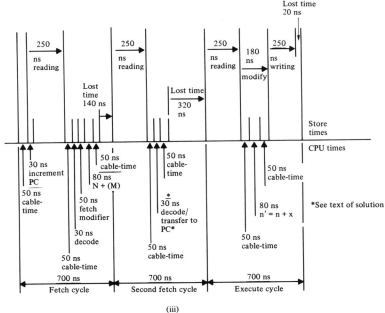

(iii)

Figure 7.6 (i) Execution of simple add order with synchronous operation. 40 ns add time. (ii) Execution of simple add order with synchronous operation. Read/write time 250 ns.
(iii) Synchronous operation indirect addressing. Read/write time 250 ns.

(c)   *Substitution of indirect addressing with retention of synchronous operation and semiconductor memory*

With indirect addressing an extra memory access is involved. Hence we have the sequence:

first fetch cycle   700 ns — to find the first address location

second fetch cycle   700 ns — to find the second address location

execute cycle   700 ns — to execute the order which was found in the second address location

Accordingly, the first fetch cycle is unchanged from part (a)(ii), then follows a second fetch cycle, similar to the first but without involving modification N + (M). Finally, the execute cycle is as in part (a)(ii). Figure 7.6(iii) illustrates the position.

Note. If the indirect access to store is the starting point for a complete subroutine, then the Program Counter must be adjusted to the 'start address' of the routine so accessed. However, if the indirect address access is a single event, the Program Counter is merely incremented in the normal way as shown on the diagram.

8 Software Systems

Objectives

This book is largely devoted to computer hardware but it has been stressed throughout that the total hardware/software system is important. This chapter is thus included to explain the important features of the software aspects of the overall computer system. Without *system software* the hardware of the machine is inoperative. The approach adopted is entirely descriptive, explaining the function of the principal packages providing the *software support* for the system. The fine details as to how the objective is achieved are not given. Such information is for more advanced computer science text books. See, for example, ref. 8.1, among many such texts.

In this chapter the distinction is drawn between system software and *applications* programs provided either by the supplier of the computer or, as is often the case, written by the purchaser of the computer system. The more general and important subject of software engineering which relates more directly to the structure of programming languages is discussed in chapter 11.

It is most important that the student understands the overall picture created by this review before moving on to more advanced works in order to understand details of Compilers or Operating Systems, etc.

8.1 Introduction

Computer programs are simply sequences of elementary binary machine instructions. By specifying differing sequences of instructions the one hardware unit can be made to perform quite different tasks. This *soft* concept is the real feature of a computer which sets it apart from any other logical device. In some cases, such as a washing machine controller, the program is committed to ROM and the soft facility is lost; it is not however lost to the designer of the controller who fully used the soft approach before finalising on the code to reside in the ROM.

Software can be usefully categorised as follows:

System Software
  Operating System
  Run-time support modules, such as handlers for various optional
    peripherals
Utility Programs
  Editors
  Assemblers
  Compilers
  Debuggers
  Linkers
  File manipulation, including disc management
  System statistics
Application Programs

This is shown schematically in figure 8.1.

8.1.1 System Software

System software is as much an integral part of a computer as is the hardware. System software is provided to present a logical and usable view of the machine, over and above the basic hardware. Thus, for instance, a user can store a program or a data file on a disc drive using a name to identify it without recourse to any detailed knowledge of the physical allocation of tracks and sectors. It also safeguards against *double* allocation of any physical sector.

The main *controlling* software is generally called an *Operating System*. In more dedicated applications such as a machine-tool controller for which there are no VDUs or discs, then only the heart of the Operating System is required and this is sometimes called an *Executive*. Operating Systems come in many shapes and sizes with differing characteristics suited to particular applications.

The fundamental Operating System functions are often enhanced by suites of subroutines which are commonly used by application programs. Often these *run-time support* modules are used extensively by high-level language compilers. More meaningful file access functions, such as indexed or keyed record access, are common features. There are no rigorous rules as to what functions are included in the basic operating-system code, and what is provided as isolated run-time support modules. Often a *system generation* (SYSGEN) routine is provided to allow a user-defined selection of modules to be *built into* a new operating system to suit a specific selection of peripherals. A standard minimum operating system is obviously required to run SYSGEN.

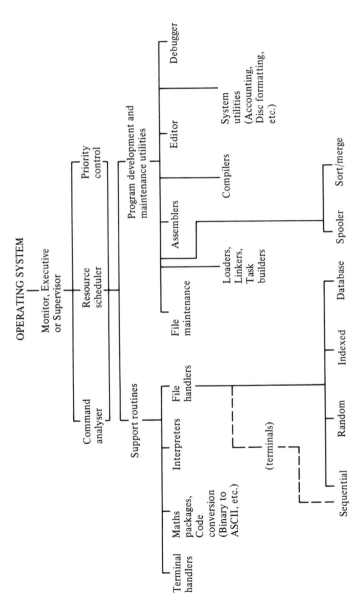

Figure 8.1 System software modules

8.1.2   Utility Programs

In addition to the run-time support modules which a programmer can effectively build into his own program, a whole set of utility programs has been developed. These are essentially tools to aid the development of private programs and general system *housekeeping*.

Text editors are used to create, store and modify programs in natural language form — that is, character strings. Other programs, Assemblers, Compilers or Interpreters, as appropriate, translate the English text into binary machine code. Further utilities are used for linking together modules of code produced by separate compilations. Modularity is essential for anything but the simplest programs.

Testing and correcting programs is one of the more arduous tasks to be faced. The problem of finding and fixing errors is aided by a Debugger. Unlike most utilities, debuggers are used while running the user's program to trap and trace *breakpoints*.

Finally, house-keeping utilities are needed to copy files, print files, format discs, copy whole discs (back-up), transmit files between machines and to report system statistics, such as how much space is left on disc.

8.1.3   Application Programs

Application programs are created to make the computer perform some specific task. Such programs turn the general-purpose hardware into a problem-solving machine. Little can be said about application programs in this book because the range is so diverse and so specific to the user.

Frequently the user writes the applications programs and thus takes advantage of the detailed knowledge of the subject area which is special to the user's company. On other occasions a *software house* writes applications programs to the specification provided by the end-user. In some cases the user needs programs which are widely employed. Such programs would include word processing, spread-sheets and in many cases those relating to accounting, calculation of payrolls, sales order processing, etc. In these cases, application programs may be developed by the staff of the computer manufacturer or by specialist software houses specialising in *packaged* solutions. As a result of substantial demand for these application programs, the development costs are widely distributed being shared by many end-users. Accordingly, this may be the only cost-effective solution in many areas.

8.2   Machine Code and Source Code

A program must comprise a sequence of binary instructions, loaded into the computer RAM, before it can be executed. An image of the program is therefore stored on disc which is transferred to memory when that program is to be run. It is an image of the actual binary machine instructions and is therefore referred to as *machine code*.

The above view, however, is oversimplified. The actual binary file stored on disc must contain some further information, stored in a *header*, a record at the beginning of the file, to define to the system details of the machine code program contained within the file. Thus the loading mechanism will read the header first and use this to help in completing the proper program load. The format of the header differs from one system to another. Thus, for instance, the loadable files with the name extension .EXE specified by the PC DOS operating system have a different header to the .CMD files specified by the more comprehensive Concurrent DOS (see section 8.8).

As will be discussed further, programs can be written in an English-like language to aid development. The user types the program as conventional text data using ordinary characters. This source program is then stored on the disc for further processing. Thus a *source code* file is simply a sequential file of normal ASCII characters, which can be printed, displayed on a screen and edited. The source code program is converted into a binary *object code* by a specialised program such as an Assembler or Compiler (more on this later).

If the program is short it can be developed as one complete entity. However, in practice, real programs are too big, so that they are developed as a set of program modules. Each source code module is converted to an object code file separately. The final object code for the complete machine-loadable image is created by *linking* the separate modules together. Thus each individual object code file must contain its own header defining specific details of how it is to be linked to other modules. An object code file is not in itself complete and cannot be loaded and executed.

Occasionally binary files of any sort are stored as hexadecimal code. In this case, each byte in the code is mapped to two 4-bit codes, each of which in turn is mapped to the equivalent ASCII character; for example, the byte 10100111 which is equivalent to $A7_h$ is stored as the ASCII characters for A and 7 — that is, 01000001 and 00110111. Such files can then be transmitted in systems which treat the 8th bit as a parity bit. Hexadecimal files must be translated to binary before they can be used.

8.3 Development Tools

The basic tools available to help develop a computer program have been outlined in section 8.2. Each of them is a specialised computer program provided with the computer, many as extra cost items however. These will now be considered in more detail. Further information may be found in such references as ref. 8.2 or 8.3.

8.3.1 Editors

An editor is a program which allows a user to create a source code file by typing on a keyboard. Simple editors work line-by-line, originating in the days of Teletypes.

Nowadays with a VDU a *full-screen* editor is possible. Not only can new text be created, but old text can be recalled and modified. The text is displayed on the screen and can be modified by typing commands on the keyboard. The cursor movement keys can be used to over-write text, to insert text, to delete text or to manipulate blocks of text.

An editor is similar to a word processor except that no automatic end-of-line wrap-around is needed. Many word processor packages, such as WordStar, have a non-document mode to support editing of source code files.

Further facilities allow for searching for character-string occurrences and for substituting one string by another.

The modular technique means that a change can be made to a program simply by editing the appropriate source code module and retranslating that to its equivalent object-code module. The new module then needs relinking with the other modules to create a new machine-code file. This leads to the concept of *libraries*. Regularly used modules can be maintained in a library ready for linking with other modules. The user may create a private library of commonly used functions but the compiler writers usually provide a *public library* of standard functions such as maths routines, I/O handlers, etc.

The overall situation is shown in figure 8.2. Note that listings and displays of source and hexadecimal files can be produced, but the full 8-bit codes of a binary file are quite meaningless to an ASCII output device. Note also that this is an iterative process. An error detected at run-time (execution) must be corrected by editing the source code, recompiling, linking, etc. The extra element indicated in figure 8.2 is a debugger. This is a special program which controls execution of the program interactively from a console. It helps greatly in tracing program errors.

8.3.2 Assemblers and Object Code

As has been explained earlier in this text, it is far easier to remember the instruction set of a computer in terms of mnemonic code than binary numbers. The mnemonic codes which make up the instructions are simply ASCII character strings. Thus a program written in terms of assembler mnemonics is a typical source code file, which can be edited.

However, the *assembly language* concept is far more than mnemonic representation. Of equal importance, addresses both for branches in the

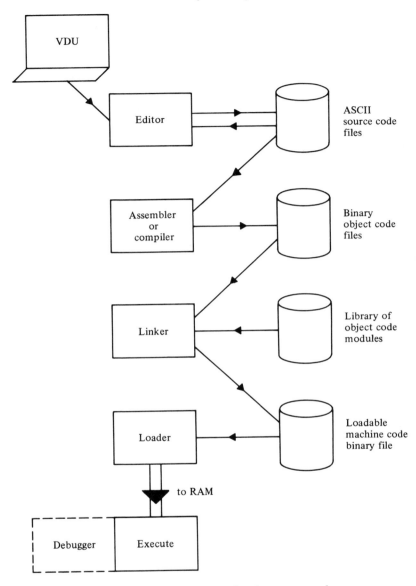

Figure 8.2 The program development cycle

program and for data items can be represented by meaningful names.
Constants can also be allocated names within the program, being given
specific values in a table at the beginning of the program. The use of names
makes debugging and maintenance practical. Any change to the middle of

a program, say, which increased its length, means that all following addresses are changed and must be corrected. By using names for the addresses these will automatically be recalculated when assembled.

Since each order must have a unique mnemonic, the translation from assembly language ASCII source code into binary object code is formal (compare this with natural language translation where the same spelling has different meaning dependent upon context and the grammar is different from one language to another). Hence the computer itself can most efficiently perform the translations. Thus the *Assembler* is a program which reads a source-code file, calculates addresses, and translates mnemonics to true binary codes. The result of the translation is written back to disc as an object-code file.

Since each CPU has its own instruction set and addressing modes, with its own related, unique, mnemonics, then the Assembler is specific to the one CPU.

The simpler Assemblers can only handle a complete program in a single source file, translating it direct to a machine-loadable binary file.

To be practically useful, the Assembler must work with a modular system. Thus the translation is from source-code to object-code format. The object-code file must contain a header with data needed by the linker. Obvious details are a list of all subroutines and data items which will be accessed by this module but which are in another module. Such addresses cannot be complete inside the object-code file since they are not known until linking is complete. Such addresses are marked with a special code in the object code to be corrected later. The second set of information contained in the header is a list of variable names and the locations of routines and variables which may be referred to from another module. In the microcomputer world the object-code file format specified by INTEL is very common.

The simple Assembler is often called an *Absolute Assembler* creating an *absolute-code* file. The one designed for modular programming is called a *Relocatable Assembler*, since it contains the pointers needed to *relocate* the addresses when linking. The object code file is therefore *Relocatable Code*.

It is possible to create code which only uses relative addressing modes and is therefore *position independent* — that is, it does not need relocating when linked. Further, some addresses must be real locations, such as loading interrupt vectors or virtual I/O. These are referred to as *absolute* addresses, and must be declared as such in the source-code files such that the assembler knows not to make them relocatable.

8.3.3　Linkers and Loaders

A *linker* is a system program which creates a loadable machine-code file by combining multiple object-code files. The linker reads the header of each object code file in order to create a complete table of all variable and routine addresses and names. It then creates the one machine-code file by copying the object code for each module and modifying the addresses to suit any previously uncompleted *externals*. It manipulates the relocatable addresses in the object-code files into the one common address space.

The linker may join object files directly specified by the user but it may also include files from a *Library*. The simpler linker will include the whole library file but the better ones will scan the library and include from it only those procedures which have been requested by the other modules, thereby saving space.

The machine-code file produced by the linker will have its own header appended giving information for the loader. It is not the same information contained in an object-code file header.

The *loader* is another program, most often part of the operating system command analyser (see section 8.4.4) which reads the machine-loadable file into memory and transfers control to the newly loaded program. The loader utilises data contained in the machine-code file header to complete the load, and to report errors. Obvious details include the amount of memory required for the code, the requirements for stack space, data arrays, initialisation of data spaces, etc.

In a simple system such as CP/M, all programs must start at a fixed location in RAM (100_h), so that the machine-code file contains absolute addresses. With the segmented architecture of the 8086 CPU, with operating systems like PC DOS and Concurrent DOS, the machine code can be linked to begin at the origin of a segment, the loader initialising the segment register value to suit. On a multi-programming system the machine code must itself be in a relocatable form since there is no knowledge beforehand of which memory sections will be allocated to it. Thus the loader must itself by capable of relocating the machine code, correcting addresses as needed during the loading process. It is thus obvious that the linker must be related to the loader, creating machine-code files to the format required by the loader. A combined linker–loader was occasionally provided but they are more often separate entities.

8.3.4 *High-level Languages, Compilers and Interpreters*

While assembly language is more straightforward to write than binary machine code it is still far from easy. Additionally assembly language is still directly related to a specific machine.

This is a serious handicap precluding widespread use of specific applications programs. Accordingly *high-level languages* have been designed. Such languages are intended to be easy to learn and since they are *machine independent*, programs written in these languages should be capable of implementation on a wide range of machines without significant modification. Individual high-level languages are directed towards specific applications areas. Thus FORTRAN finds wide use in scientific calculations and mathematics, while COBOL is used for business, etc.

A single high-level language statement may be quite complex, for example

$$X = A + B \times SIN(C/D)$$

but easy to comprehend.

When converted to machine code this one source statement will be equivalent to a number of machine-code instructions, including a jump to a subroutine to compute the sine. Note that a programmer can write his own subroutines and enter them with CALL (or equivalent) statements. Compare this with the machine-supplied subroutines such as SIN, the call to which is implied in the high-level language statement.

The support program which converts the high-level source code to machine code is called a *Compiler* and can be likened to a more complex assembler. Unlike assembly language, a high-level language has an international specification and is machine independent. Note however that the compiler itself, since it converts the machine-independent source code into machine-specific object code, must be machine dependent.

Good compilers will support modular development, creating an object-code file in a format compatible with the linker requirements. In this way it is possible to create object-code modules using mixtures of high-level languages and assembler. Some compilers in fact translate to assembly code, which then has to be assembled into object code. Most modern compilers give direct translation.

There are a number of high-level languages which have been developed for specific user types of work. Common languages are:

	Common use
COBOL (*Common Business Orientated Language*)	Commercial DP (data processing)
FORTRAN (*FOR*mula *TRAN*slator)	Scientific
ALGOL (*ALGO*rithmic *L*anguage)	Scientific
PASCAL	General-purpose *procedural* language
BASIC	Interactive scientific
Extended BASIC	Interactive commercial data processing

APL (*A* *P*rogramming *L*anguage)	Interactive with matrix/vector arithmetic — financial modelling
PL/1, conceptually a combination of COBOL and FORTRAN	Scientific and commercial data processing
CORAL	Real-time process control
ADA	Military standard for real-time systems
MODULA-2	An extension of PASCAL with concurrency
C	A system programming language made popular by the operating system UNIX

With most languages the development process requires a number of discrete actions: Edit, Compile, Link, Load, Test/Run. Any failure or modification requires the whole process to be repeated. Therefore a technique was introduced to combine all stages into one package to create an easier-to-understand environment at the expense of efficiency and flexibility. This is the concept of an *Interpeter*. The first interpreters were built around the language BASIC and were used for teaching purposes. The Interpreter is loaded into RAM by the usual means, but it then takes over the role of command analyser, program loader, etc. All programs are written in the high-level BASIC language. The Interpreter loads the ASCII source code and executes it by compiling each statement and executing that, compiling and executing the next, etc. It was also called *incremental compilation*. Now since the active program is still in ASCII form the act of editing, compiling, testing and debugging are encompassed in the one environment. Debugging in particular is powerful since direct reference can be made to variables by their names rather than obscure addresses. The interpreter efficiency has been improved by pre-compiling the true source code into a sequence of *tokens*, simply to shorten the program in RAM and to improve the time taken for the incremental compilation. Nowadays languages other than BASIC are available in interpreted versions, such as the PASCAL p-code system, BOS MICROCOBOL, etc. Conversely, BASIC compilers are also available. One recommended technique is to develop a program using the interpreter and then compile it when completed. This gives the interactive mode which is more efficient during development, *and* the compiled mode which is more efficient at run-time.

8.3.5 Debuggers

A debugger is a program which is used to help fault-find and test a new program. It is a most unusual program in that once loaded it attempts to be transparent to the operating system and is in effect a more versatile command language processor and loader. Once active the Debugger will accept commands to load programs and to execute them. However, it also includes a monitor so that it can control the execution of the program. It can be used to display the contents of memory, to change memory contents, to insert break-points into code to cause a program to execute until it reaches a specific point in the program, to execute each individual instruction and to display the resulting state of the CPU registers, etc. Some debuggers will provide a trivial assembler to help modify code in memory and a disassembler to display memory contents in assembler language mnemonics.

Special debuggers are often provided with high-level languages which make reference to the symbol tables stored on disc to access variables by name.

8.3.6   Utilities

Any system is provided with a wide range of utility programs for general *house-keeping*. The range includes programs to copy files, to back-up whole discs-to-tape or cartridge and to restore them. Programs are provided to display computer status, showing currently active programs, memory utilisation, etc. Statistics may be maintained as to the utilisation of resources by individual users, including security passwords for logging on or for protecting files, etc. The utilities provided often include simple Editors, Assemblers, etc., but these are usually inferior products and the user is required to purchase the better versions.

In systems with a linking capability, a Library-management utility is needed to create and maintain libraries of object code files.

A print spooler is quite common. This allows application programs to direct-print output to a disc file. The spooler queues such output files and prints them in sequence whenever the printer is available. Print spoolers can be very sophisticated, particularly in mainframe systems.

8.4   Functions and Elements of an Operating System

It is possible to write a program which contains all the code required to handle I/O, task scheduling, etc. Except for very small simple examples this is a dangerous practice since there is a distinct lack of structure in the coding. Lack of structure leads to repetition of coding and problems of organisation of sequency, etc. The net effect is code that is difficult, if not impossible, to debug, to maintain and to modify.

Thus an operating system presents to the user programs a logical view of the system rather than a physical one. It provides a basic control mechanism for organising the execution of code modules and by this means enables the resolution of conflicts for resources. As a simple example, if a user program includes code to output characters to a printer, then a second similar program running concurrently will interleave characters making a nonsense of the result. If both programs create printer output by requesting the operating system to perform the I/O, then the Operating System (OS) can buffer character strings and control actual printing without character interleave. In this case the user program need give no consideration to the detail of printer control.

A second need for an Operating System is to provide simpler I/O. The user program simply requests that a character be printed. The actual code for initialising a *Universal Asynchronous Receiver/Transmitter* or *UART*, used for testing status or handling interrupts and loading/unloading, is contained in the OS. Inclusion of such code in the user program would inevitably lead to repetitive coding with resulting waste of time, potential errors (assuming that the OS code is debugged) and incompatibility with other programs. Libraries of standard subroutines for inclusion in user programs would solve some of these problems, but not the resolution of conflicts.

The main functions of any operating system are briefly described below. More detailed information may be found in references such as refs 4.4 and 4.5.

8.4.1 Logical I/O

The user program can request input and output of data by a consistent reference to a logical unit, such as a console, terminal 2, printer, etc. The user need take no account of the physical addressing, control characteristics, etc. of the real device. A more advanced system will allow the user to select one of a number of physical *ports* for his own logical device.

8.4.2 Interrupt Handling

Interrupt handlers must be quick and efficient. They must handle device-dependent characteristics and pass information in a simple fashion to user programs. The information may be data (messages) or a request to start the execution of a user provided processing routine (task initiation).

8.4.3 File Handling

While memory is addressable by the byte, a disc system is only addressable by the sector. Each sector has a unique address comprising a drive number, a track number and a sector number. Actual sector sizes vary, typical values being 128 bytes, 256 bytes, 512 bytes or 1K byte. The user requires to break the physical drive into a number of subdivisions for storing individual programs and data files. Thus it is necessary to allocate a set of sectors to each file. The file then presents the logical view more suited to the user needs. The operating system allocates certain sectors on the disc to storing a directory. This directory contains a block of information for each file which defines the English language name supplied by the user, the file attributes, such as Read–only, Read–write, etc., and a list of which sectors have been allocated and in which order (they need not be sequential or contiguous). The OS will also use the total of all sector allocations to determine which sectors are free for further file allocation. Various directory concepts will be discussed in later examples.

A user program begins using a file by *opening* it, which action causes the directory to be searched and the physical allocation details copied into memory in an array unique to that logical file. This array is commonly called a *File Control Block* (FCB). When a user program requests, say, to read the 50th record in that file, the OS uses the data in the FCB to calculate the physical sector reference and causes that to be read from disc into an area in the user program designated as a file record buffer. A large file may have multiple directory entries, causing occasional re-reading of the FCB.

When a file is deleted the entry in the directory is erased and the allocated sectors are declared as *free* for reallocation by the OS. The actual data sectors are not modified in practice.

8.4.4 User Command Interface

When the OS has been initialised, as described later, it is ready for use. Some means must therefore be automatically provided to allow the user to control the system. Once loaded the OS will also load a utility program, called a *console command analyser* or *command line interpreter* or various other similar names, which requests the user to type commands on his console. Usually a normal VDU which will be used for interacting with applications programs is also part of the console. The console command program writes a prompting message to the user and then waits for a string of characters to be typed which define the action(s) required by the user. The message typed in is stored in a buffer by the *console command program* until a delimiter, usually RETURN, is detected. The message is then analysed and, if the request is legal, actioned. The command program will contain a number of simple utility functions which will be executed with an immediate return to the command program. Examples are, list the directory on the screen, print a file, rename a file and display system status. Quite the most important facility, however, is *the program load*. The name of the file is typed in by the user following which the command program causes the OS to read the directory and to copy the file sector by sector until it has all been transferred to memory. Unlike the simple commands which execute and immediately return to the console for a further command, the program load causes a jump to the first instruction in the program just loaded, thereby transferring control to that program. In many cases, the newly loaded program will over-write the command analysis program. Thus the OS must provide a trap in the keyboard input routines to detect a specific character, often Control C (03 hex) which causes the current program to be abandoned and the Command analyser to be reinstated. This is often called a *warm boot*. If an application program for any reason provides its own keyboard handler (BASIC is a common example), then the application program itself must provide a command for causing the warm boot (typing SYSTEM in MBASIC for example).

A number of utility programs are usually provided with the command analyser which are too big to be embedded. These will not be so big as to over-write the command analyser and will always return immediately to requesting a further command on completion.

The *Peripheral Interchange Program*, PIP or Copy, is a typical example, a utility used to copy files by name.

8.4.5 *Executive*

The core of the operating system is the *Executive*. The Executive is responsible for allocating resources, in particular the CPU, memory and I/O devices. The Executive maintains tables defining the current state of activity and supports queues of requests so that resources can be fairly shared and conflicts resolved without the user program having to contain any specialised code. There are many types of Executive, optimised for specific applications and these give the differing types of OS described in section 8.6. The main elements of the Executive are the *task manager* which maintains dynamic details of the status of every task in the system and the *task scheduler* which allocates resources to individual requesting tasks according to an algorithm which takes account of priority, time and availability of resources.

Further details of the Executive will be expounded in the following descriptions.

8.5   ROM-based Code

All modern computers have some code permanently stored in the computer in read-only memory*. This code is varied, dependent upon the configuration and application.

8.5.1   *Bootstrap*

In a general-purpose system with a disc or discette, new programs or data can be copied into main memory in a relatively short time. However, on power-up the computer's main memory is cleared and there is no OS resident to manage the disc. Thus a *minimum* routine is included in the system stored in ROM. This is called a *bootstrap* program. On power-up (or hardware reset) the CPU forces the program counter to a specific value — for example, 00H on a Z80, FFFF8H on an 8086. The ROM containing the bootstrap program is located such that the reset branches to the first instruction in the routine, thus executing the bootstrap routine. On older 8-bit machines, special hardware techniques were used so that the ROM could occupy the same address space as RAM. The reset selected the ROM and deselected the RAM. The last ROM instruction executed an I/O code to deselect the ROM and select the RAM. This *phantom memory* technique is not needed on 16-bit micros because of the increased address space.

A typical bootstrap program will perform the following:

(a)   Initialise all the standard LSI chips used in the specific machine; for example, set keyboard UART to asynchronous mode, set a standard baud rate, initialise the interrupt and DMA vectors, and initialise the disc controller. On many modern microcomputers the video display system is memory mapped into the main memory rather than an external VDU connected via a UART. Such a sophisticated display may need some initialisation. All I/O ports should be reset.

The whole system need not be initialised by the bootstrap, just enough to run the system load routine. Total initialisation could be completed when the OS is loaded.

(b)   Diagnostic check. This optional feature causes simple tests to be performed on the processor, RAM, ROM and some I/O. If a fault is detected, the boot will be stopped and an error message displayed. The check cannot be too rigorous; for example, RAM test will probably write a pattern through memory and read it back. A full test

---

* For the record, earlier minis used banks of switches for manual loading of initial code on power-up. The floppy disc was actually invented for the initial-program-load (IPL) of the instruction set into an early IBM mainframe.

needs to write patterns to each cell and then check that it has not affected every other location, which could take hours instead of the seconds sensible for a power-on check.

(c) Load the operating system from disc. This cannot use the *logical* features of the OS file system since the OS is not yet loaded. Therefore certain specific physical sectors (say the first two tracks) of a disc are reserved to store the system code. The bootstrap causes the heads to be positioned to read these specific sectors into memory. Thus a special *system disc* must be used which has got a copy of the OS recorded on the reserved tracks. The bootstrap thus causes the OS to be copied into memory. An error check is performed so that, if a non-system disc is incorrectly used, then an error is detected and a message displayed on the console.

On more sophisticated systems the loading process is in two parts. A simplified mini-OS only is stored on the system tracks. After loading into memory this *loader* causes the full OS to be copied from a standard directory file into memory. This has great advantages for generatable OS or for field upgrades, assuming the minimal features of the loader to be adequate and therefore static.

(d) Transfer control to the operating system. As soon as a successful OS load is complete, the bootstrap routine will jump to the first instruction of the command analyser routine in the OS, which will take over user interface to the full OS until a reboot causes the bootstrap to be reactivated.

Note that a full *cold boot* will run the complete bootstrap whereas a *warm boot* will assume that the OS is in memory and transfer control to the command analyser. In some cases the warm boot may have to reload the command analyser.

8.5.2 *Monitor*

A machine-specific monitor routine is sometimes included in ROM. The monitor interacts with the user's keyboard and display to allow a detailed control of the processor. The monitor is a simple and effective debug tool, bigger more sophisticated versions of which may be loaded from disc as debuggers, such as DDT under CP/M. To save on the size of the monitor program, it only accepts cryptic messages and commands. Thus Dxxxx means display the contents of location xxxx. More likely, the contents of a whole block of memory will be displayed to fill the screen. Hexadecimal (two-digit) codes are displayed for each byte. Gxxxx will cause transfer to location xxxx. Other typical commands are used to alter the contents of a location, search for a given pattern, fill a block with a specified character or move a block.

Some method is needed to enter the monitor. One approach is always to cause reset to enter the monitor and include a B command to cause the monitor to jump to the bootstrap code. Another approach is to cause the bootstrap to check a keyboard key before loading the OS. If a key is depressed by the user then the bootstrap transfers to the monitor rather than loading. In this case the more detailed diagnostic tests could be included with the monitor.

8.5.3   *Disc-less Systems*

Special-purpose systems do not necessarily support a VDU or disc. Further on power-up they must immediately execute the specific application program. Thus a traffic-light controller or a pocket-calculator must execute the appropriate program from power-on without any initial dialogue with a user. In these systems, the complete application program must be burnt in ROM, RAM being used only for data, buffering, stacks, etc.

Note that such a system would be impossible to develop *in situ*. All such controllers are developed on disc-based, RAM systems initially, so that debugging, monitors, displays, etc., can be used by the design engineer as described later.

An interesting development of ROM-based systems, which can be viewed as an extension of the pocket-calculator concept, is the personal computers such as the PET, APPLE II, BBC, Sinclair, etc. These machines committed a BASIC interpreter to ROM, which is automatically executed on power-up. The BASIC interpreter itself is dedicated but it includes a command analyser which will allow the user to write and run BASIC programs in RAM. A refinement allows loading and saving of programs and data on to audio cassettes (slowly). A later development allowed a discette to be used in place of the tape for faster saving/recall. This is a most undesirable concept however, which put back the development of micro OS, although in fairness the resulting low cost encouraged the growth of microcomputers.

8.6   Types of Operating System

There are many ways of classifying operating systems. Operating systems for mainframe computers are extremely complex, offering a wider variety of facilities and yet they may well be unsuitable for process control (real-time) applications. Real-time and time-shared operating systems have been developed during the last decade for microcomputers. With the advent of microprocessor-based controllers, there is a great increase in the use of ROM-based executives (no disc support).

8.6.1 ROM-based versus Disc-based

With a disc-based system the OS can be loaded initially and then used with a variety of separately loaded application programs. As such, the OS and application routines are very much separate entities. For ROM-based applications, such as a machine-tool controller, the OS code and application code are linked together, the combined code being burnt into ROM.

Many ROM-based systems are sufficiently simple for the whole code to be written into the application. At the next level of sophistication, a simple Executive is desirable (else the executive functions are being rewritten within the application), which does not need all the features of a full OS. An excellent approach to these systems is typified by Intel's RMX80 and RMX88. Effectively the Executive is a suite of routines maintained in a library on the disc of a full development system. The application program is written as a number of modules which call the procedures provided by the Executive. A linker then creates a single code entity from the user's modules plus executive modules from the library. This single *program* is then burnt into ROM. Note the use of two operating systems: the disc-based one on the development system (to create the program, to link and to maintain the library) and the specialised run-only Executive embedded in the ROM code. The library manager is sophisticated enough to include in the ROM code only those modules of the total executive library used by the specific application. There are some recent examples of run-time Executives being provided in standard ROMs, the user's code being burnt into separate ROMs to save the linking phase.

Subsets of many bigger disc-based OSs are available as ROM-able Code (for example, DEC's RSX-11S which is a subset of RSX-11M), in which case the full disc system could be used to develop the ROM-able routines.

Note that ROM-able code must be re-entrant and pure — that is, it must contain no variable data. Thus, many general operating systems cannot be used as ROM-able subsets since they were not originally designed with these limitations.

The temptation to write executive features into the application code on dedicated microprocessor systems is historically strong. It is fundamentally wrong and should be resisted. Use a standard run-time Executive, many examples of which exist.

8.6.2 Single versus Multi-user

A single-user system has only one command console. Any terminal on a *multi-user system* can be used to issue operating system commands, without reference to or interference with another terminal. One terminal will always be designated as the master console, which will be the only one live during bootstrapping, etc.

A big confusion occurs when a single-user OS is used to run a program which in itself allows multiple terminal access, such as a multi-terminal data entry system. This is not true multi-user since the users cannot individually control their use of the machines. Further confusion exists in cases where the single-program is a time-shared BASIC interpreter which allows individual users to write and run their own BASIC programs. This provides multi-user BASIC but one terminal cannot run a BASIC program while another runs a FORTRAN program say.

In summary, a true multi-user system must support multiple, independent command analysers. The term *multi-programming* is also used for a multi-user system in which each user has individual, unconstrained use of the system.

A common enhancement to the single-user system is to provide a facility for a user to start a program and then to *detach* from it so that it runs in the *background*. The user is then reattached to the command analyser in the *foreground*. Obviously, the background program cannot interact with the users terminal, but there are many uses of this technique such as background program compilation, printer *spooling* and dedicated process control programs which use special I/O devices. The user can stop running the foreground program and reattach to the background program to display messages, etc. Some multi-user operating systems allow each user a foreground and a background. The UNIX OS extends this concept, whereby each user can push (spawn) programs one after another into a queue to be executed in turn in background mode.

8.6.3   *Single* versus *Multi-tasking*

Some programs are sequential (*single-thread*) in nature, while others need to cater for the possibility of parallel processing (*multi-thread*) of events. Parallel processing is also termed *concurrent processing*.

A digital computer is fundamentally a sequential machine so that a single CPU machine can achieve apparent concurrency only by dedicating a percentage of its resources to each of the executing processes. Some mechanism is required to switch the available resources between the parallel processes. If this is done quickly and effectively, then the impression will be created that each of the processes is executing at the same time. There is some natural sharing of resources; for example, one process requests a disc transfer so that another one can use the CPU until the disc transfer is complete. Often, however, a far more complex scheduling program is present, putting demands on the operating system to act as the overall authority. Note that concurrency cannot be achieved at the application program level. Each process should appear to be progressing (albeit more slowly) as though it had sole use of resources.

The above concept could be identified with simple multi-programming, whereby each process is a totally separate program with no interaction. The multi-tasking concept, however, is much more powerful and can cope with the integration of multiple entities into one program, that program having concurrent characteristics. Examples of programs with such features are process control systems in which control loops must run sequentially but alarm monitors, operator interaction, data transmission, etc., must all run *at the same time*. Data communications programs are further examples in which the program must cater for outgoing data, incoming data (which can arrive at any time), operator interaction, buffer control, etc. such as writing to a disc while continuing to accept incoming data. Each entity of the total program is called a *task*. Thus a sequential program is termed *single-tasking* and a concurrent program *multi-tasking*.

There is no rigorous definition of a task. A useful one is that a task is the execution of a process. A task is *not* a piece of code, although it will use a specific piece of code and data during its execution. Many different tasks can actually use the same code. It is possible for a task to be initialised and never executed — for example, the task to cope with an alarm condition must be primed but hopefully will never execute.

Unlike a simpler multi-programming OS, a multi-tasking OS must provide special executive functions to control the integration of tasks. Functions must be provided:

(a) to pass information between tasks,
(b) for one task to start or stop others,
(c) to synchronise concurrent tasks based on time or the detected occurrence of external events.

More details will be given later, but note here that a multi-tasking executive is far more complex than a single-tasking one. Compare the memory requirements of a single-tasking OS like MSDOS or CP/M-86, approximately 20 kilobytes, with the multi-tasking Concurrent DOS or OS/2 which requires 256 kilobytes or so.

8.6.4 *Event-driven* versus *Time-shared*

The simplest method of sharing a CPU among multiple users is to allocate it to one user for a period long enough to execute a few thousand instructions and then to shelve that user and allocate the CPU to the next user for the next *time-slice*. This continues in a *round-robin* fashion. With n users, each user gets $1/n^{th}$ of the CPU power (less an overhead for the Executive's use of the CPU).

While the time-shared concept is generally fast enough to confuse a human user into thinking that he has continuous use of the machine, this will not suffice for so-called *real-time* systems. A real-time system is one in which external events, which can happen at any time beyond the control of the computer, will initiate a processing load. Time-sharing between all external devices will not work because the delay in working round the cycle will be too long. Microsecond response times to external events are often needed in process control. Further, time-sharing does not provide the multi-tasking features required by the real-time or *event-driven* system.

An event-driven system requires a multi-tasking Executive with both hardware and software interrupt handling. The interrupt handlers will detect and identify the external event and then schedule the appropriate processing task for execution. *The interrupt handler should not execute processing code. It should be as short as possible in order to avoid blocking further interrupts.*

While time-sharing is essentially multi-user, single-tasking a good OS will utilise interrupts internally for efficient working. The time-slicer will be more intelligent than to dutifully allocate a whole time-slice to a program which has nothing to do. Thus if a program part way through its time-slice initiates a disc transfer, then the Executive will abort that time-slice immediately, rather than waste the rest of it. The OS will use interrupt and DMA techniques to complete the requested transfer while other programs continue to time-share the CPU, missing out the disc requesting program from the round-robin. When the transfer is complete and the processing can continue, the Executive marks the list of programs so that this program is once again included in the round-robin. Similarly, a program requesting keyboard input will be taken out of the round-robin while the interrupt handlers collect the typed-in character string. It is most important to note that the multi-tasking features are used internally by the time-shared OS; they are not available to user programs. It is exceedingly difficult (and dangerous) to try to use a (good) time-shared system for any real-time work. Time-shared OS like UNIX or RSTS/E are very poor vehicles for, say, data communications in which case an intelligent interface would be needed to provide buffering.

Just as a good time-shared OS must employ multi-tasking concepts, a multi-tasking OS should use some time-sharing. The problem occurs when a high priority task gains use of the CPU and immediately requires it again on completion. Thus a lower priority task waiting to execute could be locked-out. Even a high-priority task should not be allowed to hog the processor, so that a time-out mechanism is employed to force a processor-bound task to deschedule (to be rescheduled later).

In summary, it is not possible to design one OS which is an ideal event-driven *and* time-shared system. There will always be a variety of OS available, one being more suited to a specific application area than the others.

8.7 Basic Structure of an Operating System Executive

The code which constitutes the operating system consists of a number of modules as outlined in figure 8.3.

An OS is usually built in a structured format, a common technique being the *layered* or *onion-skin* approach. Essentially, the user program(s) makes demands to the outer level of the OS which in turn makes demands on more primitive routines at the lower layers. Hardware-dependent routines can be included at the inner primitive level so that the user can have a true logical view of the system. It is possible in this way to support different physical I/O devices by device-dependent inner routines without changing the application-level interface at all. A simple example of this approach is file handling. The user merely makes a request to disc to open a file, the

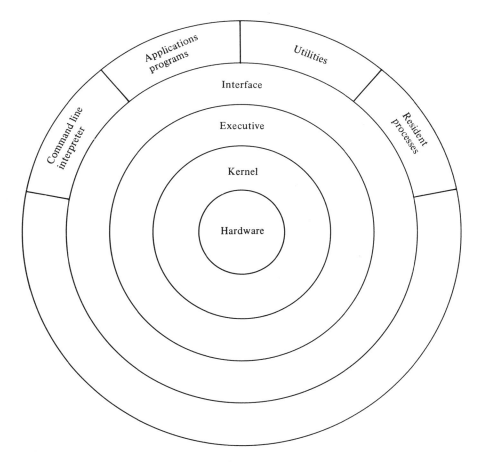

Figure 8.3 Layered architecture of system software

name of which is declared in a string. The outer level of the operating system reads the name and then makes a number of primitive level commands to the inner layer to position the head on the directory track, to read the directory, to search for a name match, to extract the physical disc parameters for the file and to return then into an array (a file control block) which will give the details for later file usage.

The basic core of the OS, the set of essential primitive routines which interact with the hardware dependent code, is sometimes referred to as the *Kernel*.

At the next level comes the heart of the OS, the *Executive* which provides all the run-time management functions, such as task and memory management, etc.

At the level above them exists a whole set of operating system functions which can be used by the application program. The Executive will schedule these to make primitive Kernel calls (sometimes many for each system level call), managed by the Executive and transparent to the user.

Finally, there must be an *Interface* between the user program code and the operating system functions. A simple subroutine call mechanism is not adequate since the user would need to know physical addresses of routines within the Executive, which may change with each system. Further, some executive calls require to transfer messages (a parameter block) with the call — for example, the address of a block of data in memory to be written to disc. Thus a very rigorous protocol must be established which must be used by the application program. This is the reason why, say, a program written in FORTRAN and compiled under DEC's RT11 OS will not run under DEC's RSX-11M OS, despite similar hardware. The calls to the OS compiled by the RT-11 compiler are not the same as those available under RSX–11M. The compiler/operating system is a strongly related pair.

From history, when the phrase *supervisor* was used interchangeably with Executive, the term *Supervisor Call* (SVC) is used to describe the calling mechanism which must be used in the user's program in order to utilise the OS functions. Some are described later.

In summary, the user programs should not make direct use of the system resources. Instead, the user program should issue an appropriate call to the OS. This will then be queued and scheduled for execution, pending the availability of all the resources needed. Only in this way can conflicting requests for services be resolved. *Any program which incorporates code which by-passes the executive and directly uses physical I/O, say, is extremely dangerous and such practices should be avoided.*

8.7.1 *Functions of the Operating System*

(i) Program Management

Once a program has been compiled and the units correctly linked, the executable code is stored on a disc file. Any program which the system may require to run can be *installed*, the OS maintaining a table of all installed tasks with appropriate attributes. An installed task can be loaded on command since all house-keeping chores have already been performed. Most installed tasks are physically stored on disc but there are facilities for keeping special programs, those which may need rapid activation, memory resident, etc., such as emergency shut-down programs in a process control system.

An installed program can be in one of two states: *dormant* or *active*. A dormant task is placed in the active state by a *run* or *execute command*, at which point control is passed from the program manager to the task manager. Note that a RUN command does not give a program CPU control; it adds it to the list of active tasks under direct control of the task manager. A program cannot be run unless it has previously been installed, to ensure completeness of the link, etc.

Program control commands can be issued in two ways:

(a) An operator command from a terminal or batch job control stream.
(b) A supervisor call from another active task.

The operator command facilities can be activated by a supervisor call so that an executing program can request further program control from the operator's console.

The operator command routines may be accessed only by the system console in a single-user system. A multi-user system allows other terminals to be declared as either slave or console mode, when commands can be entered concurrently from multiple terminals. The command routines may be shared or further copies may be attached to console-mode terminals.

(ii) Task Management

The control of CPU time among activated tasks is governed by a set of system routines called the *Task Manager*. These functions are:

Call processing — a means of interpreting a specific request for supervisor services and initiating the appropriate action.

Interrupt handling — routines to service interrupt requests, usually occurring in response to completion of events initiated by supervisor calls. They are typically integral parts of the device handlers.

Clock control — setting of time intervals for time of day or user-requested delays, etc.

Task monitoring — the current status of any task must be dynamically maintained. The task monitor is activated by the call processor and interrupt handlers.

Task scheduler — determines which task is to be given control of the CPU. Task scheduling is fundamentally ordered by one of three functions (or combination thereof): priority, time and *events*. Events are Boolean flags which can be set or cleared by an interrupt handler or another task.

Task dispatching — transferring control to the highest priority task in a state to run.

(iii)　Task Scheduling

Once active, a task can be in one of four states:

> *executing*
> *ready* — waiting to execute but pre-empted by a higher-priority task
> *suspended* — waiting the occurrence of some other event, such as a clock interval, completion of an I/O call or disc transfer
> *interrupted* — transiently suspended while an interrupt service routine executes.

In addition, a task in a suspended state (and a low-priority ready task for that matter) may be swapped out to disc. Certain suspended tasks, however, may not be swapped. This prohibition mostly relates to situations where data is being moved into memory areas in the task body or awaiting completion of a disc transfer.

Supervisor calls are also available for one task to suspend and reactivate another, including timed actions.

(iv)　Queue Management

Calls for supervisor services which cannot be immediately honoured must be queued. The issuing task may need informing of a delayed state and be asked to take alternative action if queues are full.

In some cases, queueing of data messages is also maintained. See the following section on Storage Management.

(v) Storage Management

A certain amount of memory (for example, the resident Executive) has a fixed allocation. Allocation of the rest is under control of the OS.

With an unmapped system, physical control is largely related to supervising the relocatable loader, while with a mapped system the OS must maintain the mapping registers. The OS is also responsible for error handling.

The rest of the memory is allocated between dynamic requirements of the operating system itself and the user program. The physical memory may be divided into independent partitions with either fixed or adjustable limits. Active programs may be constrained to memory or may be swappable (check-pointed).

A particular feature of storage management specific to on-line systems is I/O buffer allocation. In the simplest systems, each device handler has a fixed size buffer per terminal. Data is then passed to the user program. Certain systems allow some data transfers to take place directly to the user space. Such modules as relative-record file handling require a buffer to hold a complete disc block of data so that multiple records in the user space can possibly come from the same buffer. Similarly *write-a-record* implies reading a complete block, modifying the block in its buffer and rewriting.

The support of dynamic I/O buffers, allocated from a pool merely by updating pointers, can greatly reduce the total memory requirements for buffers. This is less applicable to disc transfers than terminals since buffers are allocated per open file (not physical disc) and records can be updated in buffers rather than reading the disc for each READ or WRITE.

(vi) Device-independent I/O

The OS maintains a *Peripheral Device Table* for each physical terminal which defines the status, points to the device service routines and provides transient data work areas. At the same time, the OS maintains a set of user *Logical Device Tables* so that the user task refers to I/O devices as logical unit or channel numbers which are mapped to the requested terminals. A different physical terminal can thus be allocated to a program by modifying the logical device tables without modifying the user's code.

If the interface between logical and physical devices is standard, device differences being catered for in the device handler, then device independence is further enhanced.

A further variant is to allow the file handling routines access to certain device handlers. Thus, print data can be transferred to a logical sequential file channel which can be allocated when the file is opened to a printer or to a disc file for spooling.

8.7.2 *Some Typical User-accessible Functions*

The range of Supervisor Calls (SVC) available to the application programmer can be split into a number of categories, as follows.

(i) *Task control functions*

These functions enable an executing task to interact with other tasks. They also enable a programmer to build a multi-tasking application, using the OS as a control mechanism. Typical SVCs are:

- Initialise and terminate a task.
- Task execution control — activate another (possibly time-related) task, suspend pending I/O or time period completion, abort or cancel current task(s), exit; orderly completion of program.
- Enqueue and Dequeue: a common method of intertask communication and synchronisation. Enqueue adds a message (containing task management information and data) to a system maintained queue. Dequeue takes the message from the top of the queue and actions it. If no message exists, it waits until one is enqueued and actions that immediately. This technique is very powerful in data communications systems.
- Get parameters: return current status of other tasks, I/O devices, flags, etc.
- Change priority level of another task; this may also include control of time-out override.

(ii) *Service functions*

In some operating systems a number of commonly used operations are provided as SVCs. On microcomputers these are more commonly written into the application programs causing inconsistencies between compilers.

- Date: functions to set the date and return the date. Sometimes coded as binary number (elapsed days) or as multi-byte character string of ASCII characters in a printable format.
- Time of day: again often in ASCII-coded format.
- Real time: typically wait for a specified number of clock *ticks* (elapse) or until a specific time (delay or until).

All these functions assume an interrupt-driven system clock to update the time/date data.

- Format translation, for example
    Binary word to ASCII character string
    ASCII string to binary
  (Support for various binary formats, such as 16-bit integer, BCD and floating point, and various character formats such as decimal, mantissa and exponent, hexadecimal.)

(iii) *Memory management functions*

In a simple single-user system, a program is simply loaded into memory at a fixed start address. The only management function required is to check that sufficient real memory exists. In a multi-programming system the memory could be split into fixed size partitions, but this is inefficient. Thus a set of SVCs are needed to allocate memory dynamically as requested. This technique is also used in multi-tasking systems for data buffer and dynamic loading of code (overlays).

Some SVCs encountered are:

- Get block of memory. The executive will allocate a block of spare memory returning the size and start address to the calling task.
- Free block of memory.
  In a variant on the above the executive reserves a block of memory (a pool) from which the users can request fixed-length *buffers*.
- Access system common memory.
- Load a program from disc.
- Load an overlay.

(iv) *Device I/O functions*

In simpler systems devices are specifically accessed:

- Read keyboard status — returns a byte indicating whether or not a character has been keyed in.
- Read keyboard — returns a keyboard character. There are many variants on the theme:
  (a) Wait until a character exists before returning or immediate return with a character or flag to indicate no character.
  (b) Translated or direct keyboard I/O. Either return character after mapping by the keyboard handler (which will strip and action certain characters such as control C) or return the 8-bit code unmapped as generated by the keyboard. A good keyboard handler is interrupt driven, placing all characters in a *type-ahead* buffer. The above functions will then actually read from the buffer rather than the keyboard hardware.
- Output character to console display. A status function is also required to ensure that the output hardware is ready to accept another character or not.
- Input and output characters to other specific devices, such as printer or auxiliary port.
- Input and output character string. The length and start address of the array to be transferred must be declared.

(v) *File handling functions*

File handling functions can be considered at two levels, the basic level and a higher level which gives the user extended methods of access to information within the file. Basic level functions include:

- Search the directory for the existence of a file.
- Create a file: adds name, etc. to the directory.
- Delete a file: removes all references from the directory.
- Maintain access privileges: establish file as read/write, read only, etc.
- Open a file: read directory data into a file control block stored in memory. This is used to map logical file transfer requests into physical track/sector data, transparent to the user.
- Close a file: purge the FCB and copy any buffers or other resident memory data to the disc. Exiting a program without closing all opened files can cause errors.
- Rewind: position the pointer to the beginning of the file. Normally when a file is opened the pointer is set to point to the next free space beyond the end of the current stored data.
- Read record: copy the current record from the file into a specified area of memory and increment the file pointer. The OS will use a specific record size normally equal to one physical sector for simplicity.
- Write a record: copy a record from a specified memory area into the current record space in the file. Sometimes an optional read-after-write error check is performed.

The above basic level file functions can be enhanced by more user-related file handlers.

- Read and write random record. Instead of the sequential access to the current record the call can specify the record number within the file to be accessed.

Far more sophisticated file handlers are available on bigger systems.

- Different sized user and physical records. The user declares the record size and the record number. The file handler then computes which physical record to access, transferring between a full-record sized memory buffer and the disc. A transfer (or partial transfer) is then made between the buffer and the user areas in memory. This is shown in figure 8.4. User records bigger than the physical record will require multiple disc transfers. Writes of user records smaller than the physical unit will require the OS to read the physical record into a buffer, update part of the buffer and then write it back in total.
- Keyed access files (commonly called, after the IBM terminology, an ISAM — indexed sequential access method — although

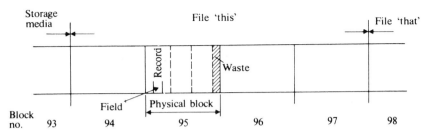

Figure 8.4 File structure

various techniques are employed). In a keyed file a record is identified by a key not a relative record number. An index file is maintained to match the key field (a character string) with the relative record at which the data is stored. The relative record is then accessed conventionally. A key-indexed access can cause 5 or 6 disc accesses in practice before actually accessing the data record proper. Far more complex data management systems allow for variable-length records, multiple keys and full *data base management*. Such software systems are more normally implemented as separate sub-systems, effectively between the user and the OS, than as part of the OS.

Cache techniques are often employed to speed up file handling, maintaining multiple buffers in RAM in the expectation that many following requests will need records just accessed, in which case the buffered data can be used without re-accessing the disc. Writes held in RAM buffers must be periodically forced to write to disc as a precaution against power failure.

(vi) *Logical I/O concepts*

VDUs, printers, disc files, etc. were treated in (iv) and (v) as special, separate devices with their own set of SVCs. A far more flexible approach is to aim for a device-independent concept when all devices are treated as files. An I/O device is allocated a *logical unit number* (LUNO) by an SVC and the standard I/O functions are used to access the logical device. It is the responsibility of the OS when allocating LUNOs to attach the I/O to the appropriate physically dependent I/O handler. Obviously the programmer must use some common sense in using this concept; for example, reading a printer, random record read from a keyboard are nonsense, but the flexibility achieved is most desirable. As an example, if a program calls a printer which is currently in use by another program, then the OS can simply open a sequential disc file, to be printed later, without any change to the user program.

8.7.3   Some Methods of Making SVCs

A supervisor call (SVC) is a mechanism by which a user program can request the execution of a block of code which must be included in the user's program. When executed, the user program will terminate operation and control will be passed to the Executive. Most often, on completion of the execution of the SVC the Executive will schedule a return to the calling program, which will then continue to execute the next instruction after the SVC. In one sense the execution of the code until an SVC occurs can be considered as a separate task (one definition encountered of a task is an execution which ends in an SVC). Our definition of a task, however, does not expect an immediate return to the sequential program.

In a sense, an SVC can be likened to a CALL statement in a FORTRAN program or a PROCEDURE call in Pascal. It must provide the following protocol:

(a)   A method for stating which of the many SVCs is required.
(b)   A method for passing parameters for the specific SVC to the Executive.
(c)   A mechanism for returning control to the next instruction in sequence.
(d)   A method for passing parameters back to the user program.
(e)   A special variation on (d) — an error report parameter so that the user program can take special action on unsatisfied calls, such as failure to open a non-existent file.

Note that while every implementation of a given operating system must be the same, no two operating systems will provide the same range of functions. Even the common ones such as get-keyboard-character will have a different protocol. Thus, while a FORTRAN program may be portable, the binary code is not. The program must be compiled for one OS and recompiled appropriately before the new binary code can be run on another OS. Most of the code from the two compilers will be similar, but the SVCs will not be identical.

Each operating system has declared a set of functions, as discussed in the previous section. Each function is identified by a unique code, normally using an 8-bit code giving up to 256 basic functions.

Unlike a subroutine call within a program, an SVC cannot pass direct to the Executive code — the Executive will schedule the processing rather than directly execute it. Thus there must be a common part of the Executive dedicated to call processing; the SVC code thus simply transfers control to the call processor. In the simple systems, like CP/M, this is just a subroutine call to a specific location in memory, dedicated to routeing to the call processor. On modern systems the preferred method is to execute a *software-interrupt*, an instruction which causes the CPU to respond as though to an external interrupt and thus invoke all the vectoring, etc., which makes such a transfer of context efficient.

There are two basic methods of passing parameters to the call processor:

(a) Use the CPU registers as direct parameters or as an address pointer to an array of parameters for those SVCs which require more data than there are registers.
(b) Establish an SVC parameter block in the user program and pass the start address to the call processor in CPU registers.

Some older systems have actually used the addresses immediately following the SVC jump instruction as the parameter block, but this is not as effective.

Case (a) is the simpler, but (b) is more powerful and makes for easier handling of queued requests in multi-tasking systems. Note that with memory-managed or segmented hardware, the executive and user program will be in different segments. Thus the executive must store the true physical address of the SVC parameter block.

Using either a subroutine call or an interrupt to enter the SVC processor, the return mechanism back to the user is straightforward. Similarly, either CPU registers or the SVC parameter block can be used to return information. Note that the user program must ensure that the array used for returned parameters is big enough. The error-code is usually coded into a single byte and returned in a register. Executive functions when executed can destroy register contents. Check the manuals carefully.

8.8 Overview of Microcomputer Operating Systems

Operating systems are available for a wide range of applications. No one operating system is even vaguely suited to all applications. A more sophisticated OS obviously needs more memory and will consume a higher percentage of CPU power. Thus, for instance, while a multi-user OS could be designed for an 8-bit processor, it is a rather pointless product since there is insufficient power to give any service to the users. Equally obviously, an extremely versatile OS will not be as efficient for a given application as an OS designed specifically for that task.

While operating systems cannot be accurately placed in categories, the following groupings may be helpful.

(i) *Single-user, single tasking*
Such operating systems do not have any control mechanisms. Apart from possible type-ahead buffering, the OS is simply a fixed suite of subroutines

which are called in-line by the application programs. The SVC is executed directly and once complete returns to the user program. If for any reason the SVC cannot finish (a common example is typing to a printer which is set in the *hold* mode) then the system locks-up. These systems, however, have the splendid virtues of being simple and therefore small. They are well suited to 8-bit micros and simpler 16-bit personal computers.

CP/M, the Control Program/Monitor of Digital Research Inc., is the common example, based on 8080 code and therefore Z80 machines as well. The microprocessor manufacturers also produced their own OS for their development systems (MDS) notably ISIS by Intel and RIO by Zilog. FLEX was a product with similar objectives to CP/M, based on the 6800 processor.

When discs were added to earlier ROM-based personal computers (for example, Tandy TRS-80, Commodore PET and APPLE II), an extended set of commands was added to access the disc, giving private and very strange disc systems, such as the BASIC interpreter controlling the Disc Operating System (DOS). No properly organised OS became popular for the 6502 processor.

Another OS, popular with universities and colleges, was the UCSD system. Designed by the University of California at San Diego, UCSD was used to support Pascal (using a p-code). It is now commercially controlled by Softech. Other languages beside Pascal are now offered and also *native-code* speed-ups since interpreted p-code is slow. The important aspect of UCSD is that the p-code concept makes portability less of a problem and the OS is available on a wide range of processors such as Z80, 8086, PDP-11, etc. Applications developed on one system will then run on another (unless native-code has been used).

With the introduction of the 8086 processor, a version of CP/M called CP/M-86 was released. It was actually preceded by Seattle Computer Products DOS-86. DOS-86 has now become the Microsoft MS-DOS. CP/M-86 and MS-DOS are very similar in concept but incompatible at SVC and disc formatting. The most important implementation of MS-DOS is the IBM Personal Computer version, called PC-DOS. The IBM BIOS (Basic Input/Output System, the hardware-dependent part) contains a number of functions which are accessible by the user (an extended set of SVCs in effect) so that a program which runs under PC-DOS will not necessarily run under another MS-DOS implementation.

(ii) *Single-user, multi-tasking*
Single user, multi-tasking OS grew out of the earlier 16-bit minicomputer field. They were major contributors to the development of operating systems. They were designed specifically for real-time process control for machines which could be configured with a wide variety of I/O devices. While most applications involved supporting interrupt-driven I/O (relay

closures, A/D and D/A converters, etc.), support for discs was built into these systems so that they could be used for simple program development as well, although not concurrently. Later versions introduced a two-partition concept, giving the user a foreground and a background region (much better when the memory-managed hardware became common) which then allowed concurrent operation of two programs. Note that one of the programs would in itself possibly be a complex multi-tasking program.

These OS were also very flexible because of the variety in I/O support needed, so that Sysgen procedures allowed user-select combinations of I/O drivers to be configured for a given application.

All minicomputers featured such an OS, the commonest examples being DEC's RT-11 and Data General's RDOS. RT-11 is still very important in the microcomputer field since DEC's LSI versions of the PDP-11 mini abound, in many cases using RT-11.

For general 16-bit microprocessors, the only product currently available in this category is CONCURRENT DOS (C/DOS). It is available at present only for the 8086 family. C/DOS must not be confused with the infinitely more trivial CP/M or MS-DOS. C/DOS is probably the first major OS to be developed specifically for a microprocessor. The SVC set contains both the CP/M-86 and PC-DOS sets (almost but not completely compatible) plus the extended calls for the more sophisticated features. The execution of the SVC by C/DOS is of course totally different from that of CP/M-86, CPM-86 being a direct-execution C/DOS using a task manager, etc. The design objectives of C/DOS are quite different to, say, RT-11. C/DOS is intended as a multi-tasking workstation operating system, taking full advantage of the modern trend for memory-mapped video systems. Being multi-tasking it will support concurrent user programs and communications programs. As such it appears an ideal vehicle for workstations on local area networks (LANs). Single-tasking operating systems like PC-DOS are being used as network workstation operating systems, but it would appear a very dangerous concept. It is probable that C/DOS can be satisfactorily used as a real-time process control OS, particularly the 286 processor version.

Concurrent DOS features multiple virtual programs for the one user, which is a far superior concept, particularly for workstations, than the foreground/background concept.

(iii) *Multi-programming (User), time-shared*
Operating systems which allow multiple terminals to be concurrently used, each running a simple single threaded program, are common for minicomputers and business machines. The share of performance available to each user is adequate for many applications, giving a cost-effective use of shared hardware. Often such systems are programmable only in high-level langu-

ages. Direct use of an assembler would allow the user to create programs which interfere with other users' programs. Some systems allow only one language and in so doing achieve higher performances at the expense of flexibility.

One some systems, each user is considered totally separate, with its own program, own data and own files. For business systems, however, it is essential that each user can access the same files concurrently. Special features of the file system are then required to allow user programs to control locking of access to files and of records within the same file.

The leading time-shared minicomputer OS is DEC's RSTS/E (Resource Sharing Time Sharing/Extended). Fundamentally, a time-shared BASIC system, RSTS now supports mixed languages. Other manufacturers supply their own, machine-dependent, business computer OS — for example, SSP for the IBM S/36.

The BOS operating system is a good example of a system dedicated to time-shared business applications. It is programmed exclusively in a languaged called MicroCOBOL. The importance of BOS is that it is designed to be easy to port and therefore is available on virtually any microcomputer or minicomputer, in stark contrast to RSTS or SSP.

MP/M and OASIS were early attempts to mount a general purpose multi-user OS on 8-bit micros. Both were unsuccessful for obvious reasons of limited address space and performance. Digital Research produced a 16-bit version of MP/M which is now superseded by multi-user Concurrent DOS.

It is an undeniable fact that most micro software has been developed for the 6502, 8080/Z80 or 8086 family. To find software for the newer microprocessors, particularly the M68000, within reasonable time scales a portable system was the only answer. The obvious choice settled on UNIX (ref. 8.6). UNIX was developed by Bell Labs on PDP-11s as a program development system. An important feature of UNIX, which gives the portability, is the extensive use of a language called 'C', specifically designed for producing systems programs, such as UNIX itself. Note, unlike BASIC and FORTRAN, C was not developed as an end-user programming tool so that the more normal languages must also be supported by UNIX. Unlike DEC's own PDP-11 operating systems, RSTS/E, RT-11 or RSX-11M, UNIX was devised to support specialist computer program development. It is a time-sharing system with no features for real-time or shared files, etc. As such, excellent utilities for program editing and maintenance were standard features.

Three major goals of UNIX are:

(a)   Efficient utilisation of disc storage.
(b)   Ability to accept *streams* of work for execution as submitted by the user while the user can continue with something else at the terminal.

(c)   An extensive *job-control language* which allows the programmer to specify whole strings of functions and operations to be performed in sequence simply by typing a command string.

Bearing in mind that in a program development system most files are program source and object code, with few data files, (a) is achieved by breaking the directory into a *tree* structure. Physical disc space is allocated in 1-sector increments (far bigger increments are common in most operating systems). For a simple directory structure a large file would require a lot of entries in the directory, a problem avoided by the *tree*. When the file grows in size requiring above a certain number of directory entries, the directory itself is split, retaining two pointers to two further sets of directory pointers. Whenever one of the second level set gets to the maximum size, it too is split. Thus the biggest wasted physical space is one sector less one byte, giving a ratio higher than 95 per cent of physical capacity allocated to actual user data compared with around 70 per cent for more standard directories.

(b) is achieved by a command queuing mechanism in UNIX called a PIPE. UNIX takes work commands and data from the pipe and executes the programs in the background. UNIX accepts a work load much bigger than the physical memory available which it achieves by *swapping* programs which are awaiting other resources in and out of a special swapping area of disc, quite transparent to the user. Further, to minimise the memory requirements, UNIX swaps less frequently used sections of its own code and utilities. Thus, during execution of a program it may be moved about in physical memory. As a result a memory management hardware system and a fast (Winchester) disc are mandatory requirements for UNIX, not desirable features

(c) is achieved by a command language processing system called a *Shell*. The UNIX Shell recognises a sophisticated range of commands and constructions but in a cryptic language suited only to specialist programmers and regular users.

As a very superior multi-user program development system, UNIX is extremely successful. It is however being used for other applications for which it is not suited, such as real-time and commercial data processing/office automation, with serious problems. Extended versions of UNIX, such as Microsoft's XENIX, Berkeley UNIX and the newer releases from Bell, are introducing methods of coping with large files (too many branches in the directory tree with megabyte data files), shared files with record locking and a user interface suited to non-computer professionals. It is disturbing to see versions of UNIX and so-called UNIX-like systems appearing without memory management hardware.

UNIX is not in practice as portable as BOS, and is in fact inferior as a time-shared business OS.

(iv) *Multi-user, multi-tasking*

There are today no generally available, sophisticated, multi-user, micro-computer real-time systems. In the mini-computer field most manufacturers offer such systems, DEC's RSX-11M being the most common. An 8-bit micro was never powerful enough to support such an OS, but 16-bit micros may be. Probably because of lower costs, multiple microcomputers have tended to replace larger single CPU systems. Intel, however, have attempted a full-blown real-time OS called RMX-86, in the main available on their own MDS units. It has not been particularly successful to date. It is more likely that specialist manufacturers, albeit using standard microprocessors, will produce their own OS to cope for multi-processor systems, rather than follow the microcomputer route. C/DOS-286 has now been adopted by IBM for this task.

(v) *ROM-based Executives*

Any program for a real-time system which is more than trivial should be built around an Executive. In this way, programs can be developed as modules (on a separate, more powerful machine with peripherals suited to development, such as VDU, discs, printer). Such a run-time Executive needs to be contained in a library so that the appropriate modules can be linked with the user-created code modules. Both the Executive modules and the user code modules must be written in pure code if they are to be burnt into ROM for the final product. In effect this means that instructions (ROM) and data (RAM) must be separated. Further, the tools for developing such a system must allow the programmer to allocate suitable addresses, for ROM and RAM; normally the OS and compilers control real address allocations in memory.

The cut-down version of RSX-11 is an early example. Other special-purpose minicomputer products included MODCOMPS MAXCOM, a run-time executive designed for data communications applications. On the micro front, INTEL introduced iRMX-80 and later iRMX-88, both with commercial constraints related to use on INTEL-manufactured products. More generally available examples are REX-80, MTOS-86 and MTOS-68, AMX and VRTX. Such Executives are often supplied in a ROM as well as in a library.

8.9 Summary and Conclusions

This chapter has in no way explained the details of any software module, rather it has explained the objectives of the commonly encountered routines. The accent has been solely on *what* and not on *how*. With this overview in mind, the interested student can now begin to study the more detailed textbooks available, a representative list of which follows this section.

System software has been viewed around the operating system, the software unit intended to ease the running of the system by handling regularly used functions. Thus I/O drivers, maths packages, etc., need only be linked into from the user's programs. The support programs or utilities used by the operating system have been briefly explained.

The availability of various high-level languages has been pointed out and the user must be aware that certain languages are suited to specific problems.

References

8.1 Goldschlager, L. and Lister, A., *Computer Science, A Modern Introduction*, Prentice-Hall, London, 1982.

8.2 Kernighan, B. W. and Plauger, P. L., *Software Tools*, Addison-Wesley, Reading, Massachusetts, 1976.

8.3 Barron, D. W., *Assemblers and Loaders*, MacDonald-Elsevier, London, 1979.

8.4 Lister, A. M., *Fundamentals of Operating Systems*, 3rd edn, Macmillan, London, 1984.

8.5 Dield, H. M., *An Introduction to Operating Systems*, Addison-Wesley, Reading, Massachusetts, 1983.

8.6 Brown, P., *Starting with UNIX*, Addison-Wesley, London, 1984.

9 Microprocessor-based Systems

Objectives

This chapter deals with microprocessor-based systems which form part of the spectrum of computing power which begins with a simple piece of hardwired logic and ends with a large multi-programming, time-sharing machine. The distinction is drawn between four types of system.

The *first system* comprises the ever popular *pocket calculator* with its fixed repertoire of operations. Such a device cannot be considered as a computer or even a microcomputer but nevertheless it has its place in the spectrum of computing power. While its mode of action is fixed it is very substantially cheaper and more versatile than a one-off piece of hardwired logic. Nevertheless it is instructive to see its architectural resemblance to such hardwired logic. Historically, one can trace the evolution of the pocket calculator from the simple calculators of Pascal, Leibnitz and Odhner and the fixed-program Difference Engine of Babbage. All these machines share the inability to handle a range of general-purpose programs and made no provision for conditional instructions. As a result they cannot be classed as computers.

The *second type* of system includes the expanding field of *small data processing systems* used by small-scale business enterprises and the home-computer enthusiast. Here the user is interested primarily in the overall system: its ease of use, the range of software provided and the possibility of writing further software in a high-level language or possibly at assembler level. Overall architecture and the details of the hardware are very much secondary considerations.

In the *third case*, the microprocessor-based system typically acts as the *controller* for a *piece of industrial* or domestic *equipment*. Production will be on a substantial scale with all the systems either identical or very similar. Here the emphasis is on an economic system design for a specific purpose. The program is likely to be fixed and will be stored in a non-volatile ROM. Any changes to the program will be infrequent. Sometimes no change whatever is envisaged. The design team will use expensive development aids. Total *design and manufacturing costs* will be *high*. However, *unit costs* will be *low*. The end user is unlikely to wish to modify the system other than in a limited way.

In the *fourth case*, the *microprocessor-based system* is designed for a *specific application* and at most may be replicated only to a very limited extent. A typical example would be a special industrial application or a final-year student project. Here the design team may constitute a single individual responsible for choice of the best combination of hardware elements and appropriate software development to implement a working system. While hardware costs may be comparatively low, system design and test, particularly as to software, are likely to be expensive in human effort.

Each of the four situations will be examined in turn. Particular emphasis will be devoted to consideration of the architecture of microprocessors and the wide variety of support chips. Attention will also be directed to an appreciation of various hardware and software development aids and test facilities.

The material in this chapter extends that of earlier chapters. It serves to emphasise that mini and microcomputer systems are not essentially different. Design techniques and hardware components are similar, though emphasis may differ as a result of diversity in applications.

Chapter 10 returns to the subject of microprocessors and microcomputers with a more detailed consideration of such systems.

9.1 Introduction

It has been seen in earlier chapters that the microprocessor is an LSI chip capable of performing basic arithmetic operations under program control. In this it can be viewed as a self-contained central processor unit (CPU) which might form the centre of a conventional minicomputer. Indeed the microprocessor plays just such a role in some minicomputer systems. However, as a result of its cheapness and the comparative ease with which it may be interfaced to other compatible semiconductor devices, primarily memory elements, the microprocessor forms the heart of a wide variety of microprocessor-based systems some of which differ significantly in emphasis from conventional minicomputer systems while largely sharing the same technology. Four significantly different roles may be seen for the microprocessor-based system. These are briefly discussed below to serve as an introduction to the more specific material of this chapter.

9.1.1 The Pocket Calculator

Recent years have seen an extraordinary growth in the popularity and use of the pocket calculator in its many forms. The sheer volume of the sales of such devices has done much to assist the parallel development in the microprocessor field since the same semiconductor technology is common to both and also equally importantly to semiconductor memory. As a result, in each case costs have fallen while the quality and versatility of the product has been enhanced.

It will be appreciated that calculators, although capable of storing and processing digital information, are limited in both the number and types of operation they perform. This is because their repertoire is fixed at the design stage and for the most part remains unalterable. The analogy with the Difference Engine of Charles Babbage may be drawn. In this machine, mathematical calculations were to be carried out, but only in a limited way. No provision was made for a general-purpose approach with a program of instructions. In contrast, the microcomputer systems based on the microprocessor to be discussed in later sections may be configured in one of a variety of ways depending on the particular application, and in addition are also programmable at will by the user. In this they resemble the versatility of the programmable Analytical Engine. In the development of microprocessor-based systems a wide variety of aids, both software and hardware, may be employed to lighten the task of both the system designer and the programmer (sometimes one and the same person) and provide a high degree of confidence in the overall system even before physical implementation is begun. These development aids will be considered later.

9.1.2 *The Microcomputer as a Data Processing Machine*

Earlier chapters have discussed the architecture of minicomputer systems. The vital role of the CPU as the arithmetic and logic unit has been stressed. The use of a microprocessor as the arithmetic and logic unit at the centre of a small computer system justifies the use of the title 'microcomputer' to describe the system. In outward appearance the system is indistinguishable from a small minicomputer system. The overall architecture is similar. The system may be used for commercial and scientific work as with the minicomputer system. In effect, the distinction between mini and micro systems is concerned with cost and the range of peripherals which may be attached to the system. The micro system constitutes the lower end of the range of computing power. However, the distinction is artificial and increasingly blurred. For example, the *single-board* minicomputer with all the essential features situated on a single printed-circuit board has been available for some years. For such a machine a microprocessor constitutes the CPU. Three classes of user may be identified for the microcomputer system used in data processing. Again the distinctions are increasingly blurred. The first is the business user. Here the emphasis is on the use of a system purchased as a complete package at a cost of up to say £10K. The microcomputer itself will be powerful and a relatively cheap element in the total system cost. Access will be via keyboard and VDU supplemented with data typically stored on floppy disc. Output will be at the VDU screen with hard-copy produced using a relatively expensive printer. A suite of software applications programs slanted towards the particular business use will be available. For widespread uses such as forward-planning involving such items as cash-flow projections, the programs should be cheap. For limited applications, such as simulation packages relating to a very narrow sector of business, the packages will be expensive representing development overheads spread over a narrow base. As confidence in the use of the system increases, further applications for the machine will arise. As a result the system may be expanded. Typical additions may comprise a Winchester disc system for increased storage (see chapter 7, section 7.6.2) and a high-quality printer. The final system may be elaborate and will justify the title *minicomputer business-system*. The users will not be interested in hardware detail though they may possibly write applications software, typically at high level, as confidence grows. The labour-intensive nature of such software development and the need for full documentation are likely to become apparent only with experience. The process is likely to be salutary.

A second important application is in *word processing*. Here the micro-computer system is used for text preparation. Text is typed using a conventional keyboard with the copy appearing on a monitor screen and stored on floppy disc. *Hard-copy* of the text is produced using a printer. Editing of the text is facilitated since corrections made on the hard-copy are carried out using keyboard and screen without the need for retyping the complete text to produce a perfect final result. The more elaborate word processors have a variety of powerful editing facilities including programs to check spelling.

A further application relates to the home-computer enthusiast who is able to use a small microcomputer system for data capture, editing and retrieval in connection with such tasks as the cataloguing of music discs and tapes, telephone numbers, address lists and the like. It must be emphasised that the home-computer enthusiast may underestimate the size of the initial task of keying-in the initial database. In all but trivial applications the task is likely to prove daunting.

9.1.3 *Microprocessor-based Dedicated Systems of Wide Application*

Microprocessors are very widely used in industrial or domestic situations to carry out dedicated tasks often with a control flavour. Thus they may be employed to control central heating plant in industry or the home, or to manage the operating of washing machines or video tape-recorders and the like. Further applications relate to the automobile industry where microprocessors monitor engine performance or via speech synthesisers request drivers to 'fasten your seat belt', warn of an insecure door, adverse weather conditions or low fuel level.

In these applications, the end user is not interested in system architecture or programming. Rather the emphasis is on low cost and the expectation of reliability.

The manufacturer on the other hand is faced with the problem of overall system design against the need for reliability and cheapness. Sophisticated and expensive hardware design tools are justified if production is large. Programs are very specific to individual applications. Once prepared they may never be changed. The programs will be entered into non-volatile ROM. Alternatively, the programs may be modified only rarely — typically on an up-grade of the microprocessor-based control device. Thus, for example, the vocabulary of a speech-based warning system for a car may be extended as additional transducers are added to the repertoire of hazard warnings provided.

In these circumstances, the stored program requires modification on an occasional basis. Various types of reprogrammable ROM are candidates for this role (see chapter 7).

9.1.4 *Microprocessor-based Dedicated Systems of Narrow Application*

In contrast to the situation outlined in the previous section, microprocessor-based systems are used also for dedicated applications where only a single or a very limited number of systems is required. This might be the case for an industrial application. Alternatively, the system might be used to monitor equipment in an on-line research laboratory. Again a prototype system might be used in a medical application.

The situation as regards hardware and software development effort is likely to be similar to that for the mass-produced case but in the present situation costs apply to the single system or are shared by only a few systems. As a result, unit costs are likely to be high. In these circumstances there will be no real incentive to cut hardware costs to the absolute minimum. Rather, attention will be directed to the reduction of software-costs. As a result, the employment of a single-board microcomputer system is likely to be useful in many cases even if certain semiconductor chips from the set provided are grossly under-utilised or indeed are not used at all. With the increase in power and fall in price, the general-purpose micro-computers such as BBC Micro, IBM PC, etc., are increasingly being used in this type of application.

9.2 LSI Technology

Before considering the ways in which the four classes of microprocessor systems discussed above are implemented, it is necessary to look briefly at large-scale integrated circuit technology (LSI) and in particular at features of microprocessor architecture. In addition, attention must be directed towards relevant software and hardware development aids and at emula-tion and simulation techniques used to ensure successful design.

First consider LSI technology. It has been mentioned earlier in this book that it is possible to manufacture single integrated circuit chips incorporat-ing thousands of transistors. Such chips involve LSI, large-scale integra-tion, technology. Each such circuit is very complex. The cost of making the masks and tooling up to make the first unit is very expensive indeed. Once in production, however, the cost of each individual unit is low. Thus it is only practical to produce low-cost LSI circuits when the design is fixed and the number of units required is well over the tens of thousands. In fact, the actual end-user cost of an LSI component is more related to the total production demand than to circuit complexity.

Random-access memory chips were early examples of LSI technology with high demand and relatively simple internal circuitry since each storage cell was similar. The pocket-calculator chip, again with vast potential demand, followed. Such a chip is a much more complex circuit than a memory chip. Its successful mass manufacture established the technology to produce ever more sophisticated units, leading to the complete single-chip microcomputer. However, the most important outgrowth from the calculator to date is the microprocessor which may be regarded as a CPU fabricated on a single chip. This chip, together with other special purpose LSI chips (for example, memory, input and output devices, decoders, etc.) can be used to build systems ranging from dedicated controllers which replace hardwired units to small general-purpose computers. The architecture of both simple calculators and microprocessors will be described in general terms in the following sections to give the reader some feel for the rapidly changing range of available units. Microprocessor architecture will receive further consideration in chapter 10.

Most LSI components are currently fabricated in metal–oxide–silicon(MOS) technology: PMOS for the older units, NMOS for performance and CMOS for low power consumption (see chapter 7, section 7.5). The current trend is towards CMOS for the most part. Silicon-on-Sapphire (SOS), Integrated Injection Logic (I^2L) and Bipolar (TTL) techniques have also been developed to give improved performance. There is also a lot of research interest centred around devices based on gallium arsenide. Most systems, including the MOS devices, use TTL logic voltage levels. Some of the special-purpose support chips, such as an 8-bit tri-state latch, use high-speed Schottky–TTL technology. In the end, the choice of which technology is used is relatively unimportant. Rather it is the power consumption–speed–cost considerations relative to a specific system which are all important.

The earlier MOS devices required ±15 volt and −5 volt power supplies, but fortunately the more recent ones only need the single 5 volt supply common on standard TTL circuitry.

9.3 The Architecture of the Pocket Calculator

In this section the internal organisation of a simple calculator, already introduced in section 9.1.1, will be discussed. Emphasis will be placed on features which distinguish the pocket calculator from the microprocessor-based computer systems to be discussed in later sections.

The calculator considered is a simple four-function device capable of addition, subtraction, multiplication and division. A 9-digit display is provided.

A schematic layout of the calculator is shown in figure 9.1. The diagram comprises the following components:

(i)   The *processor chip*. The internal construction will be discussed in detail later. Note, however, that the chip has the following input/output lines:

     segment outputs, 8 lines a to h
     scan lines, 1 to 10
     keyboard inputs A and B
     clock
     power supply, +9 volts

(ii)   A set of 9 *eight-segment, light emitting-diode (LED)* displays. Each *bar* of the display is an independent LED but with all 8 cathodes of each unit commoned. Each number is made by illuminating specific selections of seven of the eight segments, the eighth segment being the trailing decimal point, as indicated in figure 9.1. The LED will glow when its anode is made positive with respect to its cathode.

(iii)   8 *segment-drivers*, incorporated in one chip. These are simply power amplifers and current-limiting resistors combined. The segment-drivers are necessary because the processor chips cannot output sufficiently large currents to drive the LEDs directly.

(iv)   9 *digit-drivers*, incorporated in one chip. Note that these amplifiers are logical NOT gates (inverters). Thus with lines 1 to 9 from the processor chip at low voltage (logic 0), all LED cathodes are at logic 1 and the displays are disabled. If one line is switched to high, the appropriate cathode is held at low voltage and high voltages on the anodes will cause the LED to glow.

(v)   A *keyboard*. The keyboard is a series of switches arranged in a simple example as a 2 × 10 matrix. Depressing a key simply shorts a specific 'column' to a specific 'row'. The vertical lines are commoned with the digit-drivers to the scan-lines from the processor chip while the horizontal lines feed the keyboard-inputs A and B. Thus depressing the key labelled '2' shorts scan-line 2 to keyboard-input line A, without affecting the input to digit-driver 2. Note that if the keys are distributed in a more convenient physical pattern for the user, the same electrical connection pattern must be maintained.

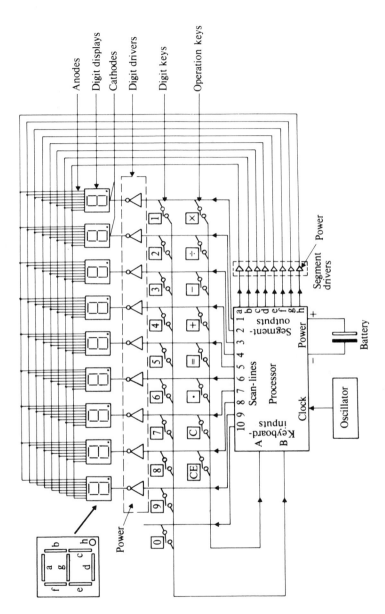

Figure 9.1 Schematic layout of a simple calculator

(vi)   An *oscillator*. This acts as the prime timing source for the clock which is used to time the sequential operations inside the processor chip and hence drive the output lines.

(vii)   A *power supply*, either a dry-cell battery or a mains operated power pack (adaptor).

It should be clear from the diagram that, with $9 \times 8 = 72$ LEDs and $2 \times 10 = 20$ keys to control with only 20 *signal* lines on the processor chip, multiplexing techniques are used.

9.3.1   The Display

Each digit is selected in turn by activating sequentially each scan-line. The actual number to be displayed is stored internally in the processor chip which is organised to activate the appropriate segment-output lines for digit 1 when scan-line 1 is selected, switching to the appropriate set for digit 2 when scan-line 2 is selected, etc. Thus to display 5.2, segment outputs a, b, g, e and d are high when scan-line 1 is high, a, f, g, c, d and h when scan-line 2 is high, all other outputs being low including a to h for the time intervals when scan-lines 3 to 10 are activated. Note that when scan-line 1 is high, the segment-outputs for the number 2 are applied to all displays. Only display 1 is lit, however, since all other cathodes are at high potential. Typically each digit is activated for around 160 μs with a delay of around 40 ms for the processor chip to reset the segment-output lines, so that with 10 scan-lines the cycle repeats every 2 ms. With every digit refreshed approximately 500 times per second, the display appears constant to the human eye.

Note that the calculator is in fact never doing nothing. While it is not actually calculating arithmetic results, it enters an *idle-routine* which continually refreshes the display.

9.3.2   The Keyboard

While the processor is continually refreshing the display, it must also be looking for fresh incoming commands from the keyboard. Thus the scan-lines perform the dual function of selecting a display digit and a column of keyboard switches at the same time. Hence as the processor drives a scan-line high, it checks to see whether either line A or B is high. This should only be possible if the appropriate key is depressed, but the processor checks again during the following scan-cycle to avoid *random-noise* inputs before taking any action. Any key depression causes internal action inside the processor chip as explained later. The processor knows which key has been depressed by a knowledge of which scan-line is activated when either A or B is read as high.

One final point to be noted is that since the calculation operation is rapid, a key could still remain depressed after the appropriate action has been completed. Thus the final part of the processing algorithm must continually check the inputs and do nothing other than refresh the display until the keyboard is clear for a few consecutive cycles.

9.3.3 The Processor Chip

The processor chip decodes key commands and controls the calculator operation, storing numbers and performing the arithmetic operations. As with a conventional computer, each function executes under control of a program. In this case, however, the programs are *simple fixed sequences* to read and store numbers obtained from key depressions and to add, subtract, etc. Further, these programs are developed by the calculator supplier and stored in a read-only memory (ROM) which is an integral part of the processor chip. There is no way in which the user can modify the program.

Figure 9.2 shows a schematic layout of the processor chip. It should first be pointed out that despite the cheapness of these devices, the control circuitry is indeed complex.

The system indicated uses 11-bit instructions with a 9-bit address, giving a maximum of 512 words of ROM (not necessarily all used for a simple calculator). A more complex calculator will probably have longer instruction words and addresses, and some of the ROM may be on an external chip.

The processor is organised as a serial/parallel arithmetic machine. This means that decimal digits are treated serially but each digit is represented by a 4-bit BCD number handled in parallel. Thus one processor storage register comprises ten 4-bit *cells*, one for each of the nine digits plus one to count the position of the decimal point. Each register is thus effectively four interlocked 10-bit shift registers. The processor shown in figure 9.2 has three such registers plus a flag register which has only two bits at each of the ten steps. All registers are continually cycled since they are of the dynamic storage type which need refreshing. The time taken to move one bit is called the *state-time* and the time for a complete cycle, ten state-times in this case, is called the *instruction-time*. The control circuitry is synchronised to the instruction-time so that the beginning of the register is clearly defined. All registers are cycled in synchronism.

The *display register* stores the number currently being entered and displayed. The *operand register* saves the previously entered number. The

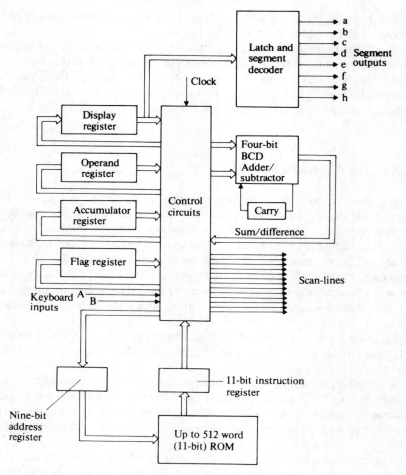

Figure 9.2 Schematic layout of a calculator processor chip

accumulator register saves the results of arithmetic operations. The *flag register* stores code to indicate the function to be performed.

The *clear* button causes the blank code to be placed into all register locations, while *clear-entry* blanks the display register only. Note that all zeros in a digit display 0, not blank.

Consider the operation to add 25.3 to 6.35. The calculator is first cleared. When the '2' key is depressed, the first cell, cell zero, reserved for the decimal-point counter, is by-passed and the code 0010 stored in cell 1. When key '5' is depressed the decimal-point counter is passed unmodified, then one state shift is missed and the code 0101 inserted into cell 1, leaving the previously entered 0010 stored in cell 2. When the decimal-point key is pressed the number 0001 is stored in cell 0, the counter. When key '3' is pressed the contents of cell 0 are now incremented, the cycle delayed by one state shift and 0011 stored in cell 1. This leaves 0010 in cell 3, 0101 in cell 2, 0011 in cell 1 and 0010 in cell 0.

All the time the display sequence goes on continuously. Scan-line 1 is made high and the contents of cell 1 are transferred to the latch where the segment decoder determines which of the segment-outputs to set high. This remains for, say, four instruction cycles when scan-line 2 is set high and the contents of cell 2 copies to the latch, etc. On one cycle, determined by the count in cell 0, the decimal point is also lit.

Next the *plus* function key is pressed which causes a code to be stored in the flag register. At the same time, routeing circuitry in the control is employed to cycle the contents of the display register into the operand register.

Next the '6' key is pressed which clears the display register before repeating the events of collecting the number 6.35.

Finally the *equals* key (or the '+' key again) is depressed. The flag register is referenced which indicates that an addition operation is now required. First the two numbers are adjusted to have the same decimal point count, in this case by adding a zero digit to the first number stored in the operand register, making it 25.30. Next the digits are presented in sequence to a 4-bit BCD adder, which is fast enough to operate in one state-time, each resultant sum digit being stored, with a copy of the decimal-point counter, in the accumulator register. Finally, in the next instruction cycle, the accumulator contents are copied into the display register, to be automatically displayed.

All the above cycles are controlled by the stored program in the ROM. Each significant event acts as a jump to subroutine by setting up the address register. Keying the first digit or the '+' key starts fixed events but the '=' key is a conditional operation with the specific arithmetic function determined by reading the flag register. Multiplication and division are performed by more complex routines involving multiple addition and subtraction operations. It is for this reason that a separate accumulator register is used rather than direct accumulation in the display register.

9.4 More Advanced Calculators

More advanced calculators are generally an expansion of the simple machine just described. Further functions, such as square root, sine, exponentials, etc., require unique keys which can initiate additional subroutines stored in an expanded ROM. Additional registers are often needed by the more complex routines for temporary working storage. User-controlled storage registers, referred to simply as *memory* are effectively further operand registers. Pressing the *memory* key copies data from the display register to the memory register while the *memory recall* key controls copying from the memory to the display register. Multiple registers are organised as a *stack* of operand registers. Pressing the memory key a second time moves the first entry one register *lower* and puts the new data in the 'top' register. The memory recall copies from the *top* into the display and shuffles the other register up. This is called a *first-in, last-out* (FILO) stack.

A *programmable calculator* does not allow user programming in the versatile sense of a normal digital computer but permits a sequence of functions to be initiated automatically rather than by pressing individual function keys. The *program* is stored in an internal RAM, which is loaded typically by pulling a pre-recorded magnetic strip across a built-in reading head. Some calculators provide the facility to record the functions of a calculation as it is keyed in the first time, hence creating individual magnetic strip records for future use.

9.5 Calculators and Microcomputers Compared

Calculators such as those discussed above differ sharply from small microprocessor-based computer systems though they share certain features and facilities. The most important difference relates to the fact that calculators are pre-programmed to carry out a limited range of mathematical tasks. Within their programs no use is made of the conditional instruction, which is a fundamental feature of the true digital computer however small.

As a result of very large-scale production for the more popular pocket calculators, unit hardware costs are very small. Similarly the software development costs are shared over a large number of units with the result that the real cost of the fixed ROM contents is also small.

Input is restricted to the use of a keypad with little more than ten push buttons for the simpler calculators. The more sophisticated devices might have twenty push buttons to accommodate various mathematical and trigonometrical functions as well as input of decimal data. Input is verified as the initial contents of a LED multi-digit display.

Output is restricted for the most part to the final contents of the LED multi-digit display. In a few of the more advanced types of calculator a thermal printer provides a permanent record of output. Speed is usually slow with little emphasis placed on this feature.

In contrast, even small microcomputer systems exhibit features over and above those of the most sophisticated pocket calculators. The distinguishing features of small computer systems have been mentioned frequently in earlier parts of this book but a brief summary should prove helpful. The list below is not intended to be exhaustive:

1. Operation on the Von Neumann principle of execution of sequential program steps from a stored program which may incorporate conditional instructions.
2. Storage arranged in a hierarchy with considerable attention devoted to the provision of random-access store of significant size. Frequently, storage of instructions and data is in a common store.
3. An instruction set of substantial size, typically say at least one hundred identifiable instructions in order to make for programming flexibility.
4. In most machines an emphasis on fixed word-length, typically 8, 16 or 32 bits, for both data and instructions. Frequently, multiple words are used for enhanced arithmetic precision and to increase the total range of store locations which may be accessed. The *bit-slice machine* (ref. 9.1) is the exception to the rule.
5. The possibility of writing programs at either low level, assembler-code level, or at high level. The provision of appropriate assemblers and compilers to permit translation to machine code for program execution.
6. Various peripheral devices which may include

   Keyboard and VDU
   printer or electronic typewriter
   magnetic disc drives either hard-disc (typically Winchester-disc drive) or floppy-disc drive
   magnetic-tape storage system

   with connection to remote terminals or other machines via twisted-pair serial link, or high-speed local area network.
7. The provision of a comprehensive operating system to permit effective computer operation and the efficient control of peripheral devices such as those listed under item 6 above.

It will be seen that the above list mirrors totally the features and requirements for minicomputer systems. With the above introduction, consideration may now be given to microcomputer systems.

9.6 Basic Structure of a Microcomputer System

While microprocessors have much in common with the LSI chips used in pocket calculators, they are essentially different in mode of operation and functional capability. Frequently, a microprocessor is described as a *computer-on-a-chip*. This is an incorrrect designation since while a microprocessor is an essential part of a microcomputer system, because it comprises the CPU and control unit of such a system, it requires several additional components before it becomes useful. The number of such components depends very much on the particular application. Thus for a specific and dedicated role, such as the controller for a particular piece of equipment, the number of external components may be limited to one or two LSI input/output interfaces together with a few memory modules. When used as an alternative to a minicomputer employed in a more general role, further support chips together with a number of peripheral devices may be necessary.

As has been mentioned earlier, the essential difference between the calculator and a microcomputer system based on a microprocessor is that the latter is programmable by the user, enabling the same basic system to solve problems which are apparently unrelated. In this lies the similarity to the minicomputer. A microcomputer system based on a microprocessor is shown in outline form in figure 9.3. The similarity with earlier block schematics relating to conventional computers is readily apparent. Note in particular the parallel bus systems interconnecting the various elements. The principal elements in the diagram are as follows.

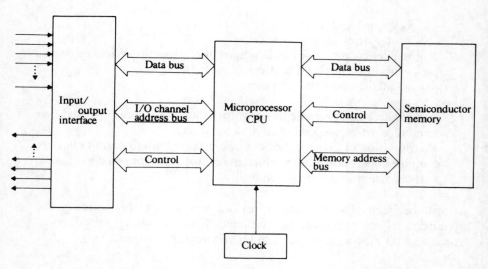

Figure 9.3 Basic structure of a microcomputer system

(i) The *microprocessor*. This performs all the CPU functions such as arithmetic, logic and transfer operations through the repertoire of instructions in its instruction set as executed through what is in effect a microprogramming unit. It modifies instructions and data and transfers program control as a result of inherent or calculated data. It incorporates an *interrupt facility* to control or to respond to the demands of external equipment. The interrupt facility is especially important for many of the applications, typically on-line control of plant, for which microprocessor-based systems are employed. Here priority must be accorded to an external significant event — for example, an outstation signalling a malfunction of some important element of plant. Accordingly, the facility is provided whereby the current activity of the CPU is interrupted, current contents of registers saved, as also is the value of the program counter, and a subroutine to deal with the special circumstances entered. Sometimes an even more important peripheral request may force a further interrupt. In these circumstances, the term *nested interrupt* or *multi-level interrupt* is employed.

In all the above activities the microprocessor is indistinguishable in its mode of operation, except as to detail, from the CPU of the modern small computer discussed in the final sections of chapter 6. The important differences are those of cost and size. Since both cost and size of the microprocessor are significantly less than the traditional CPU and control unit of a minicomputer, the microprocessor is increasingly used as the CPU and control unit of both microcomputer systems and minicomputers. Such use is particularly attractive since the cost of the microprocessor is typically no more than a few pounds (or dollars). The indication is that the unit cost for ever-increasingly powerful microprocessors will continue to fall. The sample of instructions taken from the repertoire of a typical microprocessor and shown in table 9.1 illustrates the similarity with the minicomputer. Mnemonic code is specified though small programs may be written directly in binary or hexadecimal code. As will be seen later, various types of assembler facilitate conversion from mnemonic code.

(ii)   *Input/output interface*. Interfaces permit transfer of data to and from external devices such as registers, transducers and data-transmission systems or to and from users via such equipment as VDUs or printers.

(iii)   *Memory*. Just as with larger configurations, memory plays a very important role. Semiconductor memory is used almost exclusively with microcomputer systems. Both read-only memory (ROM) and random-access memory (RAM) of the various types discussed in chapter 7 are employed according to particular requirements.

The microprocessor is thus the key to the implementation of small computer systems. Prior to the advent of the microprocessor, the choice of a system requiring only limited computational capability lay between the use of fairly complex and far from versatile hardwired logic systems using small-scale and medium-scale integrated circuits or a minicomputer which might well be under-utilised. However, advances in semiconductor technology have led to a spectrum of microprocessors ranging from cheap, slow

Table 9.1 Sample of mnemonic code for a microprocessor

Mnemonic	Instruction
ADA	Add accumulators
ADC	Add with carry
ADD	Add
AND	Logical AND
ASL	Arithmetic shift left
ASR	Arithmetic shift right
.	
.	
.	
EOR	Exclusive OR
INC	Increment
INS	Increment stack pointer
INX	Increment index register
JMP	Jump
JSR	Jump to subroutine
LDA	Load accumulator
LDS	Load stack pointer
.	
.	
.	
WAI	Wait for interrupt

and unsophisticated devices which can compete economically with hard-wired systems to more expensive and fast devices which approach the power of the CPU of conventional minicomputers.

Microprocessors are usually classified as to *word-length*, for example, 4, 8 or 16 bits, or as *bit-slice* machines which permit the coupling together of as many as 2 or 4-bit Arithmetic and Logic Unit (ALU) elements as necessary for a particular application. The most popular word-lengths used are 8 bits and 16 bits; 32-bit machines are becoming available. The restrictions caused by an 8-bit word-length are largely overcome by using more than a single word for instructions and in certain circumstances for data. Thus the instruction set of an eight-bit microprocessor is likely to approach in versatility that of the 16-bit minicomputer. Current microprocessors (see ref. 9.2 for example) have instruction sets with up to a hundred instructions. Using a variety of addressing techniques, to be described briefly later, the 8-bit micros can access up to 64 kilobytes of memory directly and multiple 64K spaces using bank-switching. The Intel 8086 family can address 1 megabyte and other 16-bit micros up to 16 megabytes. The 32-bit micros will exceed mainframes in address capability.

The semiconductor technology used in microprocessor manufacture is a further classification relating to microprocessors, as mentioned in section 9.2. Other important characteristics of microprocessors relate to register cycle-times and specific architectures as was the case with the machines discussed in chapter 6. A very wide range of microprocessors is available and new products appear constantly. Inevitably, manufacturers' literature provides the most up-to-date information though various textbooks may be consulted for fuller details (see, for example, refs 9.2 and 9.3). Chapter 10 carries the matter further.

9.7 Microprocessor Structure

It will have become apparent that the microprocessor constituting the CPU and control unit of a microcomputer system comprises the single most important element of such a system. Other elements such as memory and input/output are indistinguishable in the present application from their use with minicomputers or indeed in many cases with larger machines. Hence, systematic consideration of the structure of microprocessors is clearly appropriate at this present stage. A brief treatment of a typical simple structure is discussed below. The subject is taken further in chapter 10.

A simplified diagram of a typical internal organisation of a microprocessor is shown in figure 9.4. As with the conventional minicomputer of chapter 6, the most important feature is the Arithmetic and Logic Unit (ALU). This provides the computational and logic power and performs simple functions such as add, add with carry, subtract, subtract with borrow, shifting, logic AND, OR, etc. Again, just as with the machines discussed in chapter 6, the ALU usually operates between an accumulator and either an internal register, from the scratch pad for example, or a memory location, with the result of the operation being placed in the accumulator. Associated with the ALU is a *condition-code register (CCR)* which consists of a set of several flip-flops showing, for example, whether the result of a previous operation caused a carry to be generated, gave a zero result or gave a negative result.

The set of *scratch-pad registers* hold temporary data during a computational process. These registers are provided because they can be accessed faster and more conveniently than external memory locations. Recall that a set of six such registers constituted the scratch-pad of the 16-bit minicomputer discussed in chapter 6, section 6.6.

A distinguishing feature of microprocessors is the internal *data-highway* or *bus*. This is connected to and shared by all the internal registers and the

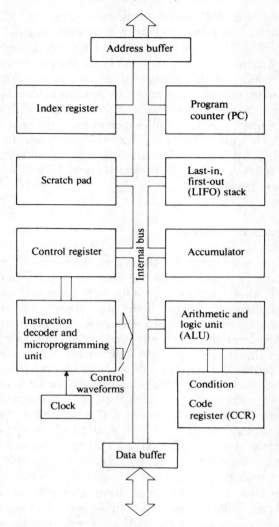

Figure 9.4 Simplified block diagram of a generic microprocessor

ALU with the precise internal timings and interconnections governed by the *control unit* which incorporates the *microprogramming unit*. The data highway is bi-directional with *tri-state logic* to control routeing and isolation of the sub-units. The concept of the data bus and tri-state logic was discussed in chapter 4, section 4.5, while its application to mini-computers was mentioned in chapter 6, section 6.4, so further stress is not necessary here.

The *program counter (PC)* permits instructions to be addressed and brought down from memory in the correct sequence. The PC contains the addresses of the next instruction that is to be loaded into the *control (instruction) register* and is normally incremented after each instruction fetch in the manner first described in chapter 6, section 6.3.2. However, certain classes of instruction can modify the contents of the program counter (PC) so that the programmer can provide branches away from the normal program flow. The branch a program takes depends upon the result of some previous computation. Sometimes the contents of the condition-code register are tested permitting conditional operation such as *branch if the carry flip-flop is set*. Such instructions as these are similar to the conditional instructions discussed in chapter 6, section 6.3.3.

Another class of instructions that modify the PC contents are the call-subroutine group. Here the contents of the PC must be stored so that at the end of the subroutine the main program will be re-entered at the correct position. This requirement has been mentioned already in association with the computers of chapter 6 (see section 6.3.8). In the present case a rather different technique is employed. The *stack* is a section of memory which is used to store the PC contents as subroutine calls are made. The stack is usually a *last-in first-out (LIFO)* type so that addresses are *pushed-on* or *popped-off* the stack as the subroutine is entered or left. With a multiple stack, subroutines can be nested up to the limits of the stack depth. This may be anything up to 64 levels or may constitute a reserved area of RAM of any size determined by the programmer. Further details will be found in chapter 10.

In addition to addressing program instructions, the microprocessor must be able to address data. Several addressing methods are used to program the data. For the most part the methods are similar to those already discussed in chapter 6 and employ the nomenclature to be found in that chapter. The availability of a wide range of addressing techniques provides programming flexibility and makes for fast execution of program. As a result, addressing techniques provide an important characteristic of specific microprocessor families.

The *instruction decoder* and *control unit* decode each instruction and under the supervision of the *external clock* the microprogramming unit controls the external and internal data paths and also the various registers to ensure the correct logical operation of the microprocessor. This activity is completely analogous to that of the control unit and microprogramming unit of conventional machines as discussed in chapter 6 (section 6.4) and chapter 7 (section 7.4). The control unit can also accept interrupts from outside the microprocessor. These permit a call to an interrupt routine.

9.8   Microcomputer System Architecture

As indicated earlier in section 9.6, the microprocessor is only one component in an overall system and it must be connected to memory and input/output to provide a practical system. In common with larger systems such as those discussed in chapter 6, memory and interface devices are connected to a common system bus structure. In addition, because of pin limitations on standard microprocessor integrated circuit packages (typically 40 pins maximum), *multiplexing* of microprocessor memory and data lines is sometimes necessary. The bus itself is usually split into address and data sections though some microprocessors have a common address and data bus. When multiplexing has been employed, address and data are demultiplexed as necessary using signals provided by the microprocessor. Such signals as memory read, memory write, data-bus ready and synchronisation signals are also provided.

The external components required to realise a microprocessor system depend greatly upon the type of microprocessor in use and also upon the particular application. However, most manufacturers supply standard *chip-sets* which are simply connected to the appropriate bus and timing lines to provide the basis of a working system. Specialised user devices may then be connected either straight on to the bus or to the interface chips provided as part of the chip-set. A typical microcomputer system configuration is shown in figure 9.5. Note the resemblance to the diagram of figure 2.2 which illustrates a small computer system in outline form. The present figure, however, stresses the bi-directional bus-system concept and mirrors the internal bus system of the microprocessor itself. In this the figure also relates to figure 6.11 which features a simple minicomputer system. Notice that in figure 9.5 the store has been divided physically into two parts, one providing for program (the *program memory*) with the other accommodating data (the *data store*). Often there are good reasons for this division which is not necessarily the case in larger computer systems. Invariably with microprocessor-based systems the store comprises semiconductor elements compatible with the microprocessor in terms of power-supply voltage levels, physical size and speed.

9.8.1   Program Memory

In dedicated microcomputer applications the program memory is of necessity non-volatile since the programs must not be lost when power is removed. Thus program memory is usually semiconductor ROM. One or other of the main classes of ROM is used in this application. Chapter 7 gave an introduction to the subject but in view of its importance the topic is reinforced through the outline provided below.

(i) *Mask programmable*. This is only suited to applications when the program has been debugged and verified. It is intended for applications in which many copies of the program are required and thus the necessarily high initial costs are spread over a large number of units. This would occur, for example, when many microcomputer systems are carrying out an identical task — say the control functions of a printer or VDU. It must be recalled that once programmed the ROM cannot be altered.

(ii) *Fusible-link programmable*. Here the program is applied by providing high-voltage pulses to the appropriate elements in the semiconductor store. These pulses blow fusible-links, impressing the relevant bit pattern on the matrix in a permanent manner. The cost of the unit, to the user, is higher than that of a masked ROM, but the initial cost is avoided and as a result the *fusible-link PROM* is well suited to applications with fixed programs but small production run.

(iii) *UV erasable*. Again these memory elements are programmed by applying a pattern of high-voltage pulses to the device. They have the advantage over the fusible-link type that they may be erased by shining UV light upon them after which they may be reprogrammed. Thus these devices, *UV erasable EPROMs*, are very useful in low volume production and prototyping systems, possibly prior to the implementation of larger schemes involving many microcomputers.

9.8.2 Data Storage

In many applications of microcomputer systems it may be necessary to change the contents of data storage between program runs and additionally during the execution of individual programs. Accordingly read/write, random-access semiconductor memory, RAM, is used for this purpose. Such memory can be either bi-polar or MOS, static or dynamic. As explained in chapter 7, bi-polar memory is faster than MOS, but it consumes much more power. Dynamic random-access memory, DRAM, is faster and cheaper than static but it has the disadvantage that refresh circuitry must be incorporated to refresh periodically the charge holding each of the memory cells at either 1 or 0. SRAM is used in simpler, small systems but DRAM is the norm.

9.8.3 The Single-chip Microcomputer

Early microprocessor-based systems involved a basic microprocessor chip together with a substantial number of support chips such as RAM and ROM chips, I/O support chips incorporating buffer registers and the like, external clocks and timers, miscellaneous peripheral-handling devices and indeed small-scale ICs to deal with a variety of supporting logic.

Inevitably the total *chip-count* diminished over the years until the appearance of the 'computer-on-a-chip' or *single-chip microcomputer*.

The earliest such single-chip microcomputers appeared in the late 1970s and currently are well established. The principal applications of such devices relate to their use as industrial controllers incorporating limited intelligence. The features provided, particularly I/O, serve to highlight these roles. Both 8-bit devices and 16-bit devices are available.

A typical software specification provides for software compatibility with other products, within the same general family of the same manufacturer. Such software capability is naturally regarded as important. On the hardware side the following list of features might be regarded as typical:

CPU with an instruction set possibly conforming to other members of the general family of 8-bit or 16-bit microprocessor devices offered by the manufacturer in question.

I/O ports, typically four, each providing for parallel operation and probably offering some bit-multiplexing capability. This feature will be important in instrumentation applications for example.

Interrupt facilities. Emphasis on the provision of interrupts from external sources. Again this feature is important for single-chip microcomputers used as industrial controllers.

Counter/timer facilities. Again useful in industrial applications.

ROM. For microcomputers, on-board ROM is provided as an essential feature. Typically, say, 4 kilobytes of mask-programmable ROM permit the storage of the limited range of programs required for specialist applications. For some single-chip microcomputers the mask-programmable ROM is replaced by EPROM. Such provision is particularly useful in applications where the end-user wishes to have flexibility in the programs employed or where it is important to change the control programs periodically.

RAM. Provision here is usually limited to permit storage of such items as program variables relating to the control programs stored more or less permanently in ROM. A typical provision might be restricted to 128 or 256 8-bit bytes of storage.

Note that in many cases the limited on-board memory may be extended through the use of external ROM and RAM chips.

By way of example a current 16-bit microcomputer offers 256 bytes of RAM, 4 kilobytes of user-defined ROM with a memory space which may be expanded to 64 kilobytes in all. System clock rate of 6 MHz ensures high-speed operation. Other features include three timers, an external interrupt controller, parallel I/O ports, a multiplexed external bus for address, data and control signals, and a serial universal synchronous/ asynchronous receiver/transmitter channel (USART) which permits data transfer at up to 1 megabits/s in synchronous mode.

The 16-bit microcomputer described above represents a very versatile device capable of use in a wide variety of applications in control and instrumentation. Robotics together with plant monitor and control are obvious examples. Single-chip microcomputers are also used as intelligent peripheral controllers.

Representative single-chip microcomputers together with typical industrial applications are discussed in ref. 9.3.

9.8.4 *Peripherals*

The discussion of single-chip microcomputers in the previous section highlighted their role as intelligent controllers for a wide range of peripheral devices. A typical example is the microprocessor interfaced to sensors monitoring parameters at various points in an industrial plant and transmitting signals back to control overall operation more effectively. Mini and microcomputers are used also in conjunction with such peripheral devices as disc drives, VDUs, printers and communication systems. Here the emphasis is on more general-purpose data transfer, usually in blocks of words rather than as single words as would be the case with the sensor-based system above. The instruction sets of both the 24-bit and 16-bit machines discussed in chapter 6 make provision for connection to peripherals. Accordingly it is appropriate to introduce briefly at this point the subject of peripherals and their interconnection to mini and microcomputer systems. The principles involved with both classes of peripherals are similar. For a fuller treatment of peripherals and I/O arrangements, readers are referred to more comprehensive texts such as ref. 9.4.

Usually a small computer system (mini or micro) suitable for peripheral connection has a *common highway* or *bus system*. This is the case with the 24-bit machine of chapter 6 where the 24-bit data highway shown in figure 6.4 is extended to permit peripheral access. This simplified diagram shows only the data highway. Figure 9.5, relating to both mini and microcomputer-based systems, gives further detail in showing both the *data bus* and the *address bus* connected to input and output interfaces. In specific systems, such as the single-board microcomputers discussed in the previous section, access to and from peripheral devices is via *bi-directional input/output ports* connected by a triple-bus system comprising data bus, address bus and control bus. Signals on the control bus determine whether data is being transmitted to or from peripheral devices.

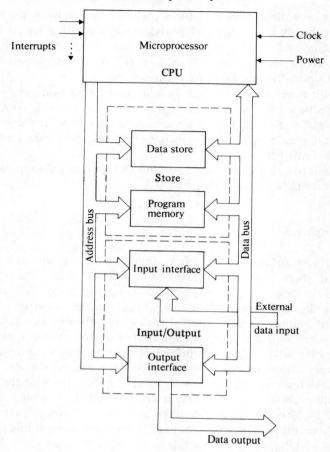

Figure 9.5 Basic microcomputer system architecture

Access to a specific peripheral is achieved by reference to its address. Two possible methods are employed. In the first, specific I/O instructions are employed. In this case the address field N of an instruction word contains the specific address in question. This technique is employed with the 24-bit machine of chapter 6. In section 6.3.9, instructions 50_8 and 51_8 relate to output of data to a device and input of data from a device repsectively. The N address field is 14 bits long and this permits access to no less than $2^{14} = 16$K devices if necessary. No confusion with N addresses located in the store is possible because of the explicit reference to the instruction 50_8 or 51_8.

An alternative technique avoids the need for explicit instructions relating to input/output. Peripheral devices bear addresses forming part of the memory-addressing range which are reserved for I/O and are not connected to the main memory. In these circumstances, access to specific peripherals is through the use of memory-access instructions. The I/O devices are said to be *memory-mapped*. While this approach avoids the need for specific I/O instructions, it results in some reduction in the size of main memory. Unless the provision for I/O is substantial, the reduction in main memory is unlikely to be significant. The technique may be put to positive advantage in that its use enables external memory to extend the very limited RAM memory of a single-chip microcomputer. In these circumstances, external memory locations beyond the limited on-board range are accessed via an I/O port. As a result, on-chip RAM of, say, 256 bytes might be extended to 64 kilobytes for an 8-bit microcomputer using two-byte addresses and a 16-bit program counter.

Block-data Transfer

Transfer of a single data word between memory and a peripheral device or vice versa typically takes about ten instructions which in a small mini or microcomputer system might require a total of say 20 μs. This rather lengthy period sets an upper limit on data transfer of about 50 000 words/s. Such a limit is unlikely to present problems when, for example, the peripheral devices to a microcomputer comprise a few hundred temperatures sampled at infrequent intervals. However, when the peripheral device is a disc store a data transfer as low as 50 000 words/s will be far too slow. It is for this reason that data is transferred from peripheral memory devices such as disc and tape systems in blocks rather than as single words.

Regardless of the method employed, the following information must be specified in respect of each block transfer: the address of the peripheral device, the start address of the block of main memory allocated, the number of data words in the block and the direction of transfer.

Transfer can occur under the direct control of the CPU. In this case the CPU must be provided with special block-data transfer instructions. While block-data transfer is in progress, the CPU is not available for other activities such as the execution of arithmetic instructions.

An alternative and attractive technique is through the use of *Direct Memory Access* (DMA). A hardware DMA controller comprises an interface unit with additional registers and logic. On receipt of a data-acquisition request, the DMA controller is loaded with the information relevant to the block transfer. Thereafter the DMA controller takes command and is permitted to override the CPU whenever both compete for the bus. Thus the CPU hesitates over operations requiring the bus but is not disabled. The process by which the DMA takes over bus control is called *cycle-stealing*.

Standard Interfaces

Peripheral equipment of every sort is produced by a wide variety of manufacturers. To permit connection to different mini and microcomputers, standard interfaces have been produced. The principal interfaces are sufficiently important to merit brief mention in a preliminary text such as the present. Further information is widely available from standard specifications, manufacturers' literature and more advanced texts.

The V24 or RS-232 Standard Serial Interface. This is frequently employed to connect a Data Terminal Equipment (DTE) such as a visual display unit or keyboard to an adjacent computer or to a remote computer via a *modem*. The *modem* (*modulator–demodulator*) permits digital signals to be transmitted over analogue telephone lines. The V24 connection is essentially a serial connection with a separate path for each transmission direction. Since various timing and control signals are also required, the connection employs a 25-way cable with connectors employing a fixed convention for the leads connected to individual pins. Transmission is normally restricted to a moderate number of bits/second.

IEEE-488 Standard. This interface is designated as a 'Digital Interface for Programmable Instrumentation'. It is also known as the Hewlett-Packard Interface Bus (HP-IB). The IEEE bus is widely used to permit a computer to control up to fourteen different instruments such as data loggers, analysers, etc. Many instruments of the above and similar types are designed to be compatible with the IEEE bus. The system provides a parallel 8-bit interconnection, though the bus itself comprises 16 lines to permit the exchange of a variety of control signals. Standard 24-way cable and connectors are employed. Stringent limitations on cable length between the instruments or peripherals connected to the bus together with an overall limit of 20 m of cable make the system specially suitable for use within a laboratory environment.

CAMAC. The aims of the *Computer Automated Measurement and Control* (CAMAC) standard are similar to those of the IEEE-488 system. The intention is to provide a standard bus system to permit sophisticated instruments to exchange data. Interconnection is via standard 86-way sockets at the back of each instrument in the set.

Various Peripheral Types. A very wide variety of peripherals may be connected to mini and microcomputer systems. Such systems themselves may be connected as peripheral devices to larger computer systems or may form elements (*nodes*) of communications networks such as an IEEE 802 local area network.

Devices connected as peripherals to small computer systems include:

(i) *Visual Display Units* (VDUs). These are of many different sorts. They may display alphanumeric character-sets from the Roman alphabet and number system. Alternatively they may display Arabic, Japanese or Cyrillic characters. A dot matrix presentation facilitates the display of such character sets. More advanced displays allow graphics presentation by directly addressing individual dots (pixels).

(ii) *Keyboards*. These are used for the entry of data to computer systems — often in association with display of the material on VDU screen. A wide variety of alphanumeric character-sets is employed.

(iii) *Printers*. Printers take a wide variety of forms. Those providing the higher quality results are expensive. The *daisy-wheel* printer is one which produces excellent results but is comparatively expensive. Most printers use a multiple-pin head to form characters by matrix printing. The resolution can be low for high-speed 'draft' printing or higher for low-speed 'near-letter-quality' print. Laser printers are becoming common for mixed text and graphics.

9.9 Support for Microcomputer System Design

For very small systems involving a microcomputer, a program may be prepared in binary or more typically in hexadecimal code. In either case the programmer will require a good knowledge of the architecture of the system and must, for example, allocate absolute addresses to instructions and data. More typically, however, a program is written in mnemonic code (see table 9.1) and translated to machine code using an appropriate assembler.

Once a microcomputer system is to be used in a more realistic role, typically for control purposes, then the question of overall system design arises. In these circumstances the preparation of program is only a part and, in many cases, a small part, of the overall design activity.

In all but the most trivial cases, a unified systems approach is necessary since the hardware and software designs modify and affect each other. Such an approach frequently involves disciplined team activity. Over recent years, overall design methodologies have been the subject of much study. The reader is directed to one or other of the specialised texts dealing with this important subject (see, for example, ref. 9.5).

A system designed around a microprocessor is inherently more difficult to test and debug than is the case with a more conventional minicomputer or hardwired logic system. Internal registers cannot be accessed, and single-step facilities for program verification are limited. Programming is usually done at low level and the final program is difficult to examine when commited to PROM.

The basic interfacing between the microprocessor and its peripherals and memory is now regarded as a routine activity. Indeed standard cards, such as processor, memory, I/O, are readily available. Accordingly, most of the design effort will be spent on timing considerations, the input/output interface between the microprocessor ports and the external process under control.

Software design has become a major feature of the overall design process and a large percentage of the design effort will be spent in program writing, testing and debugging. This is no easy task and in all but the simplest cases the designer will find it essential to use some of the powerful aids now available. The design process is of necessity an iterative one and several changes may be required before a satisfactory solution is achieved. Hardware and software functions may be defined at an early stage, but the designer must be prepared to change them in the light of experience. The software can then be written and tested using *assemblers* and *simulators*. Once a prototype system incorporating both hardware and software becomes available, *emulators* and *logic analysers*, mentioned on page 272, will help to verify the final timing and other considerations under real-time conditions. Such tests may result in modifications to either the hardware, the software or both. Development aids in almost all cases shorten the design time and in many cases are essential if the design process is to be feasible. A brief description of such aids is given in the sections which follow. These should be read in association with chapter 8. For a more comprehensive preliminary treatment, see ref. 9.6 for example.

9.9.1 Cross-products

These are true software aids in that they are software packages written in high-level languages, such as Pascal, PL/M or C, which run on *host computers* with interactive facilities. The principal aids are as follows:

(i) *Cross-compilers*. These allow the designer to write software for a microcomputer system in a high-level language which makes it independent of the microprocessor employed. The cross-compiler converts the high-level language program (source code) into binary code (object code) suitable for loading in the microcomputer system memory. Various languages such as PL/M and C, are popular for this purpose. Pascal is also widely used.

(ii) *Cross-assemblers*. These are basically translators which convert from a symbolic notation such as mnemonic code to binary code producing a one-to-one conversion of the source code. Programs written in assembler code are dependent on the microprocessor for which they are written. Most small-system software is written at this level since it produces smaller and faster programs but, as the complexity of the system increases, the effort and possibility of error also increase. For a program of 2 kilobytes or more, a high-level language approach becomes desirable.

(iii)   *Simulators.* As the name implies, these are software testing aids. The object code produced by a cross-assembler or cross-compiler is used by the simulator program which performs on the host machine the corresponding operations to those of the actual microprocessor. At the same time they provide a large number of facilities which enable the designer to follow the running of the program and to verify in detail the operations being performed. This aid is clearly dependent upon the particular micro-processor in use.

(iv)   *Interpreters.* These software aids resemble the action of a simulator program in that a program is actually run under operator control. However, an interpreter operates directly on high-level language, or partially compiled, code. The interpreter does not produce the binary code suitable for loading in the microprocessor as does a cross-compiler. A microprocessor development system (see section 9.9.2 below) could bene-fit by having a resident interpreter which would execute high-level code stored as such in its memory. The high-level code could be used to test the program at the high-level stage and, when debugged, compile the program to produce code for loading in the microprocessor memory of the developed system. The interpreter would of course use more memory and be slow compared with compiled code execution.

9.9.2   Development Systems with Resident Software

All the cross-products discussed above need large computer installations for their operation. An alternative approach is to use special-purpose systems which incorporate a similar microprocessor to that which forms the basis of the microcomputer system under design rather than rely on a different and larger host machine. To this end, most microprocessor manufacturers offer what are basically general-purpose microcomputers with associated peripherals. Complete systems are frequently comprehens-ive and include VDU, logic display panels, floppy and Winchester disc storage, generalised I/O facilities and PROM programmers. These dedi-cated systems compare in cost and range of facilities with those previously discussed in the context of host computers. Facilities include resident compilers, assemblers and interpreters. These development systems also provide the basis for hardware design-aids since they overcome the inherent inability of a software simulator to test a program under actual real-time conditions. Because many systems based on a microprocessor are used for control and monitor of real-time processes, the opportunity to test performance in a real-time environment is of vital importance.

processes, the opportunity to test performance in a real-time environment is of vital importance.

The cheaper systems relate to the products of a single manufacturer and as a result are limited in scope. More sophisticated development systems are sufficiently general-purpose to permit operation with a range of different microprocessor systems by plugging in one or other of a variety of *personality cards*. As new products appear, the range of personality cards is extended.

9.9.3 Hardware Design Aids

The microprocessor development system facilities described above as software aids have also a limited capability for the proving and testing of actual prototype systems. Their power as hardware development systems is greatly increased by the use of additional facilities. These include the following:

(i) *In-circuit emulators* (ICE). The emulator plugs into the microprocessor socket on the system under development and links by an umbilical cord to the development system. The development system with all its resources can then be used for debugging. Facilities provided by using an ICE include
(a) substituting development-system RAM for on-board ROM
(b) because of (a), insertion of break-points in programs at run-time
(c) use of a screen-based monitor
(d) tracing of the past 'n' data and addresses on the microprocessor bus
(e) by access to the original source-code on disc, debugging using symbolic names.
(ii) *Logic analysers*. Although these are not aids intended specifically for microcomputer systems, their use for this purpose is widely recognised. Since they provide storage and simultaneous display of a large number of digital signals, they are ideal for any system using a bus structure. Hence logic analysers are suitable for microprocessor systems. They are true hardware aids and in a wide range of situations they represent an essential tool.
(iii) *Limited-power development aids*. Several manufacturers have produced relatively low-cost development aids costing something of the order of say a thousand pounds (dollars) which do not have the full capability of the more comprehensive systems described above. However, such development aids enable the user to create readily microprocessor software for the entry, running, testing, debugging and display of programs. They also permit the connection of peripheral equipment via I/O channels. However, the user must provide power supplies and related facilities.

(iv) *Ready-built systems.* Built-up microprocessor printed-circuit boards are available which provide an appropriate microprocessor chip together with a certain amount of RAM, ROM, I/O and resident monitors to permit easy programming and I/O arrangements. Such boards are designed to plug into standard multi-pin sockets so that they can be incorporated with other equipment in prototype systems. Indeed, some industrial users employ such general-purpose cards as production units for low quantity runs. If a terminal is available, such built-up boards can be used as limited-power development aids.

9.10 Summary and Conclusions

In this chapter the products of the new dominant LSI and VLSI technology have been introduced. Starting with the pocket calculator, a complex but dedicated device, discussion of LSI technology was expanded to cover the CPU and support chips which form the basis of the new technology of fabricating small computers. While microprocessors dominate special-purpose devices such as intelligent terminals and machine controllers, their use in small general-purpose computers clearly points the way to the development of their ever-increasing use in complete computers which include CPU, memory and I/O on single, cheap chips. This approach has changed the face of computing. Already large computers are complemented by networks of small computers.

Even more significantly, computers have become available for all sorts of functions for which cost has previously been prohibitive. Obvious examples are in the home, the office, the shop and the car.

From the viewpoint of a technologist, the details of computer architecture will become for the future less important in the same way that detailed logic design is already of reduced value. Emphasis will be shifted to complete systems. A book such as this, intended as an introductory text, may well provide for many readers sufficient technological background in computers. For such readers, further studies would be much more concerned with special-purpose hardware for interfacing and interconnecting computers and with software for converting the available processing power into user-specific problem-solving devices.

Thus the systems aspects relating to the use of hardware and software in an integrated fashion which are already important will become vital.

For other readers, a more comprehensive knowledge of the architecture of microcomputers will be necessary. For this reason, chapter 10 provides a systematic and detailed consideration of the principal features of current microprocessor architectures while chapter 11 is devoted to software engineering.

274 Mini and Microcomputer Systems

References

9.1 Lewin, D., *Theory and Design of Digital Computer Systems*, Nelson, London, 1980.
9.2 Simpson, R. J. and Terrell, T. J., *Introduction to 6800/6802 Microprocessor Systems*, Newnes Butterworth, Sevenoaks, 1982.
9.3 Lister, P. F., *Single-Chip Microcomputers*, Granada, London, 1984.
9.4 Wilkinson, B. and Horrocks, D., *Computer Peripherals*, Hodder and Stoughton, London, 1987.
9.5 Ogdin, C. A., 'Microprocessor Project Management', in Aspinall, D. (Ed.), *The Microprocessor and its Application*, Cambridge University Press, 1978.
9.6 Ogdin, C. A., 'Hardware and Software Tools for Microprocessors', in Aspinall, D. (Ed.), *The Microprocessor and its Application*, Cambridge University Press, 1978.

10 Microcomputer Systems' Architecture

Objectives

This chapter extends the general introduction to microcomputers given in the previous chapter to cover the most relevant aspects of hardware design for microprocessor-based systems. Many of the concepts described in earlier chapters are also illustrated using examples from typical microcomputer designs.

The term 'microcomputer' can be interpreted in many ways dependent upon the context of its use. In order to provide a clear basis for further discussion, some definitions of terms are required. Following these definitions, a description of bus structures in microcomputers is given with examples from the more important system types. A detailed look at the design of memory and input/output in a microcomputer is then made.

Moving towards some more application-oriented aspects of microcomputer implementation, the control of the input/output process and the types of peripheral device available are also considered.

A significant aspect of the design of a microcomputer-based product is the choice of microprocessor to be employed. The characteristics that are most relevant to this decision are finally treated in general terms.

10.1 Introduction

In the previous chapter, the concept of a microprocessor being used to implement a small computer called a microcomputer was introduced. The term 'microcomputer' was also used to describe a single chip that contains the elements of a microprocessor, memory and some input/output facilities. The small 'personal' computers that are common in many schools and offices are also often called microcomputers. Because of this imprecision in the meaning of the term 'microcomputer', some more exact definitions are required in order to avoid confusion.

It is useful to start with the definition of the microprocessor itself. A microprocessor comprises an arithmetic and logic unit (ALU), a control unit for synchronising operations, some working registers for holding data and addresses, some dedicated registers such as the program counter, status register, etc., a clock/oscillator to synchronise internal operations, and interfaces to memory and input/output (I/O) systems. The microprocessor is often implemented on a single chip and is sometimes called a *single-chip microprocessor*. In the remainder of this chapter, the term 'microprocessor' will always imply a single-chip microprocessor unless otherwise stated. Before a microprocessor can do any useful work, it must be provided with some program and data memory and, of course, some means of communicating with external devices. As described in chapter 9, the link between microprocessor, memory and I/O is achieved using three bus systems for address, data and control signals.

When a microprocessor is combined with memory and I/O systems, it is called a microcomputer. There are several forms of microcomputer and these can be classified according to their physical implementation. Firstly, a microprocessor can be combined with a limited amount of program and data memory and some I/O facilities on a single chip, hence the term *single-chip microcomputer*. This should not be confused with a single-chip microprocessor. A typical single-chip microcomputer would have an 8-bit word-length, 4 kilobytes of program memory, 128 bytes of data memory, 2 counter/timers, 24 TTL-compatible I/O lines and perhaps a serial I/O line. Such devices are designed to be used for simple control and monitoring systems in low-cost and high production volume applications. Two examples of this type of application are domestic appliance control and engine management in automobiles. Because of their common usage in control applications, single-chip microcomputers are also called *microcontrollers*. Although single-chip microcomputers often employ a relatively simple processor architecture with a limited instruction set, they are designed for I/O-intensive applications and often have a very powerful I/O sub-system. As an example, one device has the ability to generate pulse-width modulated outputs and to count 'events' on inputs. Others provide for the direct driving of liquid-crystal displays. An example of a single-chip microcomputer application for a washing machine controller is illustrated in figure 10.1.

The next class of microcomputer describes the combination of a microprocessor, semiconductor memory and I/O on one printed circuit board (PCB). This is called a *single-board computer* and can either be of a design dedicated to one application or be general-purpose in nature and therefore applicable in many areas. Single-board computers are used in a wide variety of applications ranging from a point-of-sale terminal in a supermarket to a production line controller in a factory. Because it is not always practical to combine all the features required on a single-board computer, the boards often allow for the extension of the address, data and control buses on to an external bus via an edge connector. The format of the external bus is often to a *de facto* or approved standard to allow boards from a variety of vendors to be employed in one system. The external

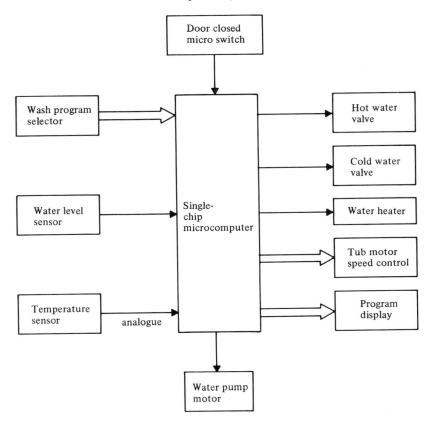

Figure 10.1 Single-chip microcomputer used as a washing-machine controller

boards may include specialised I/O functions, such as local area network controllers, disc interfaces, graphics processors or may simply be used to increase the amount of memory available. Obviously, within the limits imposed by the design of the external bus, such a multiple-board system can be expanded in a modular fashion to cater for growth in the application requirements. An example of a multiple-board microcomputer system is shown in figure 10.2. The general-purpose microcomputers used in offices, schools and the home are specially packaged systems based on the concept of a single-board computer — many also employ an external bus system or 'backplane' to allow for modular growth.

In some applications the processing power available on a single-board computer is insufficient to meet the requirements. A traditional solution to the problem would be to use a more powerful computer such as a

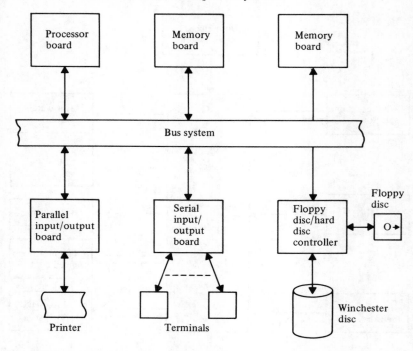

Figure 10.2 Multiple-board general-purpose microcomputer system

minicomputer or even a mainframe. An alternative that is now common is to employ several microcomputers in what is termed a *distributed micro-computer system* (ref. 10.1). Most of the standard bus systems available for single-board computers allow, as we shall see in section 10.2, for several microcomputers to reside on the same bus. This allows the processing tasks to be allocated among a number of microcomputers in either a static or a dynamic fashion. It is also possible to have a non-homogeneous set of microprocessors on the bus so that special functions such as signal processing can be executed by processors designed specifically for that purpose. Even some of the lowest cost home computers use distributed microcomputers; for example, one microcomputer may be used to execute user programs while another handles the keyboard scanning, disc accessing and display driving. Reference 10.1 provides some further reading on the increasingly important subject of distributed microcomputer systems.

There are also some more general terms that will be used in this chapter that require some initial discussion. A home microcomputer is designed purely to serve as a computer — that is, it is the end product. In contrast, the microcomputer employed in an automobile engine management system is employed for a specific function; that is, it is a 'black-box' and its implementation technology is largely irrelevant to the user. The users of the engine management system (the automobile designer and ultimately the driver) only see the microcomputer as part of an overall system, not as the end-product. When a microcomputer is employed as part of a larger system in this manner, it is described as an *embedded microcomputer*. Another contrast can be made between the use of a microcomputer in a general-purpose computer and in an embedded system. In a general-purpose system we expect the computer to respond to our commands in a reasonable time. The meaning of 'reasonable' is very subjective and function dependent. For example, to compile a 400 line program a response time of 20 seconds may be regarded as acceptable, while from striking a key on the keyboard to the character appearing on the screen might be expected to take milliseconds (that is, perceived to be instantaneous). In embedded applications such loose definitions of response time are inadequate — a guarantee must be given that a reaction to a stimulus will be completed within a specific time. If a production process is being controlled by a microcomputer, the opening and closing of valves must occur within a pre-determined time from a demand signal or the process may go unstable. These types of embedded microcomputers are described as being *real-time systems*.

Earlier in this section the concept of a distributed system was introduced. Here, to increase the effective processing power of a computer system, additional microcomputers were added to introduce parallel execution of computational tasks. Another technique that is employed with some recent microprocessors is to add a separate *co-processor* chip to increase the effective power of the processor. The co-processor typically provides an extension to the instruction set of the microprocessor and is resident on the same address, data and control bus. The co-processor intercepts and executes those instructions on the bus that do not form part of the base instruction set of the microprocessor. A good example of a co-processor is a floating point arithmetic processor which is used to enhance an integer-only instruction set to include real arithmetic and transcendental functions, etc.

Using the definitions outlined above and the concepts introduced in earlier chapters, the remainder of this chapter will concentrate on areas that are relevant to the design of microcomputer systems. In the next section the design of the microprocessor address, data and control bus is discussed, followed by coverage of multi-board bus systems.

10.2 Microcomputer Bus Systems

In this section the requirements of the interconnection between microprocessor, memory and I/O will initially be discussed. This will lead into a description of how the interconnection is physically organised in some real microprocessors. Finally, the extension of the processor bus into the general backplane bus that is needed for multiple-board systems will be considered.

Figure 10.3 shows the conceptual interconnection of microprocessor, memory and I/O. The primary routes are between processor and memory and between processor and I/O. The former is required to allow the processor to fetch instructions and operands from memory and to allow the storage of results into memory. The latter permits the transfer of information to and from the outside world to allow the microcomputer monitor to control some external system. Obviously both these routes are required for the microcomputer to perform any meaningful operations. A third route, that is not always employed, provides links between the memory and I/O systems directly, without the intervention of the microprocessor. This route, called the *direct memory access* (DMA) route, permits high-speed transfers of data between the I/O and memory sub-systems and is typically employed when the maximum I/O to processor to memory transfer rate (and vice versa) is less than the transfer rate of the peripheral devices connected to the I/O sub-system.

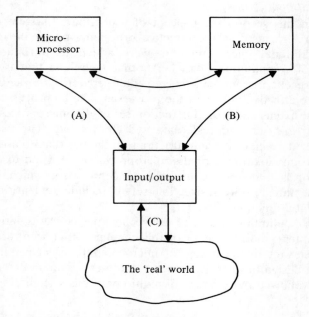

A – Normal processor – I/O data route
B – Memory – I/O data route (direct memory access – DMA)
C – Links I/O devices to real world

Figure 10.3 Processor–memory–I/O interconnection

In this section we shall be primarily concerned with the pro-cessor–memory route, many of the features of which are identical to the processor—I/O route. The detailed differences between these two routes are covered in section 10.4. The DMA route is also discussed in the same section.

10.2.1 *Processor–Memory Route*

The processor–memory route consists of not one but three routes: the address route, the data route and the control route. The address route is used by the processor to select a memory register (or location) involved in a transfer. Since we can read and write data to and from the memory locations, the data route must comprise a read data path and a write data path. The control route is a conglomeration of individual signals used to synchronise processor–memory transfers and to provide a route for general control/status signals throughout the system. The characteristics of the control route are very processor dependent and vary widely among microprocessors from the different manufacturers. Some of the more typical signals will be described to provide a broad illustration:

(1) Read/Write — this signal indicates to the memory system whether a transfer is from memory to processor (that is, a read) or from processor to memory (that is, a write). The read/write control is an output from the processor and may be implemented as either separate read and write signals or as a single signal.

(2) Memory ready — this signal indicates to the processor system that the memory system is ready to transfer data. This signal is tested by the processor during a *memory access cycle* and if a not ready condition is indicated, the processor will wait for memory ready before completing the memory access cycle. The memory ready input thus allows asynchronous transfers of data between processor and memory; that is, the memory access time can be independent of the processor cycle time. Within limits, this means that a slow memory (that is, one with a high access time) can be employed with a fast processor (that is, one with a low machine cycle time).

(3) Address valid — this signal indicates to the memory system that an address is currently established on the address bus and that the address may be used by the memory system.

(4) Data strobe — this is an output signal from the processor to indicate to the memory system that output data is established on the data bus and may be read by the memory system or that data is to be read by the processor over the data route.

(5) Halt — this processor input is used by external devices to stop the processor upon completion of the current bus cycle. This typically causes the processor to place all its address and data lines into the high impedance state and to deactivate all control signals. The use of this input will be discussed in later sections. On some processors this signal is bi-directional and may be then driven by the processor to indicate to external devices that the processor has halted.

(6) Bus request — this input to the processor indicates that some external device wishes to take control of the system bus.

(7) Bus grant — this output from the processor indicates to an external device that a bus request has been granted and that it may take over control of the system bus.

(8) Bus grant acknowledge — this input to the processor indicates that an external device has seen the bus grant signal and that it is to take over the system bus upon completion of the current bus cycle. The bus request, grant and acknowledge signals are often employed in DMA systems as we shall see in later sections.

(9) Clock in — this input determines the internal operating frequency (that is, cycle time) of the processor.

(10) Clock out — this output from the processor provides a system clock related to the processor cycle time. This signal is typically used for synchronisation and as an input to external counters and timers.

(11) Reset — is an input which causes the processor to be initialised to a known state.

(12) Reset out — is an output from the processor to indicate to the rest of the system that the processor is being reset. This output is often used to reset system components in synchronisation with the processor clock. Some processors combine the reset and reset out signals on to a single bi-directional line.

In addition to the above control routes, some processors also provide encoded *status* information to indicate, for example, that the processor is fetching an instruction, or fetching data, or writing data, or is halted, etc. Finally, an interrupt control route is normally provided. The operation of the interrupt signals will be described in detail in section 10.4 and for the moment it is sufficient to state that these signals allow the normal program flow to be modified in response to an external stimulus.

As an example, the following sequence of events illustrates the use of the above control signals in the execution of a memory read operation:

	Processor	Memory system
1.	Set read/write to read	
2.	Output address on address route	
3.	Assert address valid	
4.	Assert data strobe	
5.		Select location by address
6.		Output data on data route
7.		Assert memory ready
8.	Latch data	
9.	Remove address valid	
10.	Remove data strobe	
11.		Remove data from data route
12.		Remove memory ready
13.	Start next cycle	

We shall now consider the implementation of the address and data routes in more detail. The processor–memory routes are shown conceptually in figure 10.4.

The processor holds the current memory address in a dedicated memory address register (MAR) which is connected to the external address route. The processor data register is connected to an internal data route which feeds the processor internal registers, ALU, instruction register, etc., and to the external data routes. In the memory sub-system the address route from the processor connects to a decoder which selects an individual *memory register* from the array of memory registers. The array of memory registers is usually implemented as several chips. Each memory chip has its own data register which is enabled or selected by a combination of the decoded address and the address valid and data strobe control signals. For simplicity, figure 10.4 and subsequent diagrams show just a single data register. Similarly, for simplicity, the control routes are shown, but without any detail of their connection to either the processor or memory sub-systems.

To reduce device costs, it is desirable to minimise the number of pins on a chip. This has the additional benefit that PCB area is also reduced thereby lowering the costs of the PCB itself. Against this minimisation of pin count, the effects on performance and ease-of-use must also be taken into account. Several techniques are, or have been, employed to multiplex the processor–memory routes. The two most widely used techniques will now be considered.

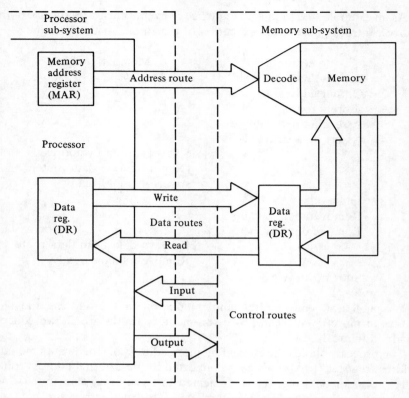

Figure 10.4 Processor–memory routes

The first and most common technique is to combine the write data paths on to a *single bi-directional route,* as shown in figure 10.5. Since the processor can only access a single memory location in any one cycle because there is only one address route, and since it can only either read or write data, we only need a single route that can drive data either to or from the memory. This effectively halves the number of data route lines required and is employed almost universally. Some microprocessors which use this pin reduction technique are listed in table 10.1.

An additional technique is to *partially multiplex* the address and data routes. The bi-directional *n*-bit wide data/address time multiplexed route is used to provide the *n* least significant address bits as well as the *n*-bit data route. The most significant address bits are provided on a separate non-multiplexed address route. An additional control signal is required to control the demultiplexing. The hardware configuration is shown in figure 10.6.

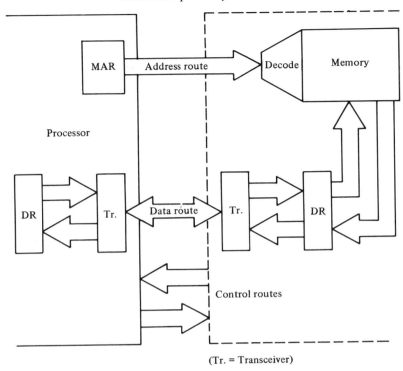

(Tr. = Transceiver)

Figure 10.5 Use of a single bi-directional data route

Table 10.1 Processors using a bi-directional data route

Processor type	Data word-length (bits)	Address length (bits)	Memory size (bytes)	Processor pin count
Intel 8080	8	16	64K	40
MOS Technology 6502	8	16	64K	40
MOS Technology 6503	8	12	4K	28
Motorola 6800	8	16	64K	40
Motorola 6809	8	16	64K	40
Motorola 68000	16	24	24M	64
Texas 9900	16	16	64K	64
Zilog Z80	8	16	64K	40

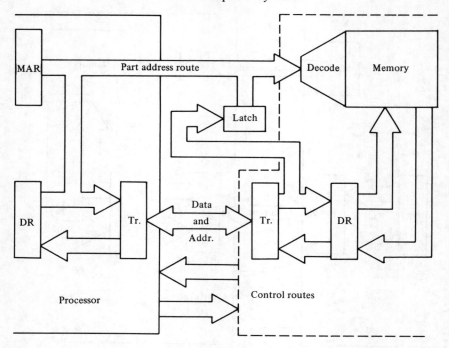

Figure 10.6 Partially multiplexed address/data scheme

The multiplexing is arranged such that the full address appears at the beginning of the memory cycle, with the least significant part being latched into the *address latch*. The data transfer then follows on the address/data route, with the most significant part of the address remaining on the address route. While there may appear to be a time penalty here, the scheme is in fact quite efficient since the time between the address appearing and the data transfer occurring allows for the access time of the memory. Figure 10.7 shows a partial timing diagram of a memory access operation using this scheme.

Because this scheme reduces the number of processor pins by $n - 1$, incurs no time penalty, and only has a hardware overhead of a single *n*-bit latch, it has become a popular technique. One of the first processors to use this scheme was the Intel 8085. This processor has a family of memory chips which incorporate the multiplexer latch, thus obviating the need for the external device. Even if these dedicated devices are not employed, a typical system will require some electrical *buffering* between processor and memory and this can be accomplished by the latch quite economically. Table 10.2 lists some of the processors that employ partial address and data multiplexing.

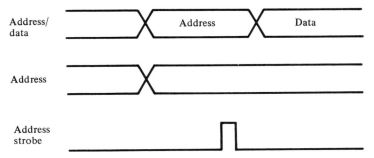

Figure 10.7 Partially multiplexed address/data route timing

Table 10.2 Processors using partially multiplexed address/data route

Processor type	Multiplexed address/data route width (bits)	Data word-length (bits)	Full address width (bits)	Mem-ory size (bytes)	Processor pin count
Intel 8085	8	8	16	64K	40
Intel 8086	16	16	20	1M	40
Intel 8088	8	16	20	1M	40
National 32016	16	16	24	16M	48

The use of a partially multiplexed address/data route with a supplementary address route is being increasingly employed for 16 and 32-bit processors with large address spaces, to minimise pin count. To minimise chip count, families of compatible memory and I/O devices are often available with these processors. These compatible devices include the demultiplexing logic required (compare the Intel 8085 family).

10.2.2 External Bus Systems

In section 10.1 it was explained that in many cases all the hardware required to implement a microcomputer system cannot fit on to a single board. In such systems it is necessary to extend the inherent bus structure of the processor on to a *backplane* into which many other boards can connect. The backplane is typically a PCB with a set of tracks and connectors designed to carry the physical signals needed to implement the interface. Careful design of the PCB is required to ensure that it has good noise characteristics and does not cause undue distortion of signals due to reflections, etc.

In the simplest case, it is sufficient just to extend the processor bus signals described in section 10.2.1 on to the backplane by providing the appropriate buffering and drive circuitry. However, in the case of systems using DMA (section 10.4) or in distributed microcomputers, there will be more than one *bus master*. A bus master is a processor that can take control of the external bus and it is obvious that in distributed microcomputers some or all of the microcomputers in the system will need to control the bus at various time to allow sharing of resources. The bus request, bus grant and bus grant acknowledge signals described in the previous section are the primitive mechanisms used to support this concept. Unfortunately, not all microprocessors provide these control signals and it is therefore necessary to provide the appropriate logic in the interface between the processor and the backplane bus. Similarly, few microprocessors implement the bus control transfers in the same manner and so it is necessary to provide a standard mechanism if a non-homogeneous distributed system is to be implemented.

Many backplane bus systems have been developed over the past decade by microprocessor and microcomputer manufacturers. A few of these systems have grown into *de facto* industry standards. Several of these industry standard buses have been adopted by the standardisation bodies and have had their specifications clarified and formalised. Three standards, approved by the Institute of Electrical and Electronic Engineers, are worthy of a brief mention: *IEE 696, IEEE 796* and *IEEE 1014*.

IEEE 696 is commonly known as the *S-100* bus and was developed in the mid 1970s by a U.S. company called MITS for use in its Intel 8080-based ALTAIR 8800 microcomputer. The ALTAIR 8800 was one of the earliest personal computers and its success led many other manufacturers to standardise on the same 100 signal line bus. Although the S-100 bus was developed for the Intel 8080 microprocessor, it was sufficiently flexible to allow many different processor types to use it, including others as diverse as the Motorola 68000 and the Texas 9900. The characteristics of the S-100 bus are briefly as follows. It employs a minimum of 16 and a maximum of 24 address lines and 16 data lines. The data lines can be configured to be two uni-directional 8-bit buses for master to slave reads and writes respectively or a bi-directional 16-bit bus. In the S-100 context, a master would be a processor or a DMA controller and a slave might be a memory or an I/O board. The bus has one permanent master — a microprocessor — and up to 16 temporary masters — DMA controllers or microprocessors. The S-100 also has status bus to define the current bus cycle type, a control bus to provide timing strobes, a control input bus to command the master to take some action, an interrupt bus to route interrupts to the master, a DMA control bus, and finally a utility bus to carry power, clock and other general signals. Reference 10.2 provides a detailed reference to the S-100 bus.

The IEEE 796 bus was originally developed by Intel and is commonly known under its Intel trademark name of *Multibus*. Multibus was developed by Intel in the latter half of the 1970s as a multi-processor bus tailored to the requirements of Intel microprocessors. Like the S-100 bus, it has also been very popular and now supports a variety of non-Intel microprocessors. Multibus uses 86 lines which are grouped as follows. There is a 20-bit address bus, a 16-bit bi-directional data bus, 8 access control lines for controlling read/write operations, 7 bus arbitration lines for controlling the handing over of bus mastership from one master to another, 9 interrupt control lines and a variety power, clock and other signals. As implied here, Multibus supports the concept of having several true bus masters with mastership controlled by parallel or serial arbitration. An Intel application note (ref. 10.3) includes a full description of the Multibus signals and their use.

Recently a number of new bus systems have been defined to provide better support for the more advanced 16 and 32-bit processors such as the Motorola 68000 and Intel 286 families. These newer systems must not only provide for the higher data transfer rates and the extra address and data lines required, but must also support the more advanced concepts employed in systems based on these processors. One example of a 16/32-bit bus system is the *VME bus* which was jointly developed by a number of chip manufacturers who supply Motorola 68000 family components (ref. 10.4). VME is based on the Eurocard format and some of its major characteristics are as follows. Firstly, VME specifies eight types of functional module that may be used in a VME system. Dependent upon the type of the functional module, there may be just a single instance of the module or there may be a multiplicity. A board in the system may also contain one or more functional modules according to its type. As a brief example, an intelligent peripheral board capable of being a bus master would contain the following VME functional modules:

1. A data transfer bus (DTB) master — this is effectively the logic required to control a data transfer between a bus master and a bus slave.
2. A data transfer bus requester — this is the logic needed to request use of the data transfer bus.
3. An interrupter — the interrupter module generates an interrupt request upon request from a local functional module and responds with an 8-bit vector number during an interrupt acknowledge cycle.

Other functional module types are a system clock driver, a DTB slave, a bus arbiter, an interrupt handler and a power module. The VME bus system is split into four sub-buses called the data transfer bus, the arbitration bus, the interrupt bus and the utility bus. Briefly, the data transfer bus has 32 address lines, 6 address modifier lines, 32 data lines and various data transfer control lines. The arbitration bus contains the four bus request lines plus ten other lines to implement the arbitration scheme. The interrupt bus has seven interrupt lines and three control lines and finally the utility bus contains power lines, system reset, system clock and a system fail signal.

10.3 Memory Organisation

In this section the memory systems that are employed in single-chip microprocessor-based designs will be treated. The primary concern is with the semiconductor memory used in the system rather than the media used for mass storage, such as magnetic discs, magnetic tape, optical discs, bubble memory, etc. Mass storage techniques differ little between micro and mini or mainframe computers and so no additional treatment beyond that given in chapter 7 is required.

In general, system designers are not concerned with the internal operation or memory cell-structure of memory components, and in this section these aspects will only be mentioned when they have some impact on the external characteristics of the devices.

Semiconductor memory systems can be categorised according to the following properties:

(a) storage capacity — numbers of bits of information
(b) storage mode — permanent, semi-permanent or volatile
(c) cost per bit of information stored
(d) reliability — expressed as component failures per million hours
(e) speed of operation — access time
                              — cycle time (data transfer rate)
(f) power supply requirements — power consumption, voltage levels
(g) organisation — bit frame structure (1, 4, 8-bit words).

The choice of components is based upon the above properties and the particular cost, reliability, and operational requirements of the desired system.

A computer program typically has four identifiable areas: *program code*, *variable data*, *constant data* and *system variable data* (or stack/heap area). An additional area, used for input/output devices, will be discussed in section 10.4 and can be ignored for the time being. These four areas can be grouped into two types: those that are constant throughout the execution of the program (that is, program code and constant data) and those that vary during the execution of the program (that is, variables and system variable data). For example, consider the Pascal program below:

```
PROGRAM demo (output);
  CONST
    volts = 240;
    limit = 100;
    increment = 2;
  VAR
    amps : real;
    resistance: integer;
    i : integer;
  BEGIN (* demo *)
    amps := 4.0;
    i := increment;
    WHILE amps < limit do
      BEGIN (* while *)
        resistance := trunc(volts/amps);
        writeln('Resistance ',resistance,' at ',amps,' A');
        amps := amps + i
      END (* while *)
  END. (* demo *)
```

The allocation of objects to memory areas is apparently obvious. For example, the variables will be in the variable data area and the statements bracketed by 'BEGIN (* demo *)' and 'END. (* demo *)' will be in the program area. The statement 'resistance := trunc(volts/amps)' is more interesting in that it calls a function. In order for the program properly to pass parameters to the function and return to the caller, some information must be placed in the systems variable area by both the calling program and the function 'trunc'. This information will include the value of 'volts' divided by the value 'amps' to be passed to 'trunc', the address of the next statement to be executed after 'trunc', and the value returned by 'trunc'. A similar process is required for the invocation of the 'writeln' procedure. In fact, the line 'amps := amps + i' will also require the use of some system variable space, since there is an implicit type change on the value of 'i' from integer to real, before it can be added to 'amps'. This type change will require the use of a function by the program.

In a general-purpose computer system there is often no distinction made between the type of memory used for constant or variable information, because programs and data are continuously being loaded and unloaded as system tasks change. For example, a payroll system may be executed, followed by a mail list generation program, followed by a resistance calculation program. However, in an embedded microcomputer system the program will generally be fixed and will not change with time. As an example, a microcomputer-controlled washing machine would be rather inconvenient to use if the user had to load in a program off floppy disc for each wash cycle! For embedded microcomputers it is thus usual to have some storage that may only be read (that is, for non-variable information) and some that may be read and written (that is, for variable information). These memory classes are *read-only memory* (ROM) and *read–write memory* (RWM) respectively, as described in section 7.5.

As explained earlier, ROM has the important characteristic that its contents are not lost when power is removed, and is described as being non-volatile. Most RWM devices lose their stored data when power is removed and are thus described as being volatile. The term 'random-access memory' or *RAM* is often used to distinguish RWM from ROM. This is sometimes misleading, however. Strictly speaking, RAM describes memory in which the contents of any memory location can be accessed directly rather than sequentially. An analogy is the comparison between finding a particular musical item on an audio record and on an audio cassette. With a record the pickup arm and cartridge is moved directly to the track to be played. On a cassette the tape must be moved forward or backward so that the read-head is positioned at the appropriate part of the tape — this requires sequentially reading through other musical items to reach that desired. In semiconductor memory, both ROM and RWM are randomly accessible and the term RAM applies equally well to both.

The division of semiconductor memory into broad categories is shown in figure 10.8.

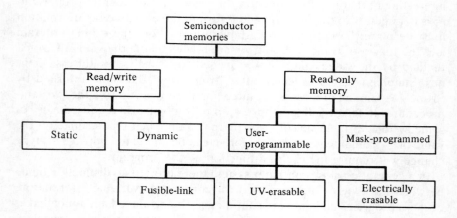

Figure 10.8 Semiconductor memory family tree

10.3.1   Organisation and Addressing

Every bit of information in a microcomputer system is stored in a separate single element or *cell*. For convenience, the cells are often grouped to represent an array of words, each of which may be 4 or 8 bits wide. This collection of bits forming a word is sometimes called a 'register'. A memory chip typically contains many such registers but its size is normally specified in terms of its *bit capacity*. For example, a 1K memory chip may be organised as illustrated in figure 10.9.

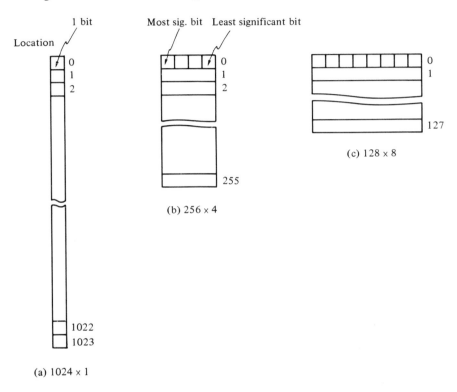

Figure 10.9 Possible organisations for a 1K memory

For a read–write memory device, each register or location is capable of two modes of operation, reading and writing. A read command accesses the information stored in a particular location and transfers it to the outside of the memory chip where it may be used or manipulated — for example, by the microprocessor. The reading of a location does not destroy the information stored. A write command transfers new information into the specified location. This process destroys any previously held information by over-writing it. The selection of a particular location within the chip is called *addressing*. It is the mechanism whereby external devices such as the microprocessor attain access to a location for a read or write operation. Since the memory sub-system of a microcomputer is likely to be made up of several memory devices, we also need a mechanism to select a particular chip. This process is called *chip selection*, and is achieved by providing a set of chip select inputs on the device. Thus a combination of address and chip selection causes the contents of a particular location to be accessed. A ROM device obviously has only one mode of operation — reading. In other senses it is similar in operation to a RWM device.

The organisation of a typical RWM chip is shown in figure 10.10 for a 1K (256 by 4) arrangement. The identification of a particular storage location from the address information on the address bus is achieved via a decoder (8 line to 256 line). The chip is connected to the microprocessor data bus via separate data in and data out lines via buffers. Separate read and write

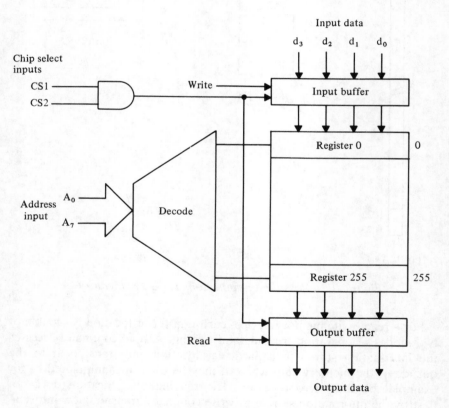

Figure 10.10 Register-based memory organisation

control lines are also provided. These enable the output and input buffers respectively when combined with the chip select signals. The chip select signals effectively enable the complete memory chip, rendering it operative for either a read or a write operation. When the chip select signals are such that the chip is not selected, the device is effectively disconnected from the data input and data output buses. This disconnection is achieved by using *tri-state buffers* on the output lines and simple AND logic gating on the inputs. The tri-state buffers have, as their name implies, three output conditions: logic '0', logic '1', and high impedance mode. In the high impedance mode the output impedance of the buffers is such that only a few microamps leakage current is sunk by the device and they act as if they are disconnected from the bus system. When a device is not selected, the contents remain unaffected by any changes on the address and data signals. The chip select inputs are primarily used to distinguish between a number of memory devices in a given system.

Once a particular memory location has been identified using the address and chip select information, data is transferred from memory or new data to the memory using the read or write controls respectively.

The memory organisation shown in figure 10.10 is typical of a register file structure which may be found on processor chips as well as memory components.

10.3.2 Read/Write Memory (RWM)

As discussed in chapter 7, there are two common operating categories of semiconductor RWM called *static* and *dynamic*, which have different operating characteristics and circuit realisations. Static RWM contains cells which are able to retain the stored information indefinitely, provided that the power supply is maintained. The cell is essentially a flip-flop or latch and thus, once information is latched, it remains until over-written. Modern NMOS static memory cells utilise four transistors and a resistor for their implementation. A dynamic RWM is only capable of retaining its stored information for a short time (milliseconds) since it relies on charge storage in a capacitor, which inevitably leaks away with time. A dynamic memory device must therefore be refreshed on a regular basis to retain its information. The refresh process simply involves reading the cell contents and rewriting an amplified version back into the capacitor. A modern NMOS dynamic cell may utilise only a single transistor.

Comparing static and dynamic RWM, it is apparent that dynamic devices have a much simpler structure and thus lead to a more dense memory chip. Dynamic memory devices also consume less power than static components since a cell only requires power when it is being refreshed or accessed. In contrast, a static cell requires continuity of supply, however it does not require the external refresh logic used in dynamic memory. Static devices are available with lower access times than those for dynamic devices. Both static and dynamic memory are available in CMOS and NMOS, while static devices are also available in the inherently faster bi-polar technology.

In choosing read/write memory for a system design a trade-off must be made between the characteristics of the two memory types. In general, for small system designs we would tend to use static devices because their simplicity outweighs their higher cost/bit. In contrast, for larger systems we would use dynamic memory because the higher packing density, lower cost and lower power consumption would be more relevant than simplifying the design.

10.3.3   Read-Only Memory (ROM)

As previously stated, this category of memory is primarily designed to hold information that is unlikely to change and which will remain preserved when power is removed. As memory technology has evolved, the distinction between RWM and ROM has become less clear since devices that have the traditional characteristics of ROM but are capable of having their contents modified at run-time are now becoming available. These devices are sometimes called *read-mostly memories*, for obvious reasons. There are also devices that can be user-programmed using external programming hardware. These form a family of programmable read-only memories (PROMs). True ROMs, PROMs and read-mostly devices will be treated in this section.

Pure ROM devices are implemented in several technologies, including CMOS, NMOS, TTL and ECL. The first two technologies are most commonly used in microcomputer systems, although bi-polar devices are sometimes used, for example, as character generators in VDUs. PROM and read-mostly memories are commonly implemented in MOS technology.

It is convenient to categorise ROM, PROM and read-mostly memory according to the technique employed to store information within the device. The most common forms of memory in these categories will now be discussed.

Mask programmed ROMs are pure ROM devices and have the information programmed into them as the last stage of manufacture. *Links* in the semiconductor structure are bridged by a *metallisation layer* according to the bit pattern to be stored. The link pattern is custom made according to a specification provided by the purchaser. Because of this customisation during manufacture, these devices are only used for large production runs where the cost of the link pattern mask generation can be amortised over a large volume of devices. A minimum production run for such devices would be 5000. Some information is used so commonly that it is worth while developing a standard ROM to hold it. Character pattern generators for VDUs and monitor programs for microcomputers are two typical examples.

Programmable read-only memory (PROM) is similar to ROM except that it may be programmed by the user after manufacture. All the links are installed during manufacture so that the device holds all ones or all zeros according to the logic polarity. A fusible material such as nichrome or polysilicon is used for the links and each link may be selectively blown or open-circuited by forcing a high current through it. External circuitry is required for generating this programming current. When a link is blown, it causes the cell at that position to take the complement of its original logic value. Once a link is blown, it cannot be restored and so PROM devices are capable of being programmed only once. PROMs are often called *fusible link devices* by manufacturers. PROM technology has not developed as quickly as in many other forms of memory and PROMs are fairly limited in their storage capacity. Fusible link PROMs are invariably implemented in bipolar technology. Their most common application in microcomputer systems is for memory address decoding. In more general digital applications, they can be used as the basis for finite state machines.

In *UV-Erasable Programmable Memory* (UV-EPROM), information may be programmed into the device by the user via external programming equipment. The complete contents of the device can also be erased by shining a UV light on to the silicon chip through a quartz window mounted on top of the component package. It should be emphasised that all the contents of the device are erased in this process and so the complete device must be reprogrammed to change a single cell location. The storage mechanism usually consists of trapping a charge in the floating gate of an MOS transistor. The charge is transferred by the application of relatively high voltage pulses (for example, 21 volts) and the presence of a charge usually represents a logic 0. The charge is removed by UV bombardment of the appropriate intensity, wavelength and duration. UV-EPROM devices were the first reprogrammable ROM devices available for general use in microcomputer systems. They were developed primarily to hold information during system development while program and data were liable to change. Subsequently the information would be put into a compatible mask programmed ROM. The situation today is still essentially the same although UV-EPROM devices are often used in products with low production runs. UV-EPROM devices will always be more expensive to produce than ROM because of the complexity of providing the quartz window in the package. A device that bridges the gap between a ROM and a UV-EPROM has been introduced recently. This is essentially a UV-

EPROM packaged in a normal plastic dual-in-line package with no quartz window. This yields a once-only programmable ROM that is compatible with both UV-EPROM and ROM devices. Because the device is packaged in this way it is cheaper than the equivalent UV-erasable device and is therefore more cost-effective in production runs that do not warrant the expense of a custom ROM.

Electrically erasable programmable ROM (EE-PROM) devices are similar in many respects to UV-EPROM, however there are two significant differences. Firstly, in EE-PROM devices there is no distinction between erasure and programming. A location is simply over-written by the new data to be stored. The programming is achieved electrically, usually by applying relatively high voltage pulses. Secondly, each location in an EE-PROM may be reprogrammed individually. Thus the complete device does not need to be reprogrammed to change a single bit or single location. As with UV-EPROM, there is a limit to the number of times that an EE-PROM can be reprogrammed. The limit is increasing as the technology develops and is currently of the order of thousands of reprogramming cycles. The time required to read EE-PROM devices is similar to that of standard MOS memories (for example, a few hundred nanoseconds). However, the programming time is significantly longer, being of the order of milliseconds. It is this time differential between reading and writing, as well as the non-volatility of the memory cells, that distinguishes EE-PROM from traditional RWM.

Because these devices are erased electrically there is no need to have a quartz window in the component package. This means that an EE-PROM is potentially cheaper than an equivalent UV-EPROM. Unfortunately this advantage in packaging is more than offset by the additional complexity of the memory cells, and EE-PROM is inherently more expensive than UV-EPROM and has a lower integration level. Some EE-PROM devices are available that are reprogrammable at standard 5 volt levels, thus simplyifying their integration into a system.

Because of their relative expense, EE-PROM devices have not replaced the UV-EPROM in the role of a development component. Also, during program development, it is unlikely that their advantage of single location reprogrammability will be of great benefit since a simple program change is likely to affect many locations in memory. For example, if an extra byte is added all subsequent locations will be changed.

The main role for EE-PROM devices is as read-mostly memory. A typical application in this category would be for the storage of calibration information in microprocessor-based instruments. As an instrument is only going to be recalibrated fairly infrequently, the limited number of times that an EE-PROM can be reprogrammed is unlikely to cause problems. Some applications require that information is modified during normal operation but saved when powered down. If the system is powered down relatively infrequently, then EE-PROM can be used as a non-volatile store for the information with RWM being used when manipulating the information during normal use. This situation occurs sufficiently frequently for manufacturers to have developed single-chip memory devices combining a RWM with an EE-PROM to hold the RWM data when powered down. This provides the best features of RWM and EE-PROM — that is, fast access for read and write operations with non-volatility.

10.3.4 Memory Timing

The timing of information transfer to and from a memory is important in synchronising activity with the processor. The sequence of events involved in a data transfer is as described in section 10.2. Timing diagrams for read and write operations for a typical RWM are shown in figure 10.11. The critical and most often quoted times are the *access* and *cycle times*, however, in designing a microcomputer memory system, all the parameters must be carefully assessed to ensure compatibility. For example, particular care must be taken to ensure that *set-up and hold times* are met and that control pulses (such as chip select and write enable) are of the appropriate width.

10.3.5 Address Map Design

The memory address register width of a microprocessor determines the *addressing range* for a system. For an 8-bit processor we have seen that a typical address length is 16 bits. This provides an address range of 64 kilobytes (that is, 65 536 bytes). More modern 16 and 32-bit designs have address sizes of anything up to 32 bits providing direct access to Gigabytes of memory. We normally visualise the address space as a linear array of memory locations whose width is the word-length of the processor and whose length is determined by the number of address bits provided by the processor. Some 16-bit processors use byte, rather than 16-bit word, width memory.

The assignment of physical memory devices to particular locations in the processor address space is a significant stage in the design of a microcomputer system. This assignment process is called *memory map design*. Figure 10.12 shows a typical address map for a processor with a 16-bit address. Note that the general layout of the address map is to some extent fixed by the microprocessor design. As an example, in figure 10.12 the lowest-order address locations are used to hold addresses that are used to point to routines for servicing interrupts. One of these lowest-order addresses in particular will contain either the address of the first instruction to be

Read cycle ① ②

Symbol	Paramé'
t_{RC}	Read cycle time
t_A	Access time
t_{CO}	Chip selection to output valid
t_{CX}	Chip selection to output active
t_{OTD}	Output 3-state from deselection
t_{OHA}	Output hold from address change

Notes

1 A read occurs during the overlap of a low $\overline{CS}$ and a high $\overline{WE}$.

2 $\overline{WE}$ is high for a Read Cycle.

3 A write occurs during the overlap of a low $\overline{CS}$ and a low $\overline{WE}$. t_W is measured from the latter of $\overline{CS}$ or $\overline{WE}$ going low to the earlier of $\overline{CS}$ or $\overline{WE}$ going high.

4 If the $\overline{CS}$ low transition occurs simultaneously with the $\overline{WE}$ low transition, the output buffers remain in a high impedance state.

5 $\overline{WE}$ must be high during all address transitions.

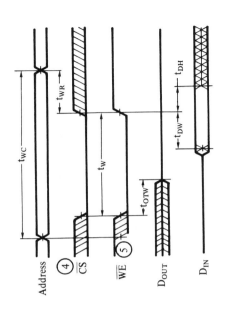

Write cycle ③

Symbol	Parameter
t_{WC}	Write cycle time
t_W	Write time
t_{WR}	Write release time
t_{OTW}	Output 3-state from write
t_{DW}	Data to write time overlap
t_{DH}	Data hold from write time

Figure 10.11 Read/write cycle timing

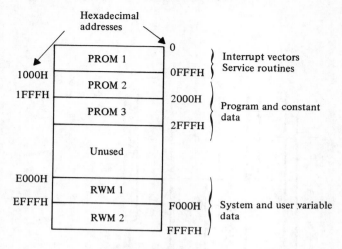

Figure 10.12 Typical address map

executed when the microprocessor is reset or the instruction itself, see section 10.5.2. This information must be held in non-volatile memory, otherwise the processor could not start up properly. A PROM is thus employed at these lowest-order addresses. Apart from this constraint, RWM and ROM can be placed as desired. The aim when designing a memory map is generally to minimise the logic required for chip selection while if possible maximising the flexibility of the map to allow more devices to be added in the future. There is a quite clear trade-off between flexibility and minimising the cost of chip selection logic.

In most applications, particularly with the large address spaces provided by 16 and 32-bit processors, it is unlikely that the number of memory devices required will fill the available address space. It is also unlikely that a single memory device will provide all the memory resources required by a processor, if only because combination RWM and ROM devices are very rare. Usually several memory devices, often with very different characteristics, will be used partially to populate the address space provided by the processor. To choose between individual devices, the address output by the processor is 'decoded' to determine which device is mapped on to that address. The particular device is selected by the chip select input described in section 10.3.1. The techniques commonly employed in implementing the chip selection logic will now be described.

The simplest technique is called *linear selection* and relies on the use of individual high-order address lines to select a memory device. For example, in a system with a 16-bit address bus, if we wish to use 6 devices each of 1K-word in size, only the 10 lower-order address lines will be used in selecting a location within a device. The residual 6 address lines can each

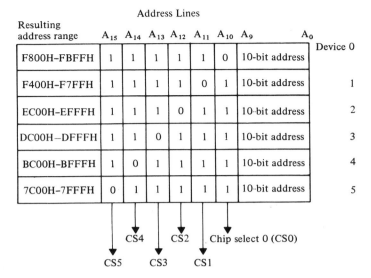

Address Lines

Resulting address range	A₁₅	A₁₄	A₁₃	A₁₂	A₁₁	A₁₀	A₉ ... A₀	
F800H–FBFFH	1	1	1	1	1	0	10-bit address	Device 0
F400H–F7FFH	1	1	1	1	0	1	10-bit address	1
EC00H–EFFFH	1	1	1	0	1	1	10-bit address	2
DC00H–DFFFH	1	1	0	1	1	1	10-bit address	3
BC00H–BFFFH	1	0	1	1	1	1	10-bit address	4
7C00H–7FFFH	0	1	1	1	1	1	10-bit address	5

CS4   CS2   Chip select 0 (CS0)

CS5   CS3   CS1

Figure 10.13 Linear selection example

be used to select an individual chip. Figure 10.13 shows a typical result of employing linear decoding. The main point to note is that the address ranges for the devices are not contiguous. This can cause problems for the programmer, particularly when using program memory where 'jumps' from one device to the next would have to be designed into the code. This would make software maintenance very difficult and would prohibit the use of high-level language compilers. Another potential problem with linear decoding is that, if the programmer makes an error and accesses an address that causes two chip selects to be asserted, two devices will be selected at once. This may result in damage to both the memory devices selected. Linear selection is only employed when a very small number of devices (such as 2 or 3) are to be used and when no future expansion is envisaged. The only merit is that it is cheap to implement.

At the other extreme in terms of cost of implementation is *full decoding*. Using this approach, chip selection logic is employed to produce a unique chip select signal for every combination of the residual address bits, as shown in figure 10.14. Full decoding is the only method which allows utilisation of the full memory space and it obviously ensures that no two devices are selected at once. The main disadvantage with full decoding is that it can require a significant amount of logic for its implementation. The use of modern programmable logic such as bipolar PROMs and PLAs can however largely overcome this.

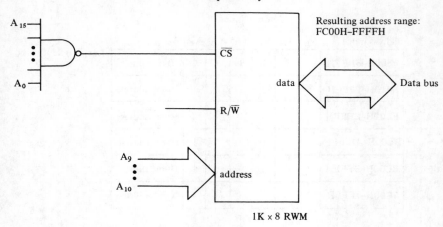

Figure 10.14 Full decoding for one memory device

A compromise between the rigour of full decoding and the limitations of linear decoding is to use full decoding on a sub-set of the residual address lines. This *partial decoding* technique allows selection of more devices than linear selection but without the complexity of full decoding. Partial decoding, if implemented wisely, can also prevent multiple device selection. A typical chip selection scheme utilising partial decoding is shown in figure 10.15. Instead of using AND logic for every chip selection, a

Resulting address range:	Address lines					Decoder o/p
	A_{15} A_{13}	A_{12}	A_{11}	A_{10}	A_9 A_0	
0000–03FFH	Don't care	0	0	0	10-bit address	CS 0
0400H–07FFH	Don't care	0	0	1	10-bit address	CS 1
0800H–0BFFH	Don't care	0	1	0	10-bit address	CS 2
0C00H–0FFFH	Don't care	0	1	1	10-bit address	CS 3
1000H–13FFH	Don't care	1	0	0	10-bit address	CS 4
1400H–17FFH	Don't care	1	0	1	10-bit address	CS 5
1800H–1BFFH	Don't care	1	1	0	10-bit address	CS 6
1C00H–1FFFH	Don't care	1	1	1	10-bit address	CS 7

(Assumes A_{15}–A_{13} are all zero)

Connect to 3-to-8-line decoder

Figure 10.15 Partial decoding

general-purpose n-bit to m-line decoder can be employed. Thus a 3-to-8-line decoder can be safely used to select 8 devices using three residual address lines. This idea can be further extended since most decoder chips have their own enable inputs. Thus a further 3-to-8-line decoder on the most significant three address lines can be used to select lower-order decoders. Such a configuration is shown in figure 10.16.

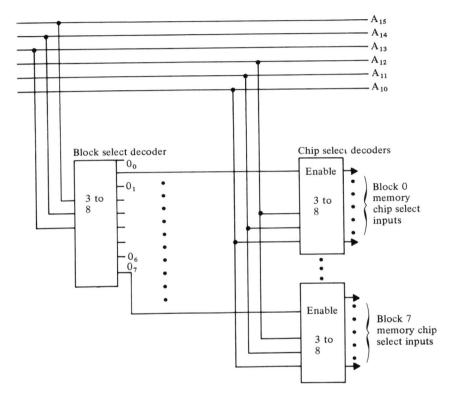

Figure 10.16 Two-level decoding scheme using standard 3-to-8-line decoders

10.4 Input/Output

The logical address space of a microprocessor system is split into two major sections: the memory area and the input/output area. In this section the implementation of the I/O addressing mechanisms in microprocessors will be considered. The features of typical parallel I/O support devices and special-purpose I/O chips will also be discussed.

10.4.1 Input/Output Address Spaces

The I/O address space can be part of the normal memory addressing range or be in a separate dedicated address space. In the former case, the system designer has explicit control over where the I/O devices are mapped on to the address space. This technique is often called *memory-mapped* I/O for obvious reasons. A benefit of memory-mapped I/O is that, since I/O devices appear to the processor to be memory locations, all the normal memory reference instructions and addressing modes can be used in I/O operations. Thus, for example, it is possible to subtract the contents of an I/O register from the contents of a processor register using this scheme. We also have the advantage of having a large address space for I/O devices, although this is of course to the detriment of memory address space. The loss of potential memory address space is, however, rarely a problem since few microprocessors make full use of the available address space. Perhaps the main disadvantage of this scheme is that if a program has an error in its implementation or design, it may erroneously access I/O locations and cause problems in the external hardware. It is also argued that programs employing memory-mapped I/O are more difficult to debug. However, both these disadvantages are minor and are counter-balanced by the flexibility and power offered by being able to use normal memory reference instructions.

The main alternative to memory-mapped I/O is to have a separate address space dedicated solely to I/O devices. To gain access to this address space it is necessary to provide some dedicated I/O instruction to the programmer. The Intel 8085 is a processor that supports a separate I/O address space and it provides an IN and an OUT instruction to transfer data from and to one of 256 input and 256 output registers respectively. There are normally severe limitations upon the addressing modes provided for I/O instructions. For example, the IN and the OUT instructions of the Intel 8085 can only transfer data between the accumulator and a directly addressed I/O register. More recent processors, such as the Intel 8086, do allow slightly more flexibility with the ability to address an I/O register indirectly through a processor register, although transfers are still limited to the accumulator. These limitations are the prime drawback of current implementations of this concept. In microprocessors that do employ a separate I/O address space, we must obviously have some means of distinguishing between the two address spaces. This is achieved by using the same address and data paths for memory and I/O operations but having an extra qualifier signal to select between the two address spaces. Processors which provide a separate I/O address space can still use memory-mapped I/O if desired and so allow the designer the freedom to choose the most appropriate technique for a given application.

10.4.2 Input/Output Registers

The physical implementation of the registers used to provide the interface between the processor and the external devices varies widely according to the complexity of the I/O function. At the lowest level the I/O registers or *ports*, as they are more commonly called, can simply be bus-compatible buffers or gates. For the input ports the connection on to the processor bus must have a high-impedance mode so that they can be selectively enabled on to the processor data route. For output ports, the inputs from the processor bus must simply be compatible with the processor bus driving capability with the outputs typically being TTL compatible.

For many input devices, the arrangement shown in figure 10.17 may be quite adequate since they either have their data permanently available for the processor (for example, toggle switches) or given an indication when they have data available for transfer (for example, an analogue-to-digital

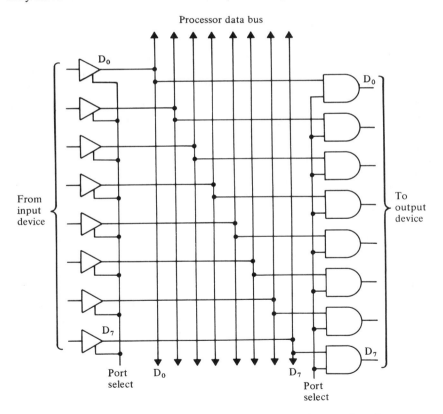

Figure 10.17 Primitive input/output connection to data bus

converter). The latter case requires special handling techniques which are discussed in section 10.5. However, the output arrangement shown is far from satisfactory for most external devices since the data will appear at the gate outputs only while the data is on the data bus and while the port is selected. We could not easily use such an arrangement for driving an indicator lamp since the lamp would be illuminated for a microsecond or less. The external device would thus have to provide its own data latch to staticise the information and be told when to expect information. A far more satisfactory solution is to use a latch interfaced directly to the data bus to staticise the information directly so that the external device is relieved of this function. This is illustrated in figure 10.18. The 8-bit port shown is simply an 8-bit latch. While the latch is enabled, the Q outputs follow the D inputs. When the enable input goes from low to high, the D inputs are latched on the Q outputs. Further changes at D do not affect Q. Most microprocessor manufacturers provide byte-wide latching ports which can be used as either inputs or outputs and provide limited handshaking and interrupt facilities.

To increase the flexibility of I/O ports, the majority of microprocessor families include so-called *programmable ports*. These are devices which can be configured under program control to be either input or output ports. The degree of control is often very high and it is frequently possible to define the individual port bits to be input, output, bi-directional or control lines. To achieve this level of flexibility it is necessary to have additional registers within the programmable device which are accessible by the processor. These additional registers control the direction of data flow through the ports (*data direction registers* or DDR) and the I/O control mechanism to be employed (*control/status registers*). I/O control mechanisms, such as interrupts and polling, will be discussed in section 10.5 and their implementation will not be further described here. If bit level control over a port is required, then the associated DDR must have one bit for each port line. As an example, consider figure 10.19 which shows one bit of a typical implementation. The DDR bit latch state determines whether the I/O line is configured as an input (DDR bit = 0) or an output (DDR bit = 1), and is set to define the port bit as an input at reset. Note that the output latch can be written into even though the associated I/O line is configured as an input. This allows the output line state to be initialised before being enabled. In addition, the port can also be read even if it configured as an output. These two conditions are obviously essential if it is required to mix inputs and outputs on one port. It is usual to have two or three such 8-bit ports in a single chip.

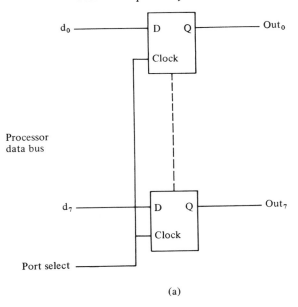

(a)

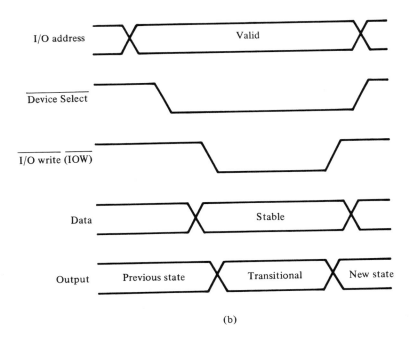

(b)

Figure 10.18 Simple latching port: (a) port configuration; (b) port timing

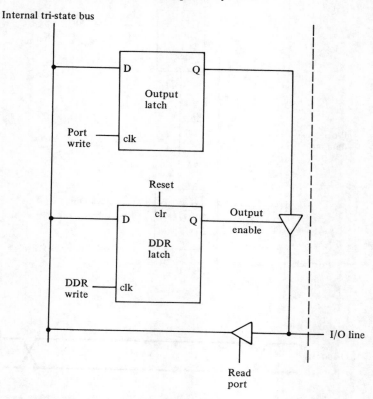

Figure 10.19 Programmable port bit configuration

10.4.3 Special-purpose I/O Devices

Many functions in a microprocessor-based design can be implemented in either hardware or in software and the choice of such a function's implementation can be a significant consideration. A good example of this choice is in counting events or time. A program module can easily be designed to count external events by simply monitoring an I/O line which is toggled for each event. Similarly, time intervals can also be calculated if the programmer can derive some relationship between the number instructions executed between events and 'real' time. However, both these processes rely on the processor being always available for their particular task. In simple systems, such a compromise may be quite realistic, but in most applications the processor is required to perform many tasks concurrently and some other technique must be employed. This generally involves delegating some functions to dedicated hardware devices. We shall briefly consider some of the more common devices in this class.

Firstly, following on from the example above, most microprocessor families have *counter/timer* chips. These are basically binary counters that are clocked by the microprocessor clock, another crystal-controlled oscillator or an external event input line. The clock source for the counters can be under program control and the current count value can be read or reset by the processor. Thus, in order to count events, the event detector is simply connected to the clock input and the counter is read or cleared as required. To time events, the event detector is used to interrupt the processor to indicate an event start or termination and cause the processor to start or stop the counter respectively. If the counter is driven by a clock of known frequency, the event time can be calculated.

Another common I/O device is the *universal synchronous–asynchronous receiver/transmitter* or *USART*. This device converts parallel data patterns into a serial format for use in data communication systems. A simple example would be in the connection of a terminal to a computer or a computer to a modem. Again, many of the functions of a USART are relatively straightforward and could largely be implemented in software. However, in this case some hardware is required to perform data sampling and clock recovery and it is therefore advantageous to combine the parallel to serial conversion and these special hardware functions on one chip.

Other examples of special-purpose I/O devices are cathode-ray tube (CRT) controllers and keyboard scanners for use in computer terminal applications, local area network controllers, graphics display controllers and data encrypters for secure data transmission.

10.5   Controlling Input/Output Operations

In the previous section the references to input and output operations tacitly assumed that an external device was available and ready to receive or transmit data to the microprocessor. In real applications this simplistic assumption is not valid. For example, there is no point in reading an analogue to digital converter if it is in the middle of a sample conversion nor in writing to a display system if it has not completed the last display function. This introduces the concept of external hardware or processes operating asynchronously with respect to the microprocessor program. In order for a program to function correctly, it must somehow be brought into synchronism with these external events. Three basic techniques are available — *polling, interrupts* and *direct memory access* (DMA).

10.5.1   Polling

Polling is a software controlled technique whereby the program regularly tests the status of a device to see if it requires an I/O operation. The polling routine is typically part of the main body of the program and in an I/O-driven system would result in a program structure like:

```
repeat
        read (device_0_status);
        if device_0_status = ready then service_device_0;
        read (device_1_status);
        if device_1_status = ready then service_device_1;
        read (device_2_status);
        if device_2_status = ready then service_device_2
until process_complete;
```

Polling thus allows a single program apparently to service several I/O devices concurrently. An implementation of the polling hardware is shown in figure 10.20. Note that a single input port can be used to allow several devices to be monitored through a single read operation.

The often cited disadvantage of polling is that it wastes processor resources by spending a large amount of time checking to see if data is

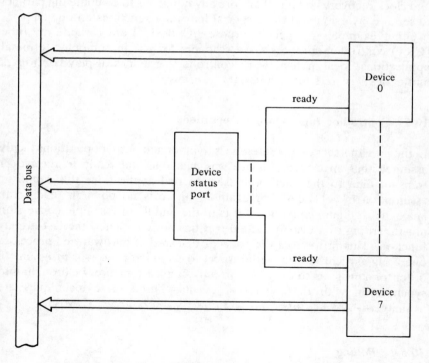

Figure 10.20 Polling hardware implementation

available. In many systems this is a perceived rather than a real problem, since the processor may not be able to do anything without any data anyway. There is, however, one limiting feature of polling, that is the *response time* to external events. For example, in the program fragment above, the worst-case delay for a response is the loop time with all devices being serviced. To some extent this can be overcome by polling those devices which have higher data rates more frequently than slower devices, but in a dynamic environment with changing priorities this may become complex.

However, polling does have some significant advantages. Firstly, the I/O operations are under program control. This leads to predictable program flow and significantly simplifies testing. Polling is also conceptually simple and just as simple to implement with minimal hardware requirements. For these reasons, polling should be the first choice in controlling I/O operations. If, because of real response problems, it is unsatisfactory, then interrupts should be considered.

10.5.2 Interrupts

In an interrupt system, the microprocessor is asked by the I/O devices for service — this is the complete opposite of polling. At the limit, an external device can demand immediate service from the processor, leading to a program flow as shown in figure 10.21. The rapid response time is achieved by the processor testing one or a number of *interrupt input pins* on the processor chip before each instruction is executed. Because of the fre-

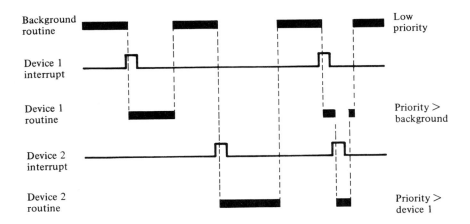

Figure 10.21 Program flow for multiple-level interrupts

quency of the test, it must be performed by hardware in the processor and is equivalent to:

if interrupt pin(s) active
    then service interrupt(s)
    else fetch next instruction;

The external hardware required to implement an interrupting device is shown in figure 10.22. In response to an interrupt the microprocessor must:

1. Save the current program counter value
2. Load the program counter with the address of the interrupt service routine
3. Save the processor register values
4. Execute the service routine
5. Restore the processor register values
6. Restore the program counter value

This process is known as a *context switch* and the rate at which context switches can take place is an important parameter for many real-time applications since it represents a bound on performance. Some microprocessors perform steps 3 and 5 automatically, others require explicit action on behalf of the programmer to save the register values. The microprocessor generally uses a stack to save the register and program counter values.

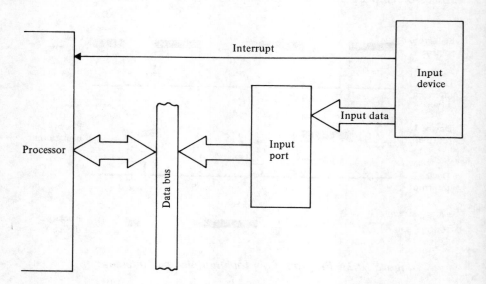

Figure 10.22 Interrupt hardware implementation

In most applications it is necessary to have *multiple-level* interrupts — that is, to service more than one device with some form of priority
between devices. For this scheme to work, the microprocessor must decide
whether a given request should be serviced and, if so, at which address it
should begin executing the service routine. Several techniques are available to implement multiple-level interrupt schemes, ranging from using
sophisticated external hardware *interrupt controllers* to simply having a
number of prioritised interrupt pins on the processor chip. No matter
which technique is employed, a method of ensuring that a low-priority
device interrupt request does not disturb a high-priority service routine
must be employed. This is called *interrupt masking* and is usually software
controlled so that priorities can be assigned according to the tasks being
executed.

It is worth briefly discussing some of the alternative techniques
employed in microprocessors to determine the service routine address for a
particular interrupt. Consider a processor with 3 levels of interrupt, level 0
being the highest and level 2 being the lowest priority. The microprocessor
has three interrupt input pins called INT0, INT1, and INT2. In addition, it
has another *non-maskable interrupt* called NMI. An NMI request is always
serviced even if another interrupt is currently being handled. Thus a total
of four interrupt service routine addresses need to be defined. Finally, we
will have a special microprocessor reset input which will initialise the
processor to a known state, typically at power-up. The handling of both the
reset and the more general interrupts is normally carried out in one or two
ways. The first causes the microprocessor to take an address from a given
location to determine the service routine address for a given interrupt, as
shown below:

Address (Hex)	Contents
0FFF6, 0FFF7	INT2 service routine address
0FFF8, 0FFF9	INT1 service routine address
0FFFA, 0FFFB	INT0 service routine address
0FFFC, 0FFFD	NMI service routine address
0FFFE, 0FFFF	Reset routine address

Each pair of address memory locations holds a *vector* to the service
routine. The alternative is for the processor to begin executing directly
from an address rather than indirectly as above. This is shown below:

Address (Hex)	
0FFEC..0FFEF	INT2 service routine
0FFF0..0FFF3	INT1 service routine
0FFF4..0FFF7	INT0 service routine
0FFF8..0FFFB	NMI service routine
0FFFC..0FFFF	Jump to program start

In this case, four address locations are used for each interrupt level. This is because, in general, enough locations are needed for a call to a subroutine instruction and a return from interrupt instruction. This allows a call and return to a more lengthy routine elsewhere in the address space. Neither this scheme nor the vectoring technique has any significant advantages over each other.

10.5.3   *Direct Memory Access*

Some peripheral devices, such as discs and graphics units, require such high data transfer rates that they cannot be handled by the execution of a microprocessor program. In these cases it is essential that the peripheral device has direct access to the processor memory whenever it requires it. This is called direct memory access and is implemented by using a special *DMA controller*. The DMA controller resides on the same data, address and control buses as the microprocessor and requests the use of these buses from the processor, as described in section 10.1. The bus request signal which is used for a DMA request typically causes the processor to halt after it acknowledges the request, with the buses floating in a high-impedence state. The DMA controller then generates the appropriate address and control signals to permit transfers of data directly between the peripheral and memory — not via the DMA controller. When the transfer is complete, the DMA controller releases the bus request signal and the processor resumes control of the data bus system. The DMA controller is itself a peripheral to the microprocessor and its internal registers must be accessible to the microprocessor to allow for the setting up of addresses, transfer modes, etc. Figure 10.23 shows a block diagram of the DMA/ microprocessor interface.

10.6   Microprocessor Features

The design of a computer-based system is traditionally separated into two distinct branches at a fairly early stage in the design life-cycle. These two branches deal with the hardware and the software design. In this section we are going to investigate the features of a microprocessor that are important to the hardware and the software designer.

Nowadays there is little to differentiate a microprocessor from any other form of CPU apart from the physical implementation. The instruction sets of most general-purpose microprocessors are similar in content to those of many minicomputers and the addressing modes provided also bear close comparison with those of larger machines. Perhaps the only significant differences lie in the provision of some specialised I/O instructions, for

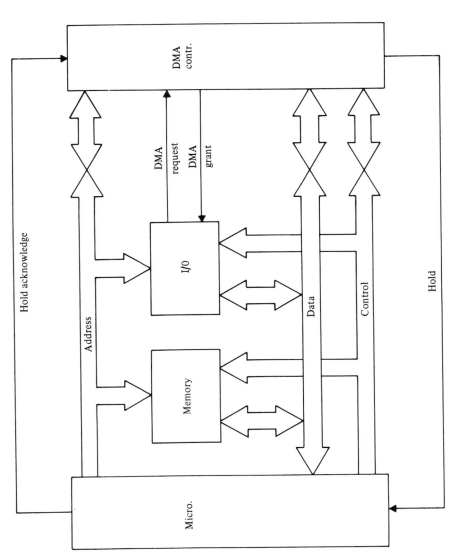

Figure 10.23 DMA–microprocessor interface

example, for individual bit manipulation. Thus the instructions and addressing modes described in section 6.6 which are attributed to a minicomputer, would also be typical of many modern microprocessors.

Rather than concentrating on the features of some particular microprocessors, it is more useful at this stage to discuss the issues that affect the choice of a microprocessor for a given application. These issues can be broadly broken down into two categories — technical and commercial. For most microprocessor applications, the factors in these two categories are traded against each other and dependent upon the specific application, different weightings will be given to each factor.

10.6.1 *Technical Considerations*

In this section, the technical factors that may be considered when choosing a particular microprocessor for a given application are enumerated. Obviously, some of these technical characteristics have an impact on the commercial considerations; for example, high performance generally implies high cost. Here are some of the more important features that may be evaluated:

(1) Word-length — the word-length of a processor defines the most natural data size for the processor to manipulate. Thus an 8–bit processor fetches 8-bit data from memory and most operators operate on 8-bit data elements. This does not preclude the processor from being able to manipulate data of greater length, indeed an 8-bit processor that could only operate on 8-bit data would be considered to be very restrictive. Similarly, a 32-bit processor will typically be able to manipulate 1, 8 and 16-bit data as well as its natural 32 bits. Some processors, although being described as 16-bit, fetch their data values in 8-bit pieces over an 8-bit data bus. Although these may have a 16-bit ALU, they are necessarily slower than a true 16-bit processor because of the greater number of memory references required for each data manipulation. The advantage of having a narrower bus width is lower cost, owing to the smaller packaging and the fewer bus buffers and PCB tracks required.

(2) Execution speed — the execution speed of a microprocessor can only be truly assessed by considering the execution time required for each instruction. A high processor clock speed does not necessarily imply a high execution rate, since the clock may be internally divided down to define the basic 'beats' of the machine, and is thus a misleading measure of true performance. In order to assess the effective performance of a microprocessor, it will be necessary to develop a benchmark program that reflects typical mix operations

for a given application and either calculate or measure the relative performances of the microprocessors being considered.

(3) Instruction set—the quality of an instruction set is to some extent a subjective measurement once certain basic instructions are included. There is still much debate by computer scientists on the most effective way of implementing an instruction set, and this basically revolves around whether it is more efficient to provide an instruction set with many specialised and powerful instructions or have one that has a few primitive instructions that can be executed very quickly. Most microprocessors have followed the former trend, but there are some notable exceptions, such as the Inmos Transputer. Some applications may have particular needs, such as the ability to multiply and divide data. Obviously, it may be more effective to choose a processor that includes multiply and divide instructions in such cases.

(4) Addressing range — the addressing range of a microprocessor is a parameter that can easily be evaluated, however there are some potential pitfalls even in this apparently simple measure. For example, some processors have a segmented address space such that at any particular instance only a small portion of the total address space can be accessed. If there is a need to manipulate data structures that are larger than a segment, some complex address calculations may be required at run time, thus putting a bound on performance.

(5) Addressing modes — for a programmer or compiler writer, the addressing modes provided by a microprocessor are one of the most significant attributes. The availability of powerful indirect addressing capabilities combined with appropriate address manipulation instructions can significantly simplify programming tasks that require data structure manipulation. Tasks such as searching or manipulating lists, which are common in many applications, benefit greatly from addressing modes which permit indirection through registers or memory locations.

(6) Data types — as mentioned earlier, many processors can manipulate data that is not the natural size for the ALU. This can extend from a single-bit, which is important in control applications, to a floating-point number which will be important in applications where a significant amount of arithmetic is required. It could make life very tedious for the programmer in a bit-intensive I/O application if bit-manipulation instructions were not available. More importantly, it could have a significant impact on the overall efficiency of the resulting code. It is therefore important that the requirements of the application are considered when looking at the data handling capabilities of a microprocessor.

(7) Interrupt facilities — many real-time systems rely on the availability of some method of handling interrupts, as described in section 10.5.2. As far as the interrupt facilities of a microprocessor are concerned, the major requirements are typically for a single non-maskable interrupt to enable a guaranteed response to a critical situation, one or more maskable interrupts for general use and, perhaps most important of all, a fast context switching mechanism to allow a rapid response to a request.

(8) Support devices — the availability of a comprehensive family of support chips such as those mentioned in section 10.4.3 can significantly reduce the programming effort, the hardware design effort and reduce overall production costs. Other effects can be a reduction in system size and power consumption and an improvement in reliability when compared with implementations that cannot make use of such devices.

(9) Power consumption — many applications have severe constraints on the power supply current available. Typical of these are portable instruments, remote monitoring systems and any application that must be battery powered. In such cases the use of low power CMOS components is highly desirable, if not essential. In some applications there may be adequate power available, but dissipating the heat generated may be a problem. Again, a CMOS-based solution may be desirable. Even where power consumption or heat generation is not a problem, it usually makes sense to minimise power usage if only to reduce the size, and therefore cost, of the power supply.

(10) Other physical considerations — certain applications have particular requirements for noise immunity, reliability, radiation hardness, operating temperature/humidity range, etc. In such cases these factors often have a dominant effect on the choice of processor and some of the other considerations mentioned above may become secondary.

(11) Development environments — an often neglected aspect of choosing a microprocessor for an application is the quality of the development tools or environment available for the various processors. The tools should support the development of both the hardware and the software, if possible in an integrated environment. The hardware support should include timing analysers for pure hardware analysis. Software support should include tools to implement the software engineering concepts described in the next chapter. This will obviously include assemblers, high-level language compilers and linkers. The software debugging should be carried out at the same level as the source code — that is, using high-level language references or assembler symbols, and not in hexadecimal or octal, etc. The integration of the hardware and software can be simplified by

the use of microprocessor emulators, which allow code to be tested before actual or *target* hardware is available, and vice versa. The integration testing should be able to be carried out in real-time; that is, at the full rated speed of the target microprocessor and without placing any restrictions on the use of the microprocessor. This requirement is sometimes called *resource transparency*. Some aids to performance measurement are also highly desirable when developing real-time programs. This will enable critical sections of code to be identified and tuned to optimise their performance. Finally, the development environment must include a convenient mechanism for programming PROMs.

10.6.2 *Commercial Considerations*

Although the technical considerations considered above have a great impact on the success or otherwise of a project, it is also important to be aware of the commercial considerations. Very often it is these considerations and not the technical features of a microprocessor that dictate the choice. Some of the major considerations are:

(1) Cost — in general, it is desirable to choose the most cost-effective microprocessor for an application. This may not necessarily be the cheapest microprocessor that is suitable — the particular technical benefits of one processor may justify its choice if it can reduce costs in other areas, even if it is more expensive than a competitor.

(2) Availability — the microprocessor must be available so that good progress can be made during the development phase. It is no use choosing the latest processor if it is not going to be available at a suitable point in the product life-cycle.

(3) Continuity of supply — many microprocessor-based products have a relatively short production life. However, it is often necessary to be able to provide maintenance support for the product for many years and so continuity of supply can be a significant issue.

(4) Multiple sources — some microprocessors are available from several manufacturers. These are often under *second-source* agreements, where the original manufacturer sells the production masks to another vendor so that the latter can manufacture and sell the same devices. The availability of second-sources can ensure continuity of supply during production and give independence from a single supplier.

(5) Support from the manufacturers — it may be important to be able to receive technical assistance from the manufacturer or its agents. This is particularly important when using new devices.

(6) Familiarity — a project can make much faster initial progress if the system designers are familiar with the microprocessor to be used, or have at least used other members of the same microprocessor family. This also applies to the programmers, if programming at the assembly language level.

(7) Compatibility — a natural extension of familiarity is the availability of proven code from previous products. Thus, if there is source or object code compatibility with a processor used in a previous project, significant savings in effort may be possible.

10.7 Summary

This chapter has described the various forms that a microcomputer can take, ranging from a single-chip to a multi-board system utilising a wide variety of peripheral devices. The bus systems to be found in a microcomputer system have been described, with reference to industry or international standards where appropriate. The implementation of microcomputer memory and input/output systems have also been discussed, with reference to both the hardware and software aspects of their design. Finally, those microprocessor characteristics that are significant in selecting a processor for a specific application have been described.

References

10.1 Weitzman, C., *Distributed Micro/Minicomputer Systems*, Prentice-Hall, Englewood Cliffs, New Jersey, 1979.

10.2 Libes, S. and Garetz, M., *Interfacing to S-100/IEEE 696 Microcomputers*, Osborne/McGraw-Hill, Berkeley, California, 1981.

10.3 Barthmier, J., *Intel Multibus Interfacing*, Intel Application Note AP-28A, Intel Corporation, 1979.

10.4 Fischer, W., 'IEEE P1014 — A Standard Bus for the High-Performance VME Bus', *IEEE Micro*, February 1985, pp. 31–41.

11 Introduction to Software Engineering

Objectives

The earlier chapters in this book have described the hardware and software components that are required to construct a computer system and have introduced some general ideas on the application of computers in a variety of areas. The concept of a general-purpose piece of electronic hardware being characterised for a particular application by a program is now very familiar. Until relatively recently the development of a computer program was in many respects regarded as being creative in an artistic sense — even as a black art by many! As computer-based systems have become more complex, this approach to systems development has become inadequate and, given our reliance on computers for our survival, distinctly dangerous. In order properly to harness the power of a computer, a more rigorous approach to the production of software systems is required — that of engineering.

In this chapter the concepts of software engineering — that is, the application of engineering practices to the specification, design, implementation, validation and maintenance of software systems — are introduced. By its very nature, software engineering is a very immature discipline and the techniques and tools are still evolving. This chapter does not therefore present the 'laws of software engineering' for they do not yet exist, but attempts to illustrate some of the generally agreed principles of good software design using some of the techniques currently available.

11.1 Introduction

In engineering the development of a product is traditionally broken down into the five major stages of product specification, design, construction or implementation, testing, and maintenance. This flow of development is usually reflected in the structure of engineering companies and is regarded as quite natural. The aim of software engineering is to employ the same strategy in the production of a software system with specialists being employed at each of the five stages. Because the five stages represent the complete life of a product, they are often called the *software life cycle*. The software life cycle will form the basis for this chapter and each of the stages will be considered in turn.

Before considering the details of the techniques and tools that may be employed at each of the five stages of a software product's life, the meaning of each stage will be briefly discussed.

The specification for a product can be based on ideas that emanate from a number of potential sources. Such ideas could come from a marketing group where an opportunity for an entry into a new market area has been recognised or from the results of a research project. The source of the ideas is not particularly relevant, what is important is that the ideas are transformed into a clear, concise, complete and unambiguous specification. This process is often difficult for a software product for the basic reason that software has no real physical form, only a function. Thus it is not possible to specify a piece of software in terms of the physical quantities that are normally utilised in an engineering specification and it is only possible to specify its function. In traditional engineering the specification of the function of a system may be defined in terms of mathematical equations which can also represent a model of the system. Unfortunately, within the current state-of-the-art for software engineering such mathematical tools are not yet accessible. Other, less formal techniques are currently available for specifying software systems and some examples of these are described in section 11.2. The producer of a software specification is sometimes called a *systems analyst*.

Having developed a specification, the next stage in the development is to translate this into a design. The aim of the designer is to take the specification and map it into a set of program modules which are the building blocks of the system. The function of each block and the relationship between the blocks will be defined. The process of developing a design from a specification is often carried out in a *top-down* manner — that is, the overall function of the system is decomposed into a set of other more detailed functions which in turn are further decomposed until a point is reached where each function is readily understandable. It is apparent that this approach is used in most branches of engineering when designing a complex system. As an example, consider the design of an aircraft. The chief designer and the aerodynamicists will develop the basic shape and form of the aircraft. This outline will then be broken down into its constituent parts, such as fuselage, wings and tail assembly, which will then be designed in detail, etc. As with a software system, the designers have to ensure that all the constituent parts fit together and operate within the specified guidelines. This is analogous to defining the interfaces between the software modules. In section 11.3 some techniques that are currently utilised in designing a software system will be described.

When the design is complete, it has to be translated into instructions that the computer can execute. This is of course achieved by writing a program and is generally described as the implementation or coding phase. The implementation phase and the design phase are sadly often treated as the same thing in many software projects and this leads to a poorly designed and implemented system. An aircraft manufacturer would not think of letting some parts of the wings be produced and attached to the fuselage while other parts are still on the drawing board; software should be no different and the design must be complete before coding starts. The coding is achieved using a programming language as described in chapter 8. In section 11.4 the choice of programming language and the important characteristics of a good high-level programming language are described.

Upon completion of the implementation, the whole system has to be checked against the original specification to ensure that it fully meets the requirements. This process is generally known as validation in software engineering. Validation is intended to *prove* that a software system meets the specification. Unfortunately, true validation is difficult to achieve in any software projects of a significant size because it is almost impossible to test a program for every possible combination of inputs that may occur in the running of the program. Thus rather than validation, testing is normally used. Testing is primarily concerned with checking the implementation phase of the project and involves using a sub-set of possible input values and program states to check operation. It is interesting to note that many other branches of engineering rely on testing rather than validation to ensure the quality of a product. Returning to the example of an aircraft, it is usual for the physical size of components to be validated using micrometers, etc., but the flight performance of the complete aircraft is assessed by test-pilots and the robustness by fatigue testing of a complete aircraft on the ground. Some approaches to software testing and validation are described in section 11.5.

When the software system is finally in use, it will in all probability have to be maintained. This is not maintenance in the traditional engineering sense since software does not wear out or otherwise degrade with the passing of time. Software maintenance is required because of changes in the environment in which it operates. This may be due to physical changes such as the addition of new hardware or it may be due to new ideas regarding the utilisation of the system — that is, a modification of the specification. Obviously, given the lack of formal validation, some maintenance may also be needed to remove 'bugs' which have slipped through the testing procedures. Research has shown that maintenance is the largest single cost item in the software life cycle and much of the impetus for improving specification, design and implementation has been derived from this fact. For this reason, maintenance is not considered in a separate section in this chapter but within each section as appropriate.

This introduction has given an idealised view of the software life cycle in that it has been presented as a linear flow from specification through design to implementation and testing. In reality the process is iterative as changes may occur in the results of earlier stages because of problems in the later stages. For example, a specification requirement may be impossible to implement and this may only be discovered in the design or even the implementation phase. One aim of software engineering is thus to minimise the number of iterations that are required in developing a product. This will not only help to ensure that a product is available on time but also that it is produced at a reasonable cost. Another aim of software engineering is to ensure the reliability of quality of a software system. One way of achieving this is to use validation techniques at all stages of development and not just at the last stage. An error caught at the specification stage is far cheaper to correct then the effects of the same error left undetected until the validation stage. Thus validation is not a single once-only process but a continuous process which is started at the specification stage.

11.2 Software Specification

In the introduction the need for a clear, concise and consistent specification for a software system was introduced. The inadequate specification of software systems has been at the heart of many problems with computer-based products and much work has been carried out in developing techniques to prevent such problems. In this section, one approach to specifying software systems will be described. This is called *structured analysis* and, while not the only technique available, is representative of much current practice (ref. 11.1). Other techniques are described in refs 11.2, 11.3 and 11.4.

A specification is the medium through which a client's ideas for a product are presented to the designer. It is thus primarily a communication mechanism and as such must use a clear but precise notation to ensure that both parties understand the full meaning of the specification. The notation must be capable of being understood by both the designer and the client since the designer needs to understand fully the needs of the client, and the client needs to ensure that the system being offered is what is required. Since the client may not be computer literate, a notation that is easily understood by laymen is required. Both the designer and the client also need to have confidence that the specification is 'water-tight' and does not contain any inconsistencies or ambiguities. A specification that is capable of being checked in these respects is therefore required. To manage the complexity of many problems, the specification must be partitioned in a top-down fashion so that an understanding of the system can be gained without having to grasp all the detail in one go. Finally, the specification should avoid dealing with implementation aspects but should concentrate on the 'logical' functionality. This leaves the designer with the freedom to choose the most suitable 'physical' implementation. Put another way, the specification defines what a system is to do, not how to do it.

Structured analysis attempts to meet the criteria discussed above in the following ways. Firstly, a largely graphical notation is used to provide a *structured specification*. The use of graphics has the obvious advantage that 'a picture is worth a thousand words'. Once the simple graphical notation is understood, the meaning of the specification is far clearer than a voluminous textual description. Because a large amount of information is represented in a relatively small set of diagrams, it is also easy to modify when a greater understanding of the problem is achieved or client requirements change. The diagrams represent the specification in a hierarchical manner. This again aids the general understanding of the problem and in addition is likely to lead the designer into employing a similarly structured top-down design. The structured specification is non-redundant in that a piece of information is held in only one place in the specification. This aids conciseness and also ensures that the specification is consistent. Finally, an emphasis is placed on the logical operation of the system being specified rather than its physical implementation, as will be shown in the following sections.

11.2.1 A Spelling-checker Program

As an example for sections 11.2 and 11.3, the specification and design of a program to check the spellings of words contained in a piece of text will be considered. The following might be typical of a requirements specification for such a system, produced by a client.

"The program shall copy a document, correcting the spelling as it goes. In order to correct the spelling, it shall isolate words in the document. A word is a contiguous sequence of letters with non-letters on either side. The words shall be compared against entries in a dictionary. This dictionary shall be a combination of the *Oxford English Dictionary* and a private dictionary specified by the user. If the word from the document or its obvious singular form exists in the dictionary, it shall be considered correct. If the word is not correct, the user shall be queried for a correction. The user shall be able to tell the checker to:
1. accept the word,
2. replace the word with a new word supplied by the user, or
3. replace the word and remember the replacement so that future occurrences of the word will be automatically replaced without querying the user."

At a first reading this requirements specification appears consistent and reasonably unambiguous. More careful consideration will reveal a number of points that would almost certainly require some clarification by the client. Some of these are to be discussed in the next section. Before reading on, think about the above specification and attempt to identify potential problem areas. Assume that the computer system to be used to run the program is defined in detail elsewhere.

11.2.2 Structured Specification Notation

A structured specification comprises three elements:

1. A set of *data flow diagrams (DFDs)*
2. A *data dictionary*
3. A set of structured *process specifications*

A data flow diagram is a hierarchical, graphical representation of the processes required in a system and the data that must flow between the processes. Four elements are used to form a data flow diagram — a *process* which is represented by a circle (or *bubble*), a *data flow* which is shown as a directed and labelled arc, a *data store* which is shown as a labelled open-ended box, and a *data source/sink* which is represented by a labelled, closed box. The data dictionary contains the definition of the data flows in a relatively formal notation. Process specifications are used to define, in *structured English*, the function of the lowest-level processes in the data flow diagrams. The use of these elements in a structured specification will be illustrated by considering the example of the spelling checker introduced in the previous section.

The first step in developing a structured specification is to identify the environment in which the software system is to operate. This is shown on the highest level diagram in the hierarchy and is called the *context diagram*. A context diagram for the spelling checker is shown in figure 11.1. From this diagram it can be immediately seen that the spelling checker interacts with four external entities: the *Oxford English Dictionary*, a user, a file system, and a private dictionary. These four entities are shown as data sources/sinks and are outside the direct control of the spelling checker. For example, although the file system provides a document for checking, the spelling checker has no control over the construction of the file system. The data flows from/to the data sources/sinks are labelled and the definitions are contained in the data dictionary.

The data dictionary entries for the complete structured specification are shown in table 11.1.

The meanings of some of the entries will now be illustrated. As an example, the 'command' and 'request' data flows represent the specification of the interaction between the user and the spelling checker. If the data dictionary entry for 'command' is inspected it will be seen to consist of

Context-diagram
Spelling_checker

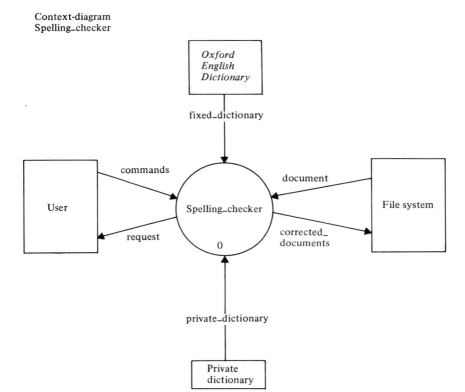

Figure 11.1 Context diagram for the spelling checker

command = [accept_command | replace_command | correct_command].

The meaning of this is that 'command' is one of the three commands 'accept_command', 'replace_command' or 'correct_command'. The definition of the three commands must also be defined in the dictionary and it will be seen that 'replace_command' is defined as

replace_command = replacement_word.

Thus a replacement command is defined in terms of another data dictionary entry, 'replacement_word', which further inspection will reveal is defined as 'word'. 'word' is defined thus:

word = 1{letter}

Table 11.1 Data dictionary for spelling checker

---

accept_command =
    * word is to be accepted as correctly spelled *
commands =
    [accept_command | replace_command | correct_command].
    * user's response to an incorrect spelling *
correct_command =
    replacement_word.
    * word is to be replaced by specified word and the
      replacement remembered *
correct_word =
    word.
    * word that has been verified or corrected *
corrected_document =
    document.
    * after corrections have been made *
dictionary =
    { dictionary_word }.
    * list of words considered to be correctly spelled *
dictionary_word =
    word.
    * word found in dictionary *
document =
    { character }.
fixed_dictionary =
    dictionary.
    * on-line version of *Oxford English Dictionary* *
incorrect_word =
    word.
    * word that could not be verified by any internal references *
internal_ dictionary =
    dictionary.
    * dictionary built from OED and private dictionary of user *
letter =
    * a–z, A–Z *
misspellings =
    { word_pair }
    * users common misspellings *
non_dictionary_word =
    word.
    * a word not found in the dictionary *

non_letter =
    * non-alphabetic character *
other_characters =
    1{ non_letter }
    * portion of document that does not need checking *
private_dictionary =
    dictionary.
    * dictionary created by user *
replace_command =
    replacement_word.
    * word is to be replaced with specified word *
request =
    * prompt to user for response to misspelling *
singular_word_form =
    word.
    * singular form of plural word *
singular_word_pair=
    non_dictionary_word + singular_word_form.
    * word from document and its singular form *
unmatched_word =
    word.
    * a word not found in the dictionary in either singular or plural
      form *
word =
    1{ letter }.
word_pair =
    incorrect_word + replacement_word.
    * misspelling and replacement *

This means that 'word' is a combination of one or more of 'letter'.
    Finally, 'letter' is defined as:

letter = * a–z, A–Z *

In the data dictionary anything between asterisks is treated as a comment
and so the final definition in this hierarchy is a comment description of a
letter — that is, an upper or lower case alphabetic character.
    This example of a data dictionary definition may appear to be very
pedantic, however it is important to define very carefully what is meant by
a 'word' in this application. Invalid 'words' in this context would be
'user's'. 'Z80', and 'I/O', all of which appear in this book!

This definition of 'command' shows that a data dictionary is hierarchical and that this hierarchy can be used as a powerful mechanism for hiding complexity. It is not important or desirable when defining 'commands' to know the detailed form of the various command options. Also, if it is decided to change the definition of 'word' to allow for some of the real examples quoted above, it would be undesirable to have to modify every data dictionary entity that is made up of a 'word' to reflect this.

Inspection of the data dictionary entries contained in table 11.1 for the data flows on the context diagram should give a powerful indication of the function of the spelling checker. The context diagram and the data dictionary should at this stage be checked against the requirements specification given in section 11.2.1 to ensure that the system specified meets the requirements. This checking process would in a real situation be carried out in a *review*. The review would be a meeting between the client and the analysts at which the analysts would present the first level of the specification for critical assessment. The process of developing the context diagram would also have raised a number of questions about the requirements specification. For example:

Which *Oxford English Dictionary* is to be used?
Can a user have more than one private dictionary?
Are any words not known in the OED but accepted as correct to be permanently added to the private dictionary?

It is essential that this kind of issue and the correctness of the context diagram/data dictionary are considered as early as possible in the development of the structured specification since corrections at a later stage can be very time-consuming and expensive.

Having agreed that the first level of the specification meets the client's needs, the next stage is to develop the next level of detail. To achieve this, the analysts must consider what the bubble in the context diagram must do to transform the input data flows to the required output data flows. This involves identifying the processes that are involved in the transformations and the data that must flow between the processes. Thus the next level down represents a view inside the bubble on the context diagram. For the spelling checker, four processes may be identified:

1. Extract words from the source document
2. Verify spellings
3. Make corrections
4. Recompose the document

These processes and the data flows between them are illustrated in figure 11.2. The data flow diagram of figure 11.2 should be self-explanatory and

Spelling-Checker

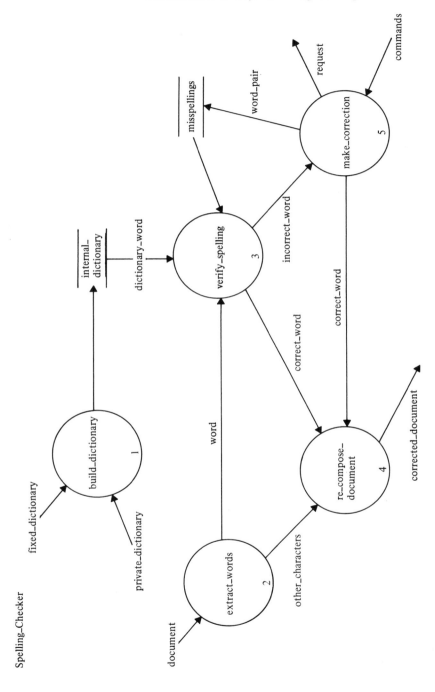

Figure 11.2 First-level data flow diagram for the spelling checker

only two items require any comment. These both revolve around the handling of misspelt words. When a word is identified as potentially misspelt, it is checked against the list of previous misspellings from a data store. This data store must maintain a list of word pairs containing misspellings and correct spellings so that the next time the same mistake occurs a request to the user will not be needed in order to make the correction. The other point is that the misspellings are shown as being held in a data store but at this stage no indication is given on how the store is to be implemented. This is intentional and an issue like this should be left until the design stage when due consideration can be given to memory requirements, performance, access methods, etc.

Figure 11.2 contains a small number of bubbles and this is very desirable in data flow diagrams. If more than nine processes are shown on a data flow diagram, then it becomes complex and difficult to understand. This second data flow diagram has introduced several new data flows and these must be included in the data dictionary. The data flows that are unconnected at one end are flows from/to the context diagram and must match or *balance* with data flows at the higher level.

When happy with this data flow diagram, the analyst will then consider each process bubble in turn and identify how their functions may be partitioned into further sets of processes. For example 'verify spelling' may be described by the data flow diagram shown in figure 11.3. A process may not require further decomposition and in this case a *process specification* is used to describe its function. A process specification is a structured English description and two for the spelling checker are given in table 11.2. Structured English is a combination of some of the structured programming constructs that are described in section 11.4 and normal English. Structured English enjoys many of the benefits that are associated with structured programming languages but without the formality. The use of a true programming language would be inadvisable at the specification stage for a number of reasons. Two of the most important are that non-programmers will read the specification and may not understand the notation and secondly the use of a programming language will constrain the analyst.

Although it was suggested that implementation details should not be included in the structured specification, it is apparent that in any real application some constraints will exist and these will influence the development of the specification. Such essentially physical details should be included as a set of notes or appendices to the specification and will typically be presented in English.

When the structured specification has been completed, it should be systematically reviewed to ensure that it meets the user requirements and that it is consistent. The former goal is usually achieved by another review with the clients, although several internal reviews will also have taken

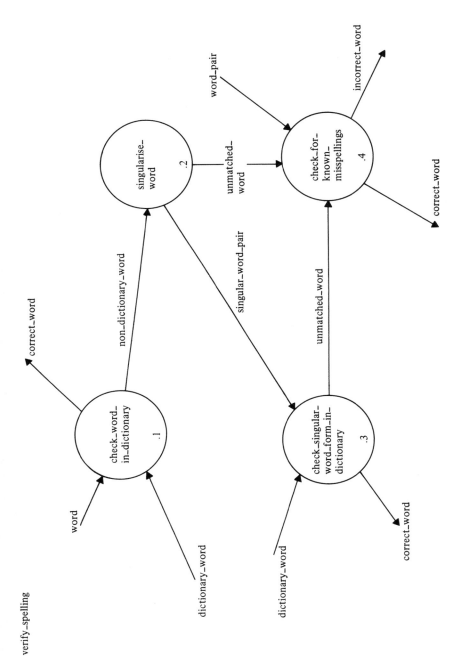

Figure 11.3 Data flow diagram to verify the spelling process

Table 11.2 Two process specifications for the spelling checker

---

TITLE: extract_words
INPUT/OUTPUT:
     document : data in
     word : data out
     other_characters : data out
BODY:
     for each character in document
          other_characters =uninterrupted sequence of non_letter
          word = uninterrupted sequence of letter
     end for
TITLE: check_word_in_dictionary
INPUT/OUTPUT:
     word : data in
     correct_word : data out
     non_dictionary_word : data out
     dictionary_word : data in
BODY:
     if word = dictionary_word in internal_dictionary then
          correct_word = word
     else
          non_dictionary_word = word
     end if

---

place before this stage. Consistency checking is a largely mechanical process since it simply involves checking the balancing of the various DFD hierarchies and ensuring that the data dictionary entries are complete and correct. Consistency checking is ideally suited for mechanisation and some computer-aided specification systems are available which provide this facility.

In this section, some of the techniques for generating a structured specification have been described. Using such techniques requires some skill and experience to yield good results. There are many guidelines for developing structured specifications which are beyond the scope of this book however; most are described further in the references provided.

11.3   Design Methodologies

Having developed a specification for a software system, the next stage is to translate the specification into a design which can be physically implemented. In this section the technique or methodology of *structured design* (ref. 11.5) will be described. The aim of structured design is to develop a plan for the implementation of a specification. The plan defines the structure of the software system and an outline of the coding required to implement the defined structure.

Structured design has a number of important characteristics which are intended to assist in the design process. Like structured analysis, it uses a largely graphical notation supported by some textual information. The notation is used to partition the design into a hierarchy of 'black-boxes' so that the complexity of the system can be hidden and revealed as required. The structuring employed is intended to reflect what is currently regarded as good programming practice and thus implies the use of structured programming, as discussed in section 11.4. Structured design has a close relationship with structured analysis in that techniques are available for transforming a structured specification into a structured design. This introduces the important concept that the form of the design should follow the function required. Finally, by analysing a structured design, an indication of the quality of the resulting product can be derived before any detailed coding takes place. In the following sections, each of these aspects of structured design will be considered. It should be noted that the result of the structured design process is a *design specification* and not the implementation of the design. The design specification will be sufficiently detailed to permit almost direct coding but will not include program code itself. The specification for the spelling checker derived in section 11.2 will be used as a basis for most of the examples in this section.

11.3.1   Structured Design Notation

A structured design specification consists of three elements:

1.   A set of *structure charts*
2.   A data dictionary
3.   A set of structured *module specifications*

A structure chart is a graphical representation of the *program modules* required to implement a software system. A program module is simply a coherent set of program statements that form a convenient unit. As examples, a Pascal procedure or function, a 'C' function, a FORTRAN sub-program and an assembly language subroutine are all valid program modules. The structure chart shows the invocation of modules (that is, which modules a given module can call (invoke)), and the communication between modules (that is, which *parameters* are passed upon invocation and return). The chart also shows the hierarchy of modules, as will be illustrated shortly. The data dictionary shares many features with the data dictionary of structured analysis except that in the case of structured design it defines the parameters rather than the data flows. The module specifications define the functionality of a program module and the interface to the module. The functionality is often described using pseudo-code. Pseudo-code is similar to structured English except that it is more closely allied to a programming language. The interface definition describes the parameter passing conventions that are employed with the module. The module specification will be used as a specification for the programmer to code against.

11.3.2 Structured Design for the Spelling Checker

A structure chart for the spelling checker program is shown in figure 11.4. The modules are shown as named rectangular boxes. The name should be a succinct description of the module function, such as 'correct_spelling'. A call from one module to another is shown by an arrow. Thus, from figure 11.4 it is clear that the module 'correct_spelling' calls 'program_startup', 'extract_word', 'provide_correct_word' and 'recompose_document'. The module 'provide_correct_word' further calls 'verify_spelling' and 'make _correction', etc. The structure chart thus clearly shows the hierarchy of the software modules in the system.

There is also some further information associated with a call; that is, the parameters passed between the caller and the called. The parameter flows are known as *couples*. There are two types of couple: data and control. A data couple, as might be expected, shows data flowing from one module to the other, in the direction shown by the arrow. 'correct_spelling' thus calls 'get_correct_word', passing the data value 'word' and receiving 'correct_word' back. It should be obvious from the naming what 'get_correct_word' is actually doing. A control couple is typically a *flag value* and an example called 'is_word' is shown being passed from 'check_dictionary' to 'verify_spelling'. In this example, 'is_word' indicates to 'verify_spelling' that the 'word' passed to it is a known word. A control couple will normally be used as part of a test in the calling module; for example, the following might appear in 'verify_spelling':

```
if not is_word then
     check_singular (word, is_word);
```

To distinguish between a control couple and a data couple, a slightly different arrow form is shown on the diagram, as in figure 11.4.

The structure chart does not imply any ordering of the invocations, so that for the 'determine_correction' module the calls to 'query_user' and

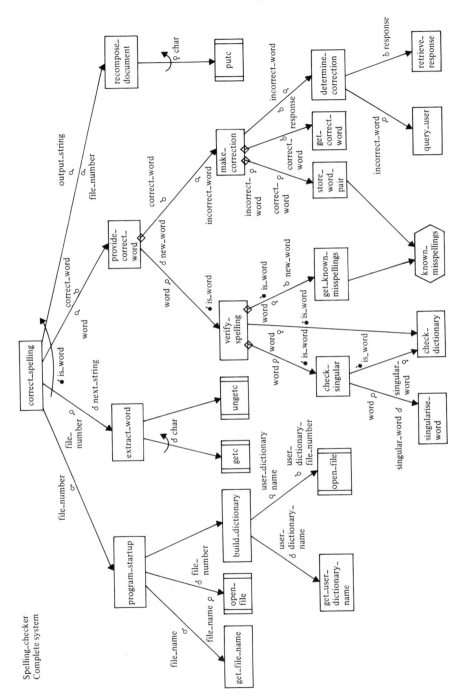

Figure 11.4 Structure chart for the spelling checker

'retrieve_response' could apparently occur in any order. The ordering of the calls, which is defined within the module specification, is clearly important in this case since a call of a response cannot be made before a prompt to the user. In this example the ordering of calls is trivial, but in more complex situations it may be impossible to define such a simple ordering. To indicate that some more complex call requirements exist, some additional items of notation are employed on structure charts. Two of these are shown on figure 11.4. The first is the curved arrow encircling one or more invocations, such as that shown around the calls to 'extract_word', 'provide_correct_word' and 'recompose_document' from 'correct_spelling'. This indicates that these three modules are called iteratively. In the same area, the call to 'provide_correct_spelling' is shown with a diamond shaped symbol at its intersection with 'correct_spelling'. This indicates that the call is *conditional*. Thus part of the module specification for 'correct_spelling' might look like:

```
while not end_of_file do
      extract_word (file_number, next_string, is_word);
      .
      .
      .

      if not is_word then
            provide_correct_spelling (word, correct_word)
      endif;
      .
      .
      .

      recompose_document (output_string);
end while;
```

There are several other notational items that may appear on a structure chart such as indicators for library modules, information clusters, page connectors, etc. These are described in further detail in ref. 11.5.

The data dictionary notations used in structured design are normally identical to those used in structured analysis and need no further discussion here. The pseudo-code that is employed in module specifications generally follows the requirements for any good structured programming language as described in section 11.4. The examples given above should indicate the form that pseudo-code will take.

So far, the notation used in structured design has been described without reference to any methodology for utilising the notation. The fundamental problem that must be resolved is — how is the structure chart developed from the results of the analysis phase? The answer is unfortunately far from simple and, although some broad advice and guidelines can be given, a satisfactory transition from specification to design requires some considerable skill and experience. As a brief example, the development of the structure chart shown in figure 11.4 will be considered.

A primitive or idealised structure chart would look like that shown in figure 11.5. A master module calls three subordinate modules to input data, process the data and output the results. An attempt should thus be made to map the design specification on to this idealised model. The first

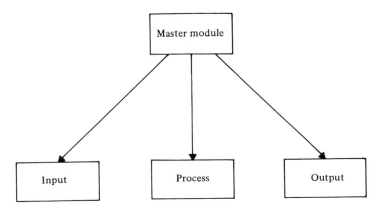

Figure 11.5 Idealised structure chart

stage in developing the structure chart is therefore to identify where on the first-level DFD there are boundaries between input, processing and output. Considering the level 0 DFD for the spelling checker, these boundaries can easily be identified by inspection. The processes 'build_dictionary' and 'extract_words' are concerned with generating input data to the spelling checker while 'recompose_document' takes the corrected words and other characters to generate the output. The two remaining processes form what is termed the *central transform* and do all the important work in the system. A module is created to manage the calling of the processes involved in the central transform. In this example, 'provide_correct_word' fulfils this role. The remaining modules which deal with input and output and the central transform module are all controlled by the master module which is 'correct_spelling' for this system. The processes 'build_dictionary', 'extract_words', 'recompose_document', 'verify _spelling', and 'make_correction' are simply transformed into modules. A similar process can then be carried out for the next level of the data-flow diagrams to yield the subordinate modules to 'verify_spelling' and 'make_correction'.

This very simplified description of the transformation from data-flow diagrams to structure chart has produced a *first-cut structure chart*. Some

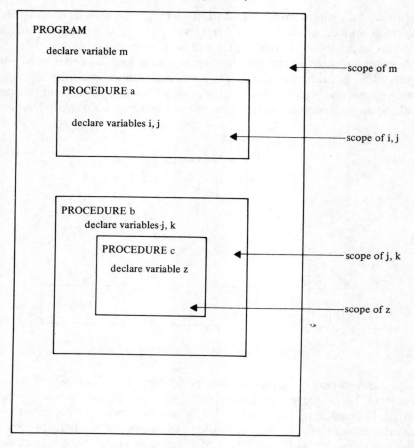

Figure 11.6 Block structured program

further work remains to be done to improve the chart so that a good design will result. This work will attempt to reduce the *coupling* between modules (that is, reduce parameter passing) and increase *cohesion* (that is, ensure that modules have a functionally related set of objectives). The issues of structure chart improvement are discussed in detail in ref. 11.5.

11.4 Program Implementation

Consideration of the implementation of a software system must include two important aspects: the programming language and the development environment to be employed. The programming language is the medium through which the implementor builds the system and its features are of obvious importance. The development environment is the equivalent of a craftsman's workshop and it describes the hardware and software tools available to the programmer. The features that are of importance to the software engineer in these two areas will now be discussed.

11.4.1 Programming Languages

Although several thousand programming languages have been developed over the last 25 years, there are only a relatively small number in wide usage today. However, in spite of the small number, there is significant controversy about the quality of existing programming languages and about the features desirable in a language. In this section, the desirable features of a high-level programming language are discussed within the context of currently agreed good practice. Initially, a consideration of how programming languages can be classified and the broader aspects of choosing a language will be dealt with.

As described in chapter 8, the lowest-level of programming language is assembly language. Assembly languages are essentially concerned with the manipulation of the processor registers and memory, rather than problem solving. In general, there is a one-to-one correspondence between an assembly language statement and a machine instruction, although many of the better assembly languages allow *macros* which enable some higher-level features to be included. Although some attempts have been and still are being made at defining standard assembly languages, most assembly languages are particular to a given processor or its relatives, and all require an intimate understanding of the processor's operation. Because it is so closely linked with machine operation, there is a large gulf between assembly language and the design notations discussed earlier. The translation from design to implementation is thus a difficult and error-prone operation. For this reason, it is difficult to justify the use of assembly language except in rare circumstances. In normal programming these might include limited areas where very efficient execution is required or applications where a special-purpose processor is being employed that has an architecture that is unsuitable for high-level language compilers.

The other major class of programming language is the high-level languages. These languages are usually related to particular applications rather than to the processor itself. Their statements allow meaningful names for the entities to be manipulated, allow relatively complex decision making and generally are easier to read and understand than assembly language (although there are one or two notable exceptions to this). Furthermore, each high-level language statement may generate a large number of machine instructions. A common criticism of high-level language compilers, particularly those for microcomputers, is that they generate inefficient code. Even if this is true, and it is certainly less so nowadays, the other advantages of high-level implementation far outweigh the potential losses in code efficiency. The ease of development and maintenance are of greater importance in almost every application.

Falling between high-level and assembly languages come what are often called *systems implementation languages*. These languages share many of the features of higher-level languages while still allowing easy access to the underlying machine hardware. Typical applications for such languages are in writing operating systems and their associated utilities. The programming language C, developed at The Bell Laboratories, is perhaps the most commonly used of this class of language and is becoming increasingly popular as an efficient alternative to assembly language for microprocessors (ref. 11.6). C provides support for structured programming and with some care can be used to produce reliable software. However, because of its terse style and its low-level features, programs written in C can be difficult to decipher.

We now come to the true high-level languages. These are sometimes classed according to the way in which they allocate storage to a program. The older high-level languages such as FORTRAN use a *static storage allocation* scheme which enables the compiler to evaluate the memory requirements for the program and its variables before execution. The use of static storage allocation is a limitation on the programmer although it makes life simpler for the compiler designer. At the other extreme are languages like LISP and APL in which all storage allocation is performed dynamically as a program is executed. There are no general-purpose languages that use full dynamic storage allocation, and those languages that exist are tailored to specific applications such as list processing.

Between these two extremes come the increasingly popular *block-structured* languages that have largely evolved from ALGOL. A widely used block-structured language is Pascal. In such languages the program is naturally made up of a set of blocks. As each block of program is entered or left, the data store required for the block to be executed is automatically allocated or de-allocated respectively. This scheme has one significant advantage which is that variables have a limited *scope*; that is, they are only accessible within the block in which they are declared. This means that variables have some protection against inadvertent interference from another part of the program. Some languages, for example, MODULA-2 and Ada, extend this concept further and permit the definition of *modules* (or packages) to provide even better security. Both MODULA-2 and Ada are significant in embedded applications in that they provide support for real-time applications; they are described in detail in ref. 11.7 and 11.8.

In the next section the major features and requirements of a modern block structured language will be discussed.

11.4.2   *Structured Programming Language Characteristics*

It is now generally agreed that the use of structured programming languages in the implementation of software systems is desirable. Structured languages allow the hierarchical decomposition of a system developed in the structured design process to be reflected in the implementation. The design of modern structured programming languages is intended to assist in the implementation of reliable systems through the provision of *abstract data typing* and a restricted but powerful set of *primitive statement constructs* within the language. A program consists of algorithms which manipulate data (ref. 11.9). It is important that a programming language is able clearly to express the underlying algorithms and data structures of a software system. There are many other desirable, but less fundamentally important, features of programming languages. For example, in real-time systems the ability to express concurrency, handle malfunctions, respond to asynchronous events and manipulate low-level hardware devices is all important. In this section, an emphasis will be placed on describing the fundamental features of a general-purpose structured programming language. Further reading on particular programming languages will provide the detail of other application-related features.

11.4.3   *Algorithm Definition*

Four concepts are required for the description of an algorithm in a structured programming language. These are *hierarchical decomposition, sequence, iteration* and *alternation*.

Hierarchical decomposition allows for the hiding of the detail of an algorithm so that a clear expression of the function of the algorithm can be achieved. In structured programming languages, the main tool of hierarchical decomposition is the procedure. As a trivial example, consider part of a program to sort words into alphabetical order. This could be implemented as:

```
read (list)
sort (list)
write (list)
```

The details of read, sort and write are hidden within their implementations as procedures. The details of the sorting algorithm(s) employed are not important to describing the overall function of the system and so are 'hidden' within the sort procedure. The sort procedure itself would almost certainly be made up of other procedures, further reinforcing the hierarchy of the program. If procedures were not employed, the equivalent could well be several pages long and be very difficult to read and understand. A procedure usually needs to pass and return data in order to do its job. In the example above, all three procedures operate on some data called 'list' and so the program variable 'list' is passed to each procedure as a *parameter*. The ability to pass parameters to procedures is thus an important requirement in a programming language.

Most structured programming languages allow two forms of parameter passing. These are known as *pass-by-value* and *pass-by-reference*. In pass-by-value only the actual value of a variable is passed to a procedure. This enables the procedure to use and operate on the value passed without affecting the original variable. This eliminates the possibilities of a procedure having *side-effects* and is the most desirable form of parameter passing. In contrast, pass-by-reference passes the variable itself to a procedure. This is achieved by giving the procedure the address of the variable and thus allows the procedure to change the actual variable itself. This can dangerous but may be required to prevent large amounts of data being passed around.

Procedures must also be able to have their own private or *local variables* that are inaccessible from elsewhere. This allows one procedure to call another without fear of its own variables being corrupted by the called procedure. Each time a procedure is invoked, it is given a 'new' set of local storage, and local variable values are not retained from one invocation to the next. The special case of *recursion*, where a procedure calls itself, relies on the generation of local storage each time a procedure is entered.

This notion of local versus *global variables*, which are accessible from any point in the program, introduces a basic concept in structured programming languages, that of block structure. A procedure is a special case of a program block and some programming languages allow for the definition of non-procedural blocks. A block is a program fragment that has a declaration part and a statement definition part. The declaration part is used to define the constants and variables that are local to the block. The statement definition part contains the operations that the block is to perform. Some languages allow a block to include further block definitions within the definition part. Those entities declared in the declaration part may only be referenced within that block and are said to have their scope limited to that block.

As an example of the rules of scope, consider figure 11.6. The program declares a variable 'm'. The scope of 'm' is the complete program and 'm' is thus accessible in procedures 'a', 'b' and 'c'. Procedure 'a' declares two local variables, 'i' and 'j'. Thus, 'i' and 'j' are accessible only by procedure 'a' and cannot be read or written by the outer program or any of the other procedures. Procedure 'b' declares the variables 'j' and 'k' and also a procedure 'c'. This variable 'j' is completely independent of the variable 'j' in procedure 'a' and no conflict or confusion will occur because the scope of both is limited to their respective procedures. The procedure 'c' is also inaccessible outside procedure 'b'. The variables 'j' and 'k' are accessible within procedure 'c' since 'c' is within the scope of procedure 'b'.

The limitation of the scope of variables and procedures have many important benefits to programmers. They basically allow the program to be implemented in a series of 'black-boxes' whose only visibility is their function and their interface. This is directly analogous to the use of integrated circuits in electronic circuit implementation. The user of an IC does not need to know the details of how the IC operates internally, just its function and its interface characteristics. Furthermore, in a system made up of a number of ICs, a change to the internal design of one IC should not affect the operation of another. The same goals apply in the implementation of reliable programs.

The statement definition part of a block will utilise the concepts of sequence, iteration and choice mentioned earlier. These concepts will now be briefly described using examples from the programming language Pascal (ref. 11.10).

Sequence is used to define a linear order of statement execution.

```
a := 1;      (* statement 1 *)
b := 2;      (* statement 2 *)
c := a + b; (* statement 3 *)
```

The symbol ':=' is the Pascal assignment operator. Thus, statement 1 is read as 'a is assigned the value of 1'. The order of execution of the above three statements is statement 1 then statement 2 then statement 3. The semi-colon is used to separate statements.

In many programming situations, it may be essential to execute a group of statements repeatedly with some controlling variable determining when iteration is to stop. Such iteration statements have a number of forms. Pascal provides three forms — FOR, REPEAT and WHILE.

The FOR statement is used when the number of iterations is known beforehand. As an example, the following statements calculate the factorial of n and the sum of the first n digits:

```
n := 10;
factorial := 1;
sum := 0;
FOR x := 1 TO n DO
        BEGIN
                factorial := factorial * x;
                sum := sum + x
        END;
```

The words shown in upper-case are *reserved words* in Pascal and have a special meaning to the compiler. In normal practice, they need not be written in upper-case, this is done purely to aid clarity in these examples. The FOR statement implies that the loop variable, which is 'x' in this case, takes the next successive value for each loop iteration until the termination value, 'n' in this case, is reached. Thus the statements between the BEGIN and END are successively executed for the values of 'x' of 1, 2, 3, 4, 5, 6, 7, 8, 9 and 10, since the loop terminator 'n' is set to 10 before the FOR loop is entered. The statements from BEGIN through END are known as a compound statement. In essence, this allows a sequence of statements to be used wherever a single statement may be used.

The REPEAT statement in Pascal is used to cause execution of a sequence of statements one or more times. The terminating condition is evaluated by the UNTIL clause. The terminating clause simply determines the truthhood or falsehood of a logical expression. As an example, consider the following program fragment which copies characters from input to output until a full-stop character is read, counting the number of characters.

```
namelength := 0;
REPEAT
        read (character);
        write (character);
        namelength := namelength + 1
UNTIL character = '.';
totallength := totallength + namelength;
```

The UNTIL statement yields a logical false value for all characters except '.', thus the execution repeatedly reads and writes the 'character' and adds 1 to 'namelength' for characters up to a '.'. When a '.' character is read, the statement adding 'namelength' to 'totallength' is executed. Clearly, the REPEAT statement is useful for any set of operations that have to be repeated an unknown number of times, but at least once, and where there is a logical test that can be performed to determine completion. In other cases, it may be required to execute a set of statements zero or more times, again using a logical condition to determine whether execution is required. In such circumstances the WHILE statement is used. Consider the following simple example to sum the reciprocals of 'number' until a value of zero is read:

```
sumofreciprocals := 0;
read(number);
WHILE number <> 0 DO
      BEGIN
            sumofreciprocals := sumofreciprocals + 1 / number;
            read(number)
      END;
```

In this example, it is essential that the body of the WHILE statement is not executed if 'number' is zero because a division by zero would result. The zero value can thus be used to delineate a list of numbers whose reciprocals must be summed. When zero is read, then execution continues from the statement after the second END.

Pascal is quite rich in its set of iteration statements. By less elegant programming, the WHILE statement could be used to implement each of the examples given but the result would be less clear and therefore harder to understand and maintain in the future. An important characteristic of all three of these iteration statements is that they have only one entry point (that is, the FOR, REPEAT or WHILE statement) and only one exit point (that is, the END or UNTIL statement). There is no convenient mechanism for jumping out of the middle of an iteration. This is a very deliberate feature of the language and aims to enforce good program structure by ensuring that the entry and exit points can only be reached in one way. It is thus always clear how an iteration has been entered and how it has been left.

The final structuring features of Pascal to be examined are the two control constructs offered within the language. In many programming applications, a choice of path through a program is required dependent upon some condition or some set of conditions. The choice may be simple, such as:

```
IF letter IN ['a'..'z'] THEN converttouppercase(letter);
buildword(letter)
```

This statement states that if the variable 'letter' has a value within the set of values 'a' to 'z' (that is, if it is a lower-case, alphabetical character), then the procedure 'converttouppercase' is invoked with the actual parameter 'letter' being passed. If this condition is not met, then the next statement, which in this case invokes the procedure 'buildword', is executed. This statement is also executed if the condition is met, but in this case after the execution of the procedure 'converttouppercase'. In some cases, there may be a choice between two statements dependent upon some test clause. For example:

```
IF temperature > limit THEN
    sendalarm
ELSE
    sendokmessage;
samplepressure;
```

In this example, one of two procedures are invoked — 'sendalarm' if the temperature is above some pre-defined limit or 'sendokmessage' otherwise. These two procedure invocations are thus mutually exclusive. Following either 'sendalarm' or 'sendokmessage', the procedure 'samplepressure' is called. Instead of simple statements, compound statements can be used in IF statements, thus allowing complex conditions to be set up:

```
IF person = male THEN
    BEGIN
        IF age < maturity THEN
            boys := boys + 1
        ELSE
            men := men + 1;
        males := males + 1
    END
ELSE
    BEGIN
        IF age < maturity THEN
            girls := girls + 1
        ELSE
            women := women + 1;
        females := females + 1
    END;
```

In the above program fragment, which could be part of a census analysis package, 'boys' is incremented if a person is a male and under the age of maturity, 'men' is incremented if a person is male and over the age of maturity, and 'males' is incremented for each male. Otherwise the person is assumed, not unreasonably, to be female and a similar set of operations performed on 'girls', 'women' and 'females'. The use of indentation to clarify the meaning of statements is often used in languages like Pascal. In the above example, the statements which belong within each arm of the IF statement can be clearly seen to be due to the use of indentation. The statement below is directly equivalent to that above, but its meaning is much less clear:

IF person = male THEN BEGIN IF age < maturity THEN boys
:= boys + 1
ELSE men := men + 1; males := males + 1 END ELSE BEGIN IF
age < maturity THEN girls := girls + 1 ELSE women := women
+ 1; females := females + 1 END;

The other control construct offered by Pascal is used when a choice is made dependent upon the value of a single variable, which must have a discrete set of values — for example, a character or a day of the week. The construct is called a CASE statement because one case from several options is matched to select an action. For example, suppose a system has to recognise and execute a command determined by a single character input by an operator:

```
CASE request OF
        'A' : append;
        'S' : substitute;
        'D' : delete;
        'C' : copy;
        'Q' : quit
    END;
(* next statement *)
```

In this example, 'append', 'substitute', etc., are procedures that are called dependent upon the value of 'request'. Thus, if the operator request 'D' is input, the 'delete' procedure is executed from the five possible procedures. It should be assumed for this example that some check is made prior to this statement to ensure that 'request' can only take one of the five values specified. Like the IF statement and the iteration statements, there is only a single entry and a single exit point for the CASE statement. The statement is entered at 'CASE' and left at 'END'.

11.4.4 *Data Definition and Manipulation*

The above concepts of hierarchical decomposition, sequence, iteration and choice are used to describe the algorithm that a programmer has chosen to help solve a particular problem. The other equally important aspect is the description of the data that the algorithm is to manipulate. In earlier chapters, the representation of some fundamental data types such as real and integer numbers using binary patterns was described. The operators needed to manipulate such numbers were also described. Such numbers and operators form a natural part of all general-purpose high-level programming languages. Many programming tasks involve the manipulation of more complex collections of numeric and non-numeric data. The representation of such data in a programming language is thus very important. Using some examples from Pascal, some of the more important requirements for data description will now be discussed.

Most modern programming languages make a clear distinction between the *declaration* of a variable and its later use. In Pascal, all variables must be declared before they can be used. The declaration defines a name for a variable and its *type*. The type of a variable is used by the compiler to check that only valid operations are performed upon a variable. Further checking may also be performed when the program is executed by the *run-time system* within which the program operates. A simple example of an invalid operation would be the assignment of a real number to an integer variable. More subtle examples will be illustrated later in this section. Pascal enforces this concept of data typing in a fairly rigorous manner and is therefore called a *strongly typed* language.

The simple data types that Pascal supports are integers, real numbers, characters and *Booleans*. An integer is a member of the set of whole numbers that can be stored in a particular computer. For a computer with 16-bit data values, integers in the range $-32\,768$ to $+32\,767$ would be available. Real numbers are normally internally represented within the computer as a signed mantissa–exponent pair. There is thus a limit to the magnitude and precision of real numbers; however, the dynamic range is greater than that of integers. A character is usually stored in some standardised code and the characters available often vary with the spoken language used in the country where the program is written or even with the type of computer employed. A Boolean can take only one of two values: TRUE or FALSE.

To illustrate the use simple data types in Pascal and the declaration of variables, consider the following program fragment:

```
VAR
        answer, i, j : integer;
        truth : Boolean;
        floater : real;
        yes, no : char;
BEGIN
        answer := 42;              (* integer arithmetic 1 *)
        i := answer * 2;           (* integer arithmetic 2 *)
        j := answer DIV 2;         (* integer arithmetic 3 *)
        truth := answer = 42;      (* Boolean assignment *)
        floater := answer / 2.0;   (* real arithmetic *)
        yes := 'Y';                (* character assignment 1 *)
        no := 'N'                  (* character assignment 2 *)
END
```

The variables and their types, integer, Boolean, real or char, are declared before their use within the 'VAR' statement. In the use of these variables there are some interesting points. Firstly, note the use of the 'DIV' operator in integer arithmetic statement 3 and the '/' operator in the real arithmetic statement. Pascal distinguishes between integer and real division, with integer division always yielding an integer result and real division always yielding a real result. Thus:

5 DIV 2 gives the integer result 2
5 / 2   gives the real result 2.5

The Boolean assignment statement also illustrates the use of different symbols to represent assignment and *equality* in Pascal. 'answer = 42' is a Boolean expression which is read as 'is answer equal in value to 42?'. The result of this logical operation is then assigned to the Boolean variable 'truth'.

Following the above declarations the following statements would be erroneous, and would be detected by the compiler:

```
answer := 42.0 ;   (* 42.0 not an integer *)
j := 1 / 2 ;       (* 1 / 2 not an integer *)
yes := "yes" ;     (* "yes" not a character *)
speed := 25.7 ;    (* speed undeclared *)
```

The use of strong type checking and the pre-declaration of variables is of significant advantage when developing programs by ensuring that some trivial errors, with dangerous consequences at run-time, are caught when the program is compiled. A classic example of a trivial typing error having disastrous effects is said to have occurred in a program written for a space mission to Mars. Instead of typing 'DO' a programmer typed 'D0' in a FORTRAN program. FORTRAN has implicit declaration of variables and so variables do not have to be declared before use. 'DO' is a reserved word in FORTRAN and is used in a similar fashion to the 'FOR' statement in Pascal. Instead of interpreting a statement as a 'DO' loop, the compiler assumed the 'D0' to be a variable and part of an assignment statement and thus generated completely the wrong object code. Unfortunately this statement was only required to be executed as the spacecraft approached Mars, with the sad result that the spacecraft veered wildly off course.

Pascal also allows the creation of *user-defined types*. For example, suppose a program has to deal with days of the week. A simplistic approach might be to say Sunday will be represented by the value 1, Monday by 2, etc. While this may produce a workable solution, the meaning of the program will not be very clear. Pascal overcomes this by allowing the definition of *enumerated types*. This is clearly illustrated by an example:

```
TYPE
        day = (Sun, Mon, Tues, Weds, Thurs, Fri, Sat);
VAR
        workday, restday, playday : day;
```

The 'TYPE' statement defines an enumerated list of all the values that a variable of that type can take. The values are also assumed to be ordered. Thus in the above example, 'Mon' follows 'Sun', as expected. 'workday', 'restday' and 'playday' are all variables of type 'day'. Some examples of the use of user-defined types are:

```
FOR workday := Mon TO Fri do
        .
        .
        .
restday := Sun;
playday := Sat;
```

It may be noted that the Boolean, integer and char types described above are effectively pre-defined enumerated types.

Pascal also allows the programmer to define *sub-ranges* of existing types. This allows the compiler to check assignment statements that use constant values for validity, and also allows the use of run-time checks to determine if a calculated value is within the desired range. Some examples of sub-range type declarations are:

```
TYPE
        byte = 0 .. 255;
        weekday = Mon .. Fri;
        binary = 0 .. 1;
```

Variables of type 'byte' can only take integer values in the range 0 to 255. Similarly, variables of type 'weekday' may only have values in the range Mon to Fri. In this case, Mon to Fri must be a proper sub-set of an existing type, such as the type 'day' defined earlier.

Many programs require more complex groupings of data in order more clearly to reflect the inherent structure of the information being manipulated by an algorithm. To cater for this, Pascal provides several forms of *data structure*. The simplest data structure, and that found in all other general-purpose programming languages, is the *array*. An array is a collection of data elements of the same type. The array is known by a single name with its individual elements being accessed by an *index* into the array. The following are valid array definitions in Pascal, followed by some typical array operations:

```
VAR
        numbers : ARRAY[1..50] OF integer;
        hoursworked : ARRAY[Mon..Fri] OF real;
        word : ARRAY[0..maxwordlength) OF char;
        matrix : ARRAY[1..10,1..10] OF byte;
BEGIN
        number[10] := 27;
        number[50] := number[10] * 5;
        hoursworked[Tues] := 8.5;
        word[0] := 'H';
        word[1] := 'P';
        matrix[3,3] := 55
END;
```

'numbers' is an array of 50 integers, with the elements being 'number[1]', 'number[2]' .. 'number[50]'. The index into the array in Pascal can be any sub-range of an enumerated type with arbitrary starting value. Thus the array 'hoursworked' has an element for each working day of the week. Pascal also permits multi-dimensional arrays such as 'matrix', which is a 10 by 10 matrix of the user-defined type byte.

A significant characteristic of arrays in Pascal, as originally defined, is that they are fixed in size, once declared. In many situations it is important to be able to increase the size of the data structure during the execution of the program. To cater for this requirement, Pascal allows for the creation of *files*, which are typically disc-resident. Rather than access an element via an index, a simple sequential access mechanism is provided. This lets the next element in a file be read or allows a new element to be added to the end of the file. More sophisticated access mechanisms may be provided by the run-time system in which the program operates but these are non-standard extensions to the language. Pascal also allows a form of *dynamic variable* creation using an area of memory called the *heap*, but a discussion of such techniques is beyond the scope of this book and is dealt with more completely in refs 11.9 and 11.10.

The final data structure mechanism provided by Pascal is the *record*. A record is a collection of related data items which may be of different types. As an example, consider a data structure to hold the details of cars. The record would need to include character-based information such as the manufacturer, model, registration and colour, numeric information such as engine size and year of manufacture. In Pascal, such a data structure would typically be declared as follows:

```
TYPE
        carmaker = (Porsche, Jaguar, Ferrari, TVR, Reliant);
        word2 = ARRAY[1..2] OF char;
        word8 = ARRAY[1..8] OF char;
        car = RECORD
                        manufacturer : carmaker;
                        model : word8;
                        colour : word2;
                        registration : word8;
                        cc : integer;
                        year : integer
        END;
```

The 'RECORD' statement defines the new type 'car' which is a structure with the elements 'manufacturer', 'model', etc. The structure 'car' could then be used as follows:

```
VAR
        mycar : car;
        carfleet : ARRAY[1..600] of car;
BEGIN
        mycar.manufacturer := Reliant;
        mycar.cc := 603;
        mycar.year := 1957;
        carfleet.manufacturer[1] := Porsche;
        carfleet.year[342] := 1987
END;
```

To reference a field of a record, the dot operator is employed. Thus 'mycar.cc' refers to the field 'cc' of the record 'mycar'. Arrays of structures can also be declared as with 'carfleet' above. Some further facilities are provided to simplify the accessing of record structures and these are fully described in ref. 11.10. It should also be noted that records can themselves include records, and that files can consist of records.

The combination of the data structures that Pascal provides, combined with user-defined types, allows a great deal of flexibility and power in defining abstract data to represent a physical situation. This results in clearer programs and permits more comprehensive compiler and run-time checking.

11.4.5 Development Environments

The environment in which a software system is developed is of crucial importance to the success of a project since it has a great impact upon programmer efficiency, documentation quality, project management and product quality. In this section, the prime concern is with the software aspects of computer-based product development and so it will be assumed that appropriate aids are available for hardware development and testing although hardware engineers would find some of the facilities useful, particularly in the production of documentation. As a first requirement of a software development environment, we need a computer. These typically have a large amount of working store, hard disc(s) and a powerful multi-user operating system such as UNIX*. The development computer may be quite distinct from the target machine and may therefore have to support some mechanism for transferring programs to the target machine. During the testing phase, this is most conveniently achieved using a hardware link or local area network (LAN).

The software development environment must obviously provide the language translators (that is, compilers and assemblers), module linkers and libraries to allow a program to be converted into machine code. An extremely important feature of the translators is the quality of the error reporting provided. Although it is a difficult task for the compiler designer to generate helpful error reports, it is essential that these are provided. The libraries provided may include standard I/O drivers, special-function routines and reusable previously developed and tested routines.

The programmer also needs an editor program to create and modify files. The most suitable type is the screen editor, which allows the programmer to view a VDU screenful of text at a time and, typically via a cursor, insert, delete and replace characters, lines and blocks of text. In addition, a good screen editor should provide character-string searching and replacement, and command repetition. Some language translators are intimately linked with a screen editor and upon detection of an error automatically invoke the editor and position the cursor at the predicted point of mistake.

Another increasingly important feature of program development environments is some means of controlling the way in which code is modified and combined. This ensures that when a system is built, it will include the latest versions of the software modules and that a standard build can be established.

As well as aids to program translation, a software development environment should also provide support for:

(a) requirements specification and validation,
(b) text processing for documentation production,
(c) testing, debugging and validation, and
(d) project management software for estimation, planning and progress monitoring.

* UNIX is a registered trademark of Bell Telephone Laboratories.

Probably the best known development environment that approaches these requirements is the UNIX Programmer's Work Bench, although this is deficient in a number of areas. Much current research effort in software engineering is directed at developing *Integrated Project Support Environments* (IPSEs) to achieve the ideals outlined in this section.

11.5 Software Validation and Testing

In this section, a brief description of some of the techniques employed in validating and testing software will be given. In section 11.1, a distinction between validation and testing was drawn. Validation attempts to show that a program has no errors, while testing involves observing the behaviour of a program for a carefully chosen set of input data, to ensure that the program behaves as expected for that test data set. Validation is thus far more thorough than testing, which by its very nature cannot disprove the existence of errors. The theory of program validation is still being developed and very few automated tools are available to support those techniques that have evolved. In section 11.5.1, some of the principles behind program validation will be described. Program testing, which is almost universally applied in spite of its shortcomings, is considered in section 11.5.2.

11.5.1 Validation Techniques

Program validation can be viewed in two lights. In the first, the structure of the program is important and the aim is to prove that the structure is sound and that the programming style is good. In the second, the aim is to ensure that the meaning or semantics of the program are sound and that it meets its specification. Distinct techniques are required to address these two different aspects of program validation.

To check the structure and style of a program, mechanised techniques can be derived which ultimately can form a part of a compiler. The three most important tools applied in this validation technique are *control-flow analysis, data-flow analysis* and *information-flow analysis.*

Control-flow analysis involves inspecting the flow of control in a program to ensure that certain errors are not present. For example, it is apparent that a program should not have any of the following characteristics:

(a) calls or jumps to undefined labels,
(b) labels which are never referenced,

(c) statements that can not be reached from the entry point of the program,

(d) statements that have no path to the exit point of the program.

The control flow inherent in a program can also be used to check that the programming style is good and that the resulting code is well-structured. To achieve this, the program is analysed to produce a control flow graph which shows all the paths through a program. From this graph, a test can be made to ensure that each program block only has a single entry point and a single exit point. A program with these characteristics is said to be well-structured. Referring back to section 11.4, it will be apparent that the control constructs provided by Pascal naturally support this concept. However, even in Pascal there is a control transfer statement which allows an unconditional transfer out of the middle of a program block and thus potential multiple exit points. This is the 'goto' statement and was specifically omitted from section 11.4 to de-emphasise its use.

Data-flow analysis aims to ensure that the data being manipulated in a program is being treated in a sensible manner. Some examples of erroneous data flow are:

(a) referencing an undefined data object,

(b) using an uninitialised variable on the right-hand side of an assignment statement,

(c) not using a declared variable.

The analysis of data flow again involves the use of a control flow graph. In this case, an additional table is generated which enumerates the points within the program that variables are used and defined. Using these two representations of the program, it is possible to check for all the above data flow problems and a number of more subtle or stylistic errors. An example of the latter is the use of a variable to hold a constant value throughout the lifetime of a program. Better programming style would be to use a constant rather than a variable.

Information flow analysis effectively takes data-flow analysis one stage further and examines how variables are related to each other in a program. For example, a simple assignment of one variable to another defines a direct relationship between the two variables. On the other hand, a variable that is manipulated within a loop is indirectly related to the loop terminating condition, which is of course dependent upon another variable. A typical error that may be found by information-flow analysis is the detection of a variable that has no effect on any output value. All variables in a program should have either a direct or an indirect effect on an output value, otherwise they are not needed.

To check the meaning of a program, a more formalised mathematical approach is required which needs considerable effort by the programmer to develop *assertions* that can be used in the proving process. The assertions define logical conditions that must be true when the program reaches a certain point. An assertion will typically define some relationship that must exist between variables or between variables and constants, for example:

(a > 0) and (b < a)

If the assertions can be mathematically proven to be met by the program, then the program will be provably correct. The significant problem with this approach is ensuring that the assertions meet the specification for the program. Very few systems have their requirements defined in a mathematically rigorous way and this is currently limiting the use of this technique.

11.5.2 Testing Techniques

In order to test a program adequately, a *test plan* must first be derived. The test plan defines the order in which modules are coded, how modules are integrated, and the methods employed to test individual modules. Like the goals of the structured methods described earlier in this chapter, a major aim in developing the test plan is to break the testing task into many smaller tasks. This will allow a complex program to be tested as a set of simpler components, with the gradual integration of the tested components into the complete system. The order of module coding is important when allocating programming tasks to individual programmers to ensure that as much programming as possible is done in parallel to make best utilisation of the staff available. In addition, it is important to observe dependencies between code modules. The coding order should ensure that when the coding of module is complete, it can be tested and is not held up because of the unavailability of other modules upon which it is dependent. The dependencies of modules upon each other can easily be derived from the structure chart for the system.

Several strategies can be considered for testing and integrating modules. These are *bottom-up, top-down, sandwich* and *big-bang*. The structure chart shown in figure 11.7 will be used to describe these strategies in more detail.

Bottom-up integration involves testing the bottom modules first, then the next higher level, etc., until the top-most module is reached. A *driver module* is employed to drive the inputs of a module under test. Thus in figure 11.7, modules E, F, G and H would be tested stand-alone with specially written modules driving them. Then modules B, C and D would

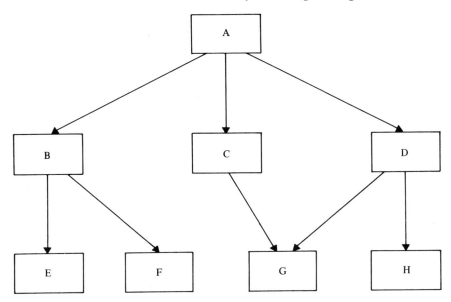

Figure 11.7 Example structure chart

be tested, followed finally by module A. The order of coding in this strategy would be to give priority to coding module G, since it immediately allows module C to be coded and tested. Then module H would be coded since D is dependent upon it and G, and so on. A module driver is a program that repeatedly calls the module under test, passing it a different test case on each call. The only disadvantages to bottom-up testing are the fact that these special driver modules have to be written and that a working program is only available when all modules have been integrated.

Top-down integration, as its name implies, turns the bottom-up testing strategy on its head. In this case, only the top module is tested stand-alone with *stub modules* being used to replace its subordinates. The stubs are minimal code modules which are not intended for exhaustive testing. Thus in figure 11.7, module A would be tested first with modules B, C and D being replaced by stubs. The modules B, C and D would be tested with stubs replacing modules E, F, G and H. Finally, modules E, F, G and H would be tested. There are two main disadvantages with top-down testing. The first is that it is harder to plan parallelism into the code development than with bottom-up integration, for example. The second is that it may be difficult to test for all parameter limits because actual modules rather than special-purpose driver modules are used at the inputs. It may be very difficult to force the normal calling module to invoke a subordinate module with particular parameter values. This operation is trivial with dedicated driver modules. However, top-down integration does have the significant advantage that a skeletal working program is available early, since the top-most module is coded and tested first.

Sandwich integration attempts to utilise the best features of top-down and bottom-up integration. As its name suggests, sandwich integration develops the top and bottom modules at the same time. This allows a skeletal program to be available early, like the top-down approach, but also allows specific-condition testing within the depths of the program, as with bottom-up.

Finally there is big-bang integration. This involves testing all modules stand-alone using both stubs and drivers. When all modules are tested, they are all combined and the complete system tested as a whole. This approach has the significant disadvantage that at integration time all modules are suspect when the program misbehaves, and it may be very difficult to isolate the culprit module. There is also the major overhead of providing both stubs and drivers. The big-bang technique may be suitable for small programs, but can be disastrous for larger systems.

In general, the sandwich integration approach is best suited for large systems because it offers a high degree of parallelism in the programming activities, early integration and a good level of testing. For smaller systems, bottom-up integration is preferred because of its simplicity. The disadvantage of not having a working program until late is not so crucial with smaller systems because of their shorter development life-cycle.

So far in this section, the overall integration and testing strategy has been discussed without reference to the actual testing techniques used on an individual module. Ideally, every combination of value and input should be tested with each execution path through the program. This form of exhaustive testing is impossible for anything but the most trivial module, and so a careful sub-set of input conditions must be chosen in order to achieve good test coverage. A reasonable approach to testing the program behaviour for inputs and outputs would be to:

(a)   check boundary conditions,
(b)   check sensitive values (for example, zero, null, round off errors),
(c)   check mid-range values in parameter range.

For execution path testing, all the conditional branches in each direction should be tested.

As an example, consider the following program fragment:

```
IF (frequency < 0.001) OR (frequency > 19999.999) THEN
    error = outofrange
ELSE
        CASE request OF
        'A' : gain(frequency);
        'C' : calibrate(frequency);
        'P' : power(frequency)
        END;
    .
    .
    .
FOR i := 1 to N DO
    a[i] := v[i] / r[i];
```

Some boundary conditions to test within this program fragment would be for:

    frequency 0.00099 – that is, just less than 0.001
    frequency 0.001 — that is, on the limit
    frequency 20000.0 — that is, just above the 19999.999
    frequency 19999.999 — that is, on the limit

These values would also check each of the possible execution paths through the IF statement, as a side benefit.

The FOR statement needs some careful checking because of the use of the variable 'N' as the terminating value. If 'N' erroneously exceeds the maximum array subscript value, then the program would fail. A sensitive value for 'N' would thus be the value of the maximum array subscript value plus one. Within the same FOR statement, the division operation is sensitive to the value 'r[i]' being zero since this would yield an overflow error. Similarly, very large values of 'v[i]' combined with small values of 'r[i]' or vice versa could also cause overflow or underflow problems.

The CASE statement should be tested for all the values of 'request' — that is, 'A', 'C' and 'P'. In addition, the program should be checked for 'request' with values outside the expected range.

The ability to test a program in this manner relies on the use of a good program development environment with the facility to control the execution of a program, modify variable values and observe the effects in a clear way. Without this kind of environment, testing of any kind will be difficult with the next result being a poorer product.

Following the module testing and integration, the next stage is to proceed through the customer acceptance tests. These tests should be part of the system specification and should have been agreed upon completion of the analysis phase described in section 11.2. The acceptance tests are used to assess whether the complete system meets the customer's requirements and are the yardstick against which the finished product should be measured.

11.6 Summary

In this chapter, the basic goals of software engineering have been introduced. Four major phases of the software life cycle — that is, specification, design, implementation and validation/testing — have been described. Some of the tools available for supporting each of these four phases have been discussed. The fifth phase, that of maintenance, has not been explicitly described since it involves identical effort to that of the four phases discussed. If the reasons for maintenance are considered, it will be seen that they fall into two broad categories. The first is that the system fails to meet the customer's expectations once in service. This can be due to a number of reasons; for example, the specification being incorrect, incomplete module testing, acceptance tests being inadequate, etc. The second cause of maintenance is that the customer's requirements have changed. Dependent upon the reason for maintenance, resolving the problem may require going back to the specification phase or may 'simply' involve correcting an implementation error. The activities involved in maintenance are thus identical to those carried out in developing the system in the first instance.

The subject of software engineering is new and therefore many of the concepts and techniques are only in their infancy. Much work still needs to be done to allow software engineers to make best use of the computer hardware available. This chapter has introduced some of the techniques currently available and illustrated their use in realistic situations. The tools available tomorrow may be very different, but their fundamental aims will be the same as those discussed in this chapter.

References

11.1 DeMarco, T., *Structured Analysis and System Specification*, Yourdon Press, New York, 1978.
11.2 Somerville, I., *Software Engineering*, Addison-Wesley, London, 1982.
11.3 Jones, C. B., *Software Development*, Prentice-Hall, Englewood Cliffs, New Jersey, 1980.
11.4 Bjorner, D. and Jones, C. B., *Formal Specification and Software Development*, Prentice-Hall, Englewood Cliffs, New Jersey, 1982.

11.5   Pages-Jones, M., *The Practical Guide to Structured Systems Design*, Yourdon Press, New York, 1980.

11.6   Kernighan, B. W. and Ritchie, D. M., *The C Programming Language*, Prentice-Hall, Englewood Cliffs, New Jersey, 1978.

11.7   Wirth, N., *Programming in Modula-2*, 2nd edn, Springer-Verlag, New York, 1983.

11.8   Barnes, J. G. P., *Programming in Ada*, Addison-Wesley, London, 1983.

11.9   Wirth, N., *Algorithms + Data Structures = Programs*, Prentice-Hall, Englewood Cliffs, New Jersey, 1976.

11.10 Welsh, J. and Elder, J., *Introduction to Pascal*, Prentice-Hall, Englewood Cliffs, New Jersey, 1979.

Index